BRITAIN ALONE

PHILIP STEPHENS

BRITAIN ALONE

The Path from Suez to Brexit

faber

First published in the UK and the USA in 2021
by Faber & Faber Limited
Bloomsbury House
74–77 Great Russell Street
London WC1B 3DA

Typeset by Ian Bahrami
Printed and bound by CPI Group (UK) Ltd, Croydon, CR0 4YY

The right of Philip Stephens to be identified as author of this work
has been asserted in accordance with Section 77 of the Copyright,
Designs and Patents Act 1988

A CIP record for this book
is available from the British Library

ISBN 978–0–571–34177–1

MIX
Paper from
responsible sources
FSC
www.fsc.org   FSC® C020471

2 4 6 8 10 9 7 5 3 1

For Felicity Bryan, an inspiration,
and for
Jess, Ben and Patty

Who controls the past controls the future: who controls
the present controls the past.

GEORGE ORWELL

Contents

List of Illustrations

Churchill, Truman and Stalin at Potsdam (*Imagno/Getty Images*)

Clement Attlee meets the crew of an American B-29
    Superfortress bomber at RAF Marham, October 1949 (*Ron
    Burton/Getty Images*)

Ernest Bevin meets Robert Schuman in Brussels, December
    1950 (*Walter Carone/Getty Images*)

Anthony Eden speaks to the nation after Nasser seizes the Suez
    Canal, August 1956 (*Keystone/Getty Images*)

An anti-Suez demonstration in Trafalgar Square, November
    1956 (*Mark Kauffman/Getty Images*)

Eisenhower is driven through London in an open-topped Rolls-
    Royce, August 1959 (*Fox Photos/Getty Images*)

De Gaulle slams the European door in Macmillan's face at
    Rambouillet, December 1962 (*Keystone-France/Getty Images*)

Macmillan and JFK in Nassau, December 1962 (*Bettmann/Getty
    Images*)

Harold Wilson in Washington in 1965 (*Rolls Press/Popperfoto/
    Getty Images*)

Devaluation paves the way for Wilson's retreat from East of Suez
    (*Rolls Press/Popperfoto/Getty Images*)

Edward Heath and France's Georges Pompidou during
    Common Market negotiations in May 1971 (*Rolls Press/
    Popperfoto/Getty Images*)

Prime Minister James Callaghan and his chancellor, Denis
    Healey, in July 1976 (Evening Standard/*Getty Images*)

François Mitterrand and Margaret Thatcher meet in November 1981 (*Jacob Sutton/Getty Images*)

Thatcher and Reagan in Washington, June 1982 (*David Hume Kennerly/Getty Images*)

Thatcher leaves 10 Downing Street for the last time in November 1990 (*Richard Baker/Getty Images*)

Tony Blair with Irish prime minister Bertie Ahern in Belfast, June 1999 (*Paul Faith/Getty Images*)

Blair with George W. Bush at the US president's ranch in Crawford, Texas, April 2002 (*Stephen Jaffe/Getty Images*)

David Cameron announces his resignation the day after the June 2016 referendum (*Bloomberg/Getty Images*)

The last laugh for UKIP leader and pro-Brexit campaigner Nigel Farage (*Richard Stonehouse/Getty Images*)

Boris Johnson and Donald Trump at the December 2019 NATO summit in Watford (*Dan Kitwood/Getty Images*)

Acknowledgements

The argument about Britain's place in the world has been an ever-present backcloth for my work as a journalist at Reuters and the *Financial Times*. Writing since the 1980s about our island's tortured relationship with Europe and its sometimes embarrassing obeisance to Washington, I have constantly caught sight of the bigger story: a nation no longer at the centre of world affairs struggling to reshape its identity. This book, I hope, tells the story.

Britain 'won' the war but lost its empire along the way. The Suez debacle laid bare the realities of post-imperial decline. Engagement in 'Europe', alongside a 'special relationship' with the United States, for a time seemed to offer a workable balance, albeit an often uncomfortable one. With Brexit, however, Britain is striking out again on its own. *Britain Alone* is an account of the array of forces – historical, political and economic, cultural and emotional – that have made it so difficult for Shakespeare's sceptred isle to settle for a role that at once matches its great strengths and admits the limits of national power.

My thanks go to successive editors of the *Financial Times* and the many superb colleagues whose knowledge and insights have helped shape my thoughts over so many years. Frederick Studemann, the *FT*'s literary editor, offered wisdom and reassurance after reading the initial draft. Much of the second half of the book draws directly on scores, no, hundreds of my conversations, on-the-record and private, with prime ministers, ministers and mandarins during my career as a writer, columnist and an editor at the *FT*. After watching Margaret Thatcher fight to cut Britain's budget contribution as a

Reuters correspondent in Brussels, I then interviewed her as political editor of the *FT*. Longer trips to the home of the European Union were interposed with press conferences marking prime ministerial pilgrimages to the White House Rose Garden. More recently, as chief political commentator, I charted the falls of David Cameron and Theresa May. The *FT* gave me a ring-side seat at all the big moments in between, including Thatcher's infatuation with Soviet leader Mikhail Gorbachev, Tony Blair's fateful war in Iraq and Cameron's defeat by opponents whom he had once described as 'fruitcakes, loonies and closet racists, mostly'.

As well as my *FT* notebooks, I have drawn on my two previous books – one about the Conservative Party's tribulations with sterling and Europe, the other an account of Blair's premiership – in charting Cameron's route to Brexit and Blair's path to war. Special mention is given in the Select Bibliography to the vivid accounts of the post-war decades written by historians such as Peter Hennessy.

Many officials in Downing Street, the Foreign Office and beyond have been kind enough to talk to me more recently in order to provide contemporaneous accounts. Some I have been able to quote directly; many others have been obliged to wear a cloak of anonymity. My long experience of British civil servants – that as well as being smart, overwhelmingly they are also generous and anxious to promote the truth – has been confirmed. They are also loyal to their political mistresses and masters, even at moments when they despair at some of the decisions they are asked to implement. They have my sincere thanks. So too do the diplomats and officials in Berlin, Paris, Brussels and Washington who have drawn a picture for me of Britain through the eyes of its friends. I am grateful also to the Robert Bosch Academy for sponsoring a sabbatical in Berlin.

I grew up in the period covered by the first half of the book, conscious I was living through a decisive break with the past, but largely unaware of the pain this was inflicting on the nation's ruling elites. Britain had grown used to reordering the world, to shaping events in far-flung colonies, dominions and dependencies. How many times we were reminded that it had stood alone against the Nazis in 1940. Adjusting to a world in which the Pax Britannica had given way to American leadership produced more than a cry of pain.

Those who are tempted to dig deeper into the post-war decades will find a number of rich histories of the leading players and turning points. I have highlighted the best of them in the Select Bibliography, as well as a number of the must-visit websites offering digitised collections of cabinet papers, prime ministerial correspondence and contemporary records of milestone events. I have devoured the accounts, diaries and memoirs of politicians, diplomats and journalists. I hope that I have done justice to the richness of the story they tell.

Felicity Bryan will be sorely missed. She was an inspirational agent. She never gave up on her charges and, in spite of a long gap since my last book, continued to nudge me along. If I have written something useful, Felicity takes the credit. Thanks too to Laura Hassan at Faber, who, having taken on the book, put up with several broken deadlines as my writing for the *FT* about the Brexit pile-up in parliament proved a constant distraction. Andrew Naughtie dug into the archives to produce some great research, and Rowan Cope, a superb editor, offered invaluable help in ordering my thoughts. I would also like to thank Ian Bahrami for his thoughtful and patient editing, and Chris Allnutt for his careful checking. Kate Ward brought it all together with skill.

For all the much-appreciated help I have received, the judgements, and any errors, belong entirely to me.

Prologue

The alarm was sounded by a distinguished Whitehall scientist. Sir Henry Tizard had served during the war as a special emissary to Washington for Winston Churchill. His task had been to supervise the exchange of advanced military technologies, from airborne radar to nuclear fission, with Franklin Roosevelt's administration. Tizard once made an Atlantic sea crossing carrying in his case the blueprints for every one of the nation's secret weapons systems. By 1949, as the chief defence scientist for Clement Attlee's government, his focus had shifted to Britain's* place in the new postwar order. Victory, it turned out, had carried a heavy cost. The defeat of Hitler had also marked the end of the Pax Britannica. Four years after VE Day, the British Empire was on the edge of dissolution and the government seemingly in permanent economic crisis. The Iron Curtain had reframed great-power relations as a competition between the United States and the Soviet Union. And yet in the corridors of Whitehall and Westminster it seemed almost treasonous to admit that Britain had slipped into the second rank of nations. Tizard was among the few urging that realism should rule emotion. 'We persist in regarding ourselves as a great power, capable of everything and only temporarily handicapped by economic difficulties,' he wrote in an official Whitehall minute. 'We are not a great power and never will be again. We are a great nation, but if we continue to behave like

---

* As in the title of the book, I have used 'Britain' and 'United Kingdom' interchangeably in the text as shorthand for the United Kingdom of Great Britain and Northern Ireland.

a great power we shall soon cease to be a great nation.'[1] A great power or a great nation? Tizard's prescient observation weaves its way through the history of post-war Britain. *Britain Alone* is a story of inflated ambition and diminished circumstance. Some called it 'managing relative decline'. The Conservative foreign secretary Douglas Hurd preferred to talk about a nation 'punching above its weight' in global affairs.

For all Britain's enduring strengths – its deep-rooted democratic traditions and culture, its language, geography and natural creativity – the journey has been painful. Much of the time it has resembled a fight with history, a struggle to hold on to the past. The dissolution of an empire that in 1945 was still home to 700 million citizens left Britain in search of a new identity, in a world where other great powers made the rules. Political leaders were from time to time brave enough to present the country with the unvarnished choices offered by relative economic decline. More often, they sought to cling on to the illusions until they were overwhelmed by circumstance. To track the big shifts in Britain's international standing has often been to note the unhappy coincidence of desperate attempts to prop up the value of sterling on international financial markets and an enforced retreat from political and security responsibilities overseas. Joining in 1973 what everyone called 'the Common Market' might have promised a workable compromise between the pull of the past and the realities of the present. Hugging America close while claiming a powerful voice in the councils of Europe was a precarious balancing act, but it provided leverage in both Washington and Brussels. The decision in 2016 to leave the European Union means Britain has to start again.

Anthony Eden's failed Suez expedition in 1956 and the referendum on Europe sixty years later are the natural bookends to this story. Both represented a lament for the past, albeit in different ways. They both asked whether Britain's identity should be set by its geography – by its Europeanness, as an island at the western edge of the continent – or by the global reach of a remarkable imperial history. In both Suez and Brexit, there was an appeal to nostalgia over reason – to a national identity moulded by past greatness rather than by the redistribution of power during the decades since 1945. Eden hoped Suez would restore the nation's standing as a world power. Sixty years later, leading Brexiters were equally insistent that Britain should not be constrained by its proximity to Europe. Boris Johnson's choice of 'Global Britain' as an epigram was no accident, though it has yet to be given much in the way of meaning. He borrowed his lines from Eden's explanation as to why Britain should stand aloof from Europe. 'Britain's story and her interests lie beyond the continent of Europe,' Eden had remarked in January 1952. 'Our thoughts move across the seas to the many communities in which our people play their part in every corner of the world. These are our family ties. That is our life.'² Then came Suez. In 1962, Harold Macmillan set out the less palatable reality: 'In the past, a great maritime power, we might have given way to insular feelings of superiority over foreign breeds . . . but we have to consider the world as it is today and will be tomorrow, and not in outdated terms of a vanquished past.'³ Johnson preferred Eden's illusions. The severing of ties with the European Union now invites another reckoning.

Above all, and how often this was said and written, Britain had won the war. The Allies, popular imagination had it, had played secondary roles in the great drama. It was all there in the six volumes of Churchill's memoirs. The rest of Europe might plan a new future, but Britain would cling nostalgically to a glorious past. Victory in 1945 fixed fast in the national psyche a self-image that set the country apart from its neighbours. Britain was a maritime power, its interests traced by global trade routes. Its political institutions and traditions had come through the war unscathed. After such courage and sacrifice, it seemed natural to assume that the nation would soon be restored to its former glory. The Victorians had been diligent in the making of Britain's national myth; the Empire was proof of global vocation. Call it manifest destiny. Conveniently, the nation had forgotten that for centuries French had been the language of the aristocracy, that the Knights of the Garter rode into battle with their standard declaring '*Honi soit qui mal y pense*', and that the House of Windsor had until the Great War been that of Saxe-Coburg and Gotha – the name change in deference to public sensitivities. Churchill remarked that Britain might be with the Europeans, but it was not of them. Yet the frontiers of empire were receding fast. The Commonwealth, a home for former colonies, was no substitute. Here was the problem – touching all the neuralgic emotions of self-image, historical memory and identity – with which Harold Macmillan and his successors in Downing Street would be obliged to grapple in the years after Suez. Too small for the world, psychologically Britain struggled to see itself as a regional power. During the sixty years from Suez to Brexit, the sense of superiority born of past glory joined battle with the insecurities that came with watching a new, economically vibrant Europe march ahead. Britain would have to find itself before it could find a role.

The possession of what successive governments have insisted is an 'independent' nuclear deterrent has been central to British illusions. Harold Macmillan's success in persuading John F. Kennedy to supply Britain with the Polaris submarine-based nuclear weapons system was claimed as a triumph. The Americans recognised the elevation of symbolism above substance. Richard Neustadt, a presidential adviser, remarked that the British deterrent was all but irrelevant to the East–West balance: 'British ministers (and services) had no intention of striking independently. To strike first was to invite the end of Britain. As for a second strike, they long since had tied all their plans to ours.'[4] Neustadt quoted the sharper observation of another official: for the British, nuclear weapons were 'the most expensive status symbols since colonies'. No subsequent prime minister has dared to question Macmillan's judgement that Britain could not hold its head high unless it had nuclear missiles sufficient to threaten the destruction of Moscow.

The post-war story has high as well as low points. At the start of the third decade of the twenty-first century, Britain remains a significant power – sixth or seventh in the economic rankings, with, most of the time, a willingness to take on the international responsibilities that come with a permanent seat on the United Nations Security Council. It can count itself among the lead architects of a multilateral liberal order that has underpinned the spread of democracy and prosperity. It was staunch in its opposition to Soviet communism. By and large, it approached the unravelling of its empire with dignity and diligence. Even now, Britain often plays an outsize role in international affairs, whether in the conduct of diplomacy, through an overseas aid budget whose generosity shames most of its peers, with intelligence services that are, in many respects, peerless, and with a military that can still fight. The persistent drumbeat, however, has long sounded a stubborn unwillingness to embrace an influential but secondary role. As Tizard feared, the attempt to hold on to the past has too often obscured the contribution Britain could make to the present.

The original sin belonged to Winston Churchill. He had sat down with Stalin and Roosevelt at Tehran and Yalta and with Stalin and Truman at Potsdam as one of the 'Big Three' world statesmen. Together they had redrawn the map of the continent,

and Churchill could never allow himself to imagine Britain joining a second tier. He refused to accept that independence for
India and Pakistan marked the end of the Empire. Britain, in the
mind of its great wartime leader, remained uniquely placed at the
intersection of three concentric circles of power – the United
States, Europe, and the Empire and Commonwealth. Others
shared his defiant optimism. Ernest Bevin, the brilliant foreign
secretary in Clement Attlee's administration, was as hard-headed
a politician as anyone could ask for. He also fell into the trap of
thinking that the privations of post-war life were just a passing
phase. Britain's great industries, its scientific and technical mastery and its natural ingenuity would see it returned to the first
rank. Fortunately, Bevin also claimed a pivotal role for Britain in
the panoply of international institutions – from the UN Security
Council to Bretton Woods and NATO – that would set the rules
for the Western order.

The restoration of British power was often viewed as a moral as
much as a selfish imperative. The defeat of Hitler may have been
a joint endeavour, but it would not have been possible had Britain
not shown the courage to stand alone in 1940. Here were the
roots of the exceptionalism that saw future generations closing
their eyes to the shifting balance of power and clinging on instead
to the baubles of national prestige. It is this mindset that explains
why Britain still has a hugely expensive nuclear deterrent in the
form of Trident – a system that is supposed to be 'independent'
yet relies completely on American technology to keep it in service – and why the cash-starved Royal Navy is putting two large
aircraft carriers into service with too few destroyers and frigates
to protect them.

Relative decline is nothing to be ashamed of. The Second
World War had crystallised a decisive shift in global power: an

island nation of Britain's size was never going to match the economic and military might of the United States and the emerging power of the Soviet Union. What really hurt was the evidence of absolute decline, particularly after Britain excluded itself from the early decades of European integration. This pain was poignantly expressed in the dispatches British diplomats sent back to the Foreign Office from continental capitals – observations on the superiority of German manufacturing processes and the punctuality of that country's trains, and questions as to why Britain's best engineers were crossing the Channel to work for French companies. What had things come to when de Gaulle could cite Britain's chronic economic weakness as cause for France to wield a second veto on membership of the European Community?

This weakness, often expressed in speculative attacks on sterling, forced retreat overseas. Those looking for the instant when Britain finally gave up on its pretensions to remain a global rather than a European power will find it in Harold Wilson's announcement in January 1968 that Britain would withdraw from all military bases east of Suez. It was no coincidence that the final curtain came down after the humiliating devaluation of sterling the previous autumn. Politicians refused to lower their sights until they were overwhelmed by countervailing forces. Attlee's government devalued the currency in 1949 only when it had exhausted all other choices; sterling's weakness forced Eden's retreat from Suez; and Wilson wasted years in a vain effort to prop up the pound.

As the decades passed, there were one or two other Tizards. Few explained Britain's dismal performance versus other European states during the immediate post-war decades better than Nicholas Henderson, Her Majesty's Ambassador to France. His valedictory dispatch from Paris in 1979, deploring the hubris of the post-war decades, should have a particular resonance in post-Brexit Britain.

A still more wounding assessment was offered by the American statesman Dean Acheson in 1962. What was intended as a gentle warning detonated a political explosion in London. His famous observation that having lost an empire Britain had not found a role struck home because it was a truth that politicians struggled to deny.

Macmillan's casting of Britain in the role of a wise Greece to America's less sophisticated Rome substituted the power of empire for a 'special relationship' with Washington – a balm to reconcile relative national decline with global pretensions. Like Acheson, however, Macmillan knew that fealty to the United States would not be enough. Geography has placed Britain at the edge of the European continent, and centuries of history should have taught it that it cannot be indifferent to the fortunes of its neighbours. Acheson touched a raw nerve. It was already clear that the Franco–German project to create a common market was leaving Britain behind.

The Americans got the answer they wanted when Britain joined the European Community in 1973; Atlanticism was henceforth to be balanced by Europeanism. The nation's security would be underpinned by a privileged position as America's closest ally, but the 'special relationship' was to be fused with political and economic engagement in Europe. In 1975, the newly elected Conservative leader Margaret Thatcher told the House of Commons that Europe had opened windows to the world that would otherwise be closing with the end of empire.[5] Other prime ministers deployed different words, presenting Britain as a 'bridge' between Europe and the United States; or, as Tony Blair once put it, a 'pivotal power'.[6] They mostly agreed, however, that a leading voice in Brussels enhanced Britain's stature in Washington, and vice versa.

America or Europe? Britain's struggle with the competing currents of the Atlantic and the Channel are at the heart of the post-war story. Atlanticists lined up against pro-Europeans – supporters of the North Atlantic Treaty Organisation (NATO) against those who favoured a bigger place for the European Union in setting the continent's political and foreign, as well as economic, policies. Should we be with the Americans and make sure that the British prime minister was always the first to meet a new president in the Oval Office? Or should we lend our weight to shape policy on our own continent? From the beginning, this was recognised by diplomats as a false choice: as early as 1945, the Foreign Office had concluded that Britain would only be able to keep a place at the top table with the Americans and the Soviet Union if it secured the leading role in Europe.[7] The greater the influence in Europe, the more likely it was that it would win respect elsewhere. Yet the temptation was to treat these pivotal relationships as separate – one being about power and security, the other about neighbourhood, trade and economy.

For prime ministers ever in search of a sprinkling of stardust, a photo call outside the Berlaymont building in Brussels would never match the click of camera shutters outside the White House. Polaris, and then Trident, was a vital status symbol. No matter that Neustadt's doubts about the 'independence' of an American-supplied deterrent were – and still are – widely echoed by British officials. John Major, Tony Blair, Gordon Brown and David Cameron – even after the Cold War, no prime minister would consider giving up such an emblem of national power.

In the tapestry of myths that inform Britain's view of its past, none is woven so brightly as the heroic years from 1940 to 1945. They began with Britain standing alone against the Nazi menace, and ended in victory. Britain was one of a handful of European nations not to have been invaded or occupied by foreign forces. This escape from subjugation – the fact that its political system, its democratic institutions and traditions and its economic and social assumptions emerged intact from the conflict – supplied the impulse for British exceptionalism. Nations that had seen their fabric torn apart by marauding invaders – some for the second time in thirty years – might well decide that exceptional measures were needed to break the cycle of history, but Britain assumed that it could carry on as before. British politicians acknowledged, of course, the role of European integration in promoting peace and reconciliation – above all between France and Germany. But only the most ardent of pro-Europeans grasped the force of the emotion in other capitals. European engagement, in the British calculus, was a question of measuring pros against cons – a subject of hard-headed cost–benefit analysis. Where Westminster has recoiled against intrusions on sovereignty, its partners have seen engagement in the European 'project' as offering a guarantee of peace and security – for these nations, the essence of sovereignty. Even for those that came late to the club – Spain and Portugal after fascism, and the countries of eastern and central Europe after the collapse of the Soviet Union – the organising emotion has been political. Greece, Portugal and Spain were willing in 2012 to take the bitter economic medicine prescribed by Germany to guarantee a continued presence in the eurozone because the European enterprise underwrote their emergence as modern democratic states. Edward Heath was alone among British prime ministers in his willingness to elevate Europe above America; for the rest, the European relationship has been transactional. Thus, Margaret Thatcher backed an acceleration of the pace of European integration through sponsorship of the European Single Market, but then railed against the federalist ambitions of Jacques Delors.

Tony Blair thought he could square the circle by being as influential in Paris and Berlin as he wanted to be in Washington – until the terrorist attacks of 11 September 2001, when he made the choice he had previously eschewed by backing George W. Bush's Iraq War.

The closer the relationship with the occupant of the White House, the easier it seemed to sidestep the issue of Britain's waning power. Wilson was heard boasting about the influence he would wield in the Oval Office even before he won the 1964 general election. Thatcher bathed in the glow of her relationship with Reagan. Even in 2017, as they put their heads in their hands at the prospect of a Donald Trump presidency, officials in 10 Downing Street pulled out every diplomatic stop to ensure Theresa May was the first foreign leader to meet him in the White House. Too often 'special' has resembled 'servile'.

For its part, the United States was brutally unsentimental – it was always about serving the American national interest. Truman cancelled the Lend–Lease programme, the financial lifeline that had kept Britain afloat throughout the war, without warning. During Suez, Eisenhower ordered the US ambassador at the United Nations to vote with Moscow, against its ally. The American Treasury blocked British access to international finance to prop up the pound – this as Soviet tanks rolled into Budapest to put down the Hungarian uprising. When Macmillan and Wilson sought to act as mediators between Washington and Moscow, the reaction in the White House travelled along a spectrum from indifference to irritation. Even during the Reagan–Thatcher dalliance of the 1980s, the American president felt no obligation to consult Britain before sending marines to invade the Commonwealth island of Grenada or proposing a deal with Mikhail Gorbachev that would have bargained away Britain's nuclear weapons. George

W. Bush was genuinely grateful for Tony Blair's backing over the war in Iraq, yet a contribution of 45,000 British troops did not buy Blair a say in what happened after Saddam Hussein had been toppled. Promises made by Bush were ignored by his vice president Dick Cheney and defence secretary Donald Rumsfeld. 'Call it a special relationship if you like,' one high-ranking US diplomat told me just before the Iraq War, 'but just remember we have lots of other "special relationships".' Churchill liked to summon up all manner of historical, cultural and emotional connections, but the Americans, by and large, thought the British should wake up to the new distribution of world power. Neustadt expressed the hard-headed view in Washington that Britain was 'a middle power, neither equal nor vassal, which history, geography or economics rendered specially significant to us for the time being'.[8]

In Europe, the formula agreed by John Major in Maastricht in 1991 – a vote in the European policy areas that most counted, along with opt-outs from those (the single currency most obviously) in which Britain wanted to retain freedom of action – might have proved a workable equilibrium. It sat easily alongside a close alliance with Washington. The permanent seat on the Security Council, a leading role in NATO and a voice heard in both Washington and Brussels held up a mirror to Britain's vital interest in preserving a rules-based international system. The mistakes were made when cool calculation fell prey to nostalgia, when eagerness to please Washington obscured independent judgement, and when the pursuit of Britain's interests in Europe was lost to political timidity at home. From the French, German or Belgian perspective, political and media convulsions in London about alleged continental plots were a mystery. They saw the British scoring significant successes in Brussels, and yet at the same time complaining about the threat of an imagined 'superstate'. The single market and the enlargement of the European Union to include former communist states of the Soviet Empire were British successes; the failure was of British leaders to claim them as such.

In the brilliant description of the journalist and historian Hugo Young,[9] Europe became the point of impact between a past Britain could not leave behind and a future it could not avoid. Jean Monnet, one of the founding fathers of the European enterprise, thought this was the 'price of victory'[10] – the price Britain paid for the version of history that said it had 'won' the war. Three-quarters of a century later, during the debates about Brexit, Tory MPs were still evoking the Dunkirk spirit. Smugness shared space, however, with spasms of fear – or you might say inferiority – about being left on the sidelines. The Tory Euroscepticism that drew the party's route map to Brexit added to the mix a paranoia about the erosion of national sovereignty through the primacy of European law and supranational institutions. Britain, ran the story, from Thatcher's famous speech in Bruges in 1988 to David Cameron's decision to hold a referendum, was being dragged into a 'United States of Europe'.

Cameron argued that the balancing act had become politically unsustainable and that the demand for a referendum on Britain's European Union membership was irresistible. In truth, the decision to call a plebiscite was self-serving. In early 2013, when he promised to hold a vote, fewer than 10 per cent of the electorate counted Europe as an issue of pressing concern. Eden's Suez expedition had been a vainglorious attempt to prove that, when it so determined, Britannia could still rule the waves. Cameron's gamble had lower motives. The prime minister wanted to snuff out a Tory rebellion to give himself a quieter life in 10 Downing Street.

There were many reasons why a small majority of those who voted in June 2016 backed Britain's withdrawal from the European

Union. Stagnant incomes, government-enforced austerity after the global financial crash, the loss of jobs to digital technology, coastal communities left behind by economic progress, and rising immigration from an expanded European Union all have a place on the list. It was striking, however, how the arguments about sovereignty were, in essence, echoes of those raised when leaders of the six member states of the European Coal and Steel Community had gathered in Messina in 1955. The elderly voted for Brexit, and the young voted against it. 'Take Back Control' reached deep into rose-tinted memories and offered an invitation to reclaim the days when Britain decided its own fate. Donald Trump caught the same tide in the 2016 presidential election, when he promised to 'Make America Great Again'.

Brexit strikes a pose, a belief that Britain can take to the seas and go it alone. It brushes aside the facts of a world in which national governments cannot act alone to meet transnational threats and opportunities. It has put a serious question mark over whether Scotland – which voted Remain – will stay in the UK union and thrown doubt over Northern Ireland's constitutional future. Real sovereignty is the capacity to rally sufficient friends and allies to the cause. The timing of the decision to pull up Britain's European anchor could scarcely have been more unfortunate. Predictions of a stable post-Cold War order have been confounded. History has moved in the opposite direction. China and Russia have challenged Western power. Donald Trump's administration in Washington discarded the responsibilities assumed by the United States in 1945, putting in question the Atlanticist mainstay of British foreign policy. Nostalgia bequeaths precious few choices. Britain cannot rebuild the global presence dismantled by Harold Wilson in 1968 and reverse the deep cuts made to its military and diplomatic capabilities during almost every decade since. For some, the alternative is a submissive relationship with the United States. For others, it is a second Elizabethan age, with a buccaneering 'Global Britain' making its mark in every corner of the world. The reality looks a lot more like Britain, or perhaps England, alone.

1

Broken Dreams

'I think champagne was produced, but there was little sparkle in the atmosphere,' the British diplomat would say of the clandestine gathering at the large but anonymous villa on the rue Emmanuel Giraud in Sèvres, a south-western suburb of Paris. 'The stars shone as brightly as I have ever seen them. It seemed wholly incongruous.'[1] Donald Logan, in October 1956 a young high-flier at the Foreign Office, was conscious of the cloak-and-dagger nature of his mission as he was driven to Villacoublay Air Base for an RAF flight back to London. But the foreign secretary's private secretary could not have guessed the magnitude of the duplicity that was to follow. Nor that history would regard him as the eyewitness to a calamity that would shatter Britain's international reputation and lower the curtain on its imperial illusions. The document that Logan carried to the prime minister, Anthony Eden, in Downing Street on the evening of 24 October 1956,[2] hastily typed in French, was posterity's proof of a dark conspiracy between Britain, France and Israel. Three months earlier, Egypt's president Gamal Abdel Nasser had nationalised the Suez Canal. The waterway between the Mediterranean and the Red Sea – Britain's strategic link to the Middle East and beyond – had been under de facto British control for seventy years. Eden's decision to retake it by military force would break the prime minister and leave Britain lost in a world over which it no longer ruled.

This had been Logan's third trip to Paris in as many days. On the first he had accompanied the foreign secretary, John Selwyn Lloyd, to the same house. On the second he had travelled back

17

to London with Selwyn Lloyd's French counterpart, Christian Pineau. He had been careful, he later recalled, to merge into the background when the French delegation arrived in London, lest his presence be noted by the waiting photographers. On his third trip he travelled back to the villa with Patrick Dean, the assistant under-secretary at the Foreign Office, to meet a French team headed by Pineau and a high-level Israeli delegation led by its prime minister, David Ben-Gurion. Dean signed, on behalf of the foreign secretary, what became known as the Protocol of Sèvres. A week later, Israeli troops advanced rapidly towards the Suez Canal after launching an invasion across the Sinai desert. Within days, RAF warplanes were bombing Egyptian airfields and British and French paratroopers were descending from the skies in a carefully choreographed operation to seize the canal. The House of Commons was in uproar, as was the United Nations in New York. A story of political folly as well as diplomatic deceit, 'Suez' was destined to become a metaphor for Britain's post-imperial decline.

Sir Anthony Eden finally claimed the keys to 10 Downing Street in April 1955. Events would show that this supremely qualified politician had served too long as an understudy. Winston Churchill had hemmed and hawed before surrendering power, torturing his anointed heir by reneging more than once on solemn pledges to make way. Wilfully blind to Britain's shrinking role, he clung on to the hope that he could serve as broker between Washington and Moscow to secure a warming of East–West relations. In the winter of 1953, Churchill's private secretary John Colville wrote in his diary that Eden's 'hungry eyes', as Churchill called them, had become ever 'more beseeching and more impatient'. By the summer of 1954, so desperate had Eden become that when Churchill decided to return to London by sea after a meeting with

President Dwight D. Eisenhower, he felt compelled to join him. The two men boarded the Cunard liner *Queen Elizabeth* in New York, and Eden confessed to Colville that he had come along only 'to get a firm date for Winston to hand over to him'. How strange, Colville mused, 'that two men who knew each other so well should be hampered by shyness on this score'.[3] Eden secured a date, but within a month Churchill had reneged once again. Eden would have to wait until the following spring.

Thirty-one years in the House of Commons and twenty-four years since his first ministerial post, with three spells as foreign secretary – no one could claim that Eden was unqualified for the job. At fifty-seven he was still significantly younger than the eighty-year-old Churchill. He had a reputation beyond Westminster as a politician who had been on the right side of the Tory party's bitter pre-war arguments about appeasement. Later, he had been at Churchill's side as foreign secretary at the Yalta Conference with Roosevelt and Stalin. Suave, self-assured and well-prepared, this was a politician who never doubted his suitability for the highest office. Within a month he had called a general election to secure a mandate. The government was returned with an increased majority of sixty against the previous seventeen.

For all Eden's confidence and experience, the wait had extracted its toll. Cabinet colleagues were soon noting he had become brittle, set in his ways and prone to secrecy. He was of a class and generation that imagined that the severe economic difficulties the country faced were a passing phase. In June 1953, the young Queen Elizabeth had been anointed at a coronation ceremony soaked in the nation's imperial majesty. Presidents and prime ministers, emirs and sheikhs, princes and princesses had travelled from all corners of the globe to join the millions of loyal flag-waving subjects who came out to pay homage to the new monarch. Special RAF flights carried canisters of newsreel across the Atlantic so that broadcasters in Canada could show it on the same day. There were carriages in glittering gold, the Household Cavalry in all its finery, and the grandeur of Westminster Abbey – this pomp and pageantry summoned up past glory, yet politicians such as Eden assumed this was also the future. India, the 'the jewel in the crown', may have been surrendered, but the Union flag still fluttered in dozens of British possessions across the globe.

After choosing the ambitious Harold Macmillan as his foreign secretary, Eden changed his mind a few months later, when Macmillan showed that he had strong ideas of his own about the nation's place in the world. He was shifted to the Treasury and replaced at the Foreign Office by the more biddable John Selwyn Lloyd – the prime minister would, in effect, be his own foreign secretary. Eden was let down by his health. A botched abdominal operation had left him weakened and vulnerable to fevers. This would matter when Nasser mounted his audacious challenge the following year. Embedded in the Suez crisis were inevitable collisions between past and future: waning imperial prestige set against rising Arab nationalism; a transatlantic relationship marked by rivalry as well as cooperation; and a world seen by Washington through the prism of competition with the Soviet Union. Each of these impulses would conspire against the prime minister, but it was Eden who set Britain's course.

The Suez Canal was the nineteenth-century vision of the French diplomat Ferdinand de Lesseps, and it had taken ten years to build. Within a few years of its opening in 1869, it had become a vital artery of the British Empire. When the ruling Khedive went bankrupt, Egypt's 44 per cent shareholding in the Universal Company of the Suez Maritime Canal was immediately snapped up by Benjamin Disraeli's government, and by 1882 it was a sufficiently vital international waterway to prompt William Gladstone to dispatch a military occupation force. Only in 1936 did the British formally quit Egypt, after half a century of effective occupation. Even then they left behind thousands of troops to defend the canal. The last of these departed by agreement only weeks before Nasser's announcement.

For a leader who styled himself as the champion of the Arab world in the fight against Western imperialism, the Anglo–French ownership and administration of the Suez Canal Company was an unacceptable symbol of past subjugation. Nasser had seized power in the aftermath of a military coup against King Farouk a few years earlier. In the interim he had successfully promoted himself as the leader of a new Arab nationalism, stirring up sporadic guerrilla attacks on the British forces guarding the canal and backing opposition to the Hashemite regimes in Jordan and Iraq allied to Britain. In July 1956, speaking to packed crowds in Alexandria, he launched a bitter attack on British imperialism and announced that Egypt would finally break free by taking control of the canal. British and French shareholders would be compensated, but henceforth Europe's vital seaway to the Middle East would be under Egypt's sovereign authority. For Britain, the canal's strategic significance was indisputable. The 'swing door of the British Empire', Eden had once called it. Safe transit was essential to keep open trade routes to the Gulf and the Far East. Oil from Iran and Iraq was carried through the canal, supplying much of the rest of Europe, as well as Britain.

The prime minister was dining in Downing Street when the news came through on the evening of 26 July 1956. His guest of honour was Iraq's King Faisal and his prime minister Nuri es-Said, with the Labour leader Hugh Gaitskell and the foreign

21

secretary John Selwyn Lloyd among the other guests. Eden was doing his best to prop up Britain's influence in the region; Faisal's Iraq, along with Turkey, Iran and Pakistan, was a participant in the British-sponsored Baghdad Pact, a military and economic alliance calculated to counter Soviet influence. Nasser stood aside from the pact, playing East against West in the cause of building his own role as a pan-Arab leader. As his guests left Number 10, Eden was joined in his study by a group of ministers and the French ambassador and American chargé d'affaires in London. The prime minister was unequivocal: a failure to take back the canal, he judged, would have 'disastrous consequences for the economic life of the Western powers and for their standing and influence in the Middle East'.[4]

In Eden's mind, national prestige counted for as much as trade and oil. He had made the same judgement a few years earlier when, as foreign secretary, he urged the Americans to mount a coup against the Iranian leader Mohammed Mossadeq, following his nationalisation of the Anglo–Iranian Oil Company. A CIA history of the coup, later published by the Washington-based National Security Archive,[5] recorded the different motives of London and Washington. 'The US State Department agreed with Eden that Mossadeq had to go,' but for distinct reasons: 'For Eden and his government, Mossadeq's policies damaged "British prestige, influence, and vital commercial interest",' while the Americans were more worried that Mossadeq would open the door to 'Soviet domination'. Britain had another perspective. Its vast, sprawling empire had been sustained by the understanding that it would act decisively if its interests were threatened. Eden feared that Nasser, if unchecked, would undermine the credibility of deterrence.

No one was more familiar than Eden with the dispute over the canal. Twenty years earlier, he had agreed the treaty with the newly independent Egyptian government that saw the British withdraw from the rest of the country. As Churchill's foreign secretary in 1954, he had negotiated an agreement with the new Egyptian regime on the future of Sudan and the subsequent withdrawal of British troops from the Canal Zone. This deal had carried political costs for Eden. Many on the right of the Tory party thought he had done too much to appease Nasser, and he had faced sharp criticism from dozens of backbench Conservative MPs, unapologetic champions of empire calling themselves the Suez Group. They included rising young figures on the right, among them Julian Amery, Enoch Powell and Fitzroy Maclean. Churchill signed the agreement, but he made no secret of the fact that his personal sympathies were with the rebels rather than his foreign secretary.

With Nasser's announcement such divisions fell away, and Eden had the cabinet behind him. As chancellor, Harold Macmillan might have been cautious. The previous few years had seen a succession of sterling crises, as the government struggled to generate the foreign currency earnings needed to meet the country's overseas commitments. Financial constraints had loomed large in Clement Attlee's decision to abandon Britain's United Nations mandate in Palestine and had forced the British withdrawal from Greece and Turkey. In 1956, the country's finances were once again in fragile condition, with the trade gap a constant source of pressure on the pound and the government's reserves of dollars and gold drained by speculative attacks on sterling. Macmillan had devoted the early months of the year to scrabbling around to find public-spending cuts in the budgets of cabinet colleagues. Only by keeping a tight rein on the public finances could the Treasury hope to sustain sterling's exchange rate against the dollar. In the circumstances, the chancellor might have cautioned against expensive foreign adventurism, but he took a different view. 'If Nasser gets away with it, we are done for,' he wrote in his diary. 'The whole Arab world will despise us . . . It may well be the end of British influence and strength forever.'⁶ The chiefs of the armed forces and the intelligence services had additional concerns. Three months earlier, a report circulated by the Joint Intelligence Committee warned of growing Soviet influence. 'Egypt is already in a position of increasing dependence on Russia . . . Moreover, the Egyptians are developing habits of collaboration with Russia; and, by way of keeping their benefactors happy, have begun to use their influence to facilitate Soviet penetration into Libya and perhaps also Syria, Yemen, Saudi Arabia and the Sudan.'⁷

When ministers met on 27 July, the atmosphere was one of shared outrage. Sir Norman Brook, the cabinet secretary, summarised the discussion. The cabinet agreed 'that Her Majesty's Government should seek to secure, through the use of force if necessary, the reversal of the decision of the Egyptian government to nationalise the Suez Canal Company'. The armed forces were instructed 'to prepare a plan and timetable for military operations against Egypt should they prove unavoidable'.⁸ The task fell to Sir Gerald Templer. Templer held the position of Chief of the Imperial General Staff, a title that spoke eloquently to the time warp in which his political masters were operating.

Ministers acknowledged that the legal position was ambiguous. The Suez Canal Company was registered under Egyptian law and Nasser had promised to compensate shareholders at a fair price. The canal had always been recognised as sovereign Egyptian territory, so Britain needed a *casus belli*. The cabinet decided that the case had to rest on the canal's status as an international waterway, as recognised by the Constantinople Convention of 1888. Eden asked colleagues if Britain should be ready to act alone if France and the United States demurred, and the answer was yes: 'Failure to hold the Suez Canal would lead inevitably to the loss one by one of all our interests and assets in the Middle East.'[9]

That day, Eden sought American support from Eisenhower in a personal note. 'We are all agreed', the prime minister began, 'that we cannot afford to allow Nasser to seize control of the Canal in this way, in defiance of international agreements. If we take a firm stand over this now, we shall have the support of all the maritime powers. If we do not, our influence and yours throughout the Middle East will, we are convinced, be irretrievably undermined.'[10] Eighteen years earlier, Eden had resigned as foreign secretary in protest at appeasement – he had kept his counsel when Hitler marched into the Rhineland, but Chamberlain's refusal to check Mussolini's Italian ambitions in the Mediterranean and East Africa was a step too far. Two years later, Chamberlain's government fell and Eden joined Winston Churchill's war cabinet – the dangers of appeasement by now printed indelibly on his worldview. Eden reminded Eisenhower of the parallel with Mussolini. 'Neither of us can forget the lives and treasure he cost us before he was finally dealt with. The removal of Nasser and installation in Egypt of a regime less hostile to the West must therefore rank high among our objectives.'[11]

A fatal asymmetry was visible here, at the very beginning of the crisis. While Britain and France, its partner in the canal, saw the crisis through the lens of empire, much of the rest of the world had an eye on the post-war institutions set up to preserve the international peace. For Eden, the threat was existential – the future of British power rested upon the outcome. It was also personal – an animus towards Nasser rooted in their past dealings. From this flowed his conviction that it would not be enough to regain control of the canal. Restoring British prestige required that Nasser be forced from office and replaced by a regime more respectful of the former imperial power. The Egypt Committee, a small group of ministers established to manage the crisis, was unequivocal in its conclusion that 'While our ultimate purpose was to place the Canal under international control, our immediate purpose was to bring about the downfall of the present Egyptian government.'[12] France, already battling a ferocious nationalist uprising in Algeria that had destabilised the government in Paris, shared this view. Beyond London and Paris Nasser's actions prompted a different reaction. Yes, the Egyptian action had been an outrage, and outside the Soviet bloc there was widespread agreement that the international community should mobilise to ensure open operation of the canal. But military force smacked of colonialism. The right answer was surely diplomacy. The appropriate forum, the United Nations.

Eisenhower's reply to Eden was firm. He had been informed of the prime minister's decision 'to employ force without delay or attempting any intermediate and less drastic steps'.[13] While the United States accepted that there might come a moment when force was required to uphold international rights, diplomacy must come first. He suggested a conference of the signatories of the Constantinople Convention: 'I cannot overemphasise the strength of my conviction that some such method must be attempted before action such as you contemplate should be undertaken.'[14] Public opinion in the United States would be outraged by precipitate action; if every peaceful means had been exhausted, opinion could be marshalled in favour of stronger measures.

Eisenhower's response triggered a sharp riposte from Sir Ivone Kirkpatrick, the permanent under-secretary at the Foreign Office. Kirkpatrick wrote to the British ambassador in Washington to arm him for his exchanges with the White House. He expressed himself in terms verging on the apocalyptic: 'If we sit back while

Nasser consolidates his position and gradually acquires control of the oil-bearing countries, he can and is, according to our information, resolved to wreck us. If Middle East oil is denied to us for a year or two, our gold reserves will disappear. If our gold reserves disappear, the sterling area disintegrates. If the sterling area disintegrates and we have no reserves, we shall not be able to maintain a force in Germany or, indeed, anywhere else. I doubt whether we shall be able to pay for the bare minimum necessary for our defence. And a country that cannot provide for its defence is finished.'[15]

Washington was no friend of Nasser. It feared he was leading Egypt – and Arab nationalism – into the Soviet camp. He had recently placed a large order with Czechoslovakia for the supply of Russian-made aircraft and tanks. But during the summer of 1956, other considerations also played in the minds of Eisenhower and his secretary of state John Foster Dulles. First and foremost was the presidential election in November. A British attack could trigger a wider Middle Eastern conflagration, and a crisis in the Middle East would be a serious distraction. Conveniently for Eisenhower, such expediency could be dressed up as principle. To British ears, the anti-colonialist lectures that Washington had pressed on its ally during and since the war verged on the sanctimonious. It could scarcely be a coincidence, ministers noted, that American influence in the Middle East had risen as British power had waned.

And in any case, the trigger for Nasser's move had been Eisenhower's announcement a week earlier that he was withdrawing Washington's promised financial backing for the construction of the Aswan Dam, a flagship project to irrigate the Nile Delta and modernise Egypt's economy. The American pull-out was calculated to show Washington's irritation at the Czech arms deal, but it backfired. Without American money, Nasser claimed, Egypt needed the dues that flowed into the Suez Canal Company. The American president reached for an argument that vexed his British ally: were the West to be seen as siding too obviously with the former colonial power, it would risk pushing other newly independent nations into Moscow's camp. The US needed Middle Eastern oil, and Egypt might lead the region into the embrace of Moscow.

The two leaders were talking past each other. Eden had not been impressed by what he saw as Roosevelt's anti-colonialist pose at the Yalta Conference. His enthusiasm for decolonisation, Eden had later observed, was 'a principle with him, not the less cherished for its possible advantages. He hoped that former colonial territories, once free of their masters, would become politically and economically dependent upon the United States.'[16] When Dulles arrived in London at the beginning of August, global opinion and the risk of Soviet intervention were front and centre of his case for diplomacy. And nothing should be done that might derail the president's prospect of re-election on 6 November. There would be moments during the following months when Eisenhower and Eden and their teams seemed genuinely to misread each other. The president and the secretary of state sometimes seemed to be sending subtly different messages. The essential divide, however, remained that between London and Washington.

If Eisenhower was worried about his election campaign, Eden felt secure that Britain would unite behind a military response. The first news of Nasser's move brought almost universal outrage: even the Labour-supporting *Daily Mirror* was firmly on Eden's side, splashing 'Grabber Nasser' across its front page, and the Tory press was gung-ho from the outset. Only the left-of-centre *Manchester Guardian* struck a restraining note. Comparisons with Hitler and Mussolini were widespread. In the House of Commons,

Hugh Gaitskell echoed the parallels Eden had drawn with the 1930s,[17] while the Suez Group of Tory MPs who had condemned Eden's earlier deal with Nasser now fell in behind him.

Across the Channel, France, like Britain, was a colonial power under pressure, and the two nations shared a determination not to bow to Arab nationalism. The French prime minister Guy Mollet was more eager than his British counterpart to confront Nasser. France had sponsored the newly established Israel, supplying it with sophisticated weaponry, including fighter jets. It had also signalled its willingness to sell secret nuclear technology to Ben-Gurion's government. The humiliation of its departure from Palestine had left Britain anxious to preserve its privileged relationship with Jordan and Iraq as head of the Baghdad Pact. A separate treaty with Jordan required the British to come to the assistance of King Hussein in the event that Israel sought to extend its territory into the West Bank. Eager as he was to act with France against Nasser, Ben-Gurion did not trust Britain. But the prize was too great to pass up. War would allow Israel to take control of the Straits of Tiran and the Gulf of Aqaba, ensuring access to the Red Sea. For Eden and Mollet, the prospect of defeating Nasser's pan-Arabism transcended tensions elsewhere in the region.

Where Eden saw a threat to Britain's status as a pre-eminent power in the Middle East, Mollet identified a more immediate danger for France. Egypt was supplying arms to the nationalists fighting against French rule in Algeria. If Nasser succeeded in Suez, the insurgency might well overwhelm the French forces. Mollet, like Eden, had not forgotten the 1930s. Appeasement was the certain route to defeat.

Eden opted for a twin-track approach. British and French military planners were set to work to take back the canal in a joint operation, with the British taking overall command. The navy began to assemble a task force based in Malta, and the RAF started to deploy fighters and bombers to Britain's sovereign base in Cyprus. However, Eisenhower and Dulles were at the same time assured that Britain would allow diplomacy to run its course. In early August, Eden agreed to a London conference of the twenty-four principal users of the canal to draw up new international guarantees for freedom of passage, which the Americans saw as a possible route to a negotiated outcome. Eden accepted the importance of persuading the new Commonwealth nations – India above all – that Britain wanted a peaceful outcome, while privately taking the view that the diplomatic game could be played as a precursor to the eviction by force of the Egyptians. The joint military operation planned with the French already had a code name: 'Operation Musketeer'.

Nasser boycotted the conference, but Dulles would not easily give up the role of mediator. He proposed the establishment of a new Canal Users' Association, which would oversee the interests of those nations dependent on free passage. If this American plan was tried and failed, foreign secretary John Selwyn Lloyd judged, Washington could be persuaded to back military action. Eisenhower showed no sign of changing his mind. 'I must tell you frankly', the president wrote to Eden, 'that American public opinion flatly rejects the thought of using force.'[18] Eden's response was to set the challenge in a wider frame. Once Nasser had established his power over the Arab world, he told the president, he would hold the West to ransom and could offer and withdraw free passage through the canal at Moscow's behest.

In Britain, the initial public support for military action began to cool. A sizeable section of the population believed the Egyptian leader should be 'taught a lesson', but, overall, opinion was less certain. As the immediate shock of the nationalisation faded, Gaitskell's Labour Party adopted a more nuanced position. When users of the canal assembled in London in late September, there were calls for the matter to be resolved at the United Nations. Had not the organisation been formed to uphold the international rule of law, so as to remove the resort to war? Sir Oliver Poole, the chairman of the Conservative Party, reported that enthusiasm within the party for armed intervention was weakening, and there were ominous signs in the financial markets of renewed pressure on sterling. India led the almost universal opposition to military action in the Commonwealth. If Britain was to go to war, Sir Edward Bridges, the Treasury's permanent secretary, told Macmillan, securing American support for the enterprise was vital. Selwyn Lloyd was sent to New York to make Britain's case at the UN, but preparations for Operation Musketeer rolled on.

The plot was hatched at Chequers in mid-October. France's Mollet had grown frustrated by what was seen as American obstructionism. By now he had concluded that the uprising in Algeria could be put down only if Nasser was removed. His government had moved ever closer to Israel, which had its own strategic interests in seizing Sharm el-Sheikh and securing unimpeded access to the Gulf of Aqaba. General Maurice Challe, the deputy chief of the French armed forces, and Albert Gazier, the acting foreign minister, arrived at Chequers with the outline of a new plan. Israel would invade, and Britain and France would send in their own forces in the guise of peacemakers. Eden was hooked: the plan could be executed before the presidential election in the United States, and Eisenhower would not risk losing the support of Jewish voters by condemning Israel's action. Selwyn Lloyd's concern was not the deception, but that the pretext was sufficiently credible.[19] He joined the conspiracy, and within days was in Paris to confer with Mollet and Pineau.

The mistrust between Britain and Israel ran deep. In 1946, ninety-one people had been killed when the Zionist Irgun had bombed the headquarters of the British Mandatory Authority in the King David Hotel in Jerusalem. Policymakers in London instinctively took the Arab side in disputes with the new Jewish state. Even as France was preparing to help Ben-Gurion's government to establish a reactor in the Negev desert, the British government was warning Tel Aviv to abandon its rumoured plans for an attack on Jordan. In such circumstances, Britain, bound by treaty to protect Jordan, would have been obliged to send military support to the Hashemite kingdom.[20] Such were the complexities of the Middle East. Field Marshal Templer, preparing for the Suez operation, laconically remarked that ministers had to be told that 'We could either go to the aid of Jordan [against Israel] with air and sea power, or we could launch Musketeer [with Israel]; we could not do both.'[21]

The Protocol of Sèvres betrayed this mutual mistrust. Each paragraph was closely negotiated by Ben-Gurion to allay Israel's doubts about British intentions. His aspiration for a complete redrawing of the map of the Middle East far outstripped Eden's willingness to put to one side old animosities. However, mutual advantage outweighed past enmity and the document provided clear testimony of the three-way collusion. Eden had found his way to war. Israel too could claim a prize beyond the opportunity to degrade Nasser's military capabilities. It was agreed that the document would remain forever secret, but Ben-Gurion had secured the written support of two great powers for a war with the Arabs – a significant diplomatic coup for the new Israeli state.

Donald Logan waited thirty years before setting out his account of the way the conspiracy had unfolded.[22] He had been vaguely aware of the talks at Chequers, but had first been told of the plan by Selwyn Lloyd when the two men travelled to Sèvres. They had been greeted by Pineau, before being ushered into a room to meet Mollet and the Israeli delegation: Ben-Gurion was accompanied by his chief of staff, Moshe Dayan, and the director general of the defence ministry, Shimon Peres. There were moments during the next two days when it seemed that the enterprise might stumble. When Logan returned for the second day, he found that Pineau was worried about Selwyn Lloyd's commitment and had decided to travel to London to speak to the prime minister. By the third day, with the conspiracy back on track, Patrick Dean and Logan were ensuring that the final agreement reflected the terms of the discussions. The protocol complete, the three parties signed each of the copies.

There is nothing startling about the Protocol of Sèvres,[23] nothing in its rhetorical style to betray the scale of the deceit. But the crude intent is indisputable: it sets out how Israel will invade Egypt on the evening of 29 October and press forward towards the Suez Canal. Acting as neutral powers, Britain and France will demand an immediate end to hostilities and the withdrawal of forces to a distance of ten miles from the canal. Egypt will be told it must accept a temporary occupation of the Canal Zone by Anglo–French forces – an ultimatum Nasser could never accept. If the appeals are not accepted within twelve hours, the two outside powers will send in their own forces, and Israel will be obliged to stop fighting only if Egypt does likewise. The agreement notes that the plan will remain secret, but that it will enter into force as soon as it is signed by the three governments.

Eden's senior ministers heard nothing of this plan. As Selwyn Lloyd and Logan headed to Paris to finalise the details of the plot, Eden told a cabinet meeting that speculation about an Israeli attack on Egypt seemed unlikely to be true. One member of the cabinet, the defence secretary Walter Monckton, had some weeks earlier raised a red flag, but in his single-minded determination to defeat Nasser, Eden had lost sight of how much was at stake. Beyond the threat to the relationship with Washington, unilateral military intervention would defy the Commonwealth and mock the government's oft-declared commitment to uphold the rules-based international system enshrined by the United Nations. Monckton did not want to embarrass Eden, and it was agreed that he would quietly be moved to the low-profile role of paymaster general. The prime minister's deal with Mollet and Ben-Gurion was to be a tightly held secret. When Logan and Dean returned from Paris with their signed copy of the protocol, Eden expressed alarm that everything had been so clearly written down. He ordered that if there were copies, they must be destroyed. Logan took up the story: 'On the following day, 25 October, we were instructed to return to Paris to ask the French to destroy their copy of the document.'[24] The mission failed. Kept waiting for hours in one of the grand reception rooms at the Quai d'Orsay, the two officials were told eventually by Pineau that Ben-Gurion had already returned to Israel with his copy, and the French government saw no reason to destroy the one it held.

The military campaign went largely to plan. If there was a miscalculation, it was that it would take several days to secure control of the canal. The Israelis faced limited opposition as they advanced. The Franco–British ultimatum was duly issued and rejected by Nasser. On 31 October, British and French warplanes took to the skies to bomb Egyptian airfields and military installations, with paratroopers leading the advance force to seize physical control of the canal. However, Eden had underestimated the strength, both nationally and internationally, of the reaction. His insistence that the British intervention represented a 'police action' did nothing to dampen angry protests at Westminster nor to dispel suspicion that the enterprise had been carefully orchestrated. The prime minister's refusal to offer a detailed commentary on the course of the military campaign prompted Gaitskell to table a motion of censure in the House of Commons. He charged that by 'a disastrous act of folly', the government had launched an 'assault upon the three principles which have governed British foreign policy for, at any rate, the last ten years: solidarity with the Commonwealth, the Anglo–American alliance and adherence to the Charter of the United Nations'.[25]

Defeat for Eden came not on the battlefield but in the court of public opinion and the international financial markets. In Britain, a sizeable section of the population held on to Lord Palmerston's faith in gunboat diplomacy, but the mood was shifting. The nation was still paying the costs of the Second World War and had little appetite for military adventurism. Some 100,000 British troops had been sent to Korea as part of an American-led United Nations force. The war against the communist-led north had ended only three years earlier, and the public was loath to see the nation's young soldiers now dispatched to the Middle East. On the liberal left of politics, the confrontation between the West and the Soviet Union had lent strength to the argument that global peace was better safeguarded by diplomacy than by military aggression. Wasn't that the purpose of the United Nations? The country was also witnessing a deeper, cultural shift. The age of deference was passing. 1956 was the year of Elvis as well as Suez. John Osborne's *Look Back in Anger* challenged the old order. The Empire was coming home in the shape of the Caribbean workers needed to sustain the nation's public services. Eden was stranded in a passing age.

Had the prime minister acted in August, he would probably have had the nation behind him, but by early November, opinion was evenly balanced. Opponents made the most noise. Gathering with his cabinet on Sunday 4 November, the day before British troops were due to land at Port Said, Eden could hear the roar of disapproval from demonstrators marching towards Downing Street from Trafalgar Square. It seemed obvious to all but the government's most ardent supporters that Selwyn Lloyd's talks at the United Nations had been a charade. There were astonishing scenes at Westminster, as MPs demanded to be told if Britain was formally at war. The *Observer*'s proprietor David Astor added a damning sentence to the newspaper's condemnation of the invasion: 'We had not realised that our government was capable of such folly and crookedness.'[26]

The anger at home was nothing compared to the outrage in the Arab world, across the Commonwealth and, above all, in Washington. Eden and Macmillan had badly misread the United States, taking the administration's slightly ambiguous signals as evidence that it would acquiesce in a military campaign. Macmillan, an old friend of Eisenhower's from their time during the war in North Africa, had visited the White House at the end of September, and the president had not raised objections to the British handling of Suez. Macmillan wrongly concluded that silence could be taken for assent, returning to London to inform Eden that 'Ike will lie doggo'.[27]

The preparations for war had not gone unnoticed in Washington. On the eve of the Israeli attack, the State Department's Intelligence Advisory Committee noted the build-up of Israeli troops, adding that 'Highly sensitive information indicates that the British have brought up their air strength on Cyprus in the last forty-eight hours to sixty-three Canberras [medium bombers], doubling previous strength. French transport aircraft to the number of eighteen have arrived within the last twenty-four hours, making a total of twenty-one and giving capability of airlifting 1,500 men.'[28] But the US administration remained in the dark about the Protocol of Sèvres. Eisenhower's blunt public response to the invasion understated his private anger: 'The United States was not consulted in any way about any phase of these actions. Nor were we informed of them in advance . . . there will be no United States involvement in these present hostilities.'[29]

Dulles set out the American position during a meeting of Eisenhower's National Security Council. Washington wanted to hold on to old allies, but also needed 'to assure ourselves of the friendship and understanding of the newly independent countries who have escaped from colonialism'.[30] Within hours of the Israeli attack, the administration convened the United Nations Security Council and tabled a motion calling for an immediate ceasefire. Britain and France found themselves wielding their vetoes against their close ally. Eisenhower had not finished and the motion was submitted to the General Assembly. Unable to exercise a veto, Britain and France saw sixty-four of the UN's member states line up against them. For the first time in the history of the organisation, the United States joined with the Soviet Union in censuring its European allies. Only Australia and New Zealand joined Britain, France and Israel in opposing the resolution. The Commonwealth was overwhelmingly hostile to the intervention, with Canada proposing the immediate dispatch of a United Nations force to supervise a ceasefire. Across the Middle East, demonstrators took to the streets to protest against British 'imperialism'. After the war, the chiefs of staff would recognise that the world had changed: 'The one overriding lesson of the Suez operation is that world opinion is now an absolute principle of war and must be treated as such.'[31]

Even allowing for Washington's anger at the subterfuge, Eisenhower's response was extraordinary. Five years earlier,

Britain had sent its troops to fight alongside the Americans in Korea. Now, even as the world's two superpowers were locked in a struggle between Western liberal democracy and Soviet communism, Washington sided with Moscow. Part of the explanation lay in events in eastern Europe. The Soviet Union faced popular uprisings in Poland and Hungary, with the new government in Budapest defiantly opposing its vassal status within the communist sphere of influence. As British paratroops prepared to seize positions around the canal and British ships carried troops from Malta to Port Said, Nikita Khrushchev sent six divisions of the Soviet army into Hungary to confront the demonstrators. Britain's colonial adventurism had effectively disarmed the West. The Hungarian revolt was crushed. In censuring the Suez adventure, as well as Moscow's repression, Eisenhower sought as best he could to take the moral high ground.

Washington went further still. As the international uproar produced a flight from the pound among international investors, Macmillan reported a rapid drain on the Bank of England's dollar and gold reserves. Doubts were raised in the Treasury as to how long the government would be able to retain sterling's rate against the dollar. Previously insouciant about the economic consequences, Macmillan now became the cabinet's leading dove. Nasser had blocked the canal with sunken ships, cutting off the route for Britain's oil supplies, and Saudi Arabia had announced an oil embargo, but the hammer blow was delivered by the Americans. As the largest shareholder in the Bretton Woods institutions, the United States blocked British access to emergency funds from the International Monetary Fund. The US Federal Reserve stood in the way of any bailout by the West's leading central banks, and Washington indicated that it would not help Britain secure alternative oil supplies. In the later description of the presidential adviser Richard Neustadt, the Treasury secretary George Humphrey offered Eden a choice between 'an immediate ceasefire and a war on the pound'.[32]

British ground troops went ashore at Port Said on 6 November. The following day, at Macmillan's insistence, Eden acquiesced to the United Nations' call for a ceasefire. It was agreed that British troops would remain in Egypt only until they could be replaced with an international force. This was total defeat – an expedition mounted to enhance British prestige had ended in humiliation. Suez had forced a breach with Britain's most important ally. Nasser had remained in power, and the Arab world, including Eden's allies Jordan and Iraq, had turned against Britain. France, which had been willing to defy the Americans, felt betrayed by the speed with which its co-conspirator buckled so quickly in the face of pressure from the White House.

Britain's ambitions to remain the leading power in the Middle East had been shattered. Ironically, Washington soon realised that this left a vacuum in the region and an opportunity for Moscow. Here was a recurring paradox of US policy. Even as it pressed Britain to roll up its empire, the United States found itself obliged to step in as a counterweight to the Soviet Union. Its commitment to the independence of former colonies was soon tempered by its perception of its own national interest. At a meeting of the National Security Council in November 1956, Dulles admitted that Washington had been walking a tightrope. A year after Suez, the US president announced the 'Eisenhower Doctrine', a security guarantee to the West's Arab allies calculated to replace British with American power.

Eden refused to admit anything of the conspiracy, even as rumours of collusion hardened into charges that the three governments had carefully choreographed the crisis. The content of the Protocol of Sèvres would remain secret until Ben-Gurion's copy was made public more than three decades later. For all that, Eden's statement to the House of Commons in December 1956 was breathtaking in its mendacity: 'I want to say this on the question of foreknowledge, and to say it quite bluntly to the House, that there was not foreknowledge that Israel would attack Egypt. There was not.'[33] Across the Atlantic, the US State Department carried out its own secret investigation into the affair, which was handed to Eisenhower in December. The report's title, 'Evidence of UK–French–Israeli Collusion and Deception in Connection with Attacks on Egypt',[34] betrayed the conclusion reached by top officials. The deliberate lies, the report noted sourly, had been directed as much against the United States as against the Egyptian dictator. The French had been more deceitful than the British, but all three co-conspirators had deliberately defied Washington. Eisenhower was puzzled why, having set out on such a dangerous path, the British prime minister had lost his nerve. The US diplomat George Kennan was more sonorous in his judgement, noting Washington's mishandling of Nasser: 'We bear a heavy measure of responsibility for the desperation that has driven the French and British governments to this ill-conceived and pathetic action.'[35] Eden's lie had hammered a final nail into a broken premiership. By January, he had shuffled from the stage and Macmillan had taken his place in Downing Street.

Suez became a metaphor for the end of empire, but in truth it was a reflection as much as a cause of the geopolitical realities of the Pax Americana. When Eden and others had looked in the mirror, they had seen a Britain that could still get its way in the world. Retreat shattered the glass. Britain was still a significant power, but it was unable to flout international opinion or defy its American ally. Whatever the United States' obligations to Britain, the starting point for US policymakers would always be the contest with the Soviet Union. Chastened by the experience of Suez, British politicians would henceforth tuck themselves in behind the American superpower. Margaret Thatcher would later reflect on the lessons of Suez.[36] One was that Britain could not embark on such enterprises without the support of the Americans. Another that, once undertaken, they must be seen through to their conclusion. A third was 'He who hesitates is lost.' The thought was at the front of her mind nearly thirty years later, when she dispatched a task force to retake the Falklands from Argentina.

The crisis would also have a profound impact on Britain's relationships with its European neighbours. The speed with which Eden had capitulated to Washington confirmed French politicians' prejudices: the English would always set their relationship with the United States above that with fellow Europeans. The conclusion drawn in Paris was that France must press ahead with the process of reconciliation and integration with the old enemy, Germany. Like Britain, France still hankered after a global role, but its chosen instrument would be political leadership in Europe. Konrad Adenauer, the West German chancellor, did as much as he could to encourage Mollet: 'There remains only one way of playing a decisive role in the world: that is to unite to make Europe. England is not ripe for it, but the affair of Suez will help prepare her spirits for it. We have no time to waste: Europe will be your revenge.'[37]

Sickly and exhausted, Eden recuperated at the novelist Ian Fleming's Jamaican hideaway, Goldeneye. A few years earlier, Fleming's *Casino Royale* had introduced the dashing figure of James Bond, agent 007 of Her Majesty's Secret Service. Suave and impeccably well dressed, as well as courageous, Bond was soon an emblem of Britain as it imagined itself. Suez turned the page. Graham Greene was soon presenting an updated perspective on the nation's standing in the world. In *Our Man in Havana,* Greene replaced the tuxedo-wearing 007 with the frayed Jim Wormold, a vacuum-cleaner salesman persuaded to moonlight for the spy-masters in London.

2

Greeks and Romans

Winston Churchill was at ease in Schloss Cecilienhof. Built for Crown Prince Wilhelm thirty years earlier, it stands in the royal park of the gilded Prussian town of Potsdam. When Kaiser Wilhelm commissioned the palace for his son, the architectural fashion of the time dictated a timbered residence in the English mock Tudor style. Britain's wartime prime minister might have been spending a shooting weekend with wealthy friends in the English Home Counties. Instead, in the late summer of 1945, Churchill was sharing the wood-panelled schloss with Joseph Stalin and Harry Truman. It was one of the few substantial buildings within striking distance of Berlin that had survived the final Allied onslaught. Hastily refurnished with what could be found in the nearby villas of the Prussian aristocracy (though Stalin brought his own less ornamented furniture from Moscow), it hosted the last of the great-power conferences. At Tehran and Yalta, the three leaders had mapped the path to victory. Now they remoulded the contours of Europe as they shared the spoils. Boundaries were changed at the stroke of a pen, populations moved like chess pieces on a board to fit the new geopolitical realities.

The schloss, preserved as a museum, still exudes the awesome significance of the moment. In the great hall, Truman, Stalin and Churchill stare down at the conference table on which the maps were redrawn. 'The Big Three', runs the simple caption below the outsize photograph of the three leaders. This was the phrase above all others that warmed Churchill's heart. Here was confirmation that the direction of world affairs would continue to be

43

set in Washington, Moscow and, yes, London. Churchill negotiated with Truman and Stalin as an equal. This, in its essence, was Britain's sense of itself at the moment of victory.

The self-image was blind to reality. The war had remade the world's economic and political landscape. Europe, a continent that had come to see itself as the centre of world civilisation and the indispensable engine of prosperity and progress, lay, literally, in ruins. The United States, the industrial motor of the Allied war effort, in 1945 accounted for about half of all global output. Unscarred by the physical destruction of the war, it stood unchallenged as the world's largest and richest economy. The war had been a boon to many of its industries, forcing the pace of technological advance and new mass-production techniques. The explosion of the atomic bombs over Hiroshima and Nagasaki attested to Washington's undoubted military primacy. The United States alone was in possession of the deadliest weapon humanity had ever seen. For its part, Stalin's Soviet Union had weathered untold hardship and the death of more than twenty-five million citizens to mobilise a vast military–industrial complex in the successful effort to halt Hitler's drive eastwards. What it lacked in technological sophistication, Moscow made up for in unswerving determination and ideological conviction. Its troops occupied most of the eastern half of the continent. The Soviet Union would not loosen its grip on the new satellite states of communism. Instead it would reach out across the globe for converts. The world would soon be described by the Cold War contest between Washington and Moscow, West and East.

At this moment of victory, Britain was exhausted, its empire precarious and its finances close to ruin. Three months before the German surrender, Churchill offered a premonition of the challenges of the peace at a private dinner. There was a fear abroad, he said, that 'We should be weak, we should have no money and we should lie between the two great powers of the United States of America and the Union of Soviet Socialist Republics.'[1] The architect of victory, he was more popular than ever when the wartime coalition government dissolved barely three weeks after VE Day. The same could not be said of the Conservative Party. Invited on 5 July to elect a Tory government, the voters delivered a landslide victory to Clement Attlee's Labour Party. 'Let us face the future,' Labour's manifesto had declared. Attlee promised post-war economic and social reform – the free health care, housing and decent social benefits that would come with the creation of a welfare state. His campaign drew a contrast between the politics of post-war revival and the harsh economic policies pursued by the Tories during the Great Depression of the 1930s. Health, housing and poverty were the issues uppermost in the mind of an exhausted nation and its returning armed forces. Attlee took Churchill's seat at Potsdam at the end of July.

Britain's place in the new order was to be half obscured behind a simple phrase – one that through the subsequent decades would be at once a proud boast of and a perennial burden on the nation's prime ministers. Britain's road to global influence would henceforth run through Washington, enshrined in a 'special relationship' between the world's foremost English-speaking powers. The phrase, and its double-edged legacy for his successors, had been deployed by Churchill during the 1930s. During the war, Harold Macmillan served as Churchill's representative at General Dwight D. Eisenhower's military headquarters in Algiers. The British role in setting the Allies' military strategy, Macmillan had remarked to his colleague Richard Crossman, was to act as Greece to America's Rome. Crossman, Macmillan said, would likely 'find the Americans much as the Greeks found the Romans – great big, vulgar, bustling people, more vigorous than we are and also more idle, with more unspoiled virtues but also more corrupt'. The answer? 'We must run AFHQ as the Greek slaves ran the operations of the Emperor Claudius.'[2]

The Americans would supply the brawn, the British the brains. This was the reassuring conceit that henceforth underwrote the British view of the 'special relationship'. The pact would be waved as a standard and, at times, carried as a boulder by future prime ministers. Waving the standard would act as a multiplier of influence: other nations, in Europe and beyond, would give closer attention to policies promoted in London if they knew the Brits had the ear of Washington. And the United States would be more easily persuaded by British arguments if it knew that its ally was shaping the debate elsewhere. But the boulder could not be ignored. Could Britain strike out on its own when to do so would incur the wrath of Washington? How was the prime minister viewed in the White House? These would become permanent neuroses. With every change of president would come an embarrassing scramble in London to ensure the prime minister was the first on the list of foreign leaders invited to the White House. The line between partnership and submissiveness was perilously thin. The Americans did not always make it easy. Macmillan noted as much after the Conservatives returned to office at the end of 1951, writing in his diary that during the war the British had been treated as being on an equal footing – a respected ally. 'Now we are treated by the Americans with a mixture of patronising pity and contempt.'[3] Perhaps it was a mistake to consider them Anglo-Saxons. Confirming his personal prejudices, Macmillan continued: 'That blood is very much watered down now; they are a Latin–Slav mixture with a fair amount of German and Irish.' On the other side of the Atlantic, Dean Acheson, Truman's secretary of state, was a self-declared Anglophile, but he barred the use of 'special relationship' within the State Department, lest it signal to other allies that Britain received special privileges.[4]

Through the subsequent decades, some prime ministers managed this delicate balance between solidarity and submission better than others. Macmillan won the respect of John F. Kennedy. Harold Wilson's refusal to send even a token military force to Vietnam produced famous rows with Lyndon Johnson, yet this decision ranks among the best in Britain's post-war foreign policy. Margaret Thatcher got on well with Ronald Reagan, yet France's François Mitterrand was the first to come to her aid after the Argentine invasion of the Falklands and Reagan saw no need to ask Britain's permission before sending troops into Commonwealth Grenada. Tony Blair once remarked that it was his 'duty' as prime minister to get along with President George W. Bush. This put him on a path that led inexorably to the Iraq War, a misadventure ranking alongside Suez as among the most calamitous of modern times.

It was too easy for British policymakers to delude themselves. The historian David Watt credited Winston Churchill with the 'beneficent myth'[5] of a unique transatlantic bond. Thrown out by the British voters in 1945, he remained as popular as ever with the American public. Early in 1946, he set out on an American tour, taking in his mother's birthplace in New York's Brooklyn, as well as making visits to Miami and Washington, before travelling to Fulton, Missouri. The measure of his stature was that Truman decided to accompany the British politician as he collected an honorary degree from Westminster College. The Fulton speech – the 'Sinews of Peace', Churchill had called it – is most often remembered for its dark predictions about the advance of communism in Europe: 'From Stettin in the Baltic to Trieste in the Adriatic, an iron curtain has descended across the continent.' All the capitals of the ancient states of eastern and central Europe – Warsaw, Berlin, Prague, Vienna, Budapest, Belgrade, Bucharest and Sofia – were imprisoned in what Churchill called 'the Soviet sphere'. Local communist parties and Moscow-backed fifth columnists were destabilising legitimate governments elsewhere in western Europe.

Churchill's bleak analysis coincided with the call for containment of the communist threat made by George Kennan, the American deputy head of mission in Moscow. Kennan's 'Long Telegram', as it was called, fitted Churchill's purpose. Communism, the wartime prime minister argued, could be countered only if the United States and the United Kingdom jointly assumed leadership of the Western democracies. America, of course, was a nation at 'the pinnacle of world power', he said, but no one should underestimate Britain's capacity to come through the dark period of economic privation it faced in the immediate aftermath of the war: 'Let no man underrate the abiding power of the British Empire and Commonwealth.' The United Nations needed leadership. 'Neither the sure prevention of war nor the continuous rise of world organisation will be gained without what I have called the fraternal association of the English-speaking peoples. This means a special relationship between the British Commonwealth and Empire and the United States.'[6]

Churchill's expansive view saw a partnership nurtured by shared history and cultural affinity, as well as a common language. The ties were as much about sentiment and emotion, kith and kin, values and ideals as about shared interests or threats. This was British myth-making at its most extravagant. True, Churchill (and Macmillan) could boast the familial bond of an American-born mother, but the century and more since British forces had sacked the White House in the War of 1812 had scarcely seen a consistently warm relationship. The alliances during two world wars had been preceded mainly by indifference and occasional hostility. The most many Americans knew about Britain was that it had once been the colonial power and that its sympathies had tilted towards the Confederacy during the Civil War. Churchill's legacy was a description of the 'special relationship' that would often buckle under the weight of competing interests. If sentimentalism was sometimes useful, firmer foundations were provided by networks of institutional cooperation established during the war and nourished beyond it. Collaboration in the military, intelligence and diplomacy spheres outlived periodic spats between presidents and prime ministers. The UKUSA Agreement, concluded in 1946, provided the basis for an extraordinarily close relationship between the Secret Intelligence Service and the Central Intelligence Agency, and the GCHQ electronic communications centre and America's National Security Agency.[7] Britain's willingness to lease to Washington outposts of its former empire, such as Diego Garcia in the Indian Ocean, strengthened military ties. The bureaucracies in both capitals established a measure of trust and habits of cooperation beyond the bounds of most alliances.

Churchill commanded the stage. Attlee preferred the cabinet committee room to the limelight. And yet he was to prove among the most effective and consequential of Britain's post-war leaders, redrawing the boundaries of the state and the government's responsibilities for national welfare. As for Britain's international role, he was with Churchill. The belief in the restoration of national power and prestige was shared across the political divide at Westminster. Attlee, no less than Churchill, was a champion of British exceptionalism. Why should the consequences of the war mark a step down in Britain's global position? After all, against all the odds, it had won. The writ of Empire, His Majesty's Colonial Office reassured itself, still ran across large tracts of the globe. The military had nearly three million troops under arms. The great trading bloc of Empire and Commonwealth, buttressed by sterling's role as an international reserve currency, would be revived.

Britain still ruled, this exercise in self-deception continued, the imperial jewel that was India. It was the dominant power in the Middle East, with control of the Suez Canal and a vital strategic foothold in the oil-rich Gulf. Much of Africa was governed from London. The English-speaking dominions – Canada, Australia and New Zealand – still flew the flag of British power. The defeat of Japan would see lost possessions restored in the Far East, reversing the humiliation inflicted in 1942 by the fall of Singapore. Even where the Empire retreated, it would leave behind a Commonwealth of nations that looked to London for leadership. Why shouldn't Britain believe in itself? The war had been testimony to the national character and to the resilience of the country's institutions. In that late summer of 1945, Britain surely had the right to imagine itself standing tall again, in the front rank of nations? The United States was a newcomer. The Soviet Union seemed an unlikely competitor. When Churchill spoke of Britain being uniquely placed at the intersection of the three circles of global power – the Empire and Commonwealth, the US and Europe – he was doing no more than articulating the opinions of the nation's political class. It was for France and Germany to build a United States of Europe.[8] Britain had made great sacrifices in the cause of freedom: the United States would surely recognise this unique contribution? It seemed obvious to the politicians gathered in the new parliament that life would be just as it had been in Tehran, Yalta and Potsdam. British politicians would cling on to this dangerous delusion for another decade.

The American worldview, as the Attlee government soon learned, did not accommodate the delicate ego of a declining power. Pragmatism and self-interest ruled in Washington, and American politicians proved as hard-headed as the British voters who had turned their backs on Churchill. Roosevelt had been persuaded during the war that America's security could not be detached from the balance of power on the other side of the Atlantic, but in 1945 this view was far from universal among American lawmakers. Most politicians on Capitol Hill wanted to bring the boys home. Even Roosevelt did not expect a long military entanglement. In wartime talks with Stalin he had suggested that Washington would disengage within a couple of years of German surrender. It looked like the Americans might repeat the mistakes of the 1920s, when the United States' isolationism had played its part in the rise of Nazi Germany. The calculation only changed in response to the expansionist plans of the Soviet Union. It was not until 1947 – a year after the receipt in Washington of Kennan's 'Long Telegram' – that the United States decided that its strategic interest lay in resisting the spread of Soviet communism.

Britain and its empire had been sustained through the war by the US Lend–Lease programme – the ingenious scheme devised by Roosevelt in 1941 in order to ship across the Atlantic tens of billions of dollars' worth of war materiel and essential supplies, while bypassing the wrath of isolationists. Described by Churchill as 'that most unselfish and unsordid financial act of any country in all history',[9] it provided the cement in the alliance once the United States formally entered the war. Roosevelt had cloaked what was effectively American aid in terms of US security, giving help to America's friends in their struggle against the Nazis in the name of an 'Act to promote the Defence of the United States'. The money came from the military budget, and the isolationists on Capitol Hill were assured that it was essential to protect the American homeland. For Britain, the arrangement was an essential lifeline and a source of the trust and intimacy that guided the two nations' planning and prosecution of the war. Congress had never been fully convinced, and as the guns fell silent, voices were raised against the diversion of American taxpayers' funds towards the reconstruction of Europe. American voters wanted their politicians to turn their attention to problems closer to home. The administration was itself at best ambivalent about how much help to offer its ally. Roosevelt and Truman both set the dissolution of the British Empire as a key post-war goal. Moral superiority and selfish interest spoke with one voice: Washington would not pay for the Empire's upkeep.

The sense of shock in London was laid bare on 12 December 1945, when MPs voted on the terms of a new financial arrangement with the United States. Four months earlier, Truman had called an abrupt halt to Lend–Lease, although after frantic representations from Attlee Britain had been allowed to keep goods that were already in transit. Amid near panic in London, a high-level delegation led by the distinguished economist John Maynard Keynes was dispatched to Washington to negotiate a peacetime deal. American dollars were vital if Britain was to hold on to its overseas territories and meet its foreign currency commitments – not least the cost of maintaining troops in countries seized from the Axis powers. A loan was agreed, but its terms saw the Americans treat the British as suppliants rather than friends or allies. Here was a glimpse of the future balance of power. The British, *The Economist* thundered in a scathing editorial, learned that 'our reward for losing a quarter of our national wealth in the common cause is to pay tribute for half a century to those who have been enriched by the war'.[10]

The measure of the Truman administration's ruthlessness was laid bare by Hugh Dalton, the Chancellor of the Exchequer, when the agreement was debated in the House of Commons in December. Dalton might have been expected to offer a robust defence of the deal. Instead he presented the terms as much in resignation as in celebration. The loan would rescue the country from the immediate prospect of economic collapse, but the chancellor could not explain why Britain should be obliged to bear so much of the burden of what had been a shared fight for freedom. The 'great load of debt' the country now confronted 'is, indeed, a strange reward for all we in this land did and suffered for the common cause'.[11] As to the financial details, Dalton admitted that talks had nearly broken down more than once. The British delegation had begun by asking for a straightforward grant from Washington in recognition of Britain's contribution to the war effort. The end of wartime aid, Keynes pleaded, had confronted Britain with a 'financial Dunkirk'. The Americans were unimpressed. Keynes's second pitch had been for an interest-free loan, but still they would not budge. Finally, Keynes had no choice but to accept an interest rate of 2 per cent on a credit line of $3.75 billion. Repayment was to be made in fifty annual instalments, starting in 1951.

The level of interest was consistent with market rates, but the Americans made the loan conditional on Britain agreeing to an array of new global economic arrangements that had been designed in Washington. The Bretton Woods system – the creation of the International Monetary Fund and the World Bank – and the provision for multilateral trade liberalisation through a General Agreement on Tariffs and Trade would later be seen as the pillars of a new economic order, from which all rich democracies, including Britain, would eventually benefit. But the American plans were born of self-interest rather than altruism. The goal was to safeguard and promote the interests of the world's largest economy and to put an end to the advantages that Britain had gained from its empire. The most damaging condition demanded of Keynes was the full 'convertibility' of sterling into other currencies by the end of 1947. Technical though this change might have seemed, it would greatly loosen Britain's economic hold over its colonies and dominions. They would no longer find themselves tied to the purchase of British goods and services and could swap sterling for dollars. This would intensify the financial strains on Britain while cementing the dollar's role as the leading international reserve currency. Those across the Empire and Commonwealth who had previously 'bought British' could choose to shop American. Before the war, Britain had been the world's largest creditor and earned significant sums from trade across the Empire and Commonwealth. Now it was a debtor, vulnerable to shifts in sentiment towards sterling. In addition, Washington insisted that all imperial trade preferences be scrapped. The rules of the Bretton Woods institutions were similarly skewed in favour of the Americans. Power was vested in nations that recorded trade surpluses, and above all the US, and countries such as Britain that were struggling with deficits would be supplicants. Years later, Dalton voiced the bitter sense of betrayal: 'We retreated, slowly and with bad grace and with increasing irritation . . . to the most unwilling acceptance of strings so tight that they might strangle our trade and, indeed, our whole economic life.'[12] As for the Americans, they would privately admit their ruthlessness. 'We loaded the British loan negotiations with all the conditions the traffic would bear,' the assistant secretary of state William Clayton confessed.

Many at Westminster refused to bow to Washington. Dalton's speech provoked outbursts of rage on the Conservative benches, articulated most violently by those on the Tory right who called themselves 'empire loyalists'. They were assured of the backing of the newspaper proprietor Lord Beaverbrook, the owner of the *Daily Express*, and other peers such as Brendan Bracken. The loan, Tory MP Robert Boothby charged, represented an 'economic Munich', and Britain would spend the money buying, among other things, American tobacco: 'There is one mandate which His Majesty's Government never got from the people of this country, and that was to sell the British Empire for a packet of cigarettes,'[13] he thundered as he tossed a cigarette packet onto the floor of the House of Commons. Churchill, now leader of the opposition, shared his disappointment, admitting to fellow MPs that it was a 'great pity' that the loan had been mixed up with other arrangements, such as those for Bretton Woods. He thought the demand for sterling convertibility so perilous that it might prove impossible – a judgement that was proven correct in 1947, when convertibility was introduced and, in the face of a financial crisis, immediately suspended again. Churchill found the bar on imperial trade preferences 'most objectionable'. Why should the opposition, he continued, 'come forward to approve and welcome a proposal which fills every party in the House with great anxiety, and which is only commended to us by fear of an even darker alternative'?[14] Ultimately, Churchill abstained, but some seventy other Conservatives joined Boothby in the No Lobby. One hundred MPs rejected the agreement, and another 169 abstained.

The arrival of Ernest Bevin came as something of a shock to the diplomats of the Foreign Office. Accustomed to serving the alumni of the finest public schools and universities – institutions they had themselves attended – Whitehall's mandarins were taken aback by the rough-hewn manners of the former dockers' union official appointed by Attlee as foreign secretary. Bevin, they would soon discover, was a politician of intelligence, courage and wit. George Brown, Harold Wilson's foreign secretary during the 1960s, was among his many admirers: 'He was a man with little or no taught advantages, who relied wholly upon his own brain, his imagination and his capacity for envisaging things and people. In this capacity he was not surpassed and I think not even matched by anyone else I have ever met.'[15] A convinced socialist but a fierce anti-communist and firm Atlanticist, Bevin was never naive about Washington's pursuit of its own interests. His relationship with James Byrnes, the secretary of state, was cool at best. The condescending Byrnes, Bevin noted, was keen to diminish Britain's role in shaping the post-war order. When, in the autumn of 1946, the Treasury objected to the cost of the secret British programme to build an atomic weapon, it was Bevin who carried the argument for a nuclear capability independent of Washington. 'No, Prime Minister, this will not do,' he remarked when others raised objections to the project. 'I do not mind for myself, but I do not want any other foreign secretary of this country to be talked at by the Secretary of State of the United States as I have just had in my discussions with Mr Byrnes. We have got to have this thing over here whatever it costs. We've got to have a bloody Union Jack on it.'[16] Bevin's Atlanticism was rooted in pragmatism rather than emotional or political attachment. The government, he told the House of Commons, did not accept 'the view submitted by the hon. Member for Devonport (Mr Foot) that we have ceased to be a great power, or the contention that we have ceased to play that role . . . The very fact that we have fought so hard for liberty, and paid such a price, warrants our retaining this position.'[17] But he also understood the immediate facts of economics. Britain needed the United States. The peace settlement in Europe had left Britain with a garrison of 80,000 troops in Germany and carrying the burden of restoring authority in war-broken nations on the continent's southern margins, including Greece, Turkey and Libya. Sustaining troops, ships and warplanes abroad required foreign currency, and Britain was not earning enough from exports to balance the books. By early 1947, it was already obvious that it could no longer afford to keep forces in Greece, where the Athens government was fighting a communist insurgency, and nor could it continue to underwrite the stability of the Turkish government in Ankara. With some embarrassment, responsibility for both was handed to Washington.

Though he was condemned by many on the Labour left, Bevin was among the first to recognise Moscow's global ambitions and to seek to involve the Americans in a permanent anti-communist partnership. History records Truman and his secretary of state George Marshall as the architects of the post-war Atlantic alliance against communism. The Truman Doctrine,[18] setting out in 1947 Washington's resolve to resist Soviet expansionism, and the European aid programme known as the Marshall Plan introduced the following year, became pillars of the new Western order. Bevin had a hand in both, and critically in the agreement that would see an American military commitment to Europe embedded in the North Atlantic Treaty. For all his optimism about a revival of British power, by supporting multilateral institutions and in his advocacy of NATO Bevin was hedging his bets. If Britain could not protect its international interests alone, what better than a rules-based system for which the United States would bear ultimate responsibility?

For its part, the Truman administration insisted that the post-war loan was the best it could get through a Congress that was still leaning towards a return to American isolationism. If officials in the state and defence departments were slow to recognise Stalin's expansionist ambitions, the House of Representatives and the Senate were still more sceptical of the need to expend financial resources in Europe and keep American forces there. The passage through Congress of the McMahon Act in 1946, calling for an abrupt halt to Anglo–American nuclear cooperation, signalled the same isolationism. Middle America didn't think the United States owed anything to anyone. If the foreign policy establishment on the East Coast seemed to take a more generous view, it was one that was rooted in strategic calculation rather than emotion. Edward Stettinius, Roosevelt's secretary of state during the war, had warned that the transition from wartime alliance to peacetime relationship would not be smooth. Britain, he observed with considerable prescience, would shun a diminished role: 'The underlying cause is the emotional difficulty which anyone, particularly an Englishman, faces in adjusting to a secondary role after so long seeing leadership as his national right.'[19]

Alongside American self-interest stood hostility towards Europe's empires. Woodrow Wilson had staked out the anti-colonialist ground in his famous 'Fourteen Points' speech towards the end of the First World War. The right to self-determination stood at its core. Roosevelt and Truman were adamant they had not fought the Nazis to see victory followed by the reconstitution of a sprawling British Empire. Roosevelt argued with Churchill about the fate of India. In a republic born from rebellion against British colonialists, antipathy to empire was part of the American political psyche. For Roosevelt, self-determination for nationalist movements was a precondition of a new international order. He pressed the case with Churchill in 1941, during their negotiations for a new Atlantic Charter, framing it as a moral issue: 'I can't believe that we can fight a war against fascist slavery, and at the same time not work to free people all over the world from a backward colonial policy.'[20] If the US was to assume leadership of the free world, the exercise of its power would be grounded in the principles of freedom and democracy. In British minds, moralism was fine – as long as it applied only to the empires of the defeated Axis powers. Churchill offered a public riposte to the Americans, when he told a City of London audience: 'I have not become the King's First Minister in order to preside over the liquidation of the British Empire.'[21] Five years later, Attlee bowed to the inevitable when Parliament rushed through Indian and Pakistani independence. The Labour politician Tony Benn noted the absence of Churchill and other senior Conservatives as the legislation was approved by the House of Lords on 18 July 1947. The dry language of the legislation scarcely captured the significance of the moment: 'The assent of the parliament of the UK is hereby given to the omission from the Royal style and titles of the words "Indiae Imperator" and the words "Emperor of India".'

American moralism was always alert to American interests. As Britain gave up its colonies and protectorates, the US began to build its own 'empire of influence'. Forcing Britain to abandon the sterling area by allowing full convertibility of its currency helped to establish the dollar as the world's reserve currency. The break-up of European empires would open new markets for American industry and offer the United States footholds in regions that were deemed vital to its strategic interests. The country's thirst for oil saw Washington displace Britain as the sponsoring Western power in Saudi Arabia. Soon it looked across the Persian Gulf at Iran and the small, oil-rich states of the Arabian Gulf where Britain controlled the oil riches.

Domestic politics also played a role in American policy. In Palestine, where British forces upholding a UN mandate faced a campaign of terrorism from Zionist groups, the US administration notionally backed an effort to mediate a two-state solution between Palestinians and Jews. But faced with strong pressure from Jewish voters in the US, Truman gave tacit support to the Zionists. The effect was to derail Bevin's efforts to hammer out a political settlement and to hasten Britain's withdrawal. By 1948, Britain had returned the mandate to the UN. The Zionists' war with the Arabs was followed by the declaration of the State of Israel. Washington was soon also trampling on British interests still further afield, signing a new security treaty with Australia and New Zealand. The surrender of Singapore to the Japanese had dealt a fatal blow to Britain's stature in the region. Australia was looking for a new guardian, and Washington, with its occupying role in Japan, was becoming the pre-eminent Pacific power.

The world was witnessing, though few in London would admit it, the formal transfer of global power from Britain to the United States – the replacement of the Pax Britannica by the Pax Americana. In the observation of the historian Michael Howard, the loss of India and the retreat from Greece and Turkey marked the first steps of Britain moving from an independent global power to membership of a US-led Western alliance.[22] The American economy had surpassed that of Britain seventy years earlier, but since then Washington had been held back by Thomas Jefferson's entreaty that the republic eschew foreign entanglements. Two world wars and the Soviet Union's global ambitions changed its mind. The transfer of power seemed brutal to the British, but its peaceful nature defied historical tradition. The Greek general and historian Thucydides had observed as early as the fifth century BC that the displacement of one great power by another inevitably led to war. Thucydides had generally been proved right as different empires waxed and waned through subsequent centuries, but this transfer did not follow the pattern. As humiliating as it was for the British, the transition to Pax Americana was accomplished without a shot being fired.

George Marshall's $12 billion plan for the reconstruction of Europe marked the recasting of isolationist America as the guarantor of freedom and democracy against the relentless advance of 'Godless' communism. Stalin's attempted blockade of Berlin in 1948 confirmed the suspicions of the anti-communists. Indifference towards Europe in Congress was replaced by a witch-hunt against anyone with the slightest connection to Stalin's Soviet Union. In 1950, the unmasking of the German spy Klaus Fuchs – a nuclear scientist who had worked on Britain's atomic programme before transferring to the US's Manhattan Project – stirred the mood of panic. Senator Joseph McCarthy found Reds under every bed, and anti-imperial moralism was tempered by realpolitik when it seemed that former colonies might choose the Soviet over the Western camp. How was it, John F. Kennedy complained to Harold Macmillan some years later, that nations that had been handed their freedom by the West could be so eager to embrace the authoritarianism of the communist bloc? Some in Washington recognised the irony that a Britain diminished by the loss of empire was correspondingly a less useful ally. Britain was among the first in the queue for assistance from the Marshall Plan. American aid for Greece and Turkey was framed as a counterweight to Soviet expansionism – the first enunciation of the Truman Doctrine. In the spring of 1949, the United States signed the North Atlantic Treaty with ten European states and Canada, establishing the alliance that would defeat Soviet communism.

NATO created an American tripwire against Soviet aggression, and Attlee and Bevin applied the same logic when they allowed Washington – without reference to Parliament – to base B-29

Flying Fortress bombers equipped to carry nuclear payloads in East Anglia. It also guided Britain's strong contribution to the Berlin airlift, when Moscow imposed its land blockade on the East German city. A desire to safeguard the American commitment to Europe shaped Attlee's decision in 1950 to meet Washington's request for a sizeable British contribution to the UN forces seeking to repel an invasion of South Korea by the communist North. NATO provided Europe, and Britain, with a guarantee that would be the pillar of European security through the Cold War and beyond. Article 5, which set out the responsibility of all member states to come to the aid of any other member who was under attack, was the great prize. Attlee's decision that Britain should be America's most reliable partner within the alliance would soon be the model for future prime ministers.

The unspoken logic was evident. Britain's economy could no longer bear the weight of its overseas obligations, and if responsibility could be transferred to new multilateral institutions headed by the United States, the pressure on sterling would be reduced. In 1952, Eden, then the foreign secretary, summarised the strategy in a cabinet paper. The aim 'should be to persuade the United States to assume the real burdens in such organisations while retaining for ourselves as much political control – and hence prestige and world influence – as we can'.[23]

America's new worldview was summed up in a paper produced by Truman's national security staff in early 1950. NSC-68, as it became known, marked the turning point for the West, setting out the existential threat of Soviet communism. The paper was used to justify the rapid build-up of US forces: 'Our overall policy at the present time may be described as one designed to foster a world environment in which the American system can survive and flourish. It therefore rejects the concept of isolation and affirms

the necessity of our positive participation in the world community.'[24] The United States, the document effectively declared, was
assuming global primacy, even if that sometimes meant treading
on the interests of its allies. In 1954, Roger Makins, the British
ambassador in Washington, wrote in a letter home that 'There is
on our side a very understandable suspicion that the Americans
are out to take our place in the Middle East.'[25] The United States,
he said, was already the dominant outside power in Saudi Arabia
and Turkey; now it had its sights on Persia and Pakistan. Makins's
mistake was to imagine that US ambitions were confined to the
Middle East.

Picking up the pieces after the Suez debacle, Macmillan set
as his first priority the refurbishment of the relationship with
Washington. At a summit with Eisenhower in Bermuda in March
1957, the prime minister offered the president a British base for
America's new Thor nuclear missiles. He was taking a political risk – the base marked out Britain as a first-line target for a
Soviet nuclear strike, but the offer would lay the foundations for
the 1958 Mutual Defence Agreement, the core of future nuclear
cooperation. Macmillan was forced to reassure worried MPs that
the rockets carrying the American warheads would be under the
control of the Royal Air Force, which would give the government
a veto over any launch. The decision had been taken as part of the
broader strategy to recast the relationship with Washington as the
keystone in the West's response to the Soviet threat. If Churchill's
claim to an equal partnership was now threadbare, Britain would
make itself the indispensable ally.

Moscow presented Macmillan with an unexpected opportunity. In October 1957, the Soviets won the race to put a satellite into space. The launch of Sputnik delivered a powerful blow
to Washington's confidence. The technological superiority that

the United States had taken for granted suddenly seemed vulnerable. Macmillan moved quickly to persuade Eisenhower that Washington needed the help of allies to re-establish its primacy. It could start with deeper collaboration with Britain and then extend to other Western allies. Macmillan was pleased with his big idea. 'Interdependence', as he called it, would suggest a more balanced relationship between the two nations. The White House offered some encouragement. Britain would soon join the thermonuclear club with its own H-bomb, and the White House persuaded Congress to repeal the post-war McMahon Act of 1946, which had blocked the transfer of atomic secrets to Britain. The stage was set for a resumption of nuclear weapons cooperation between the two countries. By the time Eisenhower and Macmillan met in Washington in October 1957, the animosities of Suez had faded. The two leaders issued a 'Declaration of Common Purpose'[26] – a rallying call against the spread of Soviet communism. At Macmillan's suggestion, joint working groups were established to promote deeper collaboration.

As ever, all this seemed more important to the British than to the Americans. The US State Department's notes from the talks recorded that the prime minister was looking for 'a formally recognised two-country relationship which could then be extended to others',[27] which implied that Britain had a privileged position over other allies. Eisenhower's preference, by contrast, was to 'turn this around and work through our alliances to maintain the closest possible contact with the British'. Subtle though this difference may have seemed, the distinction was an important one – though it did not dampen Macmillan's enthusiasm for grand strategy. During the spring of 1958, John Selwyn Lloyd, the foreign secretary, set out the plan in a secret cabinet report: Britain and the United States had been dependent on each other for some time, the paper declared with more than a hint of self-aggrandisement. 'To some extent this dependence has been one sided for, at bottom, we have needed the United States more than they us.' No matter, Russian advances in space 'have made American bases in Britain [and elsewhere] essential to the home defence of the United States and have perhaps also undermined American confidence in their technological self-sufficiency'.[28]

British power and prestige, Selwyn Lloyd's paper noted, were now inextricably bound up with the relationship with Washington. 'The United States is so much the most powerful nation in the Western camp that our ability to have our way in the world depends more than anything else upon our influence upon her to act in conformity with our interests. Against her opposition we can do little (e.g. Suez) and our need for American support is a fact which we cannot ignore. It follows that our policy should certainly be to put ourselves in the position in which we can elicit from her the greatest possible support. The policy of Anglo–American interdependence is well designed to achieve this aim.' There were risks, of course. One was the difficulty of sustaining the cooperation with the United States – what if the development of the intercontinental ballistic missile led an administration in Washington to adopt a policy of 'fortress America'? Then there were 'the dangers of becoming or seeming to become an American satellite'. It would be surprising if the United States did not exact a price for its support, and 'to some extent she does so'. To be seen as a mere agent of the United States would damage relations with others, particularly the Europeans. Britain would also lose influence with the Americans themselves, 'because this depends on the extent of our influence elsewhere'. Ministers judged the risk worth taking. Britain would be weaker for keeping its distance and it could make it clear that 'although interdependence is the cornerstone of our policy, we cannot be expected to sacrifice all our other interests to it'.

The formulation of the new strategy marked an inflection point in Britain's post-war decline. The prime minister's doctrine would serve as an elegant fig leaf, behind which Britain formally substituted status and influence in Washington for the independent action it had enjoyed during the days of empire. It was also a measure of the extent to which the policymakers in London were mesmerised by Washington, at the expense of developments much closer to home. On the other side of the Channel, the Messina Conference of 1955 had established a Franco–German-led project to create a European common market. The German economy, unburdened by the costs of sustaining military forces and starting from scratch in building a modern industrial capacity, was racing ahead. France was fast rebuilding its national infrastructure and industrial strength. Charles de Gaulle was waiting in the wings for a return to power – all the while casting Britain as the instrument of Washington's hegemonic ambitions. Among the political elites in Paris, the United States posed as serious a threat to European independence as the Soviet Union. The 'special relationship' could be rebadged as a new doctrine of interdependence, but Britain was losing sight of what was happening on its own continent.

There were times during the subsequent decades when a fair-minded audit of the 'special relationship' would identify important positive entries on the British side of the ledger. At times – such as when it pressed for a restrained response to the Soviet ultimatum demanding the West's departure from Berlin in 1958 – Britain could justifiably claim to have played as Greece to Rome. Macmillan's refusal to give up on the seemingly doomed quest for a nuclear test ban treaty often provoked irritation in Washington, not least in 1959, when he travelled to Moscow to promote an agreement. The prime minister's relatively calm response to Soviet threats was another source of friction. The US administration thought Macmillan too soft on Moscow as it sought to push the Allies out of Berlin. In 1960, an East–West summit in Paris of the leaders of the US, the Soviet Union, Britain and France was derailed when the Russians shot down an American U2 spy plane piloted by Gary Powers. A year later, hopes of a thaw in the Cold War were dashed when a meeting in Vienna between the newly installed president John F. Kennedy and the Soviet president Nikita Khrushchev foundered over tensions in Berlin. Yet persistence paid off. In August 1963, the US, the Soviet Union and Britain signed a Partial Test Ban Treaty. Macmillan could claim much credit for the first in a series of historic accords that would greatly reduce the risk of nuclear conflagration.

Whatever the mistakes – and none looms larger than Blair's decision to commit British forces to the Iraq War – or the chemistry, or lack of it, between prime ministers and American presidents, the habit and the institutions of cooperation continued to operate. The two nations worked closely together in the United Nations Security Council. The 'Five Eyes' intelligence-sharing pact, an arrangement that embraced Canada, Australia and New Zealand, spoke to an extraordinary level of trust among the nations' spy agencies. Military cooperation in NATO and elsewhere saw constant two-way traffic between senior figures in the armed forces. Britain's purchase of Polaris and the subsequent upgrading of the nuclear deterrent to Trident underpinned a unique collaboration. In 1961, a young official sent a memorandum to President Kennedy about Britain's 'dangerous' advocacy of concessions to Moscow in order to defuse tensions over Berlin. Macmillan's visit to Moscow in 1959, Henry Kissinger wrote, 'could not fail to give the impression that some Allied leaders would act as brokers because they were more reasonable, moderate or skill-ful'. The president, the memorandum continued, should tell the British leader that his attempts to act as a broker were 'unhelpful'. Yet Kissinger later remarked that the closeness between the two nations 'reflected the common language and culture of two sister peoples. It owed no little to the superb self-discipline by which Britain succeeded in maintaining political influence after its phys-ical power had waned.'[29]

Others in Washington recognised the complementary nature of British power. In May 1982, Richard Burt, at the time a rising offi-cial in the State Department, penned a memorandum about what was at stake in the looming war that would see Britain retake the Falkland Islands from Argentina. The United States, he warned, could not be indifferent to the success or failure of the naval task force that was steaming towards the South Atlantic:

> At stake is much more than the fate of a UK government
> which has proved more supportive of US policies than any of
> its recent predecessors or likely successors. Anglo–American
> relations revived relatively quickly from the trauma of Suez.
> British national self-confidence did not. The Thatcher
> government's primary achievement has been to reverse
> the thirty-year trend of British withdrawal from global
> responsibility. Failure in the Falklands will undo all that the
> Rhodesian settlement has done to revive UK national pride.
> It will leave us with no ally, save France, willing to share the
> risks and pay the price needed to protect global Western
> interests.[30]

Not everyone in Burt's department shared this analysis. The fiery Jeane Kirkpatrick, who served as Washington's ambassador at the United Nations during the Falklands conflict, was more concerned about protecting Washington's interests in Latin America. It was Burt's view, however, that prevailed.

On the debit side, the 'special relationship' would prove a constant source of anxiety – a bond that forever had to be publicly reaffirmed and substantiated. When it seemed that Eisenhower was committed to bilateral negotiations with Moscow, Macmillan despaired: 'Everyone will assume that the two great powers – Russia and the USA – are going to fix up a deal over our heads and behind our backs.'[31] Each decision taken in London had to be tested against the possibility that it would create problems in Washington. Too much time was taken presenting America's views to the rest of Europe, and not enough was spent pressing Washington to listen to the Europeans. That was not to say the two sides could not disagree – Macmillan was often at odds with Eisenhower over communist China, and Thatcher read Reagan the riot act after the American invasion of Grenada. But how elastic was this independence, and how far could the government go? The British media tested prime ministers against whether they could claim the ear of the president. Were they the first to be invited to the White House? Had they secured an invitation to the presidential retreat of Camp David in the Maryland hills, and how long an audience were they permitted? Blair had other reasons for joining Bush's invasion of Iraq, but from the moment of the Al Qaeda attacks on New York and Washington, the prime minister was determined to demonstrate that the relationship was indeed special. In 2009, Gordon Brown, Blair's successor, held a snatched meeting with Barack Obama in the kitchens of the UN headquarters in New York. His apparent failure to secure a respectful hearing saw him lampooned at home. There were ruptures – Harold Wilson's refusal to send even a token force to Vietnam. Uniquely, Edward Heath, alone among post-war prime ministers, reimagined Britain as a European power. But the habit of deference was not easily discarded. When Donald Trump won the presidential election in 2016, Britain's politicians and policymakers shared the dismay, verging on despair, of most of America's allies. When he was sworn in as president in January 2017, Theresa May rushed to Washington to be the first foreign leader received at the White House.

3

A Thousand Years of History

When the foreign ministers of France, West Germany, Italy, the Netherlands, Belgium and Luxembourg gathered in Messina at the beginning of June 1955, Anthony Eden's government declined an invitation to join the discussions about strengthening economic integration. The journey from London to the Sicilian harbour town was scarcely straightforward, a Foreign Office mandarin later explained.[1] When the leaders and foreign ministers of 'the Six' – the members of the European Coal and Steel Community – convened in Rome in March 1957 to sign the founding treaty of the European Economic Community (EEC), the British chair remained empty. Eden had thought Europe too small an arena for British engagement. His successor Harold Macmillan, picking up the pieces of the Suez debacle, had his gaze fixed firmly across the Atlantic. Britain, in the prime minister's estimation, could never again break so openly with the United States. So while others made the pilgrimage to Rome in March 1957 to sign the treaties establishing the EEC and the European Atomic Energy Community, Macmillan met with Eisenhower in Bermuda.

The closing years of the 1950s offered some succour to those still yearning for the world as it had been. The economy was strong, wartime rationing was receding in the memory, culturally and economically Britain was embracing modernity. Millions of new homes had been built – all with much sought-after inside bathrooms. The appearance of easy credit in the form of hire purchase agreements and of advertising on the new ITV commercial television channel fuelled purchases of cars, refrigerators and washing machines. Freed from national service, the young had discovered rock'n'roll. Their parents had money in their pockets. Cities such as Liverpool served as nurseries to some of the world's best pop and rock bands. Impatient with old habits of deference and eager to break free from moral straitjackets, this Britain looked to the future.

Supermac was flying high. When the cartoonist Vicky lampooned Harold Macmillan as a Marvel Comics hero, the intention had been to wound a politician never shy of self-promotion. Instead Macmillan claimed the image as his own. 'You have never had it so good,' he told the voters not long after he replaced the broken Eden in 10 Downing Street. He had a point. As the chimes of Big Ben ushered in the new decade, Macmillan could look back with satisfaction on his first three years in Downing Street. The boom had been in no small part a result of the prime minister's backing for generous public spending and low interest rates. At one point his ministerial team at the Treasury had resigned in protest at such laxity. Macmillan, though, reaped the political reward. In October 1959, the country went to the polls. The Conservatives were returned with a one-hundred-seat majority. An Edwardian toff, Macmillan was also a one-nation Tory in the tradition of Disraeli. His politics owed much to scarring memories of the misery and poverty wrought by the Great Depression. An intuitive Keynesian, he had no time for ideologues. Enoch Powell, one of the Treasury ministers who walked out in protest at the alleged profligacy, was a high priest of the fiscal fundamentalism that then, and often since, infected the bean counters who inhabited the Treasury. In Macmillan's unforgiving description, Powell was a 'fanatic'. History gave succour to national complacency. The war had shown the resilience of the nation's political institutions and economic structure. Across most of the European continent, the old fabric had been shredded. It was natural that it was now being rewoven in new patterns by politicians in Germany, France, Brussels and beyond. But why should Britain want to change the design that had delivered such a famous victory? For much of the 1950s, it had continued to bask in the reassuring glow of victory. Churchill's finest hour was replayed over and over. Old soldiers had their tales of heroism on the battlefield, and children's comics were filled with the feats of brave young RAF pilots bringing down Hitler's Messerschmitt fighter planes in the skies over southern England.

But the world was changing. British science and technology were losing their edge. The warning signs that the nation was living beyond its means began to appear even as the voters were splashing out on the bounty of the consumer age. Competing public spending demands – the remaining bills of empire, the armed forces, the new National Health Service, public-sector pay – were putting pressure on public finances. Industrial relations were poor, with key industries frequently laid low by strikes. A yawning trade deficit – the perennial concern of post-war politicians – left sterling vulnerable to attack on the foreign exchange markets. And in the industries of the future – aerospace, advanced engineering, cars – Britain was being overtaken by Germany and France.

The strains on Britain's status were building. It was far from evident that it could continue to meet its financial commitments to the Commonwealth and remaining colonies. Nor, as the Empire unravelled, was it obvious that the newly independent states would be content to carry over the old economic arrangements. The sustainability – or otherwise – of the so-called 'sterling area' had become a paralysing obsession in the Treasury. Relative economic decline seemed inevitable, but what could be done to hold on to the nation's place at the top table of international decision-making? Macmillan decided that he needed an audit, a comprehensive assessment of the nation's economic, military and political strengths and weaknesses. Projecting present trends, where would Britain and the rest of the world stand ten years later, in 1970? What needed to be done to ensure that Britain's interests and influence were protected in a world defined by the Cold War stand-off between the United States and the Soviet Union? The Europe of 'the Six' created by the Treaty of Rome was pushing ahead. Was Britain's fate, Macmillan wondered to himself, to be 'caught between a hostile (or at least less and less friendly) United States and a boastful, powerful "Empire of Charlemagne" – now under French but later bound to come under German control'?[2]

Directed by the cabinet secretary Norman Brook, government departments were put to work in the summer of 1959, crunching the numbers, assessing global trends, matching capabilities against commitments and measuring the nation's strengths and weaknesses compared to allies and adversaries. This was a formidable task made even more difficult because the work was conducted in conditions of great secrecy. Among the handful of luminaries, ministers and trusted officials assembled to oversee the project were Earl Mountbatten of Burma, a former naval officer who had served as Viceroy of India, Charles Lambe, the Admiral of the Fleet, Francis Festing, the chief of the Imperial General Staff, and Roger Makins, the former ambassador to Washington who had become joint permanent secretary of the Treasury.

France shared Britain's anxiety about maintaining its place in the world. Its foothold in Indochina had collapsed after a humiliating defeat at the hands of the Viet Minh at Dien Bien Phu in 1954. It was fighting a vicious nationalist insurgency in Algeria. Like Britain, it wondered what place in the modern world was available to a significant former colonial power whose influence was shrinking. In future years, diplomats on both sides of the Channel would regard Anglo–French relations as a lost opportunity. With similar global outlooks, permanent seats on the United Nations Security Council, fierce national pride, shared wariness about German recovery and national characters that spoke to a willingness to deploy military power, the two nations might have been the joint architects of a different Europe. Likes sometimes repel. Surveying the wreckage of the Suez debacle, France drew the opposite conclusion to that of its erstwhile partner in the enterprise. In the minds of the French, US imperialism was as serious a threat as the advance of Soviet communism. Its leaders were mindful of what Napoleon had said while imprisoned on the island of St Helena. One hundred years hence, the fallen emperor had predicted, Europe would belong either to the Americans or to the Cossacks.

While Macmillan turned to Washington, France concluded that if it wanted to retain its place in the front rank of powers, it must do so through Europe, even if that meant compromising the attachment shared with the British to national sovereignty. It received enthusiastic encouragement from Bonn. As Eden was sounding the retreat from Egypt, Konrad Adenauer, the German chancellor, was making the European case to the French prime minister, Guy Mollet. France at this point was still unconvinced of the common market sought by Germany and the Benelux states. It was more concerned about protecting its farmers. Adenauer knew that for the French, the appeal lay in the grand political purpose of the proposed European Community. 'France and England never will be powers comparable to the United States and the Soviet Union. Nor Germany either,' he told the French prime minister. 'There remains only one way of playing a decisive role in the world; that is to unite to make Europe. England is not ripe for it, but the affair of Suez will help prepare her spirits for it. We have no time to waste. Europe will your revenge.'[3]

As time passed, Macmillan could see what Adenauer had meant. The prime minister counted himself as pro-European, detached from the Empire nostalgia of much of his party, but his preoccupation had been with Washington. The Rome treaty promised to transform the performance of European economies, creating a fully-fledged customs union that would privilege member states while erecting trade barriers against those outside of the EEC. Since the end of the war, Britain's trade had been shifting away from the Commonwealth and towards other wealthy industrial nations, and the creation of the new bloc would leave it disadvantaged in some of its richest markets. The government's initial response was to create a European Free Trade Association (EFTA) of smaller nations intended to rival the European Common Market. Before long, ministers were urging their counterparts in Paris and Bonn that the two groupings be merged to create a Europe-wide free trade area – an organisation, incidentally, that would have protected Britain's trade with the Commonwealth and colonies. Macmillan had come to the party too late; France and West Germany saw no reason to adapt their project for the convenience of the British.

In London, politicians began, slowly, to wake up to the strategic as well as economic implications. However much it trumpeted its global role, Britain was a European power, and its foreign policy priority had for centuries been to ensure that no other European state grew sufficiently strong to unite the continent against it. Why else had it gone to war twice during the first half of the twentieth century? One of the ironies of the cross-Channel storms that would blow up in the decades that followed was that Margaret Thatcher was among the politicians who understood this best. By the end of her premiership, she had become the martyred prophet of the Tory Eurosceptics. Yet her Bruges speech, delivered in 1988 and subsequently a sacred text for the sceptics,[4] was anything but the paean to English nationalism it is often remembered as. The European idea, Thatcher declared, was not 'the property of any group or institution. We British are as much heirs to the legacy of European culture as any other nation. Our links to the rest of Europe, the continent of Europe, have been the dominant factor in our history. For three hundred years, we were part of the Roman empire . . . Our ancestors – Celts, Saxons, Danes – came from the Continent.' Britain, she continued, was proud to have been a pioneer of freedom and democracy, but 'We know that without the European legacy of political ideas we could not have achieved as much as we did.'[5]

The finished report of Brook and his Whitehall wise men was slipped into Macmillan's prime ministerial box in January 1960.[6] Stamped 'Top Secret', numbered copies of the 'Future Policy Study' were distributed the following month to the trusted few. Its authors, headed by Brook, had kept the secret. An early assumption that the conclusions would eventually go to the full cabinet for discussion was never realised. Macmillan, now fully engaged with events across the Channel, judged this was a policy shift that would require careful political management. The Conservative Party would have to be brought round, and so would the country. With that in mind, Downing Street ordered that discussion of the report be restricted to a handful of senior ministers.

There was nothing that could be called sensational. What counted was the accumulated weight of the evidence. The authors began by setting out the nation's prospects in the driest of statistics: relative economic growth rates, coal and steel production, energy consumption, competitiveness and population trends. The numbers spoke for themselves: 'Of all the major powers, the United Kingdom has the most vulnerable economy, because of the weakness of the external financial position.' The gold reserves stored deep in the vaults of the Bank of England covered less than one-third of the sterling liabilities to other countries – 'precarious backing for an international currency that by its nature must take the strain of political and financial pressures throughout the world'.

The economy had been growing strongly, but if times were good in Britain, they were better in its continental neighbours. Productivity – the key determinant of future wealth – had not matched that in France or West Germany. The continent – West Germany in particular – was grabbing competitive advantage, and the early success of the Common Market promised to accentuate the tilt. It was already obvious that Britain's rival trade grouping, EFTA, was no match. The danger lay ahead: 'Though in absolute terms our economic resources should grow significantly, our relative position vis-à-vis both the United States and Western Europe will nevertheless decline.' The geopolitical consequences would be grave: 'If the European Economic Community (EEC) consolidates itself into an effective political unit it will dwarf the United Kingdom, and the United Kingdom will be a small power in comparison with the three giants – the United States, the Soviet Union and EEC (with the fourth giant, China, moving up fast).' The report underlined the point: 'If, therefore, the "Six" achieve a real measure of integration, a new world power will have come on the scene.'

The authors held firm to the post-Suez foreign policy orthodoxy that the relationship with the United States was a vital multiplier of British influence and the essential guarantee of European security: 'The core of our foreign policy is and must remain the Atlantic Alliance.' But Britain could not load everything onto Washington. It would have to learn to walk and chew gum at the same time. 'As a relatively small economic power, we shall be increasingly vulnerable to the economic and trade policies carried out by the EEC, and shall risk serious damage if we fail to establish a satisfactory association with it.' The study's authors understood that America and Europe should not be seen as a choice. If the rest of the continent left Britain behind, its unique bond with the United States would suffer. This 'would seriously weaken our own standing in the Commonwealth and in the Atlantic Alliance and the cohesion of the Alliance itself if we found ourselves excluded from Europe'.

Macmillan's advisers were careful in their choice of words, but the conclusion was inescapable. What was needed was a strategy to match the vital relationship with Washington with a strong engagement with Europe: 'Whatever happens we must not find ourselves in the position of having to make a final choice between the two sides of the Atlantic.' This concurred with Macmillan's own thinking, the pro-European message he was receiving from Eisenhower's administration in Washington and the hard facts of economics. Sooner or later, Britain would have to join the Common Market.

Thus began the decades-long psychodrama that would see Britain struggle, succeed and ultimately fail to manage the collision of two conflicting emotions. An innate sense of superiority set the nation apart, mirroring Britain's past greatness, its unique parliamentary traditions, its victory in the war and its island geography. A rising insecurity flowed from the accumulating evidence that the nations that had been invaded and vanquished during the Second World War now looked set to win the peace. The secrecy surrounding the

'Future Policy Study' attested to Macmillan's recognition of how hard it would be to discard the old illusions. If pragmatism drew him towards Europe, the mood of the country leaned in the opposite direction. The national myth crafted as an explanation for the inevitability of empire celebrated English exceptionalism. Britain might now be losing the territories of empire, but it was not about to surrender the mindset. The national consciousness lagged the redistribution of power in the world.

For Britain's ruling class, Europe was too small a canvas. Eden had expressed the establishment view as foreign secretary. When voters in his constituency glanced at the letters that arrived on their doormats, he remarked, the stamps were not those of France, Belgium or Germany but those of exotic, far-flung places scattered across the globe – Malaya, the Gold Coast, Aden and Nairobi.[7] Even as the Empire dissolved, the United Kingdom remained at the head of the Commonwealth, held one of the five permanent seats on the UN Security Council, boasted a uniquely close relationship with the US and had its own nuclear weapons. In short, it remained a world power, along with the United States and the Soviet Union. Churchill's judgement that Britain should be 'with Europe, but not of it' was right.

Britain's biggest diplomatic defeat of the post-war period was self-inflicted. Encouraged by the brilliant public servant and political economist Jean Monnet, France's foreign minister Robert Schuman published on 9 May 1950 a Franco–German plan to establish a European Coal and Steel Community. Coal and steel were the crucibles of war. Merging the industries of the two nations and putting them under supranational control was a powerful signal of the commitment to post-war reconciliation. Schuman and Monnet were doing more than writing an insurance policy against future conflict between the continent's two most powerful nations. Others would be invited to join the new enterprise. Only five years after the end of the war, Paris was laying out the path for West Germany's return to the community of European nations. The new Franco–German alliance would henceforth serve as the hinge for European integration and revival. In London, the announcement was met with shock and irritation – the more so when British ministers discovered that Dean Acheson, who in 1949 had replaced George Marshall as US secretary of state, had been given advance notice of the plan. Visiting Paris on his way to a meeting of foreign ministers in London, Acheson had given the idea his blessing. With the European Coal and Steel Community, Paris and Bonn had produced the template for the future European Common Market. The message to Britain could not have been clearer: if it was not prepared to join, its neighbours would press ahead regardless, and with the backing of the Americans. Acheson found himself accused of conniving with the French. Later, he would reflect that Britain 'made her great mistake of the post-war period by refusing to join in negotiating the Schuman Plan'.[8]

Britain had spent the immediate post-war years deflecting and diluting a series of European initiatives: scuppering a plan for a customs union promoted by the Netherlands; scaling back the powers of a new parliamentary assembly, the Council of Europe, and ensuring that the new Organisation for European Economic Cooperation and Development, set up to oversee the distribution of American Marshall Aid, did not subtract from the sovereignty of its member states. If there was an organising rule in Whitehall, it was a bar on supranationalism. Any new institutions should not infringe on national sovereignty in general, and on British freedom of action in particular. Churchill, still a major figure on the international and European stages, responded to all this with majestic ambivalence. Having witnessed the devastation of the continent and proposed a union of France and Britain, how could he not be a cheerleader for a closer grouping of nations that would render a future war unthinkable? As leader of the opposition after Attlee's victory, he became an advocate of grand European designs. In 1947, he founded the United Europe Movement, which was launched at the Royal Albert Hall. The following year, he was the star speaker at a conference in The Hague that was dubbed 'the Congress of Europe'. This set the stage for the creation of the Council of Europe the following year – an assembly of European parliamentarians in Strasbourg. And yet, for all the rhetoric, and as eager as he was to criticise the caution of the government, he would not commit Britain to such enterprises. He enjoyed soaking up the applause of fellow Europeans in Strasbourg, but he never truly abandoned his conviction that European unity was something that Britain should encourage rather than participate in. When he returned to office in 1951, there was no great change in the strategy he had condemned as opposition leader. His private secretary John Colville summed up the ambiguity: 'I think Churchill considered himself a European as far as Europe was concerned – but not necessarily as far as the United Kingdom was concerned.'[9]

Attlee's government could not claim to have been taken unawares by Schuman's proposals. French officials had first raised them during the previous year. The inspiration had come from Jean Monnet, the high-ranking official responsible for France's post-war reconstruction. Monnet looms large in the gallery of dark federalist villains assembled by Eurosceptics. In real life he was an Anglophile who had worked as a civil servant in Britain during the war. With Monnet's encouragement,

Schuman had laid out his plans personally in several meetings with British officials in 1949. He was gripped by a conviction that only with collective action could the challenges facing European nations be dealt with effectively. Edwin Plowden, one of the senior Whitehall figures who heard Schuman's pitch, later told the BBC reporter Michael Charlton why the plan had been rejected: 'The Foreign Office view was that we must pre-eminently hang on to the relationship with the United States and that nothing – no matter how important France was to us and Europe was to us – should stand in the way of that.'[10] Then there was the weight of the past. As Plowden continued: 'First of all, one's got to realise that we had just won the war. We were still at the centre of an Empire, not a Commonwealth, but an Empire . . . We thought of ourselves still as one of the world's great powers.' Britain had been Monnet's first choice as a partner but, rebuffed, he turned to Germany.

The British, struggling to see how they could be at once Atlanticist and European, misread the mood of the Americans. The Foreign Office, striving to maintain a role in a world dominated by the United States and the Soviet Union, and working alongside the Americans in many corners of the globe, tilted instinctively towards Washington. So did the Treasury, mindful that the US Treasury guarded the front door to the International Monetary Fund, and thus access to funds that might be needed to prop up the value of sterling. And so did the defence ministry and the intelligence agencies, which were dependent on access to American technology and resources. Yet the dichotomy assumed by the officials was false – a leading role in its own continent's affairs could strengthen Britain's voice in Washington. As they faced up to the threat of Soviet communism, the Americans had become cheerleaders for closer European collaboration.

The grand vision of Jean Monnet, Robert Schuman and the other founding fathers sprang from a determination that, after three wars in less than a century, France and Germany should find a way to stop fighting each other. Europe would banish the demons of nationalism. The genius lay in aligning the cause of reconciliation with realpolitik. France wanted to be assured of European leadership. Germany was looking for rehabilitation. These national goals merged into an overarching one of a lasting peace. This was where the Europeans had the wholehearted support of the Americans. The Marshall Plan's programme to rebuild the continent's economies demanded an unprecedented degree of collaboration. Washington used its influence to promote integration, backing Dutch proposals for a customs union to boost trade and investment among recipients of the aid. Senior American officials viewed economic cohesion as essential for the political stability needed to counter the advance of communism. George Kennan returned from Moscow to a new role at the State Department. As the British diplomat Oliver Franks later said about his mission: 'What he [Kennan] advocated and what General Marshall accepted was that through the Marshall Plan, Western Europe must become a less fragmented economy, that it must come to have a wider market, that the people must be more – in these economic ways – at unity with each other.'[11]

Sir Edmund Hall-Patch, Bevin's economic adviser, was one of a handful of civil servants who saw through the chaff in London. The Americans, he wrote, had 'fired' the imaginations of continental governments, but his own political masters preferred not to listen. The British government had accepted the establishment of the Council of Europe – the idea championed by Churchill – in 1949, but on the understanding that it would be no more than a talking shop, operating under the direction of national governments, rather than possessing any supranational authority. Talk of a customs union was judged to be at odds with the preferential trading arrangements with the Empire and Commonwealth – a decision Hall-Patch thought flowed from 'well-established prejudice in Whitehall'.[12] A note sent to the British embassy in Washington by Sir William Strang, the permanent under-secretary at the Foreign Office, conveyed British annoyance at the American administration's support for European unity: 'Ministers here have a growing sense of irritation, amounting at times to resentment, at the lack of consideration and understanding by United States authorities in their dealings with us and other European countries; and at the implicit assumption that the European Recovery Programme is giving American agents the right to press for changes in internal policy.'[13] Strang, like his political masters, missed the logic of his own Atlanticist leanings. Bevin had done more than any other politician to persuade Washington to make a permanent commitment to Europe. It was churlish surely to stand aloof when the Americans signed up.

The Schuman Plan was received with haughty ill grace in London. A Whitehall minute of the ministerial discussion records that the chancellor, Stafford Cripps, saw it as a challenge to both Britain and the US: 'It was agreed that it showed a regrettable tendency to move away from the conception of the Atlantic Community and in the direction of a European Federation.'[14] Paris bore particular blame, he continued: 'There was general agreement that the French government had behaved extremely badly in springing this proposal on the world at this juncture without any attempt at consultation with His Majesty's Government or the US government.' This was only a few years after Churchill's proposal for an Anglo–French union. Memories were short.

Schuman outplayed his British friends. Britain, Italy, the Netherlands, Belgium and Luxembourg were all invited to join the European Coal and Steel Community, but the French and Germans made plans to prevent the British from playing a wrecking game. The project was presented to potential participants as a fait accompli. The essential parameters embedding the Community's supranational authority were non-negotiable, and a deadline was set for applications to join. Speaking from the opposition benches in the House of Commons,[15] Churchill urged the government to participate in the negotiations – even if it did not like the idea, it should have a voice. Schuman short-circuited the debate. On 1 June he told the British ambassador that France wanted an answer by the end of the following day.

Britain's peremptory response attested to the enduring strength of its post-war delusion. This was a fork in the road, a moment that would separate the country from its continental allies. Yet the cabinet rejected the plan in the absence of both the prime minister and the foreign secretary. Attlee was on holiday – in France, of all places – and Bevin was in hospital. Since they could safely assume that the other ministers would reject participation, the prime minister and his foreign secretary were content that the cabinet should take the decision without them, and without discussing the consequences of isolation. Bevin's hostility to anything that might be perceived as an erosion of sovereignty was shared by a sizeable number of his colleagues, including the chancellor, Stafford Cripps. There was no one in the cabinet to speak up for a more cohesive Europe. Harold Wilson, who was present, would later note that the issue 'was not taken very seriously at all'.[16] However, the Treasury's assessment seemed to grasp the political significance of the moment. 'The main issues', it said, are really political. The exchanges with the French government have brought out that their proposals, which started in a Franco–German context, have now been given a wider application. It is not merely pooling of resources but also, in the first place, the conception of fusion or surrender of sovereignty in a European system which the French are asking us to accept in principle. Monsieur Schuman's original memorandum said in terms that his plan would be a step towards the federation of Europe. It has been our settled policy hitherto that in view of our world position and interests, we should not commit ourselves irrevocably to Europe either in the political or the economic sphere unless we could measure the extent and effects of the commitment. This is in effect what we are now being asked to do. It is a commitment of this kind which in essence the French government is now seeking, and at the very moment when the decision has been taken to develop and give greater meaning to the Atlantic Community.

The Treasury was making the familiar mistake. Britain, it was saying, had to choose between looking west across the Atlantic or south and east across the Channel.

The cabinet's focus on sovereignty prefaced a corrosive debate from which Britain never completely escaped, either before or during its membership of the European Community. The charge ran that continental federalists were plotting to submerge nation states in a 'United States of Europe'. This may have been the objective of a handful of enthusiasts, but it was not the objective of Charles de Gaulle or his successors in the Elysée Palace. French support for economic integration was grounded in an effort to sustain national prestige. More Europe, they believed, would mean more France. For Germany, the project was about national rehabilitation. They had no plans to stop being Germans.

The significance of the moment was lost to those on the English side of the Channel. Only later would policymakers realise that in closing the door to Schuman, Britain also lost control of its own future. It ceded the authority of the victor in 1945. It could scarcely expect to map the future of a continent that had chosen its own destination. In Monnet's estimation, the first cracks had begun to show 'in the majestic ramparts of British self-confidence'.[17] For their part, the advocates of European unity had learned that it was possible for Europe to press ahead without the blessing of its island neighbour.

A pattern had been established, one that would reappear during the negotiations leading to the Treaty of Rome and then again and again during subsequent decades, when British politicians flinched at the ambitions of their European partners. The first response would be to reject the plan as impractical; the second would be to suggest that, even if the project could be made to work, there were errors in the design that would render it hopeless. When these arguments were lost, Britain would absent itself from the enterprise. This was precisely what happened when the European Commission president Jacques Delors produced during the 1980s a blueprint for a single currency. Whitehall at first scoffed that the idea would never work, but once the plan was off the ground, the Treasury offered an alternative scheme, the so-called 'hard ECU'. The others pressed ahead with their own plan. John Major was left demanding an 'opt-out' from Delors's scheme. By the time Britain voted to leave the European Union in 2016, it had opted out from the single currency, the Schengen system for borderless travel and much of the integration in legal and judicial affairs.

*

The Franco–German enterprise was not without stumbles. In 1954, France's National Assembly, unwilling to contemplate the prospect of German rearmament, scuppered plans for a European defence community. Britain's miscalculation was to interpret a temporary setback as a permanent reversal – another recurring theme. From the beginning, British politicians failed to understand the strong political underpinnings of closer collaboration. The pragmatic, transactional view in London underestimated both the emotional commitment to reconciliation and the hard-headed political calculations shaping decisions in Paris and Bonn. Britain was unwilling to give up its exceptionalism, and its neighbours were not prepared to wait. So when, in June 1955, ministers of the European Coal and Steel Community gathered in Messina to discuss closer economic alignment, they were soon discussing a plan for a tariff-free European Common Market that seemed a natural extension of Monnet's creation.

The response from London was one of insouciant disregard. Rab Butler, the chancellor, spoke for the Whitehall establishment when he dismissed the Messina talks as 'some archaeological excavations'[18] in an old Sicilian town, yet Messina was followed by a conference in Brussels that was charged with negotiating the structure of the new market. When a French official had asked his British counterpart whether London would be represented in Messina, the reply had been that it was 'a devilish awkward place to expect a minister to get to'. No such excuse was available when the bargaining moved to Brussels. Eden's government then signalled its lack of interest by sending a civil servant rather than a minister. Sir Russell Bretherton, a senior official from the Board of Trade, was instructed to attend as an observer rather than as a participant. Diplomatic folklore records that in November 1956, he made a rare intervention in the discussions: 'The future treaty that you are discussing has no chance of being agreed; if it was agreed, it would have no chance of being ratified; and if it was ratified, it would have no chance of being applied; and if it was applied, it would be totally unacceptable to Britain.' It was time to bid farewell to this ill-fated venture: '*Au revoir et bonne chance*.' The quotation is probably apocryphal and did not reflect Bretherton's personal view, but the words were true to the official state of mind in London. European vision met with intense British scepticism. Even as a member of the EC after 1973, Britain struggled to suppress a response to each new proposal that intimated it expected the project to fail. And when it worked, Britain would ask for an opt-out.

Many decades later, when Theresa May began to negotiate the terms of the British exit after the 2016 EU referendum, she would protest that she was not opposed to increased European cooperation per se. It was rather that the United Kingdom was worthy of a bespoke agreement with its European partners that preserved the UK's control over its own destiny. May's assumptions echoed the sentiments expressed by Churchill when he wished the continent well as he bid them au revoir.

For the Americans, there had been nothing altruistic about the Marshall Plan. It was all about keeping economically weakened European nations beyond the grasp of the Soviet Union. The United States judged that its own interests would be best represented in a united Europe. Unsurprisingly, Washington was impatient of British obstructionism. Britain was demanding that the United States act as a European power, while rejecting such a role for itself. For the United States, the Common Market was a buttress against the advance of Soviet communism. George Kennan's policy of containment foreshadowed a long game: the West must demonstrate the superiority of its economic system over the communist model, to show that markets rather than state planning would better deliver prosperity. Anything that promoted the cohesion and prosperity of the western half of the European continent was welcome in Washington.

Britain thus ceded the design of the new Europe. While the impulse towards Franco–German rapprochement was powerful, it was far from inevitable that European integration would take the form that finally emerged. France shared many of the British concerns about sovereignty. De Gaulle, who returned to power following the Messina Conference, later confessed that had he been president during the drafting of the Treaty of Rome, he would have refused to sign it. France initially prioritised security over economic cooperation and pressed for a new agency to pool the continent's nuclear capabilities. For its part, West Germany wanted tariff-free trade in manufactures and resisted French plans for the Common Agricultural Policy. A British government determined to shape the political agenda would have had considerable leverage in charting the course of European collaboration. Later, Anthony Nutting, who had served as a Foreign Office minister before resigning over Suez, recognised the missed opportunity: 'I think it was the last and the most important bus that we missed. I think we could still have had the leadership of Europe had we joined in Messina.'[19]

Macmillan's 'Future Policy Study' confronted the unpalatable facts: the Common Market was working, and Britain's efforts to undermine it through its EFTA arrangements with Sweden, Norway, Denmark, Portugal, Austria and Switzerland had failed. In the absence of France or Germany, EFTA lacked sufficient economic clout. 'For the first time since the Napoleonic era', Macmillan said, 'the major continental powers are united in a positive economic grouping, with considerable political aspects which ... may have the effect of excluding us both from European markets and from consultation in European policy.'[20] The dawning truth was that the British had been mesmerised by the false choice between Europeanism and Atlanticism. This was a point that Kennedy made to Macmillan, and one that Barack Obama repeated half a century later, when he backed the campaign for Britain to remain in the European Union.

Macmillan's about-turn recalled a prophecy made by Monnet at the very beginning. Asked in 1950 whether France and West Germany were prepared to press ahead with the European Coal and Steel Community in the absence of Britain, Monnet had told Stafford Cripps, the Labour chancellor, that 'I hope with all my heart that you will join in this from the start. But if you don't then we will go ahead without you. And I'm sure that, because you are realists, you will adjust to the facts when you see that we have succeeded.'[21] Monnet inadvertently provided a perfect description of the journey from nostalgia to realism that came to define the British relationship with Europe: aloofness, hesitation and resentment, followed, when all other options had been explored, by an unseemly scramble to climb aboard the European train.

Much as Macmillan had grasped the narrowing political choices, he was not prepared to take bold risks. When the 'Future Policy Study' was presented to a small group of ministers in March 1960, the conclusions were not met with enthusiasm. Some thought it 'defeatist'. The Treasury was accused of underestimating the worth of the Commonwealth and being overly pessimistic about the nation's economic prospects. Rab Butler, now home secretary, exchanged the scepticism he had shown towards Messina for a bald assertion that Britain should simply seize the leadership of Europe. As the historian Peter Hennessy noted tersely, there was no accompanying explanation as to quite how this might be achieved.[22] Whitehall's mandarins were slowly shifting from a position of disdain to one that pointed up the risks of exclusion. Most politicians would take longer to be convinced that Britain should throw in its lot with 'lesser' nations. Macmillan was trifling with closely held perceptions of national identity, history and self-government.

Among Tory and Labour sceptics alike, sovereignty was the most painful issue. For its ruling class, England was self-evidently a superior democracy, with institutions, habits and traditions embedded through struggles and compacts that reached back centuries. Continental neighbours had been scarred by upheavals, wars and revolutions. Britain had been free of such upheavals, Margaret Thatcher told the French president François Mitterrand on the two-hundredth anniversary in 1989 of the storming of the Bastille – conveniently glossing over the English Civil War and the Glorious Revolution of 1688. Across the Channel, Britain's MPs saw nations that were new to democracy. When Attlee's government had considered Schuman's plan, his deputy prime minister Herbert Morrison had remarked that 'the Durham miners' would not accept any such constraint on national economic management. Churchill sometimes took a more nuanced tack, remarking in Parliament in 1950 that 'We are prepared to consider and, if convinced, to accept the abrogation of national sovereignty, provided we are satisfied with the conditions and safeguards.'[23] However, he left open the question of whether such a condition could ever be satisfied. On the right of the Tory party, Enoch Powell made English nationalism his own. For Powell, the Treaty of Rome was an abomination, a lethal affront to self-government. It would pull down the very pillars of democracy. Of the six nations that had signed the Rome treaty, Powell noted, four had come into being only during the previous two centuries. Europe was not Powell's only enemy. The Common Market would subvert Britain's democratic institutions, while immigration from the Commonwealth undermined the country's ethnic and cultural cohesion. Here were the antecedents for the xenophobic campaign – take back control from Brussels and keep out Turkish migrants – waged by hardline Brexiters in 2016.

The debate confused symbols with substance, constitutional theory with the realities of cross-border interdependence in the modern world. In theory, sovereignty confers the power to act, but this is a capacity that in reality is often as dependent on cooperation with like-minded nations as it is available through unilateral action. In the second half of the nineteenth century, at the height of empire, Lord Palmerston famously remarked that Britain had no need for permanent alliances. The nation's interests were paramount. The distinction was a plausible one when a quarter of the globe was coloured pink, but in the second half of the twentieth century Britain had no such choice. Alliances and national interests could not be disentangled in a nation that had lost its pre-eminent global role. By the lights of English nationalists, an individual marooned on a desert island can claim absolute sovereignty, and yet the castaway is entirely powerless.

The prosaic truth was that Britain had long been a prolific signer of treaties and an energetic joiner of international institutions. In 2015, the Foreign Office calculated that the nation had since 1834 put its name to more than 13,000 treaties, spanning everything from defence pacts, fishing-rights arrangements and trade deals to the treaties marking accession to the United Nations and NATO. Each of these chipped away at theoretical sovereignty, whether by providing for others to resolve disputes or by imposing restraints and reciprocal obligations. Yet none of these commitments fettered Parliament's absolute sovereignty – the right of MPs to overturn any such arrangement. What Westminster had devolved yesterday it could reclaim tomorrow. Macmillan grasped the vital distinction between sovereignty and power.

The supporters of British sovereignty were not alone in their objections to European entanglement. The former nations of empire, now gathered together in the Commonwealth, spoke to Britain's experience as a global rather than a European power. The 'White Dominions' – Canada, Australia and New Zealand – were counted in an Anglosphere of English-speaking nations that embraced Britain's relationship with the US. The Commonwealth operated its own system of trading preferences, which would be put at risk by a decision to join the European Community's customs union. Edward Heath, chosen by Macmillan to lead negotiations with 'the Six', recognised the tension when he set out Britain's goals in October 1961: 'Some people in the United Kingdom have been inclined to wonder whether membership of the Community could in fact be reconciled with membership of the Commonwealth . . . It would be a tragedy if our entry into the Community forced other members of the Commonwealth to change their whole pattern of trade.'[24] The circle would have to be squared during the course of negotiations.

Macmillan's response to the voices of scepticism was to move slowly. The 'Future Policy Study' was followed in the summer of 1960 by what looked like another objective stocktake. Whitehall was set a series of questions to test the progress of the Common Market against that of the smaller EFTA. In truth, many of the questions were rhetorical. The purpose was the prime minister's desire to show that circumstances had changed since Messina. The officials concluded that Eden's government had been wrong on two counts: the feasibility of the Common Market project and the assumption that Britain could set its own terms for association. France and western Europe, the report said, were 'no longer weak'. On the contrary, 'The Common Market is becoming a powerful and dynamic force, economically and politically. In 1956,' they continued, 'we thought that joining the Common Market would weaken our special relationship with the United States. The position has now changed and the United States is attaching increasing importance to the Community.'[25] As for the Commonwealth, any loss of direct ties as a consequence of membership might well be outweighed by the loss of global influence if the country stayed out – and that would be damaging to the Commonwealth. Britain, it concluded, was falling behind economically. Membership of the Common Market would give it access to a market of 200 million people and amplify Britain's influence in Washington. Yes, there would be some diminution of sovereignty, but a place in the Council of Ministers would allow the government to apply a brake on the ambitions of the European federalists.

The debates within Whitehall turned on the practicalities of knitting together obligations to the Commonwealth and the Common Market. The cabinet's starting point was that Britain could negotiate special arrangements that would preserve its ties with former colonies while also bestowing the benefits of a European vocation. This was the balance imagined by Macmillan in July 1961, when he opened formal negotiations with 'the Six'. From the beginning, the tone was defensive. The decision to apply for membership was taken by the full cabinet. As the Foreign Office historian Gill Bennett puts it, there was no air of celebration – more 'a mood of gloomy resignation'.[26] Yes, Europe was an opportunity, but no, Britain would not shrink its ambitions.

'Euroscepticism', as it came to be known, was not the sole property of nationalists and nostalgists on the right of the political spectrum. The political divides on the European question were as much within the two main parties as they were between them. The political left prided itself on its internationalism, but this did not extend to sharing control of trade policy. Herbert Morrison's observation about the Durham miners spoke to a deep suspicion among trade unions that Europe represented a threat to British industry. A market that was open to German manufacturing would seriously jeopardise British employment. Faced with the cabinet's decision, the Labour leader Hugh Gaitskell decided to tread carefully. He did not share the conviction of those on the left that the EEC was a 'capitalist club' posing a mortal threat to the nation's working classes. Nor was he instinctively pro-European like some of his shadow cabinet colleagues. So he sat on the fence, insisting that Her Majesty's Opposition would set out a position based on the terms secured by the negotiating team. By mid-1962, however, anti-Europeanism in the Labour Party was hardening. Gaitskell had lost the 1959 election to Macmillan. With another poll due by 1964, a successful bid to join the European Community could underwrite Macmillan's bid for another term. Gaitskell did not relish a battle with the anti-European left, led by the rising Harold Wilson.

What startled the country – and shook Macmillan – was the nature of Gaitskell's turnabout in October 1962. In place of a judicious speech suggesting that Britain was better off outside, the Labour leader used his appearance at the party conference in Brighton to issue a thundering denunciation of the entire enterprise. The economic gains, he started, had been exaggerated, but the political price was one that no British politician should consider. The surrender of sovereignty, he charged, would mean 'the end of Britain as an independent European state'. Plunging deeper into the nostalgia that had previously been the property of the Conservatives, Gaitskell went on: 'It means the end of a thousand years of history.'[27] As a piece of political oratory, this was Gaitskell's finest hour, and the conference hall erupted in applause. It fell to his wife Dora to puncture his satisfaction. 'All the wrong people are cheering,'[28] she told him, noticing that his traditional supporters on the social democrat wing of the party were silent.

When the Conservatives gathered for their annual conference the following month, Rab Butler, who had so brusquely dismissed the Messina gathering, offered the rejoinder: 'For them, a thousand years of history. For us, the future!' Butler saw Europe through a lens of condescension: why could those wretched continentals not recognise the natural order of things and bow to British leadership? All these debates, in cabinet, at Westminster and beyond, were conducted in splendid isolation. British politicians assumed that the country's relationship with the rest of the continent could be settled in London. Sure, the Europeans might ask for a refinement here or a small adjustment there, but Britain would set the parameters. It was a mindset that the nation would never shake off.

For Macmillan, Europe had become a question of power. The 'special relationship' with the United States was a necessary but insufficient buttress for British power. Outside 'the Six', he judged, its influence would quickly wane. Ten years earlier, Eden had set out the contrary case: 'Britain's story and her interests lie beyond the continent of Europe,' he had said. 'Our thoughts move across the seas to the many communities in which our people play their part in every corner of the world. These are our family ties. That is our life.'[29] Macmillan knew the options had narrowed. 'In the past, a great maritime power, we might have given way to insular feelings of superiority over foreign breeds . . . but we have to consider the world as it is today and will be tomorrow, and not in outdated terms of a vanquished past.'[30] For all that, the prime minister's speech to the House of Commons in August 1961, in which he announced the start of formal negotiations with the EEC, was defensive. The emphasis was almost entirely on the economic case. As he assured MPs, the Rome treaty did not deal with defence or foreign policy. The promises and conditions – that Britain would retain its global role and ties to the Commonwealth, that it would not sacrifice cheap food supplies from Australia and New Zealand – outweighed any vision of the opportunities that might accrue. For all that the sovereignty question had been closely discussed in cabinet, Macmillan glossed over it, giving the impression that Britain would join the EEC on its own terms.

The harsher reality was that Britain could not assume it would be welcomed with open arms. The retreat at Suez was still fresh in the minds of the French; while Britain had resolved never again to fall so far from the orbit of the US, France was building Europe as a defence against American power. No one was more convinced of this, and more suspicious of collusion between the Anglo-Saxons, than Charles de Gaulle, who had returned to power in 1958. The general nursed all manner of grievances against *les Anglais*, some real and others imagined. He had never forgotten his exclusion from the great-power conferences during the war, Britain had reneged on a promise of nuclear cooperation and Macmillan was a creature of the Americans. It was with de Gaulle that Britain would have to negotiate. The prime minister hoped that their wartime relationship in North America would help. He was disappointed at almost every turn. An invitation to de Gaulle to his country house, Birch Grove in Sussex, served only to stir despair:

'De Gaulle now hears nothing and listens to nothing.' The problem was 'his pride, his inherited hatred of England (since Joan of Arc), his bitter memories of the last war and, above all, his intense "vanity" for France'.[31]

Macmillan assembled a formidable negotiating team, including Edward Heath, destined to become the only post-war prime minister whose support for European engagement was unconditional. The Foreign Office, which had until recently been scornful of the enterprise, put its shoulder behind a diplomatic drive in the capitals of 'the Six'. Konrad Adenauer, a pivotal figure alongside de Gaulle, was closely courted. As the bargaining continued through 1962, Whitehall realised that concessions would have to be made and ties with the Commonwealth recalibrated.

On 14 January 1963, de Gaulle brought the process to an abrupt conclusion. Macmillan had been forewarned when he met the general the previous month at Rambouillet. The meeting, just ahead of a summit in the Bahamas with John F. Kennedy, had been painful. Though the prime minister refused to admit as much, the French president had already made up his mind. Even so, he was not prepared for the fusillade de Gaulle fired after summoning the media to the Elysée Palace in January. Twenty years earlier, as the head of the French government in exile in London, de Gaulle had flirted with Churchill's idea for a new Anglo–French union; now he concluded that Britain could not be trusted as a member of the European Community. 'The Six' had chosen to make Europe their future, but Britain would not loosen its ties with the US. When Macmillan had met Kennedy in Nassau a month earlier, he had petitioned for – and secured – access to America's submarine-launched Polaris nuclear missile programme, spurning French offers of a European nuclear programme in the process. This could not go unpunished.

De Gaulle's statement listed the many practical, and politically charged, obstacles to British membership of the Common Market. One was the collision between the subsidies provided by the Common Agricultural Policy (CAP), designed to protect French farmers, and Britain's imports of cheaper food from the Commonwealth, which were 'obviously incompatible with the system which the Six have established quite naturally for themselves'.[32] The CAP had been France's triumph in the negotiations that led to the Treaty of Rome and the price that Adenauer's German government had paid to cement Franco–German reconciliation. French farmers and wine growers could not be sacrificed to the interests of dairy producers in New Zealand or sugar growers in the British Caribbean.

Beneath the economics lay the philosophical divide. De Gaulle had followed the debates in Westminster. Echoing the view that Britain was a global rather than a European power, he said: 'England in effect is insular, she is maritime, she is linked through her exchanges, her markets, her supply lines to the most diverse and often the most distant countries.' British membership of the EEC would change its nature. If it was admitted, the other EFTA states would follow, and then 'The cohesion of its members . . . would not endure for long and ultimately it would appear under American dependence and direction.' The radioactive phrase there was 'under American dependence and direction' – Britain, to put it simply, was Washington's Trojan horse. It was possible, de Gaulle concluded, that 'England might transform itself sufficiently to become part of the European community . . . and in this case the Six would open the door to her and France would raise no obstacle.' But he was not hopeful.

In the general's mind, the Polaris agreement struck in Nassau had confirmed the Anglo-Saxon conspiracy. Kennedy had offered to match it with a similar deal for France, but the offer only deepened de Gaulle's conviction that France needed its own nuclear deterrent. France would soon withdraw from the NATO command structure, and three years later the organisation was effectively expelled from French soil.

The general's statement was as surprising to France's partners as it was to the British. The other five, led by Adenauer's West Germany, backed British membership. The negotiations had thrown up obstacles, but none that could not be surmounted. Macmillan concluded that de Gaulle's objections were as much about historic rivalry as they were about Europe. The general had never forgiven his exclusion from Tehran, Yalta and Potsdam, and perhaps he had not forgiven France's age-old adversary its victory in 1945. He feared that British membership would dilute French leadership. Whatever the precise balance of motives, the ambivalent and hedged manner of the British application gave the French president his excuse. Here was proof of the prescience of Edward Stettinius's message to Roosevelt that Britain would not easily fit within a club it could not presume to lead. For 'the Six', Europe represented a project to banish the past and safeguard the future. The British view was transactional: was it better off in than out, and what could it gain without giving up what it had? Here was a foretaste of the stubborn exceptionalism that would forever set Britain apart from its neighbours. A week after de Gaulle's veto, France and West Germany signed the Elysée Treaty – a unique political agreement to bind together the fortunes of the continent's two most powerful nations. The exclusion that Macmillan had feared was complete: 'All our policies at home and abroad are in ruins,' he wrote in his diary on 28 January 1963.[33] The political columnist David Watt was more sympathetic to de Gaulle's reasoning: by negotiating so hard for

Polaris, Macmillan had shown that Britain's standing in the world mattered more than Europe. In any event, Europe had now moved to the centre of British politics; it would remain there for more than half a century.

4

A Very British Bomb

'National prestige'. The phrase ricocheted around Whitehall. The more relative economic decline chipped away at the substance of national power, the more neurotic Britain's leaders became about clinging to emblems of power. None was more important than the bomb. In December 1962, after a series of miscalculations and mishaps, the country's future status as a nuclear-weapons state hung on the outcome of a summit between Harold Macmillan and the young American president John F. Kennedy. The loss of the nuclear deterrent would require Britain to radically rethink its defence strategy. Much more importantly, what would Britain be without the bomb? In Macmillan's mind, its loss would be a fatal blow to the country's international standing.

Summit meetings of world leaders rarely change the course of history. They are choreographed for the cameras, their outcomes pre-cooked and pre-packaged in the dark back rooms of official-dom. The purpose of the final communiqué is to codify the choices made and decisions already taken. When Harold Macmillan left behind the winter chill of London in December 1962, his premiership rested on the hope that his talks with Kennedy in the warmer climes of the Caribbean would turn out to be the exception that defied the rule. And, for once, a summit did indeed rewrite the script. More, the American sale to Britain of the Polaris nuclear weapons system set a course for British foreign and defence policy for the next half-century and beyond. The nuclear deal that was struck underwrote Britain's membership of an exclusive club and paid, in effect, its subscription fee as a permanent member of the

United Nations Security Council. In the process Macmillan built a psychological prison from which his successors would never escape. When, in 2016, David Cameron announced that the government would purchase from the US the latest Trident nuclear missiles, he was merely renewing, as Margaret Thatcher had done before him, the bargain sealed by Macmillan beside the glistening waters of the Caribbean. No relationship has more closely defined Britain's post-war place in the world than that with the United States. No other single encounter between its leaders did more to shape the terms of the relationship.

The crackling commentary of the Pathé news report on the two leaders' arrival in Nassau paid unconscious homage to Britain's global pretensions. The 'Big Two', it said, would be discussing how to shore up 'a rapidly deteriorating Anglo–American alliance'. It might have added that Macmillan's political future hung on the outcome. The month just passed had seen a string of bad by-election results for the Tories. Macmillan's efforts to negotiate entry into the Common Market faced a French roadblock in the shape of President de Gaulle. And Washington's apparent determination to cancel the Skybolt missile system it had promised Britain threatened to cut the ground from under Britain's nuclear deterrent. 'The Sunday press is hysterical about Europe, about Skybolt, about the Tory party,' the prime minister wrote in his diary on 9 December.[1] Three days earlier, he had felt under sufficient pressure to tell backbench MPs that he was ready to stand aside should they think this would solve the government's problems. 'This is the first time I have had to use this weapon,' he wrote that evening.

Britain had been rudely confronted with the facts of global power just two weeks before the Nassau summit. Dean Acheson, Truman's secretary of state, was an informal adviser to Kennedy.

A scion of America's East Coast establishment with a liking for well-tailored suits, he was also an Anglophile, well known and highly respected in Whitehall's corridors of power and not out of place in London's smartest salons. But Acheson, one of the principal architects of America's post-war commitment to Europe, was above all a hard-headed foreign policy practitioner. He had always doubted his country's interests were well served by talk of 'special relationships' with individual allies. During his time in the State Department he had heard of a departmental project to codify the 'specialness' of the relationship with Britain. He had ordered it to be halted and all the paperwork destroyed. How would other allies respond, he asked officials, if they thought Britain was getting special treatment?[2]

For all that, his intentions in addressing the West Point Military Academy at the beginning of December 1962 were not hostile. Most of his speech amounted to a set of reflections on the future of the transatlantic alliance and NATO. Wrapped up in the broader argument was a gentle warning to good friends in London. He had no inkling that his words would detonate like a bomb in London. 'Britain has lost an empire and has not yet found a role,' Acheson said, in the most oft-quoted of his observations. Then came the wounding strike at the heart of the course Britain had set for itself since the war: 'The attempt to play a separate power role,' he explained, 'that is, a role apart from Europe, a role based on a "Special Relationship" with the United States, a role based on being head of a "Commonwealth" which has no political structure, or unity or strength . . . this role is about played out.'

British prime ministers could not dictate the terms of the superpower relationship: 'Great Britain, attempting to work alone and to be a broker between the United States and Russia, has seemed to conduct a policy as weak as its military power,' Acheson said.[3]

Acheson was unaware of the febrile mood in London. In British terms, his words were devastating, and newspapers on the right and the left reacted angrily. The *Daily Express* declared the speech to be 'a stab in the back', and the *Daily Telegraph* called Acheson 'more immaculate in dress than judgement'. The *Daily Mirror* went further, reminding its readers that the Americans had also written off Britain at the time of Dunkirk in 1940. Then, Franklin Roosevelt had been acting under the advice of the US's ambassador in London, Joseph Kennedy, the father of the current president. The White House announced that Acheson had not been speaking for the administration. In an attempt to calm the waters Kennedy gave Macmillan the same message in a private telephone call. As Tory and Labour MPs alike joined the chorus of condemnation, however, the prime minister reacted publicly. In what was said to be a reply to 'representations' from the former Conservative minister Lord Chandos, Macmillan invoked Britain's glorious history. Acheson was guilty of an error 'which [had] been made by quite a lot of people in the course of the last four hundred years, including Philip of Spain, Louis XIV, Napoleon, the Kaiser and Hitler'.[4]

Macmillan later confided in his diary that Britain would have looked stronger had it felt able to shrug off the speech.[5] Acheson's rebuke had drawn blood because he was speaking the truth. The more the British felt obliged to talk about their privileged position in the affections of the Americans, the more unequal the relationship appeared. The defence secretary Peter Thorneycroft grasped this following a series of fiery exchanges with his American counterpart Robert McNamara in the week before the summit. He could not, he said, 'be seen to plead on my knees with the Americans'.

The further irony for Macmillan was that Acheson had done little more than put into blunter language the conclusions of the prime minister's 'Future Policy Study'. Macmillan's response

– the application to join 'the Six' in the Common Market – was his answer to the question about Britain's future. In Macmillan's design, the US and Europe would serve as the two, mutually supportive, pillars of Britain's global role. The practice was not quite so straightforward. De Gaulle wanted Britain to choose. Neither the cabinet nor the Conservative Party had come around easily to an acceptance that Britain should throw in its lot with the French and Germans. Many still hankered after the Churchillian vision of concentric circles of power. Now, when he met Macmillan at Rambouillet, de Gaulle was preparing to block the path to Europe. The general would often cite an exchange he had had with Winston Churchill on the eve of the Normandy landings. If Britain had to choose between Europe and the open sea, Churchill had admitted, 'she must always choose the open sea'. Now de Gaulle charged that Macmillan would not break free of Britain's American shackles. The prime minister had found the encounter exhausting and depressing. De Gaulle reported to the French cabinet that his guest had been driven almost to tears. Macmillan knew he could not afford to return from the Bahamas with the 'special relationship' in a similarly sorry condition.

The two leaders who settled with their delegations into separate beachfront villas in Nassau were an unlikely couple. One was a patrician Scot born into a previous century. A high Tory, and a protestant, Macmillan was a decorated hero of the Great War – a conflict that was coming to its close when his interlocutor was born. David Bruce, the US ambassador in London, warned the president not to be misled by the conversational style; Macmillan was as hard-headed as they came. As for the dashing forty-five-year-old occupant of the White House, Kennedy's background as a Catholic Irish American from Boston did not suggest a natural Anglophile. His wealthy businessman father had served as ambassador in London during the 1930s and had sided with Chamberlain's policy of appeasement. 'Democracy is finished in England,' Joseph Kennedy had remarked. At the opening of the 1960s, the young Jack carried the standard for modernity. No one would ever accuse Macmillan of being 'hip'. Pre-summit nerves among officials on both sides underestimated both men – the guile of an old hand who understood the pull of history, and the youthful wisdom of a president who knew when to temper policy with politics. The tensions were noted by the veteran *Sunday Times* journalist Henry Brandon, who had reported on many such summits. Brandon sensed a mood of nagging exasperation and bitter indignation 'such as I have never experienced in all the Anglo–American conferences I have covered over the past twenty years'.[6]

Macmillan's pre-summit nerves were understandable. One by one, Britain's pretensions to the great-power role it had enjoyed as one of the Big Three had crumbled. Now it faced another threat to its international prestige. As Ernest Bevin had insisted it should, Britain had built its own 'bomb', but the RAF's ageing fleet of Vulcan bombers would soon go out of service. Britain's own 'Blue Streak' programme to put nuclear warheads on home-made rockets had ended in expensive failure two years earlier. The government lacked the money and the technology to follow the Americans and Russians by building massive intercontinental ballistic missiles. How could it threaten – or deter – the Soviet Union if it lacked the means to use this most lethal of weapons? To remain a nuclear power, it needed an American delivery system.

Macmillan had no intention of surrendering this emblem of national prestige. His pitch, he decided in advance of the talks, would fall back on the notion of interdependence, which he had raised with Eisenhower in 1957. The West could confront the challenges of the modern age only if they acted in concert. But interdependence did not mean the sacrifice of national power. For Britain, this rested on the closeness of its relationship with the United States and its status as a nuclear power. Arthur Schlesinger, the American historian and a close associate of John F. Kennedy, understood the stakes. For Macmillan, he observed, the 'special relationship' and possession of a deterrent 'were at once essential to Great Britain, good for Tories and adornments of his place in history'.[7] As he arrived in Nassau, Macmillan understood that the statement released at the end of the talks would determine whether Britain could call itself a global player any longer. Kennedy had prepared diligently for the summit, at one point telephoning Dwight Eisenhower to clarify what his predecessor had promised during earlier discussions. He could not know that the decisions taken in the Bahamas would set the course for British policy well into the next century.

Flanked by the foreign secretary Alec Douglas-Home and the defence secretary Thorneycroft, Macmillan said nothing of de Gaulle's rebuff. He could not afford to expose his weakness. In Nassau, as at Rambouillet, the prime minister was the supplicant. De Gaulle had the power to shut Britain out of Europe; Kennedy had it within his grasp to shut down Britain's nuclear weapons programme, an emblem of its status in the world. It had joined the 'thermonuclear club' with the explosion of an H-bomb in 1957. As Bevin had demanded, the device was stamped with the Union flag. But attempts to build a missile to carry a nuclear payload had ended in expensive failure. Blue Streak, commissioned in 1955, had been cancelled in 1960 without ever being properly tested. More recently, the Americans had raised serious questions over the suitability of their Skybolt system, which had been offered by Eisenhower after the failure of Blue Streak. By the time Macmillan reached Nassau, the last remaining credible option was the submarine-launched

Polaris missile system. If Kennedy said no, the much-vaunted 'special relationship', rebuilt so painstakingly after the Suez fiasco, would be shredded. So too would be Britain's claim that it continued to sit in the front rank of nations. Yes, Macmillan reflected, this was a summit that might well break him.

Despite their different backgrounds, Macmillan and Kennedy had struck up a trusting relationship. The wily Macmillan made the most of his American heritage and appointed David Ormsby-Gore, a close childhood friend of the president, as ambassador to Washington. Ormsby-Gore soon established himself as a White House insider, a rare foreign emissary with direct access to the president. Against all protocol, and to the irritation of Kennedy's own staff, he was offered a seat on the presidential flight from Washington to Nassau. Kennedy's advisers were unmoved by such connections – the United States, they judged, had nothing to gain from a deal with Macmillan. To the contrary, these hard-headed policymakers told the president, American interests argued against the perpetuation of a separate British nuclear capability. It was time, some thought, that Britain was put in its place.

The most powerful weapon ever invented might have belonged to Britain. The scientific breakthrough that gave the world the atomic bomb was made in a laboratory in Birmingham. In the spring of 1940, the German-born Rudolf Peierls and the Austrian-born Otto Frisch, both exiles from Hitler's Europe, discovered how to create a chain reaction with a small amount of uranium-235, generating a huge explosion. The group would soon be joined by other refugees, including two French scientists who had produced pioneering work on a plutonium-based weapon. By the time the government-established MAUD Committee completed its top-secret report the following year, Britain was so far ahead in the nuclear game that when the information was shared with the Americans, Washington urged a pooling of resources.

The British government decided to press ahead with an independent programme, badly underestimating the scale of the American effort. Within a year, having thrown its superior scientific and industrial resources into the Manhattan Project, the United States had taken a decisive lead.[8] When Hitler's advance brought the front line of the war to the Channel, Churchill agreed that the British team should be dispersed. Most joined the US programme, and some continued their work in Canada, a collaboration formalised by the Quebec Agreement in 1943. Neither nation, they agreed, would use such a weapon without the consent of the other. When US bombers caused unprecedented destruction in Hiroshima and Nagasaki in August 1945, they did so only after Britain had given formal approval. Leonard Cheshire, the RAF's most decorated pilot, joined the airborne observation team that monitored the explosion at Nagasaki.

The war over, the Americans turned inwards. Congress passed the McMahon Act, which overturned all previous nuclear understandings with the United Kingdom and barred any future collaboration. The Soviet Union had its own nuclear project, and the key question for British policymakers was whether the United States would risk a nuclear conflagration in defence of Britain. Beyond that, of course, there was the issue of national prestige. Lord Cherwell, an adviser to Churchill, answered for much of the establishment: 'If we are unable to make the bombs ourselves and have to rely entirely on the United States for this vital weapon, we shall sink to the rank of a second-class nation, only permitted to supply auxiliary troops, like the native levies who were allowed small arms but not artillery.'[9] The imperative was to hold on to the nation's global status.

Bevin's insistence in 1946 that a British bomb be stamped with the Union flag fitted the national self-image. Many Labour MPs were still hoping for rapprochement with Moscow, but the Attlee government made a decision that none of its successors would challenge. Five years later, a mushroom cloud above the Montebello Islands off the coast of Western Australia signified Britain's entry into an exclusive club. Churchill, returned to power in the 1951 election, was initially hesitant about the test, but his scientific adviser William Penney had had no such doubts: 'The discriminative test for a first-class power is whether it has made an atomic bomb and we have either got to pass the test or suffer a serious loss in prestige both inside this country and internationally.'[10] By now the Soviet Union had exploded its own device, and with Attlee's permission the United States had stationed nuclear-armed bombers at bases in the United Kingdom. Churchill, visiting the Queen at Balmoral, was asleep when the first British bomb exploded. It was only the beginning of the race.

The atomic bomb changed decisively the calculus of war. The advent of the hydrogen bomb a few years later threatened the very future of the planet. Barely a week after the first British atomic test, the Americans exploded the world's first thermonuclear device on Enewetak Atoll in the Pacific Ocean. The mushroom cloud rose more than forty kilometres into the atmosphere and the explosion produced a yield equivalent to more than ten megatons of TNT; 'Little Boy', the bomb dropped on Hiroshima, had yielded about fifteen kilotons. Britain had been kept in the dark about the H-bomb, but the price of great-power status had been raised. When the prime minister and the leader of the opposition clashed in the House of Commons over the relationship with Washington, Attlee's demand of Churchill inadvertently betrayed the shared assumption about Britain's post-war role: 'The heads of the three states ought to meet,' the Labour leader demanded. 'The three states' – no one could admit that in reality it was already two. Moscow would soon have its own H-bomb. Britain could not stand aside. 'We must do it. It's the price we pay to sit at the top table,' Churchill told Edwin Plowden.[11] By the time the chiefs of the armed forces had completed a comprehensive review of defence options in 1954, they felt confident enough to argue that 'Our scientific skill and technological capacity to produce the hydrogen weapon puts within our grasp the ability to be on terms with the United States and Russia.'[12] 'On terms', 'the three' – wherever you turned in Whitehall stood a politician or mandarin fretting about Britain's waning global power.

Attlee, Churchill and, later, Macmillan at various times grew alarmed at the way the Americans set nuclear weapons alongside their conventional arsenal as instruments of war. In 1951, Attlee and Truman agreed on procedures for the use of those weapons based in Britain. The accord was reaffirmed during the following year by Churchill and Eisenhower. A joint communiqué stated that 'Under arrangements made for the common defence, the United States has the use of certain bases in the United Kingdom. We reaffirm the understanding that the use of these bases in an emergency would be a matter for joint decision by His Majesty's Government and the United States Government in the light of circumstances prevailing at the time.'[13] Whether, in practice, an American president would wait for the permission of a British prime minister was less obvious.

The gulf in understanding was brought home to Churchill when he met Eisenhower in Bermuda in December 1953. Churchill, his private secretary John Colville noted, saw the H-bomb as 'something entirely new and terrible' – a threat to the very existence of the civilised world. By contrast, the president 'looked upon it as just the latest improvement in military weapons. He implied that there was in fact no distinction between "conventional weapons" and atomic weapons; all weapons in due course became conventional weapons. This of course represents a fundamental difference of opinion between public opinion in the USA and in England.'[14] Colville was right. This difference – amplified by the emergence in Britain of the growing Campaign for Nuclear Disarmament – would inform nuclear diplomacy between the two capitals for the next decade. When war broke out in Korea, Attlee flew to Washington to seek a renewal of the wartime understanding that atomic weapons would be used only with the consent of both governments. Truman gave an assurance that Washington would 'consult' before taking such a decision.'[15] Attlee's concerns were shared by his successors. Elaborate underground command centres were built at secret locations in the English Home Counties, and shelters across the United Kingdom. Nuclear drills were introduced and local authorities drew up plans of how to respond in the case of nuclear attack. This was a charade. The advent of the H-bomb meant that any nuclear exchange with the Soviet Union would lead to something approaching national obliteration.

For Churchill, an attempt to engineer a rapprochement between Washington and the post-Stalin leadership in Moscow would become something of an obsession. Its failure would lead him into retirement. Macmillan would pick up the baton, with sustained attempts to persuade first Eisenhower and then Kennedy to agree a nuclear test ban treaty with the Soviets. Attitudes in Washington seemed far less cautious. The mediating role sought in turn by Churchill and Macmillan in part reflected an eagerness to keep Britain at the top table of world powers, but it also showed an understanding that the costs of a superpower war would fall much more heavily on Britain than on either of the two main protagonists, a realisation that gave force to the rapid expansion of CND and the anti-nuclear movement.

Whatever people's fears, this was not a game that Britain's leaders thought they could opt out of. In 1954, Oliver Franks – public servant, scholar and ambassador in Washington between 1948 and 1952 – gave the BBC's Reith Lectures, with 'Britain and the Tide of World Affairs' as his title. The world was in tumult, but Franks's assessment of Britain's role was clear: whatever the shifts in the geopolitical plates, 'Britain is going to continue to be what she has been – a great power.'[16] Three years later, in 1957, Britain would explode its own thermonuclear device. Britain's global status and its bomb had become inextricably linked, and as Macmillan and Kennedy met in Nassau in 1962, Washington threatened both.

By the end of the 1950s, Britain was developing the capacity to produce thermonuclear warheads in sufficient numbers to meet its assumed needs. What was required was a delivery mechanism with the capacity to penetrate Soviet defences. American policy was set out in a secret paper produced by the White House National Security Council in April 1961, just months after John F. Kennedy's inauguration.[17] The organising assumption was that the US national interest would be best served by securing control of the West's nuclear arsenal. As long as Britain had the bomb, France, who had already tested a bomb in 1960, and Germany would want to catch up. 'We must try to eliminate privileged British status . . . our minimum objective should be to persuade him [Macmillan] to commit his atomic warheads to the NATO atomic stockpile and his delivery weapons to NATO commanders. Beyond this we should try to move him to cease the production of fissable material for weapon purposes.' Distilled, the message was that America alone should have a finger on the West's nuclear trigger. Kennedy concurred with his advisers, adding a note to the paper: 'It would be desirable for the British in the long run to phase out their nuclear deterrent, since their activity in this field is a permanent goad to the French.'

Macmillan, of course, was not party to such American deliberations and was relying on a deal he had struck with Eisenhower in 1960. Washington had sought access to a British port for its fleet of Polaris nuclear submarines, and the prime minister had offered a base at Holy Loch in Scotland. The quid pro quo for Holy Loch – for Britain's willingness, in effect, to offer itself as a target for Soviet war planners – was the US's readiness to supply Britain with its Skybolt air-launched missile system. Russia's launch of the Sputnik satellite had propelled the world into the missile era. The US had reshaped its nuclear forces around Minuteman missiles scattered in silos across the vast deserts and prairies of the United States and submarines that prowled the deepest oceans carrying Polaris. The failure of Blue Streak left Skybolt as the only remaining option for Britain. Under development by the Pentagon, it promised to extend the life of the British deterrent well beyond that of the Vulcan bombers, which already looked vulnerable to Russian air defences.

By mid-1962, however, a series of failed tests was casting doubt on the viability of Skybolt. The air-launched missiles had run significantly over budget. If they worked, the technicians concluded, they were unlikely to be particularly accurate. Early autumn saw the Pentagon questioning publicly whether Skybolt would ever be cost-effective. There was no great alarm – for the Americans, it was an optional rather than vital programme. The British, though, began to suspect ulterior motives. Nothing was said directly to Macmillan's government about the possibility of cancellation, but the mood music changed. Robert McNamara, the US defence secretary, gave a speech in which he set out publicly what senior policymakers were thinking privately. McNamara announced that the Kennedy administration was opposed to all 'national' nuclear forces within the Western alliance.[18] The 'all' could only mean the British. Within the context of NATO, McNamara told an audience in Ann Arbor, Michigan, independent nuclear forces were 'dangerous, expensive, prone to obsolescence and lacking in credibility as a deterrent'.

America's own arsenal, of course, was inviolate. McNamara's views were shared in the State Department and by Kennedy's national security adviser, McGeorge Bundy. George Ball, the official charged with relations with Europe, was an enthusiast for European integration and feared that the British bomb would damage the process and give France an added incentive to develop its own independent *force de frappe*. Before too long, Ball and others argued, West Germany would also want the bomb. The fear that Bonn would renege on Konrad Adenauer's promise not to pursue nuclear weapons research had become a recurring theme of American defence diplomacy. The State Department was particularly vociferous, with Ball arguing that supplying Polaris would encourage British 'delusions', hinder efforts to nudge it towards Europe and block progress against nuclear proliferation. In the summer of 1961, Kennedy wrote to Macmillan, explaining why he had decided to refuse French requests for help in developing its nuclear programme: 'If we were to help France acquire a nuclear weapons capability, this could not fail to have a major effect on German attitudes . . . the likelihood that the Germans would eventually wish to acquire a nuclear weapons capability would be significantly increased.' Any such move would 'shake NATO to its foundations'[19] and proliferation would become unstoppable. Kennedy was persuaded – particularly by Ball – that an extension of the UK's privileged arrangement could damage Washington's relationship with the rest of Europe, especially France. On that point, he was at least half right: de Gaulle's decision to veto Britain's membership of the EEC was followed by the expulsion of all foreign troops from France and the nation's withdrawal from the military wing of NATO.

Washington's alternative to national deterrents was the creation of a new multilateral nuclear force among America's allies, to which the United States would commit part of its arsenal and to which Britain would assign its national force. The assumption was that this would be largely sea-borne, with crews drawn from across the Western alliance. One way or another, Washington wanted control of the West's bomb. British defence strategists mocked the American idea for a multilateral force as a recipe for paralysis; it would be impossible to reach agreement across governments on the firing of such shared weapons. More to the point, a multilateral force would put an end to Britain's privileged position as Europe's only nuclear power. Macmillan protested to the president that *in extremis*, simply going it alone would be 'better than putting a British sailor aboard ship to have tea with the Portuguese'.[20] Britain, in other words, was not just another European ally.

The administration's tough stance did not go unnoticed in the American media. 'The government of the United States,' the *Washington Post* declared in an editorial on 15 December, 'has handled its relations with Great Britain with little consideration for British feeling and not much evidence of real concern about the British position.' That said, McNamara recognised privately that the prime minister faced serious political troubles, and the secretary of state Dean Rusk wanted to avoid an open breach with the British. His attachment to the notion of a 'special relationship' was pragmatic rather than sentimental. It was the best Washington had as a result of its weak ties to de Gaulle and Adenauer. 'The secretary [Rusk] said he wasn't against the special relationship until he could see something better to take its place,' one official note recorded.[21] Those just below him in the department's Bureau of European Affairs took a more uncompromising line: it was time Britain owned up to its diminished status. So the American side landed in Nassau with three potential offers for Macmillan: the US would press ahead with the Skybolt programme, with the cost shared with the UK. Macmillan could have Hound Dog, a missile system already in service with the United States Air Force, though it would need considerable adaptation to operate from British aircraft. Or Britain could take its place as a member of the new multinational nuclear force that Kennedy was seeking. All three options fell below Macmillan's ambition.

The Caribbean had become a regular venue for Anglo–American summits. The Americans did not have far to travel, and the British could say they were meeting on 'British' soil. With ministers and officials in tow, these gatherings would often run on for two or three days. In a world without twenty-four-hour rolling news and digital communications, leaders had the time to work through extensive agendas. Kennedy and Macmillan had met previously in Bermuda. Those talks had gone well, though the president had later grumbled that the water in the rather cramped governor general's mansion had been insufficiently hot for a decent shave. The British valued relaxed beachfront settings for the sense of informality and intimacy. They put the leaders beyond the noise of Westminster and the glare of political Washington. Macmillan liked to charm. Nassau would demand his best performance.

Macmillan's demand was simple: a missile system that could deliver Britain's home-grown nuclear weapon, thus allowing the country to assume its place on the front bench of world powers.

That meant Polaris. He did not dare contemplate rejection. One question could never completely be resolved: how 'independent' could such a system be? Under what circumstances could a British government make a unilateral decision to fire such missiles? Though he was viscerally opposed to the idea of a multilateral nuclear force, the prime minister was prepared to compromise, as long as he would be able to say on his return home that Britain had safeguarded its nuclear independence.

The State Department's minutes of the negotiations at Nassau[22] convey Macmillan's determination and desperation. The prime minister began, this report notes, with an emotional appeal, recapping the history of Anglo–American cooperation and pointing out that the bomb had started out as a British project. Churchill and Roosevelt had agreed it should be a cooperative venture, but in 1946 the McMahon Act blocked British participation. Britain had been generous a decade later, the agreement to allow the United States to base its submarines at Holy Loch a token of its good faith.

The appeal was accompanied by a pre-emptive strike against Kennedy's concerns, particularly the fear that Washington's other European allies would react badly to a new Anglo–American deal. Saying nothing of his recent blunt exchanges with de Gaulle, Macmillan said he was sure that the implications of a nuclear deal for Britain's Common Market application would be 'frankly, absolutely none'. One question, the US note recorded, was whether the switch from Skybolt to Polaris would upset other allies. The prime minister thought not: 'If it did, we could make some gesture. All these things we were discussing were gestures, in a sense, since the only reality was US power.' This was an admission no British prime minister before or afterwards could make publicly. When push came to shove, Washington decided.

Kennedy's opening gambit was to suggest that Skybolt could be revived as a jointly financed project. The missiles were less than accurate and air-launched nuclear weapons were an imperfect deterrent, but for a modest investment – $100 million was the figure he had in mind – Britain would get a capability that would meet its needs at least until the early 1970s. The president returned again and again to the dangers of proliferation, though he was prepared to consider giving Britain access to the Hound Dog system, which could be adapted for its Vulcan bombers. Macmillan had no intention of buying into a project that the US military had deemed a failure, and nor would he accept Kennedy's assessment that a Polaris agreement would encourage proliferation. He conceded that Germany was 'dangerous', but felt the international threat was not comparable to that of the 1930s because of the emergence of the two superpowers.

Macmillan wove desperation into a thinly veiled threat. Drawing a parallel with the isolation Churchill had faced in 1940, he said he faced the same dilemma – whether 'to chuck it, or go on'. This comparison was far-fetched by any standard – Churchill had been facing an enemy that had swept aside all before it, while Macmillan confronted rejection by an ally – but the prime minister was unabashed. There were plenty of people in Britain, he told the president, who thought the defence budget could be better spent on things such as higher pensions. Without a deal in Nassau he would have to consider whether to press on alone and build a British missile system from scratch. For its part, the United States should consider what sort of ally Britain would be if the Labour Party came to power.

Macmillan ended with an ultimatum that exaggerated the alternatives to Polaris. He would first try to press ahead unilaterally, cutting military spending in the Far East to pay for a British programme. Such a course, he expected, would lead to 'a deep rift with America'. Expectations that Britain's conventional forces could carry the burden of defending Europe would be impossible to meet. If Macmillan determined Britain could not stay in the nuclear club? He would resign. The United States would then find itself dealing with a succession of 'Gaitskells', a reference to the Labour leader's support for multilateral nuclear disarmament. This argument went back and forth over two days, interspersed with discussions that ranged from the conflict between India and Pakistan over Kashmir to China's place at the United Nations. As far as the British side was concerned, all roads led to Polaris.

In the end, Kennedy relented. Macmillan could have Polaris, and at a price the British delegation took to be entirely reasonable. The bargaining, however, was not over. America's missiles would come with strings attached. The president insisted that the submarines carrying Polaris were assigned to the command of NATO. No one – least of all the Germans – could be left in any doubt that these weapons were at the disposal of the alliance rather than Britain. Macmillan had anticipated the demand when he made his opening pitch, stating that 'he would be prepared to put in [to NATO] all of his part of a Polaris force, provided the Queen had the ultimate power and right to draw back in the case of a dire emergency similar to that in 1940'. Kennedy proposed a tougher form of words: 'Only in the event of a dire national emergency – an emergency in which it might be necessary to act alone – an emergency which we cannot envisage and which we all trust will never occur – would Her Majesty's Government be faced with a decision of utilizing such forces on its own – of course after adequate notice to all its partners.' The defence secretary Thorneycroft was outraged and advised Macmillan to break off talks. Calmer voices soon prevailed, and after further negotiation a new formula was agreed: Polaris would be supplied on the understanding that it would become part of a NATO multilateral nuclear force. 'The prime minister made it clear that except where HMG may decide that supreme national interests are at stake, these British forces will be used for the purpose of international defence of the Western alliance in all circumstances.'[23]

Among Britain's defence strategists, Polaris was presented as an insurance policy. In 1962, Britain sat under the American nuclear umbrella. The Thor missiles, submarines and nuclear bombers sited in Britain by the United States carried the clear implication that a Soviet attack would inevitably draw American retaliation. As Macmillan pointed out to Kennedy, however, circumstances could change. A future US president might baulk at risking an all-out Soviet nuclear strike against New York and Washington if Britain were attacked. And there was a third possibility. Even if future administrations were indeed ready to honour commitments made to Britain, Moscow could miscalculate. The Soviet Union might launch an attack on Britain in the mistaken belief that the United States would sit on its hands rather than risk a much wider conflagration. The existence of a British deterrent, capable of inflicting devastation on Moscow and perhaps a dozen other Soviet cities, would be a guard against such miscalculation.

The question left hanging was whether the Nassau agreement would allow for sufficient independence of action in such circumstances. Macmillan knew the language was ambiguous. He was nervous of the response in London, where opponents would condemn the claim of 'independence' as a mirage. Such was his concern that the cabinet was convened in London under the chairmanship of Rab Butler, the first secretary of state, to review the wording. Ministers had mostly been kept out of nuclear decision-making from the moment that Attlee's government had decided to secure the bomb, but Macmillan needed political cover. He got it – but not without some equivocation. The official cabinet minute shows ministers congratulating the prime minister on 'persuading the president to move away from the original United States positions'.[24] The joint wording had the effect, in the prime minister's mind, of 'giving us the sole right of decision on the use of our strategic nuclear forces'. The foreign secretary and defence secretary, with him in the Bahamas, concurred. Yet the cabinet minute shows that some ministers were not entirely content. The communiqué, these ministers said, seemed ambiguous in its meaning. Was it saying that Britain had the right to withhold its nuclear weapons from the alliance in a case of supreme national interest? Or did it permit the United Kingdom to use the deterrent in cases other than the defence of the Western alliance? 'It was clear', the cabinet minute continued, that 'the prime minister intended the exception to cover both cases. If he were free to make this interpretation public, with the consent of the president, this would safeguard the principle of independence; but there would be advantage in clarifying the terms of the statement and removing the ambiguity.' Across the Channel in France, de Gaulle was committed to an independent nuclear capability, the *force de frappe*.[25] Clarification of Britain's position, the cabinet concluded, 'was especially important in view of Western European opinion. We might easily suffer from the growth of a suspicion that our military independence was, or might be, less secure than, for example, that of the French.'

By the time these misgivings reached Nassau, Macmillan had concluded that it was unlikely he would be able to secure any further concessions. He would have to make the best of what he had. The government had rescued the future of Britain's nuclear deterrent and would buy Polaris at cost, making a small contribution to the research and development outlay shouldered by the United States. Britain would also lease its airbase on the island of Diego Garcia, in the Indian Ocean, to the Americans. Macmillan was satisfied, writing in his diary: 'We have had a tremendous week – three days of hard negotiations, nearly four days in reality. The Americans pushed us very hard . . . Whether parliament and the country will think we have done well or badly, I cannot yet tell. Yesterday's press was quite good (except of course Lord Beaverbrook's). Today's is very bad.'[26] 'The sell-out', screamed Beaverbrook's *Daily Express*. 'Macmillan's nuclear folly', echoed the *Daily Herald*. Ministers had been obliged, as they would be many times in the decades to come, to recognise the limitations of British power, but much of the media found the adjustment harder to make. Macmillan's diary entry gives a fair-weather description of the compromise. 'Broadly I have agreed to make our bomber force (or part of it) and our Polaris force (when it comes) a NATO force for general purposes. But I have reserved absolutely the right of HMG [Her Majesty's Government] to use it independently for "supreme national interest". These phrases will be argued and counter-argued.' That said, 'the cabinet did not much like it [the agreement]'.[27]

By the accounts of the Americans, Macmillan had got the best deal on offer – a better agreement than some on his own side had expected and one more generous than the officials and presidential aides on the other side of the table had wanted Kennedy to concede. The president's advisers had urged him to tough it out. Another prime minister probably would have failed in Nassau. To a great extent, Macmillan depended on persuasion and trust. The dynamics of great-power relations are generally ruled by interests rather than sentiment, but there are occasions when history is written by personal chemistry as much as by the facts of relative power.

So why had Kennedy given ground? His adviser Richard Neustadt thought that whatever the leaders' backgrounds, 'in temperament, taste and wit, the two were strikingly compatible'.[28] The prime minister had worked hard to build the relationship. His links with Eisenhower had been close, and Macmillan had continued to nurture them with Kennedy. When Eisenhower visited London in August 1959, the prime minister personally supervised the schedule. An open-topped white Rolls-Royce was borrowed from the Hollywood actor Douglas Fairbanks Jr so that president and prime minister could be driven together in style to a service at St Paul's Cathedral. Macmillan had followed Kennedy's inauguration in 1961 with a stream of letters and suggestions. Sometimes they had an element of 'Greece-to-Rome' pomposity – the prime minister's initial papers were dubbed a 'Grand Design' for the future of the West – but the goal was to position Britain as the president's most reliable ally. Macmillan had reflected on the task before Kennedy's inauguration: 'With Eisenhower there was the link of memories and a long friendship. I will have to base myself now on trying to win him [Kennedy] by ideas.' Just two months before Nassau, the world had looked into the chasm of nuclear Armageddon following Washington's discovery that Moscow had sited nuclear missiles in Cuba. During the Cuban Missile Crisis, Kennedy had pushed back against an American military that was pressing for strikes against the missile sites. More than once he picked up the telephone to London to rehearse his arguments for a diplomatic settlement with the Soviet leader Nikita Khrushchev. Macmillan had offered sympathy and support. Kennedy had appreciated both the reassurance and the absence of lectures. Against all precedence, David Ormsby-Gore had been invited to sit in on the White House crisis meetings.[29]

The State Department's George Ball attributed the Nassau agreement to a mutual feeling of 'great warmth' between the two leaders: 'My own view is that Kennedy simply responded to the despairing cry of a politician in distress, a kind of fellow feeling.'[30] Arthur Schlesinger remarked that the two men got on 'as if they had known each other all their lives'. Neustadt later prepared a detailed assessment of the Skybolt Affair and subsequent deal. His judgement was that Kennedy had faced 'an impassioned older man embodying a valued weaker ally who invoked in his own person a magnificent war record, an historic friendship and a claim upon our honour – in Eisenhower's name – to say nothing of one politician's feeling for another'.[31] In the arguments before Nassau, Neustadt concluded, 'Robert McNamara and Peter Thorneycroft had spoken different languages; these two [Macmillan and Kennedy] spoke the same.' The prime minister's skill had been in playing at once on 'our friendships and fears'. Ormsby-Gore, a frequent visitor to the Kennedy compound at Hyannis Port, was a pivotal figure in building trust. The official and social sides of his relationship with Kennedy almost merged in the ambassador. To some around the president, he was a cuckoo in the American camp – an impression that was confirmed when he joined the president's Christmas party in Florida following the Nassau meeting.

Kennedy secured from Macmillan public assurances that the acquisition of Polaris would not be used as an excuse for further cuts in Britain's conventional forces, a reflection of what was to become a constant complaint of the Americans – that Europe was 'free riding' on their defence spending. Why should the United States invest in the defence of the continent if the Europeans themselves were not prepared to play their part? In December 1962, however, the immediate challenge for the president came from the French. The US administration wanted the Europeans to integrate their efforts in order to solidify the Western alliance against the Soviet Union. It also wanted to discourage nuclear proliferation – above all to Germany. Eager to avoid charges of favouritism, and in an attempt to square the circle, the White House offered de Gaulle the Polaris system on roughly the same terms as provided to Britain. The French president slammed the door – even as he prepared to put an end to Macmillan's attempt to join the European Community.

De Gaulle made the strategic case for an entirely independent bomb that Macmillan and the British could not admit. 'In case of a general atomic war,' he said, 'there would inevitably be terrible and mortal destruction for both countries. In such conditions, no one in the world and in particular no one in America can say whether or where or how or to what extent American nuclear weapons would be used to defend Europe.'[32] Maurice Couve de Murville, de Gaulle's foreign minister, marked out the contrast between Britain and France: 'We never imagined our deterrent as anything other than a French deterrent . . . Britain never imagined that its deterrent could be built without the help of the US; that means inevitably without it being controlled by the US.' Of course, de Murville's 'controlled' was a word that Macmillan and each of his successors would never admit. What was clear – and the oddity was apparent – was that Britain had, in effect, bought an American nuclear system as an insurance policy against a decision in Washington to withdraw the US nuclear umbrella. In the end the symbolism provided by the escape clause in the Nassau accord was enough for the British prime minister. De Gaulle decided that to depend on a deterrent that had been made in America would by definition mean it was less than wholly independent. The French, strangely enough, were following the path marked out by Ernest

Bevin: they would have the Tricolour stamped not just on their bombs but on the missiles that would take them to their targets. Britain would have to live with the ambiguity. To the extent that the bomb was an emblem of national prestige, Macmillan thought the doubts manageable. That France had tested a weapon in 1960 (and China would follow in 1964) made it all the more important that Britain remain a nuclear power. If not one of three, then it would at least be one of five – each of them permanent members of the UN Security Council.

For all that, the sensitivity remained. Henceforth no British government would refer to the nuclear deterrent without first prefacing it with the word 'independent' – an insistence that in its way served only to underline their doubts about the circumstances in which Britain could act without American consent. Twenty years later, when Margaret Thatcher wrote to Ronald Reagan seeking to replace the ageing Polaris with the US navy's Trident missiles, the ghosts of Nassau were still in the room. In 1980, the then president Jimmy Carter had agreed to sell the Trident I system to the UK. By 1982 the US navy had opted for the more advanced Trident II. It was this that Thatcher now requested, but she had to be mindful of the Nassau conditions. 'Like the Polaris force, and consistent with the agreement reached in 1980 on the supply of Trident I missiles,' Thatcher wrote, 'the United Kingdom Trident II force will be assigned to the North Atlantic Treaty Organisation; and except where the United Kingdom Government may decide that supreme national interests are at stake, this successor force will be used for the purposes of international defence of the Western alliance in all circumstances.'[33]

Thatcher also felt obliged to echo Macmillan's commitment to maintaining Britain's conventional forces:

It is my understanding that cooperation in the modernisation of the United Kingdom nuclear deterrent in the manner proposed would be consistent with the present and prospective international obligations of both parties. I would like to assure you that the United Kingdom government remain wholly committed to the strengthening of the Alliance's conventional forces. The United Kingdom Government have in recent years substantially increased their defence spending and further increases are planned for the future in order to sustain the United Kingdom's all-round contribution to allied deterrence and defence.[34]

Reagan's reply followed the same template. 'The United States' readiness to provide these systems is a demonstration of the great importance which the United States government attaches to the maintenance by the United Kingdom of an independent nuclear deterrent capability,' he said. Then came the strings: 'I attach great importance to your assurance that the United Kingdom Trident II force will be assigned to NATO and that the economies realized through cooperation between our two governments will be used to reinforce the United Kingdom's efforts to upgrade its conventional forces. Such nuclear and conventional force improvements are of the highest priority for NATO's security.'[35]

More than three decades later, in the summer of 2016, David Cameron's government replayed the routine when parliament approved the construction of four new submarines to carry the latest American version of the Trident missile system. 'The nuclear deterrent', the prime minister told a NATO meeting in Warsaw, 'remains essential in my view, not just to Britain's security, but as our allies have acknowledged here today to the overall security of the NATO alliance.'[36] Twenty-five years after the collapse of the

Soviet Union and the end of the Cold War, the British government's reasoning was as it had been in 1962, when the world had teetered on the edge of nuclear conflagration.

Some in parliament raised questions about the nature of the deterrent. Did Britain still need a system that provided, in the jargon of the navy, 'continuous at-sea deterrence' (CASD) – at least one submarine ready, at a moment's notice, to fire a fusillade of nuclear missiles at an enemy? The Liberal Democrats, in coalition with Cameron's Conservatives between 2010 and 2015, leaned towards a cheaper, cruise missile-based deterrent. Others questioned whether Britain still needed the assurance of CASD. Even with a bellicose Vladimir Putin in Moscow, the prospect of a surprise nuclear attack was remote. By opting for three submarines rather than four, the government might have saved billions of pounds, but the prime minister pressed ahead regardless.

Some senior officials around Cameron expressed deeper concerns. The austerity budgets that followed the 2008 global financial crash had seen defence badly squeezed, and the nuclear deterrent promised to take more and more from a shrinking allocation. When Macmillan met Kennedy in 1962, defence spending accounted for more than 6 per cent of Britain's national income; by the time Cameron opted for modernisation, the figure was barely 2 per cent. The army, the navy, the Royal Air Force – all had faced severe cuts. Another thirty years of Trident would impose a further, persistent squeeze. 'Top-of-the-range nukes and no soldiers,' one high-ranking official in the Ministry of Defence remarked privately of the Trident decision.

Others in Whitehall raised the issue of independence. Cameron wanted a new form of words that would give greater credence to British freedom of action, but the Americans were clear that was not on offer. Beyond the assignment of the submarines to NATO, the Nassau arrangement had created a technological dependence on the US that France would never have accepted. Cameron's agreement also included provision for American servicing and refurbishment of the missile system. The Americans controlled the software and the missiles could be serviced only at a US facility. Did this really give the prime minister a free hand in the event of a national emergency?

This was not the British bomb as Bevin had imagined it, and nor did it match the independence of the French one. Peter Westmacott was Britain's ambassador in Washington when Cameron negotiated the terms that would keep Trident operational until 2060. Beyond the assignment to NATO, he said, there were other constraints on Britain's freedom of action. The missiles were not only built in the US but for the lifetime of the systems would require servicing and maintenance at the Kings Bay naval submarine base in Georgia. As for independence, Westmacott highlighted a contradiction. 'We may want to remain as a power with what we call an independent nuclear deterrent, but we have long since given up the option of doing that without the Americans. We are dependent on them for it to work.'[37] Westmacott, who also served as ambassador in Paris, drew a contrast with the French nuclear force. 'The French [nuclear system], on the other hand, functions independently, even if they've worked with the Americans on upgrading some of their warhead technology.' So why did British politicians not seem to have a problem with the fact that Polaris and Trident were not independent? According to Westmacott, 'They pretend it is. And, of course, there isn't actually an American finger on the trigger.' The American historian Kenneth Waltz was scathing. A deal struck 'to put the "great" back into Great Britain turned England into a nuclear satellite of the United States'.[38]

This was the prison Macmillan had constructed, from which his successors were either unwilling or unable to escape. Prime ministers continued to offer a strategic case for Polaris and Trident, but the political reality was that possession of nuclear weapons had become inextricably tied up with official notions, and public perceptions, of national prestige. No subsequent prime minister would dare challenge Churchill's assertion in 1954 that the bomb was 'the price we pay for sitting at the top table'; to suggest that Britain should give up the deterrent was to admit that it was no longer a front-rank power. Other governments, it was said, would then ask why Britain should hold on to its permanent seat on the UN Security Council when the other four permanent members were all nuclear powers.

Nuclear disarmament, wrongly but fatally, became a synonym for political and military weakness. For a brief period during the early 1980s, the Labour Party under Michael Foot shifted in that direction. It fought the 1983 general election on a platform of unilateral disarmament. But Foot's policy was tainted by a wider perception that he was unwilling to sustain strong military forces. Margaret Thatcher secured a landslide victory and Labour, under Neil Kinnock, John Smith and Tony Blair, concluded that it had best embrace the bomb. No one would say that Germany was any less safe for its lack of such a weapon. But Britain, of course, was not Germany.

5

Power and the Pound

'He will be a tough nut to crack,' David Bruce telegraphed to Washington, as the new prime minister picked up the keys to 10 Downing Street in October 1964. 'We will find Mr Wilson a resourceful, tough, realistic, opinionated bargainer.'[1] In the description of his biographer, the United States' ambassador to London was 'The Last American Aristocrat'. The scion of a grand Baltimore family, Bruce also kept a large antebellum mansion in Virginia. He was among the State Department's most gifted diplomats. At ease in John F. Kennedy's Camelot, he was equally at home in the Belgravia drawing rooms of Tory high society. David Ormsby-Gore opened the door to Kennedy's White House for Harold Macmillan; Bruce had an open invitation to Number 10.

Kennedy's assassination and Macmillan's resignation during the closing months of 1963 robbed the transatlantic relationship of its intimacy. Macmillan's chosen successor, the Scottish aristocrat Alec Douglas-Home, had to give up his peerage to take the job. History would record his role as that of caretaker. The Conservatives were exhausted. Douglas-Home was a polite footnote to thirteen years of Tory rule. On the other side of the Atlantic, Lyndon Baines Johnson, a rough-hewn Texan politician who had made it to the high reaches of the Democratic Party through his ruthless leadership of the Senate, was unlikely to be seduced by the patrician manners of the English upper classes. A Southern Democrat, he was unimpressed also by the avowed socialism of the new prime minister.

Bruce was the bridge in a relationship that was more often strained than convivial. As ambassador he saw himself as a mediator as well as a servant of the president. The Atlantic, he wrote back to Washington after Labour's election victory, might get a little choppier in the short term. Wilson had a reputation as 'a tricky customer', but the White House could be assured that 'if nothing else, self-interest dictates that he must risk no serious split' with Washington. 'It is tempting to try to analyse Mr Wilson's character,' he wrote, 'but to do so would require a magazine-length report. No telegraphic summary could do justice to his complicated, often inconsistent, personality; only his future actions will disclose whether his numerous detractors or admirers have properly assessed his intentions and capacities.'[2] Wilson's left-wing agenda and connections with Moscow had not gone unnoticed in the US capital, but Bruce was confident the new prime minister was not a Soviet spy. 'I do not think that in his frequent trips to Russia he has been hornswoggled, but he has certainly cajoled himself into believing he can negotiate more successfully with the Soviet government than any other allied statesman.'

'Hornswoggled' – the term presumably owed more to Bruce's roots in Virginia than to the family townhouse in the smartest neighbourhood in Baltimore. His assessment stood the test of time. Wilson was never easy to read; detractors and admirers would argue long beyond his premiership over whether he was a cynical opportunist devoid of political principle or a master political strategist successfully navigating rough waters.

In one respect, though, he was an entirely conventional prime minister: he intended to be a player on the global stage. A familiar pattern was set to repeat itself. One by one, post-war leaders arrived in office certain that Britain remained in the front rank of global affairs. Their expectations were gradually deflated by harsh economic realities and the shift in the balance of international power. Leadership then became a game of maximising influence and persuading voters that the prime minister still held the respect and attention of his peers abroad. Wilson was no exception to the rule. Before the election he had imagined himself whispering words of wisdom to the US president on the White House lawn, in the full glare of the television cameras. Britain had given up its empire, but not its global interests. The nation's frontiers, Wilson declared soon after entering Number 10, extended well beyond its own continent to the distant Himalayas.[3]

Wilson would soon learn that photo calls at the White House came with a price tag. Repeated sterling crises would highlight the limits to the nation's reach overseas. Denis Healey, Wilson's defence secretary, was hard-headed in his assessment. He understood that the cost of sustaining military bases reaching across the Middle East to South East Asia, as well as the 55,000 troops in the British Army of the Rhine, would collide with the large trade deficit, limited foreign currency and gold reserves, and unforgiving financial markets. Britain, Healey would later write, had more troops in the Middle East and Asia than facing the Soviet threat in Germany. Bases in Singapore and Aden, Borneo and Bahrain, and Hong Kong and the island of Gan in the Indian Ocean were post-colonial commitments that the country could ill afford. As for Wilson's 'Himalayan frontier', Healey thought it an 'embarrassing farce'.[4] It was exposed as such when India and Pakistan turned to Moscow rather than London to mediate a settlement to the 1965 Indo–Pakistani War.

Macmillan had hoped to cement Britain's place in the world. He departed Downing Street a disappointed man. He had successfully rebuilt trust in the relationship with Washington. He could also draw satisfaction from the signing in autumn 1963 of the Partial Test Ban Treaty. This was the first in a series of international treaties that over time injected a vital measure of predictability into the nuclear stand-off between the United States and the Soviet Union. Macmillan played no small part in the treaty's successful conclusion. Engagement with Europe, however, was unfinished business. Playing Greece to America's Rome might amplify British influence, but he had come to understand that closeness to Washington was not enough. De Gaulle's veto had stymied his effort to find a new equilibrium. Acheson's critique of the nation's post-imperial drift went unanswered.

Wilson had campaigned in the election as the champion of modernity – the dynamic, self-made leader who would sweep away thirteen years of Tory complacency. He stepped into Downing Street promising a 'New Britain' – a slogan, incidentally, with which Tony Blair would take the Labour Party back into power in 1997, after eighteen years of Tory rule. At Labour's annual conference in Scarborough during the autumn of 1963, Wilson promised 'planning on an unprecedented scale to meet automation without unemployment; a pooling of talent in which all "classes" could compete and prosper; a vast extension of state-sponsored research; a completely new concept of education; an alliance of science and socialism'.[5] The nation's economic fortunes and political strength would be recast in the 'white heat' of technological invention. Science would serve the cause of prosperity.

Overblown as it was, the enthusiastic embrace of the future caught the nation's mood. Macmillan had resigned in October 1963, never having quite recovered from the blow of de Gaulle's European veto. The general's *'non'* had been followed by the Profumo affair, a seedy story of sex, spies and the 'anything goes' entitlement of the ruling classes. John Profumo, the minister for war, had shared a lover, Christine Keeler, with the Soviet naval attaché. It did not seem that secrets of state had passed between them, but Profumo lied about the affair to the House of Commons and was forced to resign. In other circumstances, the prime minister might have taken the scandal in his stride, but the Conservatives had been in power for too long. In October 1963, a scare about his health, later found to be a false alarm, persuaded a dispirited Macmillan to step down. Eschewing a search for a dynamic young successor, the Conservatives settled on Alec Douglas-Home, a politician who seemed visibly puzzled as to why voters might want to leave behind the drab conformity of the post-war years for the raucous modernity of the Swinging Sixties.

Wilson's illusions reached beyond his imagined stature in Washington. He was among the first to his feet to applaud Hugh Gaitskell's 'thousand years of history' address to the Labour conference in 1962, and he had also opposed Macmillan's application to join the European Community. Britain had not properly exploited its rich scientific and technological base, he said – too much of its endeavour had been allocated to sustaining a military budget in excess of those of its more economically dynamic European neighbours. Labour's National Economic Plan and a new Whitehall Department of Economic Affairs would harness state intervention and the latest technologies to rejuvenate the economy. There was a lot of hot air in all this, but Douglas-Home presented an easy target. In Wilson's description, 'We are living in the jet age but we are governed by an Edwardian Establishment mentality.'[6]

Gaitskell, who had died suddenly in January 1963, hailed from the Labour right, while Wilson won the leadership as a standard-bearer for the left. His supporters would have had no truck with Macmillan's vision of Britain as a bridge between America and the European Common Market. They were suspicious of both

Washington and Brussels. British influence, they thought, should be embedded in the burgeoning Commonwealth of nations emerging from empire – a unique opportunity to create a new, multi-ethnic association spanning the world's richer and poorer nations. Wilson warned that joining Europe risked forgetting 'the four-fifths of the world's population whose preoccupation is with emergence from colonial status into self-government; and into the revolution of rising expectations'.[7] The new world should reflect their enthusiasms and aspirations. The Labour left fixed its gaze on the United Nations in New York, it was prominent in the Campaign for Nuclear Disarmament and it fiercely opposed Washington's military entanglement in South Vietnam. The party's manifesto for the 1964 general election thus disowned the nuclear deal Macmillan had struck at Nassau. Polaris, it declared, 'will not be independent and it will not be British and it will not deter. Its possession will impress neither friend nor potential foe'.[8] The furthest a Labour government would go was to accept a version of the multilateral nuclear force promised for Europe by the Americans. Britain would draw power and prestige, the manifesto proclaimed, from 'a great Commonwealth of 700 million people, linked to us by ties of history and common interest'. Yet even as he played the left's tunes, Wilson continued to look to Washington as a source of the influence he craved.

Wilson's talent was that of the accomplished political operator. None was more attentive to the fissures and fractures in his party, nor to the possibility that rivals were gathering their forces against him. As prime minister, he did not intend to be held prisoner by socialist idealism. If awkward political swerves were needed to align party aspirations to foreign policy truths, he would be prepared to make them. It was soon evident that the Commonwealth was no substitute for a central role within the Western alliance. Richard

Neustadt wrote to Johnson, predicting that Wilson would disappoint anti-nuclear campaigners on the Labour left. 'Power breeds realism,' he advised, 'but there is a gestation period.'[9] David Bruce was similarly confident that Washington would call the shots. For all Wilson's toughness, only 'our own lack of equal resourcefulness and determination would enable him to profit at the expense of our more powerful position'.[10]

Deference to the Commonwealth was no more than obligatory political baggage. Wilson shared the conventional wisdom that safeguarding national prestige demanded a strong relationship with the US president. 'We cannot afford to relinquish our world role,' he told the House of Commons in December 1964, on returning from his first visit to the White House.[11] The prime minister had never doubted his personal stature. Tony Benn was among those attending a private dinner hosted by the *Guardian* a few months before the election. Wilson had boasted to his hosts, Benn wrote in his diary, that he would have a more intimate relationship with Washington than any of his predecessors. He thought 'that he can telephone [the US president] and fly over as and when necessary, without the usual fuss'.[12] Here, as plain for Wilson as for Macmillan, was the lure of the 'special relationship': reflected power. Before his first visit to Washington, Wilson quietly dropped his pledge to renegotiate the Nassau deal.

Britain's retreat from empire during the early 1960s required the maps of several continents to be redrawn, yet for the most part this momentous transfer of power was conducted with neither great excitement nor upheaval at home. Twenty years earlier, while war was still raging in Europe, Winston Churchill had declared that this moment should be postponed for ever. History was on Roosevelt's side; by the time Wilson reached Downing Street, the number living under British rule beyond its shores had fallen below twenty million. The dissolution happened at a speed no one had predicted when India and Pakistan were given independence in 1947. Churchill had succeeded in stalling the process of decolonisation on his return to Downing Street in 1951, but after Suez there was an unstoppable acceleration of the demand for national self-determination. In February 1960, Macmillan travelled to Cape Town to read the last rites on empire, in a speech that gave more energy to the departure of Britain's African colonies: 'The wind of change is blowing through this continent and, whether we like it or not, this growth of national consciousness is a political fact,' the prime minister declared.[13] What mattered now, Macmillan added, was which side the new nations would choose. Could these newly independent states be kept in the Western camp, or would they defect to the Soviet sphere of influence? Macmillan was correct, but a few on the Tory right would continue to see the Commonwealth as a vessel for British power.

The embers of empire still glowed here and there. John Kerr, later one of the nation's top diplomats, joined the Foreign Office in 1966. Within his first year as a desk officer in the Arabian department, he witnessed from London 'the last British-arranged coup in the Persian Gulf, when we evicted the sheikh of Abu Dhabi – took him to a Land Rover, put him on a plane and off he went to Saudi Arabia, where they looked after him very nicely'. Later, employees of an American oil company visited the young Kerr to ask 'if they could dig a hole in Qatar and look for oil. And I said: "Certainly not."'[14]

However, what had started as a slow, orderly march for the exit by the 1960s resembled an avalanche, as colony after colony stood in line at the United Nations to take their places as fully independent states. The UN had started out in 1945 with fifty-one members. The addition of Malawi, Malta and Zambia took the total to 117 by 1965. Overall, twenty new states emerged from the Empire between 1957 and 1964. Nigeria, Tanzania, Sierra Leone, Kenya, Uganda, Cyprus, Malaysia and Trinidad and Tobago led the march from empire to Commonwealth. They were soon joined by dozens of smaller possessions scattered across the globe – the Maldives, Singapore, Malta, Mauritius, the Seychelles, Tonga, the Bahamas, Grenada, the Solomon Islands and Papua New Guinea among them. Alongside came the dissolution of what remained of the informal empire of protectorates and dependencies in the Middle East and Gulf. Qatar, the United Arab Emirates, Bahrain and Yemen all claimed independence. The historian Robert Self calculates that during the thirty years between 1945 and 1975, the population of the Empire fell from 700 million to less than five million,[15] and four million of those remaining lived in Hong Kong. The rest were scattered across tiny territories such as the Falklands, Ascension Island, Pitcairn and Tristan da Cunha.

This comprehensive remaking of the map of the world was largely unremarked upon by voters at home. There were debates aplenty in parliament about the impact of decolonisation on trade and, in several instances, about the rights of white settler populations in places such as Kenya and Rhodesia. Macmillan was accused by the Tory right – the old Suez Group – of proceeding with indecent haste. There was also some grumbling in the English Home Counties about what would become of a generation of young men from the second-tier public schools that had previously built their business on producing administrators to run distant parts of the Empire. The transition on the ground was not universally smooth: the Mau Mau Uprising in Kenya, and the ferocious response of the colonial authorities, left a dark stain on the record of colonial administration in East Africa. In South East Asia, British troops spent much of the 1950s fighting a communist insurgency in Malaya. And in 1964, Wilson was obliged to deploy tens of thousands of soldiers to defend the newly independent state of Malaysia against the territorial ambitions of President Sukarno's autocratic Indonesian regime.

White South Africa's imposition of the racist and repressive apartheid regime – and the failure of successive British governments to respond with serious sanctions on Pretoria – became a running sore within the Commonwealth. It was settled only when the whites accepted majority rule at the end of the 1980s. In 1965, Ian Smith's unilateral declaration of independence, designed to preserve white power in Rhodesia, greatly increased the tensions between Britain and other African states. Wilson bowed to Commonwealth demands for an arms embargo, but this was far short of the military intervention demanded by many newly independent African states. Rhodesia would absorb copious amounts of political and diplomatic energy in Westminster and Whitehall, until the Lancaster House Agreement in 1979 finally provided a path to majority rule.

Cyprus, the scene of a violent insurrection by Greek nationalists and divided between its Greek and Turkish communities, seemed forever to be tipping over the edge into crisis. And no one could have guessed that Britain's decision to hold on to the Falkland Islands in the South Atlantic would plant the time bomb that would eventually explode with the Argentine invasion in 1982. The occupants of the Chagos Islands, thrown out of their homes on their island territory in the Indian Ocean and transported to Mauritius in order to make way for the Diego Garcia airbase leased by Britain to the Americans, would have to wait half a century before the British courts recognised the injustice.

The minutes of cabinet meetings from the time record the many mistakes and embarrassments as ministers sought to balance the impatience of nationalist movements to move immediately to independence with the practicalities of British retreat. At the back of many minds was the bloody conflict between India and Pakistan after the Attlee government rushed for the exit in 1947.

Yet these momentous shifts to self-government in former colonies rarely grabbed the sustained attention of most Britons. The nostalgists on the Tory backbenches struggled to mobilise public opinion. Outbreaks of fighting in far-flung places struggled to make the front pages. Once started, decolonisation had an irresistible logic. To the extent that the Empire and the Commonwealth came into sharper view, it was more often in terms of controversy about the numbers of immigrants from former colonies in the Caribbean, India and Pakistan arriving in Britain to fill vacant jobs in public services and in the textile mills of the north. The Notting Hill race riots in 1958 saw mobs of young white men attacking families recently arrived from the West Indies. Far-right groups such as Oswald Mosley's Union Movement and the self-styled White Defence League stoked the fires of racial hatred. In 1962, Macmillan's government imposed restrictions on Commonwealth immigration. Enoch Powell began to rehearse the 'Rivers of Blood' speech that six years later would see him thrown out of the Tory party for outright racist incitement. In opposition, Labour denounced all restrictions on arrivals from the Commonwealth. Once in government, the party tightened the rules further. For all that, the unwinding of empire for the most part represented a dignified departure. Given the rush to independence, the task of building democratic institutions in places that had never known an election and avoiding tribal and ethnic rivalries where new national borders criss-crossed former imperial boundaries was never going to be easy. Britain could claim to have made a fair job of it.

The country could no longer afford the Empire. Before the Second World War, Britain's control of imperial trade and capital flows had made it a wealthy net creditor. Insurance, finance, shipping and the services needed to oil the wheels of trade and finance generated more than enough to bridge a long-standing deficit between exports and imports of physical goods. The pound was the reserve currency held by central banks and private investors across the dominions and Empire; in 1945, about half of all world trade was still conducted in sterling. The war had, however, cost Britain all its overseas assets and more, leaving it a net debtor. During the 1950s, the government became addicted to loans from the International Monetary Fund and foreign currency support packages put together by the US Federal Reserve and other central banks. So-called 'invisible' earnings from insurance and the rest no longer offset the widening deficit in food and manufactured goods. And as Britain struggled, America boomed. With the productive capacity of much of Europe in ruins, the US accounted for 40 to 50 per cent of the world's global output. The sheer scale of its industrial production lines gave it an unbeatable competitive edge. Technologically it had bounded ahead.

Politicians of both left and right, however, shared a misunderstanding: the assumption that in one form or another the Commonwealth could become a surrogate for empire, an alternative source of British power and prestige. They thought the newly independent states would assume a debt of gratitude and be content to amplify Britain's voice in the councils of global affairs. The arrangements would be underpinned by the long-established trade patterns of empire and by sterling's place as a reserve currency. Here were the last imperial delusions. It should have been obvious that independence would encourage new nations to reassess their interests and make their own choices. Why would they mark self-government by submitting to direction from London? British politicians might have grasped this when India lined up with most of the Commonwealth and joined the United States in publicly condemning the Suez adventure. Jawaharlal Nehru, the first prime minister of India, formalised the break when he co-founded a new international grouping of non-aligned nations in 1961. Still, a small band of nostalgists imagined that things would soon be otherwise and that the Commonwealth would pay fealty to the former mother country. Strong echoes of this were still being heard in 2016, when Brexiters summoned up the Commonwealth as the foundation for a 'Global Britain' that would regain the authority lost to the European Union.

The backdrop for Wilson's first visit to the White House in December 1964 was inauspicious. The government had inherited an economic crisis, but Wilson had ruled out a devaluation of the pound, seeing it as an admission of weakness. The only alternative was a package of measures including temporary import levies, higher interest rates and a rise in taxes. The reverberations were felt in the United States, where Lyndon Johnson feared that the dollar could come under pressure. He had also been irritated by Wilson's shifting position on nuclear cooperation. As it turned out, the talks were more cordial than officials on either side expected. The prime minister was eager to please, while the president took the advice of the Anglophiles among his officials who cautioned against an open rupture. Churchill would have made more of a fuss about the 'special relationship', but Wilson, a Huddersfield boy who had won a scholarship to Oxford University, was smart enough to know that emotional imagery would not impress the unpolished Texan. Instead Wilson showed himself as willing to compromise, softening his pre-election dismissal of Kennedy's plan for a multinational European nuclear fleet by suggesting an alternative Atlantic nuclear force. He offered the promise the Americans wanted: Britain would retain its military bases east of Suez in order to allow the United States to concentrate its efforts on fighting communism in Vietnam. At the White House banquet given in his honour, Wilson spoke of a 'close' rather than a 'special' relationship.

The officials in Johnson's White House counselled that for all its economic weakness, Britain remained a useful ally. Neustadt noted that the prime minister had arrived in Washington 'with recollections of the Anglo–American relationship and hopes for his own personal relationship, which are quite different from perceptions of reality held by many American officials'.[16] Britain had still to accept its place as a junior partner. The meeting would be 'more of a chore than a major act of policy'. For all that, he urged Johnson to recognise that Wilson's pro-American stance faced significant opposition within his own party. Washington would not gain from a British retreat from the world. A decade earlier, Eisenhower's White House had been pressing Downing Street to wrap up what remained of its empire. Now, as it was drawn deeper into the war in Vietnam, the United States needed Britain to stand watch against communist uprisings elsewhere in Asia.

The summit saw one or two sharp exchanges. Johnson took issue with Wilson's decision to increase spending on public services and welfare, a move that had unsettled financial markets and raised fears that the dollar could get caught up in speculation against sterling. He made it clear that pressure on the pound should not be an excuse for further British defence cuts that would increase the burden on American forces in Europe. Inexplicably, the president then launched a stinging attack on the decision of Macmillan's government to approve the sale of a fleet of British Leyland's famous red buses to Cuba. The deal broke the American trade embargo on Cuba, but scarcely amounted to a security threat. On the other hand, Johnson was also at pains to thank Wilson for the help Britain had provided for a rescue mission for American and Belgian hostages held by rebel forces in the Congo.

All this, of course, was small change. The foreign policy issue that kept Johnson awake at night was Vietnam – a tragedy in the making that would consume his presidency, fan the flames of anti-Americanism around the world and shake the foundations of the American republic. Vietnam would impose severe strains on the Anglo–American relationship. Although Wilson would continue to regard himself as a privileged adviser to the president and a broker between the great powers, his refusal to send British troops to Vietnam would ensure the 'special relationship' never reached beyond the politely transactional.

Wilson's biographer Philip Ziegler records that Johnson waited until the two leaders were alone in the White House Rose Garden before raising the subject of Vietnam.[17] A year earlier, a group of pipers from the Black Watch of the Royal Highland Regiment had joined America's day of mourning for Kennedy. The pipers played 'The Brown-Haired Maiden' and 'The Badge of Scotland' as Kennedy's funeral cortège wound its way from the White House to Washington's St Matthew's Cathedral. Perhaps recalling the occasion, Johnson asked Wilson to send a battalion of the Black Watch to support the American forces in Vietnam. By his later account, the prime minister did not respond and insisted to colleagues that he had made no commitments. This, though, was only the first of many such conversations during the following three years. Johnson's requests for British boots on the ground and Wilson's refusals became an ever-present source of grit in the relationship. The outcome was a sullen truce punctuated by occasional angry exchanges. For Wilson, Vietnam also emerged as the issue that underlined, almost as vividly as it did for Eden during the Suez crisis, the debilitating link between Britain's economic weakness and its freedom to map an independent path on the international stage.

His premiership, like those of his predecessors, was dogged by sterling crises. Washington served as the gatekeeper for the International Monetary Fund and central bank rescue operations that had become a feature of Britain's economic life. With a nod from the White House, the IMF and the central banks would step in to prop up the pound. Equally, the United States had shown during the Suez crisis that it could slam the door on international assistance. This was something to be remembered each time Wilson said no to Johnson's requests for military support.

Malleable on most things, Wilson stood his ground. 'Why don't you run Malaysia and let me run Vietnam?' The telephone line to London fairly crackled as Johnson spoke his mind. It was February 1965, two months after their first White House encounter.[18] Amid rising Viet Cong attacks on American forces – technically still only 'advisers' to the South Vietnamese forces – the prime minister feared that Johnson was about to order a serious military escalation. Brushing aside the advice of his officials, he decided to travel to Washington to caution the president personally against deeper entanglement. The world would see Wilson the statesman whispering words of advice to the president of the United States. The White House, unsurprisingly, rebuffed the suggestion. The best he was offered was a late-night telephone call with the president. Johnson, the White House note of the conversation records, fired every barrel. No, he did not want the prime minister to fly over. A visit would have no impact on his decisions. Wilson should decide which side he was on. The United States, Johnson reminded him, had sent forces to help the British fighting an Indonesian-backed insurgency in Malaysia, without reciprocal help in Vietnam. There was nothing to be gained from the two leaders 'flapping around the Atlantic with our coat-tails out'. Would the prime minister be content if the president announced to the American press that 'he was going over to London to try to stop the British in Malaysia'?[19]

Johnson would soon send tens of thousands of combat troops to prosecute the war on South Vietnam's behalf. Wilson's fears were realised, reflected in Britain in rising public protests against the war and growing disgruntlement within the cabinet as well as the Labour Party at the prime minister's refusal to speak out against Washington. For his part, Wilson feared a serious rupture in Anglo–American relations – a break, he told Bruce, that would compare with that over Suez. The outcome was an uneasy modus vivendi. Wilson continued to offer political and diplomatic support to Washington, punctuated by occasional nods in the direction of the anti-war movement. Johnson pressed for military assistance. He was not going to take advice from anyone who refused to accept a stake in the outcome. When his advisers – notably McGeorge Bundy and George Ball – reported that Wilson faced real political problems, Johnson accused them of being 'dangerously sympathetic to the UK'.

Wilson had made up his mind ten years earlier, when France's humiliating defeat at Dien Bien Phu ended its attempt to hold on to Indochina. 'We must not join or in any way encourage an anti-communist crusade in Asia under the leadership of the Americans,' he had said.[20] On that occasion, Churchill had delivered a brusque rejection to Truman's request for British support. Now opposition to the war in Vietnam spread well beyond the Labour left.

For many others in Wilson's party, it was essentially a colonial war. The prime minister settled on an awkward balancing act. He would continue to publicly support America's backing for the South Vietnamese regime in Saigon, but would not go any further. As the United States slipped deeper into the mire, Johnson kept on asking. A token force would be sufficient, he would suggest. Wilson's answer was always no. The formal explanation was that as a co-signatory of the 1954 Geneva Accords ending France's war in Indochina, Britain could not be a party to the new conflict. In truth, the dispatch of British troops would have been an act of political self-immolation. As it was, his refusal to condemn the American intervention provoked serious unease among Labour MPs. Sending just a handful of British troops could well have lost him his party. Whatever the motive – and with Wilson political expediency always loomed large – the rebuff probably counted as his most important foreign policy decision. The price – Johnson would never fully trust him – was worth paying.

That is not to say the arrangement was stable. In the summer of 1966, Wilson provoked Johnson's wrath by publicly distancing the government from the American decision to extend its bombing to Hanoi and Haiphong. In the opening months of 1967, he took it upon himself to act as a mediator between Washington and Moscow, reprising the honest broker role once sought by Macmillan. The British even gave the operation a code name: 'Sunflower'. In February, Wilson told MPs he had put forward a plan to end the fighting during talks in London with the Soviet premier Alexei Kosygin. He wanted Johnson to extend the 'Tet' ceasefire in Vietnam. Washington was dismissive. The United States by now had half a million troops in the war and no confidence that the regime in Hanoi would seriously engage in peace talks. The prime minister's secret plan 'amounted to nothing so much as some ideas recycled from the United Nations',[21] the State Department said in a circular sent to American embassies around the world. Vietnam had become a transatlantic sore that could be salved but never fully healed. An exchange with the British journalist Louis Heren at a party to mark Dean Rusk's departure from the State Department gave a flavour of the resentment. By Heren's account, Rusk said: 'All we needed was one regiment. The Black Watch would have done. Just one regiment, but you wouldn't. Well, don't expect us to save you again. They can invade Sussex, and we wouldn't do a damned thing about it.'[22]

Anger in Washington did not dispel a suspicion in Whitehall that, inadequate as it might have been deemed in the White House, Wilson's political backing for the war reflected a secret understanding with Johnson to prop up sterling. The prime minister's commitment to defending the pound at times bordered on the obsessive. The defence secretary Denis Healey would later say that Wilson 'regarded the sanctity of sterling as so absolute that he allowed cabinet to discuss the issue only once, on 19 July 1966; and he refused to circulate the minutes of that meeting, even to the cabinet ministers who attended it. Thereafter he vetoed all attempts to discuss the exchange rate in cabinet, or even in any of the cabinet committees on economic affairs.'[23] Holding the exchange rate, however, required help from Washington – at the very least, the assurance that it would come to Britain's aid when sterling was hit by speculative pressure. A quid pro quo in the form of British backing for the president's Vietnam policy would not have been extraordinary.

Wilson certainly needed help. If keeping British troops out of Vietnam was one of his most intelligent decisions, setting his mind so firmly against devaluation was perhaps his worst. Given the mismatch between Britain's foreign currency earnings and the much higher cost in dollars of its overseas obligations, attacks on the pound had become an uncomfortable fact of economic life. The currency's weakness had come to illustrate Britain's failure to match the economic performance of its European neighbours, the frailty of its hopes for a continued global presence and its economic dependence on the United States. Wilson might have sought to break the cycle straight after the 1964 election. He resisted, fearful that immediate devaluation would undermine his great project to modernise the economy. Attlee had devalued in 1949 and faced heavy losses in the general election the following year. Wilson's stance, however, left him exposed to the 'stop–go' economics that bedevilled Eden and Macmillan. As long as Britain's overseas commitments ran ahead of its earnings and drained its reserves of gold and foreign currency, a crisis was always around the next corner.

Britain's problem was not cyclical – a matter of economic fortunes that swung this way or that over time – but systemic. Without a step change in the nation's economic performance – in its productivity, industrial relations and innovation – and thus its foreign currency earnings overseas, sterling would be vulnerable. Wilson could indulge in rhetoric about Britain's place at the top table, its role in policing the global peace and its place at the centre of a Commonwealth. The claims had substance only to the extent that the government could pay for the nation's presence overseas. The result was the fundamental mismatch between national self-image and domestic economic capacity.

Washington played a double game. Successive US administrations determined that the dollar would replace the pound as the international reserve currency, yet they were also ready to organise a series of international rescue operations to support sterling when it suited their foreign policy interests. Sterling was set at a rate of $4.03 when the Bretton Woods system of fixed but adjustable exchange rates came into force in 1946. In September 1949, the rate was cut to $2.80. Sensible economics proved to be bad politics. Devaluation became fixed in the public mind as a measure of national weakness.

Wilson always denied the rumours of a secret understanding with Johnson. Yet, even if nothing was said explicitly, it was obvious that US support for sterling and Wilson's backing for Washington's Vietnam policy had become entangled. Just as Johnson was dispatching tens of thousands of troops to Vietnam during the summer of 1965, sterling faced a new wave of selling on the international currency markets. Wilson's government needed dollars to restore market confidence, while Johnson wanted proof that America's allies backed his Vietnam policy. In June, he wrote to Wilson and asked for the 'most earnest consideration to increasing the assistance in ways which will give a clear signal to the world – and perhaps especially to Hanoi – of the solidarity of international support for resistance to aggression in Vietnam and for a peaceful settlement in Vietnam'.[24] Johnson's aides, led by the national security adviser McGeorge Bundy, thought the trade-off should be explicit. He told Patrick Dean, who had replaced David Ormsby-Gore as ambassador in Washington, that there had to be a 'quid pro quo'. All the president asked for was the dispatch of two platoons of troops or even a military hospital – what mattered was the symbolism. In a note to the president, Bundy was blunt. He said that it made 'no sense for us to rescue the pound in a situation in which there is no British flag in Vietnam, and a threatened British thin-out in both East of Suez and in Germany . . . a British brigade in Vietnam would be worth a billion dollars at the moment of truth for sterling'.[25]

Johnson rejected the advice, ruling out so direct a link as too dangerous. He did, however, set conditions for the sterling rescue package that was put in place in September 1965. Wilson was obliged to offer assurances that an accompanying set of public spending and defence cuts would not weaken Britain's commitment to its military role east of Suez. A decade earlier, the United States had been keen for Britain to retreat from empire. Now, as it slipped deeper into the mire of Vietnam, Washington feared that Britain's departure from Singapore and Malaysia would leave a vacuum that would soon be filled by the Soviet Union. If Britain would not join the fight against communism in Vietnam, the very least the United States could expect was that it would continue to defend Western interests in South East Asia. Wilson agreed. Military bases in the Mediterranean and Middle East bore the brunt when the defence secretary Denis Healey announced another round of cuts in the spring of 1966.

The moment of truth arrived on 18 November 1967, when Wilson lost his battle with the financial markets. Suez had brought down the curtain on Britain's imperial delusions. The 1967 devaluation forced it to realign its international ambitions with its European geography. Eighteen months earlier, the Labour leader's gamble on a snap general election had paid off, increasing his wafer-thin parliamentary majority to a more comfortable ninety-eight seats. Politics could not fix the economics. The grand modernising strategy had stalled and the cycle of sterling crises and deflationary spending cuts was becoming ever more frequent. The American-led bailout in the autumn of 1965 had been followed by another rescue operation in the summer of 1966. The clouds gathered again just a year later, when the Arab–Israeli Six-Day War closed the Suez Canal and threatened Britain's access to oil supplies.

Confidence on the markets was further hit by worsening industrial strife. By October, the Bank of England was haemorrhaging dollar reserves in its attempt to prop up sterling. The prime minister bowed to the inevitable: a 14 per cent depreciation that cut sterling's value from $2.80 to $2.40. Wilson tried to put a brave face on things, appearing on national television to assure voters that 'It does not mean, of course, that the pound here in Britain, the pound in your pocket or purse, or in your bank, has been devalued.' Business leaders launched a campaign to harness the patriotism of the nation. 'I'm Backing Britain' lapel badges, emblazoned with the Union flag, were distributed across the nation's factories and offices. In a kindly mood, the *Financial Times* called the movement 'a beacon of light in an otherwise dismal economic and industrial prospect'. In truth, it threw the thinnest of cloaks over the country's humiliation. Struggling to find spending cuts, the cabinet even considered withdrawing from the Concorde supersonic aircraft project with France, which a few years earlier had been among the shiniest emblems of Wilson's quest for a great technological leap. Only the realisation that the government would face massive financial penalties now saved a vital statement of national prestige.

The last veil had been torn from the pretence that Britain remained a global power capable of projecting military force well beyond European shores. Talk of a withdrawal from East of Suez had been in the air for some years. Provisional plans had been drawn up in 1966 for a deferred retreat during the 1970s. Confronting the need for another round of cuts in public spending, Wilson had run out of options. Plans were laid for the closure of all naval and military bases east of the Suez Canal. Beyond giving up responsibility for the defence of Malaysia and Singapore, this meant abandoning Britain's informal empire of influence in the Gulf. Aden, which as recently as 1962 had been seen as a permanent garrison, had already been surrendered to insurgent nationalists. Britain would at last admit the truth its leaders had been determined to avoid: its place was as a European power.

The withdrawal was finalised in January 1968, when ministers huddled in Downing Street over several days to confront the unavoidable logic of the devaluation. Outside, the hands of Big Ben had been brought to a halt by the snowstorms battering the capital; inside, the discussions were steeped in gloom. The cabinet met eight times over eleven days. The budgets for services such as education, health and welfare took large cuts, as the Treasury attempted once again to shift resources in the economy from consumer spending to exports. The government would within three years withdraw all its forces from East of Suez. Some 35,000 service personnel and 12,000 dependants would be brought home by March 1971.

The earlier plans sketched out by the defence secretary Denis Healey would have kept most of them in place until the mid-1970s. The United States led the protests at the accelerated timetable. Wilson reported to the cabinet that Lee Kuan Yew, the prime minister of Singapore, had become 'excitable' when told about the withdrawal.[26] Johnson had been doubly angered by an associated plan to cancel a £400 million order for the fifty American F-111 advanced fighter aircraft that had been intended for the RAF's bases in the Far East and Persian Gulf. The president warned that taken together, the measures would signal British disengagement from its international security obligations. Britain had reneged on the understanding that US-led rescue operations for sterling would guarantee a British willingness to share global security burdens. George Brown, the foreign secretary, reported in a similar vein on his conversations with Dean Rusk. Brown suggested delaying the withdrawal of troops from East of Suez, in the hope of retaining as much goodwill as possible among allies. 'Even if we ceased to be a world power,' he told the cabinet, 'we should continue to retain world interests and to need friends and allies to defend them.' The former minister Duncan Sandys spoke for the Tory opposition when the debate moved to the House of Commons: 'What right does the prime minister think he has irrevocably to abdicate Britain's role in the world without even giving parliament an opportunity beforehand to discuss the grave implications involved?' The new chancellor Roy Jenkins (James Callaghan had moved to the Home Office) responded with a candour that was generally absent from such debates:

> The changes which we have announced are no more than the recognition – some will say the belated recognition – of basic currents in the tide of history. We are no longer, and have not been for some time, a superpower. It does not make sense for us to go on trying to play a role beyond our economic strength. From here forward . . . our part in world affairs must be underpinned by economic strength and not undermined by economic weakness.[27]

The *New Statesman* saw this public admission of geopolitical reality as 'comparable in importance to Mr Attlee's granting of Indian independence and the Tory government's evacuation of British Africa'. As for Wilson's assurance that devaluation would not affect the pound in voters' pockets, this was, at best, economical with the truth. A lower pound would put up the price of imports, fuel domestic inflation and put pressure on living standards. The voters would bear the costs. Devaluation followed by retrenchment overseas spoke to the unavoidable truth: the weight carried by post-war Britain on the international stage was intimately linked to its economic performance at home. Beset by industrial strife and suffering from poor productivity growth, the British economy had fallen behind that of its European peers. The retreat from East of Suez was the latest painful expression of the enduring tension between waning economic power and post-imperial illusions.

For all the sense of humiliation, the retreat also engendered a curious feeling of relief. Keeping up global appearances had placed an intolerable strain on the government's resources, and the military could now be reshaped to focus on the defence of Europe. The cabinet minister Patrick Gordon Walker observed that the devaluation crisis had 'made articulate a decision that had subconsciously already been reached, but which the cabinet as a whole and the prime minister had flinched from recognising'.[28] For Wilson, it was a second rendezvous with reality.

The politician who had mocked Macmillan when de Gaulle vetoed Britain's application to join the European Community soon performed a U-turn. Britain had been left 'naked and shivering in the cold' after de Gaulle's rejection, Wilson had taunted Macmillan in January 1963. The attempt to join the Common Market had brought 'national humiliation'. Wilson thus arrived in office possessed with the blithe overconfidence that had seen Britain stand aside from the European Coal and Steel Community and the Rome treaty, yet the facts of economics were against him. Britain's output had been growing at a respectable 3 per cent each year, but France and Italy were recording rates of 5 per cent and West Germany's growth was 6 per cent. The difference showed. Malcolm Muggeridge captured this parting of the ways in a gloomy piece for *Encounter*: 'Each time I return to England from abroad,' he observed, 'the country seems a little more run-down than when I went away; its streets a little shabbier, its railway carriages and restaurants a little dingier; the editorial pretensions of its newspapers a little emptier, and the vainglorious rhetoric of its politicians a little more fatuous.'[29]

For a moment it looked as if de Gaulle himself might rescue Britain from its predicament. Having dispatched the British in 1963, he had turned his wrath to the European Community institutions in Brussels. The general was at odds with the other five founding members over the financing of the European Community budget. The Common Market was pointless for France without the promise of generous support for the country's agriculture. De Gaulle also wanted to slow the pace of institution-building and integration. He saw the project as essentially intergovernmental – a confederation of nation states, or '*Europe des patries*' – rather than the exercise in supranationalism envisaged by the founding fathers, or the federal construction imagined in Bonn. It was an abiding irony that the French view of supranationalism and inter-governmentalism within Europe was much closer to the British outlook than that of the more federalist Germany. Yet British, and for that matter French, politicians would never find a way of turning this meeting of minds into an agreed direction for the enterprise. In 1965, the French president was discovering that the architecture of the Community carried with it an institutional bias towards deepening integration, which Jean Monnet and the founding fathers had always intended. For a time, de Gaulle expressed his displeasure by leaving an 'empty chair' at meetings in Brussels, derailing much of the Community's work. It seemed to some that the enterprise might collapse and Britain might be spared its dilemma over whether to sign up. This was too much to ask. The general's rage passed.

Wilson wore his convictions lightly. His goal was to hold his party together. If the left could be brought round, he decided, membership of the Community might give the economy a much-needed jolt. Europe was not a capitalist club set on stealing Britain's sovereignty after all. The shock of the sterling crisis in July 1966, which forced another round of deflationary spending cuts, sealed the decision. Con O'Neill, the leader of a swelling number of senior Whitehall officials who were convinced that Britain could not stand on the sidelines for much longer, was invited to prepare a paper for ministerial talks at Chequers. The cabinet was split, but the appointment of the strongly pro-European George Brown to the Foreign Office tilted the balance in favour. In October, O'Neill set out the awkward truth for the cabinet. 'For the past twenty years,' he began,

> this country has been adrift. On the whole it has been a
> period of decline in our international standing and power . . .
> We do not know where we are going and have begun to
> lose confidence in ourselves. Perhaps the point has now
> been reached when the acceptance of a new goal and a new
> commitment could give the country as a whole a focus around
> which to crystallise its hopes and energies.[30]

If membership of the Community would provide a challenge around which the nation might coalesce, O'Neill might have added, it would also provide a purpose for Wilson's government.

Macmillan had spent more than a year persuading his cabinet and MPs to back him before lodging a formal application for membership. Wilson initially pretended to be similarly open-minded, announcing at the end of 1966 that he would embark on a tour of European capitals to investigate the terms should Britain decide to join. The 'probe', as it was known in Whitehall, was a charade. Macmillan's mind had been made up from the beginning, and so it was with Wilson when he launched Britain's second bid.

The game continued through the early months of 1967, as Wilson toured European capitals with George Brown. 'We mean business,' he had announced in the Commons. Brown was the convinced European, although, as Hugo Young records, his utility as a negotiator was frequently put in question by his liking for the bottle: 'His behaviour, in any case, was often an embarrassment. He was frequently drunk, as was his habit at home as well.'³¹ But even for the French he was a Brit whose motives could be trusted. For his part, Wilson was shameless and openly played to French prejudice towards the Americans. In 1962, London and Paris had agreed to build the supersonic Concorde. Five years later, Wilson held out the prospect of Britain and France leading a new 'technological community' rooted in the European Community. Addressing the Council of Europe in Strasbourg in January 1967, he appeared at the podium as a politician who had never doubted that Britain's destiny lay in a partnership with its continental neighbours:

> For if the nineteenth century, the age of nationalism, was
> illuminated by the heroism which created the great nation
> states, the twentieth century, equally, will go down in history
> as the age in which men had the vision to create, out of those
> nation states, out of the destruction of two world wars arising
> from the conflicts of European nationalism, a new unity based
> on cool heads and warm hearts.

This was cynicism in a heroic cause, but in the end it counted for nought. By May 1967, Wilson had announced to the House of Commons Britain's second application to join the EEC. On 27 November, as the government emerged from the trauma of devaluation, de Gaulle gave his second *non*. Britain, he said, was still not ready to choose Europe over the United States. And Europe

– and this was the most painful barb – was not prepared to accept a nation so burdened with external debt and unable to stabilise its currency.

The general had a point. Washington was a source of power and prestige and, post-Suez, the 'special relationship' underwrote Britain's pretensions to remain a global player, if not a great power. The Nassau nuclear deal attested to the unique nature of the security relationship. As the gatekeeper to the International Monetary Fund, Washington was also the lender of first resort when Britain ran into financial trouble. Europe, or at least Europe in the shape of the emerging Common Market, presented an unwelcome challenge: a warning that the superiority over its neighbours assumed by Churchill had been lost. By the mid-1960s, however, the strategy had, as Dean Acheson put it, been played out. Standing aloof had not worked. Nor had the effort to undermine 'the Six' through the creation of the European Free Trade Association. Europe had become a reproach to Britain's relative economic decline. As Germany and France powered ahead, Britain fell behind. And now it was stranded on the sidelines.

6

Missed Chances

From the beginning, British politicians treated European unity as an issue best wished away. As what the French called 'the construction' of Europe gathered pace, the abiding hope on the English side of the Channel was that the enterprise would founder. Britain could then avoid an agonising choice: abandon its great-power pretensions and join the club, or risk being locked out. Here was the recurring collision between insecurity and superiority that over the decades shaped the European discussion in London. Churchill could never descend from the pedestal on which he had stood during the war – above all at those three-power summits where, with Roosevelt and Stalin, Britain's prime minister redrew the maps. His response to Europe's founding fathers was one of lofty condescension: let the others build a 'United States of Europe'. Eden, unable to resist the magnetic pull of empire, left empty the British seat at Messina. Post-Suez, Macmillan came to see the imperative of British engagement, but not so clearly that he would risk jeopardising a place at the right hand of the US president. For the opportunistic Wilson, what mattered more than anything was the preservation of Labour Party unity.

The arrival of Edward Heath in 10 Downing Street in June 1970 changed everything. In its way it was a revolutionary moment. It broke – smashed – the mould of hesitation and prevarication. For the first and, as it would turn out, the only time since 1945, Britain had a prime minister whose organising goal was to shift the nation's gaze from America to Europe. Turning ambition into reality required extraordinary political commitment. Heath took office at the beginning of one of the most turbulent periods in post-war history. His government faced an unprecedented challenge to its domestic authority from increasingly militant trade unions. In Northern Ireland, what began as a protest to secure civil rights for the province's Catholic community was turning into a bloody war waged by the Provisional Irish Republican Army against the British state. Bombings and shootings claimed hundreds of lives, and the violence spilled over to the British mainland. Events abroad – America's decision to ditch the post-war international currency system based on gold and the quadrupling of oil prices in the wake of the first Arab–Israeli war – derailed attempts to stabilise the economy. The Empire was gone, but Ian Smith's white supremacist government in Rhodesia proved a constant sore in relations with the Commonwealth. Post-colonial upheavals in Malta and Cyprus joined the lengthy list of problems that were demanding prime ministerial attention.

Such tumult saw Heath make several U-turns. His startling swerve from the free-market economic policies with which he had arrived in office towards the embrace of unabashed interventionism prompted many in his own party to mark him out as an unprincipled pragmatist. Yet on Europe the prime minister was immoveable. Britain's place, he understood, was as a European power. He had no fears about loosening the bonds with Washington so carefully tended by his predecessors. In his own words, there was nothing to be gained from 'sitting on the shoulders of American presidents'.[1] Tradition had it that new prime ministers dashed off to Washington to kiss the ring of the American president. Heath made no such request of Richard Nixon's White House. Instead Nixon travelled to Britain. The two men's first encounter – some four months after the prime minister's election victory – saw Heath receive the president at his country residence, Chequers. The agenda was deliberately short, the conclusions unremarkable. Two months later, the two sat down again for more substantial talks in Washington. Again, the proceedings were polite but without warmth. Heath was not innately hostile to the United States. Rather, he saw no reason or purpose in subservience. The United States would have to adjust to the fact that Britain intended to take a leading role in Europe.

Class set Heath aside from past Tory leaders. His predecessors in the role had been drawn from the aristocracy or, at the very least, the landed gentry. Heath was a grammar school boy, the son of a carpenter. Brought up on the Kent coast, in sight of France on a clear day, personal experience, temperament and conviction all propelled him in the direction of Europe. Twenty years earlier, as a new MP at Westminster, he had voted for British participation in the Schuman Plan. In 1962, he served as Macmillan's chief negotiator in the first abortive attempt to join the European Community. There was no truer believer. His response to de Gaulle's veto was unequivocal: Britain would keep pushing at the door until eventually it was opened: 'We are part of Europe by geography, tradition, history, culture and civilisation.'[2] Heath possessed an understanding, relatively rare at Westminster, of the important role that Franco–German reconciliation had played in the drive to blur national frontiers. The British debate about the Common Market centred largely on the economic pros and cons, the pooling of sovereignty or the risks of exclusion. Heath grasped the emotional underpinnings of the enterprise. As a student at Oxford during the 1930s, he had travelled widely in Germany and, in 1937, had attended one of Hitler's Nuremberg Rallies. The experience confirmed a fierce opposition to Neville Chamberlain's policy of appeasement of the Nazis. A trip to Barcelona during the Spanish Civil War saw him witness at first hand the effects of Franco's bombing of civilian targets. Military service as an artillery officer during the march towards Berlin after the Normandy landings left its own imprint. Heath shared the passion for a peaceful continent. 'I saw in German cities practically everything was destroyed,' he told the BBC television journalist Michael Cockerell, 'and I was convinced then that what my generation had to do was to create a unity in Europe which would mean that this would never happen again.'³ Nor was he embarrassed by the language of the European federalists, underscoring his own commitment to 'true European unity' in a letter to Belgian prime minister Paul-Henri Spaak after de Gaulle's veto. As his biographer John Campbell records, there was nothing mushy or sentimental about this. European engagement belonged to hard-headed geopolitics rather than faith in abstract notions of federalism.⁴ Wilson had looked for international prestige in the reflected glow of the US president. Heath thought Britain could exercise influence on the global stage only if it had established itself as one of Europe's leading powers.

His credentials in other European capitals – underscored by his role as Macmillan's negotiator and the close contacts he had maintained since 1965 as leader of the opposition – prised open the door to Britain's third application for membership. As significant was de Gaulle's departure from the Elysée Palace in April 1969, after his failure to win a national referendum on reform of the French constitution. His successor Georges Pompidou had his own doubts about Britain's intentions towards Europe. He made it plain that there was no prospect of admitting *les Anglais* until the Community had fully set the terms – to French advantage, of course – of its financing and disbursements to farmers through the Common Agricultural Policy. But his scepticism lacked the visceral animus of his predecessor. Unlike the general, he did not have old scores to settle or humiliations to avenge. He was conscious that West Germany and the other founding members of 'the Six' had grown impatient. Britain was not alone in seeking admission; Denmark, Norway and Ireland had also lodged applications. West Germany's Willy Brandt was successfully lobbied by Heath for support in persuading the French to relent. At every turn, however, driving the process forward was Heath's personal conviction.

The moment of decision came at a Paris summit with Pompidou in May 1971. The two leaders met at the Elysée Palace. Aware as anyone of Macmillan's failed efforts to persuade de Gaulle, Heath put immense effort into preparing for the encounter. Every argument was explored and the answers rehearsed. His officials pronounced him the master of every detail of the negotiations under way in Brussels. Talks between the two men lasted twelve hours, spread over two days. On the British side nothing was left to chance. Pompidou was feted lavishly at the grand residence of the British ambassador, just a stone's throw from the Elysée. What counted in the conclusion was not so much policy substance as the forging of mutual trust. Paris well understood that Britain's approach to the Community had been instrumental. Membership was viewed as a useful adjunct to British power, and a commitment, presumably, that could be discarded should circumstances change. Pompidou was looking for deeper commitment. 'The crux of the matter', he told a BBC correspondent in advance of the summit, 'is that there is a European conception or idea, and the question to be ascertained is whether the United Kingdom's conception is indeed European. That will be the aim of my meeting with Mr Heath.' Heath gave him the answer he was seeking. Marking out his independence from the general, Pompidou chose the Elysée Palace's elegant Salle des Fêtes for a joint press conference to announce that Britain's application now had France's blessing. It escaped no one's attention that this was the room in which de Gaulle had handed down his first veto in 1963.

For all that, the detailed negotiations in Brussels that followed Pompidou's *oui* offered a salutary lesson that future British governments would habitually forget and be obliged to relearn many times over. The Community is a law-based institution. Its authority and legitimacy are rooted in its rules rather than in its own demos. This body of law – the *'acquis communautaire'* in the language of Brussels – is the product of the myriad compromises and trade-offs made by member states when they pool sovereignty to advance shared interests. As Con O'Neill, the leader of Heath's official negotiating team, would observe: 'Almost every conceivable Community policy or rule or enactment is the result of a conflict of interest between members, and has embedded in it features representing a compromise between the interests.'[5] The implication was clear: Britain would have to accept the rules as others had made them. Any attempt to rewrite the *acquis* to accommodate a new member of the club would unravel these historical compromises, leading founding members to make new demands of their own. The rules, therefore, had to be considered inviolate. Accepting them was the price Britain would have to pay for coming late to the club.

O'Neill, who later wrote the Foreign Office's official history of the negotiations, understood. He was careful when pitching British demands to ensure in advance that they did not cross this red line. There could be compromises at the margin – measures to soften the blow to Commonwealth nations of new barriers to imports of dairy products and sugar, transition periods to soften the shock of change – but the essential architecture would remain as originally designed by the founding members. Days and nights were spent negotiating the terms under which Britain would continue to buy New Zealand lamb and Caribbean cane sugar. The country's contribution to the Community budget absorbed weeks and months. But, in the end, Britain was always going to be disadvantaged by its absence at Messina. It would thus make hefty net contributions to the Brussels budget for the benefit of French farmers and would be forced to open up its rich coastal waters to the fishing fleets of its continental neighbours. Here were the seeds of future conflict, put to one side in the cause of the bigger prize of opening the door. Con O'Neill, the chief negotiator, acknowledged as much: 'What mattered was to get into the Community and thereby restore our position at the centre of European affairs, which since 1958 we had lost.'[6]

Heath was certain the strategic gains would outweigh the initial costs. 'For twenty-five years', he declared when the deal was finalised in July 1971, 'we've been looking for something to get us going again. Now here it is . . . we have the chance of new greatness.' Public opinion had waxed and waned since Britain's first application to join the Community, and at the start of the 1970s it was generally sceptical. On the prime minister's side, however, there was a mood for change – a sense of the need for a fresh start for the nation. The Queen's consort Prince Philip, speaking to the country's business leaders on the same day, framed the challenge with inimitable bluntness: Britain had to start paying its way in the world. 'We are, in fact, rapidly reaching the position of a man living beyond his means. In simple terms, as a nation we are becoming poorer.'

The parliamentary debate in October 1971 on the principle of membership ran for six full days. At its close, the House of Commons voted by 356 to 244 to back membership – a resounding majority that seemed to fulfil Heath's pledge to secure the nation's wholehearted consent before pressing ahead. Some 196

MPs spoke in the debate. The corresponding vote in the House of Lords was 451 to 58. After two decades of dithering on the sidelines of European integration, it seemed to many as though the issue was settled permanently. Harold Wilson ensured it was otherwise. His U-turn in favour of membership during his premiership was followed by a second reversal after he had lost the 1970 general election. There was nothing of any considered reassessment of Britain's interests or regard for changing international circumstances in this. Since de Gaulle's second veto, the balance in Wilson's party had turned against membership. The leader followed, waving the smallest of fig leaves. Labour was not against joining in principle, Wilson declared. Rather, it rejected as unsatisfactory the terms negotiated by Heath. With a majority of only thirty and facing a revolt by perhaps three dozen or more anti-marketeers on the Tory backbenches, the prime minister won House of Commons approval only with the votes of rebel Labour MPs.

Here was a harbinger, later apparent in the referendums on membership in 1975 and 2016, of the unique challenge that the European question would henceforth pose to the equilibrium of Britain's national politics. The first-past-the-post electoral system all but ensured that the big votes at Westminster were decided on a straightforward left–right axis. When it came to Europe, the differences defied these traditional party lines. Europe was not a left–right argument. Instead the cleavages appeared within the parties themselves. Conservatives counted among their ranks a broad swathe of one-nation pragmatists for whom European engagement was above all about protecting Britain's position in a world where power was shifting elsewhere and, alongside them, a smaller but vocal group of English nationalists who could not accept the transfer, as they saw it, of national sovereignty to supranational institutions in Brussels. On the other side of the Commons, Labour, in the form of such centrist figures as Roy Jenkins, Shirley Williams and William Rodgers, embraced a social democratic tradition that saw Britain as part of the European mainstream, alongside a socialist left that saw the European Community as a threat to its ambitions for public ownership and state direction of the economy.

Enoch Powell was by the early 1970s the loudest and, by virtue of his chilling 'Rivers of Blood' speech against Commonwealth immigration, the best-known champion of English exceptionalism. Having left the Conservative Party, he signed up with the Ulster Unionists. There were others, however – Tory MPs beyond the public limelight – whose concern about sovereignty pre-dated Powell's embrace of xenophobic populism. Derek Walker-Smith, MP for East Hertfordshire and later Lord Broxbourne, had led the sovereignty charge against Harold Macmillan's application. What concerned such critics was the primacy of European Community laws over national ones in areas where governments had decided to transfer competences to Brussels. These were the arguments that would prefigure the 'Take Back Control' campaign of the Brexiters in 2016. Walker-Smith offered a flavour of the onslaughts on establishment 'elites' that would loom large forty-five years later. Thus, during the 1971 debate, he told the Commons that MPs had been asked

> to say that entry will involve no sacrifice of essential sovereignty. Of course, it depends on what is meant by 'essential' – not essential, perhaps, if only the Executive matters, if Members of Parliament are to be seen and not heard, to acquiesce and not decide; not essential, perhaps, if one believes in elitism, to use the new fashionable expression.

I am indebted to the *Financial Times* of 9 July, in a discussion of this very subject, the Common Market, for this illuminating definition: 'Elitism means decisions being taken by an extremely small section of people at the top of the pyramid.'

This new elitism, he continued, was 'old autocracy writ French'.[7] Substitute 'German' for 'French' and Walker-Smith might have been speaking alongside Boris Johnson and Michael Gove in the 2016 referendum campaign. The Commons exchanges gave the lie to subsequent claims from the Eurosceptics that the political significance of membership was never properly explored – that the nation was tricked into believing that in joining the Community, Britain was signing up to nothing more than a trading bloc. More accurately, debates about sovereignty took their place in a hierarchy of priorities, at the top of which was how to revive Britain's economic performance and, with it, its capacity to secure its national interests.

As often as not, the anti-European case was sepia-tinted. Some imagined that the Commonwealth might yet serve as a surrogate for empire, providing Britain with a network of influence and outposts across the globe. The foreign policies these nations had asserted since independence – usually at odds with British views – went unnoticed. Another group, Atlanticists, made the case for a close relationship with Washington, unbalanced as it might be, above entanglement with Europe. Cheerleaders for the 'Anglosphere', an imagined construct that saw Britain and the US joining with the old white dominions of the Commonwealth – Australia, New Zealand and Canada – called for a global alliance of the English-speaking peoples. The post-war 'Five Eyes' accord, under which the five nations had agreed to share the work of their intelligence services, was held up as a model.

Labour had its own sovereigntists. James Callaghan, an instinctive Atlanticist, worried aloud that the primacy of French in the day-to-day business of the European Community would threaten the language of 'Chaucer, Shakespeare and Milton'. Callaghan later made his peace with Europe, coming to see it as a necessary insurance policy against overdependence on Washington. Tony Benn, the self-styled champion of the left, travelled in the opposite direction. As Anthony Wedgwood Benn, during the early 1960s he had pressed the case for closer engagement with the continent, warning that the alternative was to be left stranded by the economic and technological progress of Britain's neighbours. A decade later, as plain Tony Benn, he raised the standard of sovereignty.

What this meant, then and during the decades to follow, was that the traditional, party-based rules of Westminster politics did not apply to the question of Europe. A governing majority of even a handful of seats would generally guarantee the prime minister of the day the support of the House of Commons. But in the absence of a majority sufficiently large to shake off significant recalcitrant minorities, the same prime minister could never be quite sure of the outcome when the vote was about Europe. In 1971, Heath secured a healthy majority of 112 for Britain's entry only because he was persuaded by his party's whips to declare a 'free' vote. This is turn allowed Roy Jenkins, the deputy Labour leader, to head a rebellion against Wilson. Some sixty-nine Labour MPs backed membership and another twenty abstained, more than cancelling out the thirty-nine Tories who defied the prime minister. The subsequent passage of the necessary legislation pointed up another paradox. Counted across all the parties, the pro-European side of the argument could claim a 'natural' majority of all MPs. There was no guarantee, however, that this majority could be mobilised for each and every vote. After backing the principle of entry in October 1971, many fewer Labour MPs were prepared consistently to defy their own leadership on the details of the legislation, often leaving Heath with the thinnest of majorities. Yet a third complication – and this was to create immense problems after 2016 – lay in the fact that a parliament firmly on the pro-European side of the argument might not always represent the mood of the country. The 1975 referendum saw parliament and voters in accord. In 2016, however, the small majority in the country who voted for Brexit did so in defiance not only of David Cameron's government but of the cross-party majority of pro-European MPs at Westminster – a dangerous collision between parliamentary and plebiscitary democracy.

By its own lights, Washington should have been fully behind Heath's push into Europe. From the beginning, American policy had been to encourage European integration and to seek to nudge Britain into the process. The strategic calculation was straightforward: a united Europe would provide a more reliable partner in the confrontation with the Soviet Union. It would also constrain the resurgence of German nationalism, an abiding fear of American policymakers. This remained the formal position of the Nixon administration, but the United States had grown accustomed to a different relationship with Westminster. British prime ministers were eager to please, and if the Brits' insistence on a 'special relationship' was self-regarding, it provided the White House with useful leverage. So Washington took umbrage at Heath's reordering of Britain's foreign policy priorities. Secretary of state Henry Kissinger, charged by Nixon with steering the transatlantic relationship, later complained that Heath had 'dealt with us with an unsentimentality totally at variance with the "special relationship"'.[8]

In part, this reflected calculated positioning on Heath's part. De Gaulle's charge that Britain was Washington's Trojan horse in the European Community had not been completely dispelled. When de Gaulle held up British subservience as sufficient cause to bar its path into the Community, Heath did not entirely disagree with him. He also understood that as long as such suspicions prevailed, it would be harder to claim a leading role in what was now a Community of nine – Denmark and Ireland had joined alongside Britain. So when Nixon offered the prime minister a 'hotline' telephone link to the Oval Office, Heath accepted, but then made little use of it. Macmillan or Wilson would have shouted from the rooftops about such an intimate connection as proof of their international standing. Heath told Kissinger that he did not expect treatment above that offered to the leaders of France and Germany.

Nixon, bogged down in Vietnam and engulfed from 1973 in the Watergate scandal, showed little personal interest in Britain. Raised on the West Coast, the president felt no great affinity for the transatlantic alliance. He left the diplomacy to Kissinger. The secretary of state's self-proclaimed affection for Europe, however, did not always extend to keeping his allies informed. Washington's unilateral decision in 1971 to collapse the Bretton Woods currency system threatened to shred the entire fabric of the post-war economic order. It was made without reference to European leaders. The American opening to China, with its strategic implications for the West's relationship with the Soviet Union, was also kept secret. Heath shared the resentment of other European governments. When Kissinger suggested that 1973 be designated the 'Year of Europe',[9] Heath's response was studiously cool. Europeans would not dream of patronising Washington by declaring a 'Year of the United States', he told Kissinger. Pompidou's riposte was the more sardonic: for Europeans, the French president remarked, every year was the 'Year of Europe'. Heath's barb was the one that hit home.

So too did the prime minister's decision to coordinate Britain's foreign policy positions with its European partners before settling on any agreement with Washington. The Community's smaller nations, Heath wrote to the president in July 1973, resented the privileged access to US thinking afforded to Britain, West Germany and France; in future, 'the Nine' would coordinate their reactions to US policy proposals: 'The French have been exploiting our failure to keep our partners informed. The Nine [foreign] ministers have now decided they will exchange the information which they obtain in the framework of bilateral conversations with the United States and try to harmonise their reactions.'[10] For Kissinger, this did not sound like the 'special relationship' of old.

In the summer of 1973, Kissinger was sufficiently upset to order diplomatic retaliation, so as to remind Heath where the balance of power lay in the relationship. Restrictions were imposed on the highly sensitive intelligence exchanges between London and Washington that took place under the wartime BRUSA Agreement. James Schlesinger, the defence secretary, sent a similar message about nuclear cooperation when he stalled talks on Britain's programme to upgrade the Polaris nuclear system. Britain's nuclear deterrence doctrine required the possession of weapons that could threaten the destruction of Moscow. That capability was threatened by new Soviet anti-ballistic missile defences, but Heath's programme to upgrade Polaris, code-named 'Chevaline', depended on American assistance. In September 1973, Heath wrote to Nixon offering assurances that Europe was not seeking to 'gang up' on Washington. There was no contradiction, he said, between Britain's determination to align its thinking more closely with Europe and its close alliance with the United States. But the president should understand that 'Europe is struggling to achieve a new identity and develop a distinctive viewpoint of its own'.[11]

The US administration's tactics unsettled Whitehall officialdom, but if Kissinger thought they would bring Heath back into line, he was disappointed. When the Arab–Israeli war broke out in October 1973, Heath, like almost all his European counterparts, was inclined to support the Arabs, while Nixon gave full-throated backing to the Israelis. The prime concern of most governments was to protect oil supplies. What shocked the White House was Britain's agreement that American aircraft should be denied the use of European airspace to resupply the Israeli forces. Kissinger noted that this was 'a new experience for American leaders: a British prime minister who based his policies toward the United States not on sentimental attachments but on a cool calculation of interest'.[12] Heath broke other taboos. Alongside the 'Chevaline' programme, he raised the possibility of cooperation with France in the development of a new generation of nuclear weapons. He enthusiastically backed the revival of proposals for a new European defence community, a project seen by Washington as undermining NATO's role in the continent's defence, which caused Kissinger to grumble that he was dealing with a 'benign version of de Gaulle'. At home also, Heath was determined to set his own course on Europe, ignoring those in his own party who wanted the government to tread carefully. Even before Britain had signed the Treaty of Rome, the prime minister defied the Tory sovereigntists by agreeing to a plan that committed the Community to the creation of a monetary union and single European currency within the following decade. In November 1973, an increasingly frustrated Kissinger warned Lord Cromer, Heath's ambassador

179

in Washington, that the 'special relationship' was 'collapsing'. In the event, relations were patched up. The two leaders faced more pressing troubles at home: Nixon with Watergate, and Heath with his looming battle with the mineworkers. Heath would be the first to fall.

The 1960s had been a story of opportunities lost – a failure to capitalise on the nation's industrial and technological strengths and align its global aspirations with the economic realities. London had put itself at the heart of the 'Swinging Sixties'. British rock bands conquered America. The nation took an international lead in art and design. But the industries that drove the economy – steel, shipbuilding, cars and aerospace – stalled. Productivity stagnated and employers and trade unions seemed to be in permanent conflict. Wilson had tried and failed to overhaul industrial relations before crashing to defeat in the 1970 election. Heath's inheritance was the promise of national decline. Briefly, it looked as if EEC membership might break the cycle. David Hannay was then a young diplomat: 'It looked like a glad, confident morning. For the first nine months, everything went well. Then came the Yom Kippur War, the quadrupling of the oil price and the slow collapse of the Heath government.'[13] The next few years saw Britain plunged, literally, into darkness as the government's battles with the unions coincided with soaring oil prices after the 1973 Arab–Israeli war. In Northern Ireland, the civil rights protests of the minority Catholic community against the discrimination operated by the Protestant, unionist majority mutated into something akin to a civil war on the streets of Belfast and Derry. The IRA's bombing campaign exported the violence to the British mainland. In the face of a national miners' strike, the government ordered industry to operate a three-day working week in order to conserve stocks of coal. A fifty miles per hour speed limit was imposed on motorways to reduce petrol consumption. Television programmes were cut short at 10.30 p.m. each evening. Voters were urged to clean their teeth in the dark to save precious energy supplies. On the fringes of the far right, renegade former military and intelligence officers hatched far-fetched plans to seize control of the state in the event of a breakdown of civil authority.

In February 1974, Heath called a snap election. Wilson's return to Downing Street, first at the head of a minority government and then, after another election in October, with a small majority, did little to dispel the gloom. Heath had framed the election around the question of who governed Britain. Though they had rejected Heath, the voters showed no great enthusiasm for Wilson. The historian Andy Beckett caught something of the contemporary mood:

> On the evening of 4 March 1974, Harold Wilson returned to Downing Street as prime minister. As he emerged from his official car, there were cheers and boos from the crowd waiting in the cold . . . Wilson walked slowly – almost trudged – the few yards to the front door of Number 10, with his shoulders slack and his back to the crowd. On the doorstep he turned and waved, a little woodenly, without any apparent joy. He gave the briefest flicker of a smile.[14]

Across Europe, the question only half answered by the British voters was reframed: does anyone run Britain?

Wilson had put Europe at the heart of his campaign. In 1966, he had promoted membership of the European Community as an overdue rendezvous with a long history of collaboration with Britain's continental neighbours. The withdrawal from East of Suez after the 1967 devaluation had confirmed Britain's transition from a global to a European power. Defeat in 1970, however, changed the Labour leader's political calculus. In opposition, his organising goal was to keep his party together in the face of rising Euroscepticism among left-wing MPs. The antis in the Conservative Party were a sizeable minority, but very much a minority. Among Labour MPs there were now roughly equal numbers on either side of the European line and, among party activists, a big majority for leaving the Community.

Wilson's election pledge to hold a referendum on membership was an effort to bridge this divide. The idea had first been pushed by Benn and others on the left, but Jenkins and other pro-Europeans vigorously opposed it. Wilson initially expressed severe doubts, while James Callaghan prophetically predicted that a referendum would be 'a rubber life-raft into which the whole party may one day have to climb'.[15] Wilson set the vote for the spring of 1975, promising to renegotiate the terms of membership before putting the issue to the people. He soon discovered, as Heath had before him, that the other member states would not unpick the careful political compromises that constituted the rules of the club for Britain's benefit. There could be some shading here and there and perhaps some small technical adjustments, but nothing that changed fundamentally the basis of Britain's membership. This reality was spelled out when talks opened at the end of 1974. As Michael Palliser, the British ambassador in Brussels, told Hugo Young: 'It soon became clear to me that the whole object of the exercise was to keep Britain in, and get something that could be presented to the British as politically adequate. What was actually obtained mattered much less than the impression that, whatever it was, it was quite enough.'[16] If staying in was one of Wilson's objectives, the other was to hold the government and party together through the referendum campaign. Wilson kept his own thoughts closely guarded. He must have understood, however, that quitting the Community after two years would be a political as well as economic calamity. Britain's troubles had already seen relative turn into absolute decline. How would the country fare if thrown back on its own devices?

The 'No' campaign, run by an alliance of Tory sovereigntists and Labour left-wingers, saw Enoch Powell join hands with the future Labour leader Michael Foot. Membership of the Community, the campaign declared, 'sets out by stages to merge Britain with France, Germany and other countries into a single nation . . . those who want Britain in the Common Market are defeatists; they see no independent future for our country'.[17] The campaign featured such left-wing figures as Peter Shore and Barbara Castle alongside Foot and Benn, and, on the right, the Ulster Unionist Ian Paisley, the Tory maverick Alan Clark and Powell. A decade or so later, a new generation of Tory Eurosceptics would argue that the electorate had been told during the campaign that they were being asked to ratify membership of the Common Market rather than a broader political enterprise. By the late 1980s, these zealots had gathered around the banner raised by Margaret Thatcher in her famous Bruges speech. Yet they ignored her contribution to the 1975 campaign. Newly elected as leader of the opposition in place of Heath, she laid out a trenchantly pro-European position as one of the leaders of the 'Yes' side. More, she emphasised that the purpose of membership went well beyond the assumed economic advantages. The paramount case for being in was the political case for peace and security.

The deal that Wilson secured at a summit in Dublin in March 1975 included nothing in the way of a fundamental shift in the terms of British membership, but it met Palliser's test of giving the impression that the government had done enough. A change in the way Britain's contributions to the Brussels budget were calculated could be presented as a remedy for the unfair system under which it joined. In the event, the new rules made no significant difference. And thanks to adjustments to the regimes for imports of New Zealand lamb and dairy products and Caribbean sugar, the prime minister was able to claim that he had secured something for the Commonwealth and for British consumers. Public opinion was willing to be led. The country was still living through the consequences of the oil price shock. Inflation had jumped to above 20 per cent and unemployment was rising. The IRA campaign in Northern Ireland added to the national sense of insecurity.

The cabinet voted by sixteen to seven to back the new settlement. To preserve party unity, Wilson then broke with the convention of collective cabinet responsibility and allowed ministers as well as backbench MPs a free vote on the issue, with the seven from the cabinet joining the 'No' campaign. More than half of Wilson's own MPs counted themselves as anti-marketeers, but the prime minister was assured a majority through the support of an overwhelming number of Conservatives. On the campaign trail, business and the media gave near-unanimous support to the pro-European side. A decade or so later, Rupert Murdoch's *Sun* newspaper led the right-wing media's charge against Brussels, but in its 1975 referendum editorial it stated simply: 'We are all Europeans now.'[18] *The Times*, not yet under Murdoch's ownership, was equally unequivocal: 'Since the national decline of Britain became fully apparent after the war, there has never been a rational alternative to a European base for the redevelopment of Britain.'[19]

The nation was in no mood to take risks. The chaos of the three-day week was fresh in the minds of voters. Though Wilson himself rarely emerged from the shadows, the 'Yes' campaign united the leaderships of all the main parties. Even the Church of England was signed up to the cause, with, by Hugo Young's account, 'every Anglican bishop' backing the 'Yes' side. In Young's description, 'All the acceptable faces of British public life lined up on one side.' Staying in was the safe option, the voters concluded, with the final tally 67 to 33 per cent.[20]

'Goodbye Great Britain' ran the headline in the *Wall Street Journal* in April 1975, just a few weeks before the referendum. In a damning report on the condition of the country, the influential American newspaper urged investors around the world to sell their sterling assets. Many were already doing so. Beset by trade and budget deficits, Britain had already been given the epithet of 'the sick man of Europe'. The break-up of the Bretton Woods system of currency arrangements might in other circumstances have offered Britain an opportunity to step out of the shadow of repeated sterling crises. As Attlee and Wilson had discovered, the post-war system of semi-fixed exchange rates had hardened the link between devaluation and political defeat. Propping up the pound had required repeated bouts of fiscal austerity. After Nixon's decision to abandon Bretton Woods, the Heath government linked sterling to other European currencies in the so-called 'snake' currency mechanism, but the short-lived experiment ended in devaluation. The Treasury then decided to deprive currency speculators of a fixed target by introducing a free-floating exchange rate; old-fashioned sterling crises could be confined to history. If that was the economic theory, the financial storm that broke over the government in the late summer and autumn of 1976 was as humiliating as anything seen since the war. Britain was broke. The price of financial rescue by the International Monetary Fund would be complete submission.

*

The clouds gathered in early 1976. Harold Wilson, exhausted by trying to hold Labour together in the face of rising economic troubles and union unrest, had finally called time on his premiership. The financial markets were frightened that he would be replaced by the left-winger Michael Foot, but in the event, the moderate James Callaghan secured the succession. Denis Healey, another of the party's big political beasts, was in charge at the Treasury. For a time, the markets stabilised. But the structural weaknesses of the economy could not be wished away. Inflation ran at more than 15 per cent and wage demands were chasing prices higher. Public spending ran far ahead of tax revenues, adding to public borrowing, and the trade deficit was widening. In June, Healey negotiated what the *Daily Express* called 'the biggest overdraft in British history' – a $5.3 billion standby credit from other central banks – to help the Bank of England stabilise the pound. The money was to be repaid by the end of the year.

The crisis broke in September. The chancellor had made it as far as the VIP departure lounge at Heathrow Airport on his way to a meeting of Commonwealth finance ministers in Hong Kong. Accompanied by Gordon Richardson, the governor of the Bank of England, and a clutch of Treasury officials, he planned to travel from there to the annual meeting of the International Monetary Fund in Manila. A telephone call to his private office at the Treasury before departure put paid to his travel plans. Healey had intended to use the Manila meeting to seek a $3.9 billion loan from the Fund in order to prop up the currency. Events had outpaced him. The sterling exchange rate against the dollar was falling towards $1.60. He returned to the Treasury.

The succeeding months were as traumatic as any seen in Whitehall since the Second World War. The Fund, under pressure from other shareholders, including the United States, had tired of providing repeated bailouts. It demanded a fundamental reshaping of the nation's public finances as the price of the support the government needed to repay the central banks' loan. What followed for the government were two months of acrimonious negotiation: firstly, with the Fund, about the terms of a new loan; secondly, within the cabinet, where Callaghan faced intense pressure from ministers on the left to abandon talks and opt instead for a siege economy, with import and capital controls to cover the trade deficit. Callaghan was caught between the tough line adopted by the Fund's managing director Johannes Witteveen and cabinet colleagues such as Tony Benn and Peter Shore, who demanded the government slam the door on international capitalism. More than once Callaghan sought to soften the conditions for a loan by enlisting support directly from the US president Gerald Ford and the German chancellor Helmut Schmidt. The allies had run out of patience, and Britain had run out of road. Ford and Schmidt stood solidly behind the IMF's prescription of tough spending cuts and tax increases – the 'conditionality' attached to an IMF loan. The US Treasury and the Federal Reserve took an equally tough line. So much, the Atlanticist Callaghan discovered, for the 'special relationship' with Washington. Whitehall was all but paralysed. Peter Ricketts joined the Foreign Office in 1974. At first, 'It felt like we were America's number-one partner, closer to them than any other country.' The IMF crisis, however, was 'a very cold shock, another of those intake-of-breath moments when people realised the weakness of our position in contrast to the Churchillian rhetoric.'[21]

The crisis ended in a submission that was as humiliating as any Britain had known. During early December, the cabinet met almost daily. Callaghan's tactics, Healey would later write, had been to 'allow his colleagues to talk themselves to a standstill'.

One by one, the supposed alternatives to signing up to the Fund's terms were discussed and dismissed. Benn's 'Alternative Economic Strategy' for the state direction of industry, import quotas and restrictions on outflows of capital was judged wholly impractical by the majority of his peers. Witteveen shaved the harshest edges from his original demands, but there was no hiding the abject surrender in the letter of intent Callaghan finally agreed to in return for the loan. Spending cuts of £3 billion over two years touched every corner of the nation's public services. 'Britain's Shame', screamed the headline in the *Sun* on 16 December, when the chancellor unveiled the deal. 'Chicken Chancellor', echoed the *Daily Mail*. The insults came thick and fast when Healey laid out the terms to the House of Commons. Two months earlier, Callaghan had read the last rites over the Keynesian demand management that had been the post-war economic orthodoxy. Governments, he told an angry Labour Party conference, had been living on borrowed time, ideas and money: 'We used to think that you could spend your way out of a recession and increase employment by cutting taxes and boosting government spending. I tell you, in all candour, that that option no longer exists.'[22] The prime minister's realism did not cushion the blow. Britain had in effect transferred sovereignty over the management of its economy to the international bureaucrats who inhabited the IMF's offices in Washington. Never before had one of the advanced industrial nations faced such conditions. The twelve-page letter sent to the Fund set the parameters for the decisions of British ministers in every significant area of economic policy. Power and the pound, ministers had again discovered, were indivisible.

Britain's troubles scarcely went unnoticed in capitals around the world. The American diplomat Raymond Seitz, who served at the US embassy in London during the 1970s and would later return as ambassador, caught the temper of the times. 'The nation', he later wrote in a memoir, 'sat with its head in its hands bemoaning its fate, once so grand and now so grim. Britain then was a hang-dog nation.'²³ It fell, though, to a British diplomat to write the definitive national report card at the end of the decade.

Sir Nicholas Henderson was a diplomat of the old school. Tall, urbane and possessed of a rumpled elegance, he carried the nat-ural authority of the Foreign Office mandarin. He had started out as a junior official at the Potsdam Conference, and in March 1979 was approaching retirement age. Writing his valedictory dispatch after four years as ambassador to France, he imagined this would be his last word on the country he had represented abroad for more than three decades. He approached the task with a mix of exas-peration and scarcely concealed anger. By tradition, these end-of-posting ambassadorial dispatches blended rhetorical flourish with unvarnished candour. They focused on the strengths, weaknesses and foibles of the host country. Henderson turned the telescope around, offering the outsider's view of the nation he represented. He admitted the observations 'may go beyond the limits of an ambassador's normal responsibilities'. Dated 31 March 1979 and addressed to the secretary of state for foreign affairs, the paper was headed, with ruthless honesty, 'Britain's Decline; its Causes and Consequences'.²⁴

As it turned out, Callaghan had been unlucky in 1976. The economy, benefiting from the tax revenues from North Sea oil, began to recover even as the ink dried on the IMF agreement. But the malaise ran deeper than the balance of payments deficit, and as Callaghan would later write, the tide of history had turned against Labour. Rubbish piled up on the streets as the industrial strife that had broken Heath's government also brought down its successor in a rancorous winter of discontent. Henderson, writing before the

May 1979 general election that would see Callaghan swept from office, pulled no punches. During the past generation, he began, 'our foreign policy has contributed to our economic decline just as the latter has undermined our diplomacy'. Here was the proof, in Henderson's mind, not just of the interplay of domestic economic performance and international influence but of the unwillingness, even in 1979, of the ruling classes fully to own up to the central fact of Britain's post-war place in the world – that it was now a European rather than a global power. Relative decline against the superpowers – the United States and the Soviet Union – had been inevitable. Henderson charted Britain's poor performance against France and Germany with painful precision – absolute decline. Germany and France had intensified their collaboration, while Britain found itself pleading poverty in Brussels in an effort to secure a rebate on its contributions to the European Community. It might have been otherwise: 'We had every Western European government ready to eat out of our hand in the immediate after- math of war. For several years our prestige and influence were paramount and we could have stamped Europe as we wished.' Instead Britain had been trapped by history.

Henderson's dispatch, which ran to sixteen pages, was packed with statistics showing how Britain had fallen behind. Income per head, to take one measure, had fallen below that of France for the first time in three hundred years. 'We are scarcely in the same economic league as the Germans or French.' To make matters worse, 'We talk of ourselves without shame as being one of the less prosperous countries of Europe.' In 1954, France's national output lagged behind that of Britain by 22 per cent; by 1977, France was ahead by 34 per cent. The figures for Germany were more alarming: Britain's output, once 9 per cent higher than Germany's, was now 61 per cent lower. Stirred in with the cold figures was a withering anecdote: 'You only have to move about Western Europe nowadays to realise how poor and unproud the British have become in relation to their neighbours. It shows in the look of our towns, in our airports, in our hospitals and in local amenities; it is painfully apparent in much of our railway system.'

The price of this economic weakness, Henderson continued, was everywhere visible in Britain's diminished standing in the world. Britain had lost its position as the predominant power in the Middle East. It had surrendered the will and authority to shape events in other former outposts of empire. Even its special position with the United States was under challenge. One particularly painful irony was that Paris got more attention in Washington: 'France, in fact, over a period of nearly two decades pursued a blatantly anti-American policy, but its importance to the US is much greater now than at the beginning of that period, because of its economic strength.' Through the ages, Britain's role in Europe, the departing ambassador noted, had been that of the hinge power ensuring balance across the continent; now 'the fact must be faced that for the first time for centuries British policy cannot be based upon the prevention of any single power dominating the continent because, out of weakness, we would be unable to do this'.

The failure went beyond economic management. For the Foreign Office's man in Paris, the associated political sin was the reluctance to seize the initiative in redrawing the geopolitical map of the continent after 1945. The success of the European Community stood in rebuke to the British policy of self-exclusion. 'Because we had survived the war intact,' Henderson said, 'we did not realise fully the motives or strength of the European search for unity. We underestimated the recovery powers of the continental countries and the great boost that could be given to their industrial development by membership of a common market.' Politicians and policymakers, he continued, had underestimated the change in Franco–German relations and overestimated the importance of the Commonwealth to Britain. Even after the belated decision to join the EEC in 1973, 'there is no doubt that our general stance in the Community has made us look an uncooperative member, with inevitable results'.

The dispatch arrived in London during the spring of 1979, when rubbish was still piled high in the streets as a result of the strikes. With an election unavoidable, David Owen, the Labour foreign secretary, recognised the damage such a judgement could inflict on the standing of the government. Circulation of the dispatch was strictly limited, though Henderson's colleagues thought he had always intended the document to reach an audience well beyond the ornate corridors of the FCO in King Charles Street. As it turned out, it was leaked and published in *The Economist* soon after the election, with Margaret Thatcher already in Downing Street. Retirement would have to wait: Henderson found himself summoned to return to the Foreign Office, where Peter Carrington, the new foreign secretary, sent him to Washington. His years there would see Britain's international standing begin to recover, not least during the Falklands War, though his plea for wholehearted engagement in Europe would be lost on the new prime minister. Rather, Thatcher's single-minded quest to 'get our money back' by securing a rebate on Britain's contributions to Brussels would deepen the sense that this was an enterprise defined by 'them and us'.

7

Cold Warrior

Margaret Thatcher arrived in 10 Downing Street with a portrait of Winston Churchill under her arm. Britain's wartime leader would gaze down on her ministers as they assembled in an anteroom before cabinet meetings. Britain had to pick itself up and make itself heard again. There were battles to be fought against the socialists and trade unions at home. There was also a foreign enemy to slay. Churchill had battled the Nazis. Thatcher would fight communism. Unburdened by self-doubt, the Lady defined herself against her enemies; in her mind, domestic and foreign policy were inextricably linked. Charles Powell, Thatcher's closest foreign policy adviser, recounts that 'The point of her foreign policy was to strengthen Britain . . . beating Galtieri in the Falklands, dealing with the trade unions back in Britain, winning the Cold War, getting rid of socialism at home and so on . . . they were all seen through that prism.'[1]

As a minister in Edward Heath's government and as Conservative leader during the subsequent 1975 referendum, Thatcher had shown herself committed to Britain's place in the European Community. But defeating the Soviets would be done with the United States. And in Ronald Reagan, who soon replaced Jimmy Carter in the White House, she would have a close partner on the world stage. The 1970s had seen the flowering of detente with the Soviet Union. The Helsinki Accords on security and cooperation in Europe marked an uneasy accommodation with Moscow. The United States and the Soviet Union had begun to build a framework of treaties to contain the nuclear arms race, and the threat of mutually assured destruction had receded. When Thatcher looked back, she saw a decade of retreat. To her mind, after Vietnam the US had dropped its guard against the communist menace, even as Moscow's surrogates were advancing into Central America and southern Africa. An Atlanticist by instinct, Thatcher put two items at the top of her foreign policy agenda: modernising the ageing Polaris nuclear deterrent and bolstering NATO's resolve to deploy new medium-range nuclear missiles in Europe.

Churchill and Macmillan had devoted much of their diplomacy to positioning Britain as the mediator between the two superpowers. The two men were forever proposing great-power summits to defuse nuclear tensions. This was partly about sustaining Britain's place at the top table, but it also reflected a genuine fear of nuclear conflict. During the Berlin crisis of the late 1950s and early '60s, Macmillan had acted as a check on American impatience. Later, he took much credit for the signing of the Partial Test Ban Treaty in 1963. Thatcher saw herself in an entirely different role. In Powell's description, 'She had no ambition for Britain to play any sort of independent role between the United States and the Soviet Union.' Rather, Britain would enhance its influence by being the faithful friend: 'We must play the role of America's ally and that will give us considerably enhanced national power.'[2]

An unabashed cold warrior, she intended to stiffen what she saw as a Europe drifting towards appeasement and an America that had allowed the Soviet Union to close the nuclear arms gap. The hostility towards communism was deep-rooted. Thatcher would later write that as a Conservative Party student activist at Oxford towards the end of the war, she had been unsettled by Churchill's decision to put his name to the Yalta pact with Franklin Roosevelt and Joseph Stalin, which divided Europe into Western and Soviet spheres of influence.[3] She had been greatly relieved when, in 1946, Churchill delivered his famous 'Iron Curtain' speech. To Thatcher's mind, he had recognised the special responsibility of the United States and Britain to defend freedom and democracy. She would later widen this alliance to include the Commonwealth nations of Canada, Australia and New Zealand, cherishing a unique role in the world for 'the English-speaking peoples'. Europe was a second-order priority. To her mind, anti-communism and pro-Americanism were welded together as one.

'Russia', Thatcher had declared three years earlier, in a speech setting out her policy as leader of the opposition, 'is ruled by a dictatorship of patient, far-sighted men who are rapidly making their country the foremost naval and military power in the world.'[4] Bent on 'world dominance', the Soviet Union was 'rapidly acquiring the means to become the most powerful imperial nation the world has seen'. For its part, the West had gone soft: 'They put guns before butter, while we put just about everything before guns.' The speech caused something of a stir, prompting the Soviet ambassador in London to lodge a formal protest and an editor at *Red Star*, the country's military newspaper, to call Thatcher the 'Iron Lady' of British politics. It was a sobriquet she accepted with enthusiasm.

The prime minister's convictions might have received no more than a polite hearing in Washington. Jimmy Carter was putting his name to the SALT II nuclear arms limitation treaty recently negotiated with Moscow, and discussion of the planned NATO deployment of medium-range nuclear missiles was provoking a wave of protests across Europe. Thatcher's relationship with Carter was cordial but hardly close. Her occasional commentary on the president's approach to Moscow carried as much an air of exhortation as of support. 'I share your concern about Cuban and

Soviet intentions in the Caribbean,' she remarked in a letter to Carter in October 1979, before adding, 'This danger exists more widely in the developing world. It is essential that the Soviet Union should recognise your resolve in this matter.'[5] In this respect, she had been 'encouraged' by Carter's recent statements.

Events, however, were on Thatcher's side. The Soviet regime's rounding up of dissident intellectuals during the summer of 1979 – in obvious violation of the Helsinki Accords – and its invasion of Afghanistan that December jolted the confidence of the standard-bearers for detente. By the end of 1979, Thatcher had secured her first goal, when NATO gave the go-ahead for the deployment in Europe of cruise and Pershing II medium- and short-range nuclear missiles as a counter to Moscow's new generation of SS-20 missiles. The decision was far from popular. West Germany's Social Democrat chancellor Helmut Schmidt had been among the first to call for the deployment but faced a powerful backlash from voters, while the Dutch and Belgian governments came up against similar protests. In Britain, the arrival of the American missiles provoked the creation of the Greenham Common peace camp. Throughout the 1980s, women protesters periodically blockaded the RAF station in Berkshire where the missiles were based. The Greenham peace camp mirrored demonstrations across the continent against the acceleration of the nuclear arms race. Thatcher was unmoved. To her mind, the new missiles simply reinstated the balance of nuclear forces and reaffirmed America's commitment to the defence of Europe.

The prime minister also secured the modernisation of Britain's nuclear deterrent. In 1980, she agreed with Carter's administration that the Polaris force should be replaced with the new Trident I missile system. Britain would continue to produce its own warheads and build the submarines that would carry the American missiles. In 1981, however, the incoming Reagan administration decided to press ahead with the development of the more advanced Trident II. A year later, amid some doubt in the cabinet, Thatcher pressed the president to supply Britain with the new system. The financial terms, she would later say, were reasonable, but what irked her was the American insistence that the deal include a British commitment to increase its conventional defence forces. Washington, unconvinced that Britain's nuclear capability made a serious contribution to the defence of the West, was determined that Trident should not be used as an excuse for cuts in its contributions to NATO. Reagan also pressed another issue: the US wanted to further expand the military base it had established at Diego Garcia in the Indian Ocean – a base that had become pivotal to US operations in the Middle East, and from which Carter had launched the abortive attempt to rescue the American hostages in Iran. Finally, Britain was obliged, in addition to the bill for Trident, to bear the cost of manning a new air defence system for American bases in the United Kingdom.

Thatcher's logic through all this was straightforward. Beyond national prestige – how could Britain continue to play a leading international role if it was giving up its nuclear weapons? – Trident was also a guarantee. In the event of an escalating East–West confrontation, Soviet nuclear planners might conclude that Washington would be reluctant to launch a strategic nuclear strike – and thus risk a global conflagration – in defence of Britain. As Thatcher wrote in her memoir, 'They [the Soviets] would never doubt that a British Conservative government would do so.' Publicly, she glossed over the US-imposed limits on the use of Britain's arsenal. When John F. Kennedy struck the Polaris deal with Harold Macmillan at Nassau in 1962, he insisted that the missiles be assigned to NATO. Only if 'supreme national interests' were at stake could Britain act alone. Thatcher wanted the condition removed – or at least diluted – in order to strengthen Britain's claim that the deterrent was truly 'independent'. Washington demurred.

Ronald Reagan was as sympathetic a president as Thatcher could have hoped for. She had met him twice during her time as leader of the opposition and decided then that he was an ideological soulmate. He seemed charming and unaffected, and shared her small-state, low-tax approach to the market economy and her implacable hostility to communism. The admiration was mutual. 'I couldn't be happier than I am over England's new prime minister,' Reagan, at the time a candidate for the Republican presidential nomination, remarked in an American radio broadcast after her election victory.[6] Like the prime minister, he was a nostalgist. 'If anyone can remind England of the greatness she knew during those dangerous days in World War II when, alone and unafraid, her people fought the Battle of Britain, it will be the prime minister the English press has already nicknamed "Maggie".'

Forsaking modesty, Thatcher's memoir says of Reagan's victory in November 1980 that it was 'as much of a watershed in American affairs as my own election victory in May 1979 was in those of the United Kingdom'.[7] While others talked of containing the Soviet Union, Reagan's plan for the Cold War was to 'win it'. There would be many occasions during the next eight years when the two leaders were at odds – including about the role of nuclear weapons in preserving the global peace – and moments when Thatcher would bridle at Reagan's broad-brush worldview, his limited appetite for intellectual engagement and his careless disdain for detail. Sometimes she overestimated Britain's influence in Washington, and once or twice she showed a curious timidity.

What mattered most for Thatcher was the meeting of minds. All the same, the asymmetry in the relationship showed itself in the eagerness with which she sought to be the first foreign leader to receive an invitation to the White House. Then, as for other prime ministers before and after, Britain's diplomats secured the prized invitation. A warm reception left her in upbeat mood. The West faced many dangers, she said, 'But I believe the tide is beginning to turn in our favour. The developing world is recognising the realities of Soviet ambitions and Soviet life . . . there is new leadership in America, which gives hope to all in the free world.'[8]

Thatcher's enthusiasm was not universally shared. To many British and European politicians, Reagan was a Hollywood cowboy catapulted by a mysterious American electoral system into the position of the most powerful man in the world. His homespun aphorisms were a source of mockery. Later in her premiership, Thatcher would also remark on his failure to engage whenever complexity hove into view. In the first years of his administration, however, Reagan presented a paradox – one neatly summarised in the autumn of 1982 by Oliver Wright, who had replaced Nicholas Henderson as British ambassador to the US. In a dispatch to Francis Pym, the foreign secretary, Wright set out the puzzle:

We have self-evidently a president – how shall I put it? – whom it is difficult to engage in a serious discussion on any subject of contemporary politics; and yet at the same time a president who is effecting a radical change in the nature of these politics. He has attracted a team of intelligent, hard-working and reasonably sophisticated men and women of conviction to translate his simple beliefs into policies, programmes and action. Moreover, despite appearances, he is not a man whom it is wise to take lightly.[9]

Reagan had clashed with European leaders on the issue of sanctions against Russia when they met at a Group of Seven summit in Versailles during the summer of that year. As Wright noted: 'Word circulates quietly in Washington that what really made Reagan mad at Versailles was that Helmut Schmidt made it all too obvious that he thought that what Reagan was saying was not worth listening to.'

The Falklands War was the making of Margaret Thatcher. In the spring of 1982, her administration looked distinctly shaky. The economy was trapped in recession, unemployment had reached three million, and public spending cuts and an overvalued exchange rate had led to the collapse of many of the nation's traditional industries. This was the moment the military junta in Argentina decided to seize the Falklands, a handful of islands in the South Atlantic that were among the eclectic collection of overseas possessions comprising the remnants of empire. Until the Argentine troops took the capital, Port Stanley, at the beginning of April 1982, there was precious little public consciousness that Britain remained the sovereign power over territories that had first been claimed more than two hundred years earlier and were now inhabited by fewer than 2,000 people. The Falklands and the associated dependencies of South Georgia and the South Sandwich Islands had a British governor and a handful of Royal Marines as a token defensive force. Beyond its revenues from sheep-farming, the islands' governing council earned a large slice of its income from the sale of stamps. Now this tiny settlement would demand that Britain send an expeditionary force halfway across the world. By the summer, the Union flag would fly again over Port Stanley. Thatcher's victory would transform Britain's image in the world. For those who looked closely, it would also mark the limits of Britain's global reach and its dependence on the United States.

British sovereignty had been periodically challenged by Argentina ever since 'Las Malvinas', as the territories were known in Buenos Aires, had been carved out of the former Spanish Empire and designated a Crown Colony in 1840. Britain's claim was not entirely straightforward, but neither was Argentina's. During the twenty years before the invasion, there had been various efforts to achieve a settlement. The Foreign Office at one point suggested a leaseback arrangement, under which sovereignty would be transferred and the administration of the islands would remain with Britain, but the suggestion came to nothing. What ministers and diplomats missed during the opening months of 1982 was the intense focus placed on the islands by the military regime of General Leopoldo Galtieri. The latest in a line of military dictators, the general had seized the presidency in December 1981 and almost immediately made the recovery of the islands his central goal. Publicly, the British government remained as determined as ever to uphold the rights of the Falkland Islanders to remain part of Britain. The islanders had the support of a vocal group of MPs on the backbenches at Westminster. But the government was prepared neither to invest in building up the Falklands' faltering economy nor to bolster their defences. As the historian Lawrence Freedman would write: 'To the Foreign Office, British interests with Latin America as a whole ranked higher than those of a couple of thousand islanders.'[10]

In Buenos Aires, the messages from London were read as signalling indifference. A year before the invasion, the defence secretary John Nott had announced the latest in a series of deep cuts to the government's military programmes. The decision to buy the Trident II missile system – at an estimated cost of £7.5 billion rather than the £5 billion originally allocated for Trident I – had added to the financial pressures. The axe fell heaviest on the navy: the number of destroyers and frigates was to be reduced by a third, to about forty ships. The implication this carried was that Britain was retrenching, concentrating its military forces on the defence of Europe and its role in NATO. Among the ships to be decommissioned was HMS *Endurance*, the icebreaker that patrolled the waters of the South Atlantic, providing protection for the Falklands. Although the government promised to defend the islands, Nott was cutting back necessary resources.

The timing of the Argentine invasion was half planned, half opportunistic. The flying of the Argentine flag by a group of scrap-metal merchants who had landed on South Georgia in March 1982 elicited a slow response in London. HMS *Endurance*, which had not yet been decommissioned, would be sent south again. There were suggestions that nuclear submarines might also be directed towards the South Atlantic. Galtieri, with his navy already at sea, decided to pre-empt any such moves. On 2 April, Argentine forces invaded the Falklands and South Georgia. Peter Carrington, who as foreign secretary had been responsible for the negotiations with Argentina, took the honourable course and resigned. Nott held on to his post for a further six months. Thatcher prepared for war.

There was something anachronistic, almost surreal, about the idea of a British naval task force sailing from the English south coast to fight a war 8,000 miles away in the South Atlantic, but Thatcher's decision was also in its way inevitable. As Michael Heseltine, secretary of state for the environment, remarked at the emergency cabinet meeting summoned to discuss the crisis, if ministers had done otherwise, they would have been out of office within days.[11] The mood was fixed when parliament met for a rare Saturday session; the invasion was a humiliation that could not be allowed to stand. Thatcher allowed herself no leeway for subsequent compromise:

> The people of the Falkland Islands, like the people of the
> United Kingdom, are an island race . . . They are few in
> number, but they have the right to live in peace, to choose
> their own way of life and to determine their own allegiance.
> Their way of life is British; their allegiance is to the Crown. It
> is the wish of the British people and the duty of Her Majesty's
> Government to do everything that we can to uphold that
> right. That will be our hope and our endeavour and, I believe,
> the resolve of every Member of the House.[12]

The opposition Labour Party was led by Michael Foot, a veteran left-winger who backed unilateral nuclear disarmament. He would have no truck with Galtieri:

> There is no question in the Falkland Islands of any colonial
> dependence or anything of the sort. It is a question of people
> who wish to be associated with this country and who have
> built their whole lives on the basis of association with this
> country. We have a moral duty, a political duty and every other
> kind of duty to ensure that is sustained.[13]

George Foulkes was among just a handful of Labour MPs calling for negotiation over war:

> My gut reaction is to use force. Our country has been
> humiliated . . . But we must also be sure that we shall not kill
> thousands of people in the use of that force. I am in favour of
> the firmest possible diplomatic action and sanctions against
> the Argentine. I am in favour of asking the United States
> and all our allies to unite against the Argentine. However, I

am against the military action for which so many have asked because I dread the consequences that will befall the people of our country and the people of the Falkland Islands.[14]

Such disquiet spread after the loss of more than 320 Argentine lives a few weeks later, when a British submarine sank the cruiser *Belgrano* in waters outside the official maritime exclusion zone declared by the government. Yet to argue against invasion seemed to a majority to be taking the side of a ruthless military dictator. Within days, the task force, headed by the aircraft carriers HMS *Hermes* and HMS *Invincible* and including requisitioned luxury liners such as the *QE2* and *Canberra*, had been assembled at Portsmouth and Plymouth.

The Argentine invasion was condemned by the United Nations Security Council. The French president François Mitterrand was among the first foreign leaders to offer Thatcher unequivocal support. West Germany's Helmut Schmidt did the same. And in spite of doubts in some capitals, the European Community was persuaded to impose sanctions against Buenos Aires. Mitterrand's offer of help was particularly striking. France's socialist president and Thatcher were scarcely kindred spirits, and France had supplied Argentina with the Super Étendard fighter planes, equipped with Exocet missiles, that would present the biggest threat to British ships. The sensitive technical information about the aircraft and missiles which the Paris government now passed secretly to London was critical in allowing British forces to devise countermeasures.

The response of Thatcher's soulmate in the White House was more surprising. On the eve of the invasion, when Argentina's intentions were already obvious, Reagan telephoned Galtieri at Thatcher's request. The general refused Reagan's appeal to stand down. Once Argentina had taken control of the islands, Reagan was quick to condemn the invasion, but his administration fell short of offering unqualified support for Thatcher's plan to retake the islands by force. Thatcher soon learned, as her predecessors had done, that there was nothing sentimental about America's view of the 'special relationship', particularly when it collided with its own national interests. In this case, Washington saw Central and Latin America as a pivotal battleground in the Cold War. Galtieri was an important ally. Washington did not want to be seen to take the side of an old 'colonial power' in its defence of what Reagan called 'that little ice-cold bunch of land'. The president offered Thatcher warm words, but his State Department, led by Alexander Haig, struck a more neutral pose. Haig assumed the role of broker in an effort to negotiate a settlement before the British task force reached the South Atlantic. Washington did provide discreet military assistance to the UK – its base on Ascension Island was a vital stopping-off point on the way to the South Atlantic and a base for British Vulcan bombers – and British commanders were dependent on US intelligence and surveillance capabilities to track the Argentine forces. But Reagan refused the wholehearted public commitment sought by Thatcher.

The US defence secretary Caspar Weinberger did his best to circumvent the hesitation. Dismayed that the administration was drawing equivalence between a fellow NATO member and the Argentine dictatorship, he broke ranks and provided support. He was an important counterweight within the administration to Jeane Kirkpatrick, America's forceful envoy to the United Nations and a hard-headed neoconservative, who often took the Argentine side. In a cable to London, the British ambassador Nicholas Henderson abandoned diplomatic niceties to describe Kirkpatrick as 'more fool than fascist'.[15] Kirkpatrick, he continued, 'appears to be one of America's most reliable own-goal scorers: tactless, wrong-headed, ineffective and a dubious tribute to the academic profession'. For his part, Weinberger was subsequently rewarded for his steadfast support with an honorary knighthood from the Queen.

Thatcher was immoveable: Argentina had used military force to seize British sovereign territory, and the invasion could not be allowed to stand. This was a principle that reached well beyond the fate of the Falklands. Britain would not accept anything less than a restoration of the islands to its control, and only then would it talk to Argentina about the future. Within the cabinet Francis Pym, who had replaced Carrington as foreign secretary, sometimes took a more conciliatory line. To the prime minister's mind, as she told Haig during his attempt at shuttle diplomacy, it was 'essentially an issue of dictatorship versus democracy'.[16]

The collapse at the end of April, four weeks after the invasion, of Haig's attempts at mediation saw the US administration come off the fence publicly. British forces had retaken South Georgia. But even as Reagan blamed Argentina for the breakdown in diplomacy and announced that the US was ready to supply Britain with military equipment for the task force, he continued to press Thatcher privately to negotiate. The exchanges were often bruising. In one difficult telephone call, the prime minister reminded the president 'that he would not wish his people to live under the sort of regime offered by the military Junta'. In another, she remarked that she was sure that he would have acted in the same way if 'Alaska was invaded'.[17]

The British military victory in mid-June transformed the public perception of Britain and Thatcher. The invasion had been a humiliation – a failure of diplomacy and testimony, so it seemed, to Britain's diminished power. The success of the task force had been far from inevitable. The navy lost several ships. The aircraft carriers provided only limited air cover. Had a few more of Argentina's Exocet missiles hit their targets, the landing of British forces would have proved impossible. By the time Argentina surrendered the capital Port Stanley, 255 members of the British forces and 649 Argentine troops had lost their lives. The victory was not without controversy. The sinking of the *Belgrano* while the warship was outside a declared military exclusion zone and heading away from the islands was particular cause for dispute. Britain could have devoted, at least initially, more time and energy to securing a peaceful outcome through a combination of economic sanctions and coercive diplomacy. Most governments in the region backed Argentina's claim to sovereignty. When the House of Commons met to mark the victory, the far-left Labour MP Martin Flannery struck a discordant note: 'Will the prime minister not close her mind completely to some discussion, under the auspices of the United Nations, on the ultimate sovereignty of the islands? Is it not a profound anachronism in 1982 for any state to have sovereign territory 8,000 miles away?'[18] Mrs Thatcher would have none of it. And yet her government had been engaged in just such discussions before the invasion.

Thatcher's luck had turned; the 1983 general election was won in the South Atlantic. Dispensing with any pretence of humility, Thatcher offered her own view on the significance of the war a few weeks after the retaking of Port Stanley: 'We have ceased to be a nation in retreat. We have instead a new-found confidence – born in the economic battles at home and tested and found true 8,000 miles away.'[19] Even the Russians were impressed. Nigel Sheinwald was a young desk officer in the Soviet department of the Foreign Office and recalls the reaction in Moscow: 'They respected the fact that we decided to do it and the way our military went about it. I remember having a conversation with the person we thought was head of the KGB operation in London. He said how much respect people at home had for our victory.'²⁰ More than fifteen years earlier, in a defence White Paper published in 1966, Harold Wilson's government had concluded that Britain would no longer be able to fight an expeditionary war against a sophisticated enemy without the benefit of land-based air cover and the support of allies. The belated American assistance aside, the Falklands campaign seemed to defy that prediction. Yet – and here was the irony – Thatcher would soon preside over cuts in the defence budget that removed any possibility that the feat could be repeated. By the time she left office, Britain had all but admitted that henceforth wars could be fought only alongside the Americans.

The Falklands conflict cemented Thatcher's reputation as a conviction politician. Even for the Iron Lady, however, there were limits to conviction. Twice in the first half of her premiership she faced foreign policy choices where her preferences and instincts collided with the hard facts of power. Like the Falklands, they looked back to Britain's colonial past. In both instances, albeit only after some resistance, the prime minister came down on the side of realism.

Rhodesia had been a running sore since Ian Smith's white minority government's unilateral declaration of independence in November 1965. Harold Wilson's government considered and then dismissed the possibility of military intervention. After abortive diplomatic interventions – Wilson met Smith on HMS *Tiger* in 1966, and again on HMS *Fearless* two years later – successive governments had relied on a strategy of economic sanctions and international opprobrium to force white Rhodesians to accept majority rule. Most recently, a US-backed peace initiative led by David Owen, James Callaghan's foreign secretary, had been

TOP The Big Three: Churchill, Truman and Stalin at Potsdam

BOTTOM The Yanks are back. Clement Attlee meets the crew of an
American B-29 Superfortress bomber – soon to be armed with
nuclear bombs – at RAF Marham, October 1949

The final throw. Anthony Eden speaks to the nation after Nasser
seizes the Suez Canal, August 1956

LEFT Eisenhower is given the royal treatment by Harold Macmillan. The American president is driven through London in an open-topped Rolls-Royce, August 1959

BELOW *Non*. De Gaulle slams the European door in Macmillan's face at Rambouillet, December 1962

Striking an unlikely nuclear deal: Macmillan and JFK
in Nassau, December 1962

Harold Wilson says no. The prime minister, in Washington
in 1965, refuses to provide even a 'platoon of pipers' for
President Johnson's war in Vietnam

LEFT The pound in your pocket? Devaluation paves the way for Wilson's retreat from East of Suez

BELOW A true European. Edward Heath persuades France's Georges Pompidou to say *oui* during Common Market negotiations in May 1971

RIGHT Another sterling crisis looms. Prime Minister James Callaghan and his chancellor, Denis Healey, in July 1976

'The eyes of Caligula and the mouth of Marilyn Monroe' –
François Mitterrand's reported description of Margaret Thatcher.
The two meet in November 1981

LEFT Cold warriors. Thatcher and Reagan in Washington, June 1982
RIGHT Enough. After more than eleven years as prime minister,
Thatcher leaves 10 Downing Street for the last time in November 1990

Peacemaking in Northern Ireland. Tony Blair with Irish prime
minister Bertie Ahern in Belfast, June 1999

... And preparing for war in Iraq. Blair with George W. Bush at the
US president's ranch in Crawford, Texas, April 2002

Loser. Brexit means exit for David Cameron as he announces his resignation the day after the June 2016 referendum

The last laugh for UKIP leader and pro-Brexit campaigner Nigel Farage, whose supporters had been described by Cameron as 'fruitcakes, loonies and closet racists, mostly'

Populists in arms. Boris Johnson and Donald Trump at the December 2019 NATO summit in Watford

rejected by the Salisbury government. Facing a rising guerrilla war waged by the ZANU–Patriotic Front of Robert Mugabe and Joshua Nkomo, Smith had imposed a new political settlement, providing for majority rule but enshrining the privileged position of the white minority. Once in Downing Street, Thatcher's instinct was to recognise the government led by Abel Muzorewa elected in the spring of 1979. Privately, she dismissed ZANU–PF as the representatives of 'terrorists'. Recognition would have left Britain isolated. The United States, European governments and the leading Commonwealth nations had all declared Muzorewa's election to be illegitimate. She found it hard to disguise her sympathies for the white settlers. That said, facing isolation within the Commonwealth, she allowed her head to rule her heart, telling the House of Commons in July 1979: 'At this point, we should like to make clear that we are wholly committed to genuine black majority rule in Rhodesia. We believe that it is possible in Rhodesia, as in other countries to which Britain has granted independence, to reconcile reasonable reassurance for the white community and the protection of their rights with black majority rule.'[21] By the time she reached Lusaka in Zambia for a Commonwealth Heads of Government Meeting in August 1979, Peter Carrington, the foreign secretary, had persuaded her that the government should sponsor its own plan for a constitutional settlement. Under prime ministerial protest, the parties, including ZANU–PF, were prevailed upon to meet at London's Lancaster House in September to thrash out an agreement.

The accord reached three months later, in December 1979, was Carrington's achievement. After a brief interlude during which sovereignty reverted to Britain, it gave the renamed Zimbabwe independence under majority rule. Thatcher's contribution had been to contain her objections; as her official biographer Charles

Moore would note, she remained sympathetic to the white minority. Her husband Denis, who had family and business connections in the region, 'had an unreconstructed belief in the political and economic incompetence of black regimes and a natural sympathy, based on ethnicity and sport, for the whites of southern Africa'.[22] In the prime minister's mind, one senior diplomat would later remark, the whites belonged to the 'family' of English-speaking nations. She tended to gloss over, the official added, the blood that had flowed in the Boer War.[23] Once the Lancaster House deal had been done, she was pleased to take the credit due to Carrington. She would later write that 'political and military realities were all too evidently on the side of the guerrilla leaders', but, as Moore observed, 'The Rhodesian settlement never made her happy.'

Hong Kong presented a sterner test of the prime minister's conviction politics. Travelling to Beijing in 1982 to discuss the handover of the colony when Britain's lease on it expired in 1997, Thatcher assumed that she could set the terms of the transfer. Hong Kong, after all, was a great success story and a tribute to over a century of British rule. There was a legal obligation to return the New Territories, which accounted for 90 per cent of the colony, to China, but because the city itself had been ceded to Britain by treaty, China required the agreement of the British government. And whatever the legal fine print, surely it was obvious that Hong Kong should continue to benefit from British administration? Britain's duty, she thought, was to the people of Hong Kong. From the beginning, there were glaring inconsistencies in Thatcher's stance. Britain's presumed duty to the citizens of the colony, for example, had not persuaded the government to offer them full British passports. And the contrast she drew between the authoritarian rule of the Chinese Communist Party and British oversight of Hong Kong glossed over the fact that Hong Kong was scarcely a model for democracy.

Thatcher's pitch to Chinese leader Deng Xiaoping when the two leaders met in September 1982 was that Britain would be ready to discuss the return of sovereignty once agreement had been reached on a continuation of British oversight. The Chinese leader's response was abrupt: China would recover sovereignty, which was inseparable from administration. The talks ended badly, and the only agreement about sovereignty was that the word would not be included in the communiqué. Travelling on to Hong Kong, Thatcher was expansive in her public promises to uphold the rights of the people. On her return to London she was told that it would be impossible to hold on to the colony if Beijing decided to take it over when the lease expired.

What followed during the next few months were two sets of negotiations. The first saw the foreign secretary Geoffrey Howe and his officials deliver to the prime minister a lesson in realpolitik. Howe, switched from the Treasury after the 1983 election, was everything that Thatcher wasn't – careful, deliberative and mindful that banging the table was not an invariably successful negotiating tactic. China, Thatcher had to acknowledge, would accept nothing less than full sovereignty and administration. The second negotiation, between London and Beijing, focused on the guarantees that Britain could extract in return for agreeing the smooth handover that would assure the colony's future economic contribution to China. The outcome was as good an agreement as any that might have been expected. The Sino–British Joint Declaration signed by Thatcher and Deng in December 1984 enshrined the idea of 'one country, two systems'. Rule of the colony would revert to China, but democratic protections for the people of Hong Kong would be guaranteed for at least fifty years. The bargain left a number of issues unresolved – John Major would be obliged to settle them nearly a decade later – but it was enough to save China's face and see Thatcher adopt a pragmatic line.

On a third troublesome hangover from empire Thatcher was much more reluctant to budge. By the 1980s, apartheid South Africa had become a pariah state. It had left the Commonwealth more than twenty years earlier – withdrawing before it was expelled – and faced rising isolation within the international community. Thatcher, however, battled tirelessly against moves within the Commonwealth and the European Community to impose sanctions against the regime. The official policy was that engagement was the best route to apply pressure on the regime, but in truth her views were rooted in a mix of empathy for the white settlers and the calculation that they provided a bulwark against the advance of Soviet communism. She viewed the African National Congress as a front for the terrorists waging war on the white regime. Sir Oliver Wright, the permanent under-secretary at the Foreign Office from 1986, later recorded Thatcher's views: the answer, she suggested, was a return to pre-1910 South Africa, with a white mini-state partitioned from neighbouring black states. When Wright protested, he received a sharp rebuke: 'Do you have no concern for our strategic interests?'[24] Thatcher's obduracy on the issue brought the Commonwealth close to breaking point and Geoffrey Howe to the point of resignation. Ultimately, she was forced to accept an extension of sanctions. The release of the ANC leader Nelson Mandela after twenty-seven years in prison and the transition to black majority rule would leave her marooned by events.

The privileged relationship with Washington was cherished as much by officials as by the politicians, even if by the 1980s senior

British diplomats worried that the phrase 'special relationship' signalled an uncomfortable neediness on the part of the British. The broad and complex web of relationships between the two nations' defence, nuclear and intelligence establishments had created an unmatched basis of trust that most of the time gave the British a 'first look' at ideas as they emerged from Washington. The closest comparison was the framework of political and bureaucratic cooperation established in 1963 by France and West Germany through the Elysée Treaty. For the Treasury, close ties with Washington were deemed vital in the event of sterling crises because the route to the International Monetary Fund ran through the US Treasury. The Foreign Office, with its close contacts with the State Department, liked to think it was in at the ground floor of US policy-making. The traffic in secrets between the Secret Intelligence Service and the Central Intelligence Agency and GCHQ and the National Security Agency flowed in both directions. Sir John Scarlett, who later led the SIS, says the relationship between the agencies was 'a great national strength. It was much more of an equal partnership than people might think . . . It came from years and years of working together and the trust that comes from it.'[25] British generals, admirals and vice-marshals managed to embed themselves in US military command centres. All this came at a price: if Britain wanted special access, the Americans expected British loyalty. They also felt perfectly free, when it suited them, to do as they pleased.

The first Thatcher heard directly from Reagan about his decision to invade Grenada was after the marines had been dispatched. The small Caribbean island remained a member of the Commonwealth and, with the Queen as its head of state, still retained a British governor general. In October 1983, the government of Maurice Bishop – Marxist in theory, more pragmatic in real life – was overthrown by communist hardliners in a military coup. The new regime's links to the Soviet Union caused alarm in Washington, where the administration had put in place a strategy to forestall Cuba's efforts to spread its influence. Some other small Caribbean states called for intervention. Thatcher's government thought the threat exaggerated. Cuba certainly saw Grenada as a useful staging post for the troops it sent to fight in the East–West proxy wars raging in Angola and Ethiopia, but British officials doubted the Soviets had a direct role. They were content to wait and see. The news from Washington, however, was that the US intended to respond to a request from Caribbean governments asking them to intervene to topple the military regime.

After a series of frantic ministerial meetings, a blunt message was dispatched to the White House: an invasion would be seen as an unwarranted intervention in the affairs of a small independent nation. It would complicate the government's efforts to face down opposition to the deployment of cruise and Pershing missiles in Europe. The prime minister was 'deeply disturbed' at the plan. A telephone call followed soon afterwards. Reagan agreed to consider her objections, and then admitted that it was too late to halt the operation. Howe had a day earlier told the House of Commons that the government had no knowledge of any planned invasion. Now, in Thatcher's words, 'He and I would have to explain how it had happened that a member of the Commonwealth had been invaded by our closest ally.' Reagan knew she was angry: 'If I were there, Margaret,' he said, 'I'd throw my hat in the door before I came in.'[26]

Sir Peter Ricketts, then an official in Howe's private office, recalls that once the marines had landed, they put the British governor in a helicopter and took him from the island to an aircraft carrier. 'There he signed an antedated letter giving them approval to come in.'[27]

Thatcher accepted a half-apology from Reagan, deciding that the episode did not merit a serious rupture. She would soak up the accusations that Britain had acted as America's poodle. The same charge was heard again three years later, when US bombers took off from Britain to launch air strikes against Muammar Gaddafi's Libyan regime. The proposed attack was in retaliation for Libya's support for Palestinian groups waging a campaign of terror against civilian targets, and followed skirmishes between American and Libyan forces in the Mediterranean. France denied the Americans the use of their air space, so Reagan messaged Thatcher and asked for permission to use F-111 aircraft based in the UK. Thatcher responded urging caution; she was concerned not just about protests at home but also feared retaliation against the 5,000 British citizens living in Libya and British hostages held in Lebanon. British diplomats warned that an attack could start a chain reaction of violence across the Middle East. After another day of deliberation, the prime minister gave Reagan her backing. The public response in Britain was overwhelmingly hostile, with the opposition suggesting that Thatcher had behaved as Reagan's lapdog. Later, she said she feared the implications of a refusal: 'Whatever the cost to me, I knew that the cost to Britain of not backing American action was unthinkable.'[28] It was a curious admission – by her own account, the 'special relationship' had never been stronger.

Many in Whitehall judged that the overall gains to Britain more than repaid such occasional embarrassments. John Sawers, a Foreign Office diplomat who would later become head of the SIS, says the bond was 'genuinely close and hugely valuable for the UK . . . relationships with the US military, the US nuclear forces, US special forces, the intelligence community . . . greatly enhanced Britain's position'.[29] And the traffic was not one-way: once the administration had taken a decision, 'The first place America would come to was London. There would then be another set of arguments. The Americans basically, I think, took the view that if they couldn't persuade London, they wouldn't be able to persuade anyone in Europe.'

There were occasions when Thatcher stood her ground. In 1982, the British company John Brown Engineering was swept up in the US administration's sanctions against European companies supplying oil and gas equipment to the Soviet Union. The measure was aimed at a pipeline that would carry Siberian gas into western Europe. Thatcher joined other European leaders in condemning the imposition of American policy on European business. Washington retreated under protest. She also turned her back on Washington to back a more pro-Palestinian position taken by the European Community in promoting peace between Israel and the Palestinian Liberation Organisation. Yet, for all the exceptions, the closeness of the Reagan–Thatcher relationship often seemed to underline the extent to which Britain's policy choices were reactive, driven by decisions taken in Washington. Thatcher's reflexes anticipated Tony Blair's support for George W. Bush's administration in the approach to the Iraq War. It was his 'duty', Blair would say, to keep Britain close to Washington.

On one issue – many would say the most important one – Ronald Reagan was misunderstood in Britain. The president denounced the Soviet Union as an 'evil empire' and set in train a steep rise in American defence spending. He also launched the Strategic Defence Initiative (SDI), popularly known as Star Wars, to build a defensive shield in space against Soviet nuclear missiles. And he put cruise and Pershing missiles into Europe to counter the threat from Soviet SS-20s. All this made the US president a target for growing anti-nuclear protest movements in Europe.

Behind the shared determination to defeat communism, however, there was a profound difference between the two leaders. Even as he modernised the vast US nuclear arsenal, Reagan held the scrapping of all these weapons as a long-term goal. A president whose public image suggested a careless disregard of the risk of mutually assured destruction, he was in truth horrified by the prospect of a nuclear exchange. The Soviet Union viewed Reagan's SDI programme as a shield from behind which the United States could launch a nuclear first strike. Reagan considered the SDI as a route to neutralising – and eventually removing – the world's nuclear arsenals. This set him apart from Thatcher. The divide was not immediately obvious but, according to Charles Powell, 'they developed completely contrary views'. Reagan had not been anti-nuclear when he became president, but 'became convinced they [nuclear weapons] were a great evil'.[30]

To Thatcher's mind, nuclear weapons provided the West's essential safeguard against the triumph of Soviet communism. They were the guarantee of, rather than the threat to, global peace. And the threat was greatest in Europe. Outgunned in terms of conventional weapons, Europe, and Britain, would be completely disarmed were the US to abandon its nuclear posture. The Soviet Union would be deterred only if it knew that at every stage of escalation of conflict it would be met with a countervailing response from NATO, leading at some point to a nuclear exchange. This had been her argument for the deployment of short- and medium-range missiles to match Moscow's SS-20s. It explained also her distinctly cool reaction when Reagan announced his plans for SDI. The debate took place behind the scenes but was no less intense for that.

By the autumn of 1983, Geoffrey Howe, aided and abetted by a group of senior Foreign Office diplomats, was pressing the case for a more subtle approach to Moscow. For all the immutable differences, the West had to do business with the Soviets, and a strategy of engagement did not require it to drop its guard. The deaths in quick succession of the Soviet leaders Leonid Brezhnev and Yuri Andropov and the frailty of Konstantin Chernenko marked the passing of the old guard. Western leaders should at the very least test the intentions of the new generation in Moscow. Thatcher signalled a willingness to shift after a seminar of Soviet experts at Chequers in September 1983. This led her in turn to a decision to attend the funerals in the succeeding two years of Andropov and Chernenko. It also mapped the path to one of the most unlikely but intense relationships of her premiership. In December 1984, months before Chernenko's death the following March, Thatcher hosted at Chequers the man who would succeed him. 'I like Mr [Mikhail] Gorbachev,' she declared before the television cameras. 'We can do business together.' During lengthy but relaxed talks, the two leaders disagreed on everything. Thatcher, however, admired Gorbachev's candour and his willingness to engage in debate. To one or two of her officials, her enthusiasm verged on infatuation. It was the first time she had encountered a communist leader with a mind of his own. Before long she was telling Reagan of her discovery.

Thatcher was influenced also by the messages being conveyed to her via the SIS from the Russian double agent Oleg Gordievsky. A senior officer in the KGB and notionally a diplomat at the Soviet embassy in London, Gordievsky had been supplying the SIS with high-grade intelligence since the mid-1970s. In 1983, his reports on the thinking in the highest reaches of the Kremlin began to give his handlers cause for alarm. The briefings provided an insight that Thatcher had not previously considered: the ratcheting up of Western anti-communist rhetoric might be taken by Moscow as a signal of darker intent. The story in the West was about Soviet expansionism, but the communist leadership had its own deep fears. As absurd as it might seem to Western leaders that the US could launch a pre-emptive attack on the Soviet bloc, that was not how it looked in Moscow. Gordievsky provided warnings as to just how dangerous these fears had become. Monitoring a regular NATO exercise – code-named Able Archer – in the autumn of 1983, some senior figures in the Soviet system believed it was a prelude to a real strike. Moscow's own forces were put on alert. The world was on the road to nuclear war by accident, until a reassessment led the Kremlin to stand down. Thatcher alluded to such risks at a press conference in Moscow following Andropov's funeral in February 1984. Her approach, she said, evolved over time. 'I believe as strongly as ever in basic Western freedoms – and I make it plain to all in the East privately and publicly that I will defend them anywhere any time. But we must avoid the terrible dangers that could flow from misunderstandings.'[31]

Much as she felt she could do business with Gorbachev – a view that strengthened when he took the top job – she harboured severe doubts as to how much would change. In an aide-memoire written after Chernenko's funeral in the spring of 1985, she noted that she had carefully read Gorbachev's recent statements during the flight to Moscow: 'All confirmed the impression gained at Chequers the previous December, that even if he wished to change matters he wouldn't know how to, because a rigid communist system was the only one he had ever known.'[32]

Nuclear business, Thatcher was soon reminded, was done by the Americans. And here she was seriously at odds with the US president. The SDI was still at its research stage. There was no certainty that the system would ever work, but it represented an important challenge to her priority of retaining the existing architecture of deterrence – and specifically ensuring that the Americans kept nuclear weapons in Europe. Increasingly, she expressed doubts about whether the ageing president had the intellectual capacity to grasp the complexity of the arguments. For his part, Reagan would not be budged from the belief that space defences would lead to disarmament and the eventual abolition of all nuclear weapons. He would share the technology, he told the prime minister, with the Soviet Union. To complicate matters further, many other Europeans – the Germans most prominently – sympathised with Gorbachev's view that the SDI was an obstacle to further arms control agreements.

During her Chequers talks with Gorbachev, Thatcher had betrayed her own doubts about the SDI, characterising the space defence programme as naive. A week later, she travelled to Camp David for talks with Reagan, in one breath reporting on her talks with Gorbachev and in the next laying out her objections to the Star Wars project. The British note of the meeting reports her telling Reagan that Gorbachev was 'an unusual Russian in that he was much less constrained, more charming, open to discussion and debate, and did not stick to prepared notes'. She had told him, the note continues, that there was no point in Moscow

> trying to divide Britain from the United States. This ploy will never succeed. Britain is part of the Western Alliance of free nations and the Soviets should drop any illusions about severing Europe or Great Britain from the United States. She also told Gorbachev that she and the president have known each other since long before they assumed their current positions and dividing Europe from America is simply 'not on'.[33]

Thatcher was by now feted in Washington as a fearless ally. Her access to Reagan was the envy of other European leaders. Yet she had also begun to overestimate her own influence. She supported the idea of research into space defence, she told the president, but she was fearful of its consequences. The existing deterrence structure, she said, had served the West well in preserving the peace; scrapping nuclear weapons would disarm America's European allies. A White House record of the meeting listed her objections:

> Nuclear weapons have served not only to prevent a nuclear war, but they have also given us forty years of unprecedented peace in Europe. It would be unwise, she continued, to abandon a deterrence system that has prevented both nuclear and conventional war. Moreover, if we ever reach the stage of abolishing all nuclear weapons, this would make conventional, biological or chemical war more likely. Hitler won the race for the rocket; the US won the race for the nuclear bomb. The technological struggle goes on, she observed. There are all sorts of decoys, jamming systems and technological developments, such as making the missile boost phase even shorter. All these advances make crisis management more and more difficult.[34]

Reagan held to his position, speaking, according to Thatcher's adviser Charles Powell, with 'notable intensity'. The Strategic Defence Initiative would be a defensive system, one that if successful could lead to the elimination of nuclear weapons. The US would make it available to all countries. A joint communiqué at the end of the talks glossed over the differences, noting, in deference to Thatcher, that the two leaders were agreed that the West should not undercut deterrence. The words dampened speculation of a serious rift. Reagan did not change his mind. As he told

Thatcher again some months later, he wanted 'to render obsolete a strategy based on the nuclear destruction of populations'.[35] This moral dimension worried her. It chimed too easily with the demands in Britain of those who were calling for nuclear disarmament, including the opposition Labour Party.

There were no great pronouncements after Reagan and Gorbachev met in Geneva for their first summit during the autumn of 1985. But the meeting changed the dynamics of the relationship, serving as a prelude for the resumption of talks on reducing or scrapping intermediate-range nuclear missiles and regular direct contact between Reagan and Gorbachev. In the description of Anatoly Chernyaev, a senior adviser to Gorbachev, what changed was the mutual recognition that neither wanted to start a nuclear war. The theme of correspondence between the two leaders became the need to reduce nuclear weapons stocks to a level of 'reasonable sufficiency' that would provide security rather than superiority for both sides.

A year later, when the two leaders met in the Icelandic capital of Reykjavik, they came tantalisingly close to a historic accord that would have seen massive cuts in their nuclear arsenals. The talks broke down at the last moment – ironically, because Gorbachev could not accept that Reagan genuinely saw the SDI as the route to complete disarmament rather than American impregnability. At one stage in the discussions Reagan suggested he would go to 'zero'. Presented with a proposal that both sides scrap half of their strategic weapons within five years and abolish their remaining ballistic missiles within ten, Reagan said that he was ready to eliminate all nuclear weapons. But in refusing Gorbachev's demand for the Star Wars programme to be shut down, paradoxically he scuppered a deal. The negotiations underscored the chasm that had opened up between Thatcher and Reagan. In the description of Powell, 'She nearly had a heart attack when she heard what was going on in Reykjavik.'[36]

For the prime minister, the summit was a merciful failure. It had underscored as never before Britain's complete dependence on US nuclear policy. France had its own nuclear capability – the *force de frappe*. Britain relied for Polaris and Trident on a United States that was now considering scrapping all nuclear weapons. Publicly, Thatcher sought to hide her horror at the agreement that might have been. Privately, she used all her energies to persuade Reagan that he would have left Europe defenceless. He might also have persuaded British voters that the opposition Labour Party was right in pressing for comprehensive disarmament. The Reykjavik moment passed. A year later, Washington and Moscow concluded an agreement to remove all short- and medium-range weapons from Europe, but the 'zero option' for strategic weapons was never revived. Reagan was entering the twilight of his presidency, his authority undercut by revelations that his administration had been using arms sales to Iran to raise secret funds for anti-communist groups in Nicaragua. Imperceptibly, the magic drained from the Thatcher–Reagan relationship. Much to Thatcher's irritation, George H. W. Bush would distinguish himself from his predecessor by stepping back from such an intimate relationship with Britain's prime minister. Washington's attention turned more closely to Bonn and Paris. The more worried she became about Reagan's nuclear stance, the more beguiled she was by Gorbachev's efforts to reform the Soviet Union. Two world leaders loomed large over Thatcher's premiership: the partner she most needed was Reagan, but the leader who intrigued her was Gorbachev.

When the first British-built VC10 took to the skies at the beginning of the 1960s, the new passenger aircraft had been at the cutting edge of aviation technology. A sleek, narrow-bodied plane, it had broken the record for the fastest commercial crossing of the Atlantic. It represented the best of advanced engineering, proof that Britain was embracing, in Harold Wilson's phrase, the 'white heat of technology'. A quarter of a century later, the aircraft was no longer quite such an emblem of modernity. Long out of commercial service, the small number that remained belonged to the Royal Air Force. Most had been converted into airborne tankers; a handful were kitted out to carry VIP passengers. Cramped, noisy and with a limited range, they were not the most comfortable way to criss-cross the globe. Margaret Thatcher thought otherwise. While officials sometimes prevailed upon her to travel on roomier aircraft leased for the purpose, the prime minister preferred the VC10. Her personal accommodation was comfortable; more importantly, the aircraft was crewed by the RAF. The Boeing Corporation's 747 jumbo jets might be bigger, more efficient and more luxurious, but with its spartan interior and uniformed stewards, the VC10 spoke for Britain.

In September 1989, after a short visit to Japan, the prime minister set off for home. The plan was to stop over in Moscow on the way back to London. Prime minister, Number 10 staff, a couple of officers from the secret communications agency GCHQ and a dozen or so journalists loaded themselves onto her favourite plane. Such were the limits on the range of the VC10 that it could not make it from Tokyo to Moscow in a single hop. The prime ministerial party kicked its heels for a couple of hours at a Soviet airbase deep in frozen Siberia while the aircraft was refuelled. The VC10 would be filled up again in the Russian capital, where Thatcher had scheduled a meeting with Gorbachev.

Thatcher and Gorbachev had built quite a relationship. Two years earlier, the prime minister had been given star treatment during a four-day visit to Moscow and Georgia. So careful had her preparations for that trip been that she arrived with an entirely new wardrobe designed by Aquascutum, the British luxury fashion house. Gorbachev was invited to take tea with the Queen during a return visit to London the following year. Thatcher's admiration for the Soviet leader's domestic reform programme, or 'perestroika', and his determination to pursue a policy of increased openness towards the West, or 'glasnost', built bridges over the ideological gulf between the two leaders. The prime minister saw in Gorbachev's determination to recast the Soviet system something of a mirror of her own economic and social revolution. Her growing doubts about Reagan's intellectual capacity were matched by her rising enthusiasm for Gorbachev. Here was a leader who seemed to share her reforming courage. By 1988, she had travelled sufficiently far to declare: 'We are not in a Cold War anymore.' Closeness to the Soviet leader conferred the international stature she so enjoyed. Gorbachev saw in turn that the relationship could operate to Moscow's advantage. Three years earlier, reporting to the Communist Party's Central Committee on his latest talks with the British prime minister, Gorbachev observed that Thatcher saw that Reagan was getting old, Mitterrand had been weakened by enforced political cohabitation with a right-wing government led by Jacques Chirac, and Kohl had his own difficulties. 'So it is her chance to stand out,' the official note of Gorbachev's remarks recorded. Thatcher was 'acting out the desire to raise her authority by dealing with Moscow'.[37] Other leaders, including Kohl, would take the message that 'those who do not have relations with us' will lose at home. On the substance of nuclear disarmament, though, 'her position in favour of nuclear weapons is like paranoia. I simply shamed her. I told her that her position goes against worldwide sentiments. The US and USSR are beginning a process of disarmament; we are upholding a moratorium, while Great Britain does nothing.'

Thatcher arrived in Moscow with a lot to talk about. The democracy genie was by now out of the bottle and Soviet-sponsored regimes across eastern and central Europe were under siege. Hungary had opened its borders to the West, and among the tens of thousands fleeing the other countries in the Warsaw Pact were large numbers of East Germans. How long could the Berlin Wall, to borrow one of Thatcher's favourite epithets, imprison the people of East Germany? As Douglas Hurd, Thatcher's foreign secretary, noted: 'The East Germans were kept as prisoners within a communist system which depended on Russian military power.'[38] Now the system was fracturing. For the Iron Lady, this should have been a moment of unrestrained celebration.

It was no such thing. Instead, unfolding events became a source of fear. For a decade she had seen her role as stiffening the spine of the West, but with the Soviet Empire crumbling, she became disorientated. Her mind turned to the implications, and above all to Germany. The Cold War, European integration and a Germany divided between East and West had sidelined the thorniest issue in European politics. Through the post-war decades, the prospect of German reunification had been no more than an occasional topic of conversation. Now, as East Germans flooded westwards via Hungary and the erstwhile Soviet satellite states staked their claims to democratic independence, the 'German question' returned to the centre of European politics.

In temperament and outlook, the Federal Republic of Germany was Britain's natural ally. Atlanticist in its worldview, it also shared Britain's commitment to a rules-based international order and its preference for liberal, open markets. Sure, Britain did not share Bonn's ambitions for a federal Europe and often resented the strength of the Franco–German alliance, but the German representation in Brussels had become a first stop for British officials seeking allies to reshape European policies. Ministers never gave up on the idea that, with shrewd diplomacy, the Bonn government could be detached from its French ally. If nothing else, West Germany saw Britain as an important foil against France. Unification, however, would change everything, reopening the prospect that Germany could once again become the continent's dominant power. Thatcher's response was generational, driven as much by emotion as diplomatic or strategic calculation. Could the Germans be trusted? Had they really changed? A unified Germany, re-establishing its economic hinterland in the newly free countries of eastern and central Europe, would reorder the balance of power. The question that gnawed at her was whether the post-war transformation in the political culture, geopolitical outlook and territorial restraint seen in the Federal Republic would carry through in a united Germany. She doubted it. The national character was too deeply embedded.

Thatcher had additional concerns. She feared that events in eastern and central Europe would derail Gorbachev's programme of reform. He'd had the courage to dismiss the received wisdom of his country's politics, to take on powerful enemies and to allow conviction to set his course, but German unification would empower those in Moscow who had always opposed glasnost and perestroika.

The September 1989 meeting between the two leaders was one of the most remarkable of the Cold War. The Iron Lady and the leader of the 'evil empire' were at one in their opposition to German unification. For a political lifetime Thatcher had argued that the freedom and democracy seen in the West belonged to all the peoples of Europe, from the Atlantic to the Urals. Confronted with the possibility that the goal was within reach, she was now prepared to make extraordinary compromises with her principles. Realpolitik counted above the rhetorical commitment to freedom, hard-edged calculations of interest above conviction. The official British note of the conversation between the two leaders gives a flavour of Thatcher's concerns about any premature move towards German unification: 'Mr Gorbachev said that he could see what the prime minister was driving at. The Soviet Union understood the problem very well and she could be reassured. They did not want German reunification any more than Britain did. It was useful that the matter had been raised and that he and the prime minister knew each other's mind on this delicate subject.'[39] The Russian record, written by Gorbachev's adviser Anatoly Chernyaev, offers a much sharper summary. It notes that such was the prime minister's sensitivity about what she was about to propose that she asked at one point for the note-takers to stop.[40] Chernyaev filled in the gap immediately after the meeting had ended.

Thatcher's words were those of a leader stranded by the advance of history. 'Britain and Western Europe are not interested in the unification of Germany,' the note records her saying. 'The words written in the NATO communiqué may sound different, but disregard them. We do not want the unification of Germany. It would lead to changes in the post-war borders, and we cannot allow that because such a development would undermine the stability of the entire international situation and could lead to threats to our security.' For four decades the West had done its best to challenge the legitimacy of the communist regimes in the Soviet Union's satellite states; now Thatcher promised a change of course. Of course, nations such as Poland and Hungary must be allowed to make their own domestic choices but, as Thatcher said, 'We are not interested in the destabilisation of Eastern Europe or the dissolution of the Warsaw Treaty either . . . we are in favour of those processes remaining strictly internal; we will not interfere in them and spur the decommunisation of Eastern Europe. I can tell you that this is also the position of the US president.'

This was a truly extraordinary démarche. Just a year earlier, Thatcher had fired her famous fusillade against the plans of Jacques Delors, the president of the European Commission, for a federal Europe. Brussels, she said, must stop looking inwards: 'We must never forget that east of the Iron Curtain, people who once enjoyed a full share of European culture, freedom and identity have been cut off from their roots. We shall always look on Warsaw, Prague and Budapest as great European cities.'[41] But now the revolutionary had become a reactionary. As great tears appeared in the fabric of the Iron Curtain, Thatcher was assuring the leader of the Soviet empire that she would do nothing to spur the decommunisation of these great nations. Charles Powell skipped over most of this in the formal record of the talks, which was distributed widely across government. But a separate note, restricted to just a handful of people in Whitehall, echoed Chernyaev's account. On the flight back to London, Thatcher invited the travelling journalists to join her for a glass of champagne. A regular on these flights, it was the only time I can recall her doing so on such a trip. She was in an ebullient mood – fizzing almost – and gushing in her praise of Gorbachev. Nothing was said of the private part of their conversation. Within weeks of her return, the Berlin Wall had fallen.

Thatcher was not alone in her fears. The stand-off between the United States and the Soviet Union bestowed a certain stability on the international system. The communist threat in many respects unified the West and encouraged awkward questions of history to be put to one side. Sir Patrick Wright, the permanent under-secretary at the Foreign Office, wrote in his diary of the prime minister's growing 'Germanophobia'. Thatcher was apparently 'appalled to see pictures of the Bundestag singing "Deutschland über Alles", which she described as "a dagger in my heart"'.[42]

The French president François Mitterrand hailed from the same generation of Europeans, for whom the prospect of a powerful, unified Germany stirred visceral fears. When he met with Thatcher at the European Council meeting in Strasbourg in December, he encouraged talk of a new Anglo–French entente to contain German power. Kohl, Thatcher said, seemed to have forgotten that 'the division of Germany was the result of a war Germany had started'.[43] Mitterrand spoke of the threat of a Germany 'pressing forward' as it had done during the 1930s. The president's words marked a false dawn. The Foreign Office diplomat David Hannay was in the British delegation's room when she returned from the meeting. '"It's wonderful," she said. "He [Mitterand] agrees. We're going to stop this nonsense about Germany."' Hannay and others suggested caution: 'Prime minister, don't believe a word . . . When the chips are down, the French will stand with the Germans.' The French president was indeed an unreliable ally, too shrewd in the end to be left trailing behind events. The prime minister soon found herself isolated. For all the doubts he expressed, Mitterrand concluded that unification was unstoppable. The answer was to contain Germany within Europe. France would use Kohl's hopes of unification as a bargaining chip to press its demands for the creation of the single European currency proposed by Jacques Delors. Critically, Thatcher also found herself on the opposite side of the argument to Washington. Reagan had gone. President Bush's administration had decided it would go with the grain of history. Once Bush threw himself behind unification, the argument was lost.

Thatcher did not give up immediately. In Hurd's explanation: 'She did not seriously believe that Chancellor Kohl was a new Hitler or that a united Germany would coerce Europe into a Fourth Reich under the jackboot. But she argued that unification would unbalance Europe by adding fifteen million disciplined Saxons and Prussians to what was already Europe's leading economic power.' More than that, 'Nothing had entered her own life to erase vivid memories of the German past. She did not believe that Germany would subordinate itself to a process of European integration.'[44] In March 1990, a group of academics were summoned to Chequers to offer a historical perspective. A note summarising the discussion written by Charles Powell makes plain the depth of Thatcher's concerns, while the scholars took a more sanguine view. The historian Timothy Garton Ash recorded that 'the overwhelming message of all the historians present was that the Federal Republic, as it had proved itself over forty years, must be trusted and supported in carrying through the unification of Germany in freedom'.[45] The simple fact of the seminar, however, was seen in Bonn as a measure of Thatcher's hostility. Three months later, Nicholas Ridley, one of Thatcher's favourite ministers, gave an interview to the *Spectator* magazine in which he called the plans for a single currency 'a German racket designed to take over the whole of Europe'. He was not against pooling sovereignty in all circumstances, but 'not to this lot. You might as well give it to Adolf Hitler, frankly.'[46] The resulting furore forced Ridley's resignation from the cabinet, but the real damage lay in the widespread belief in Washington and Europe that he was giving voice to the prime minister's own instincts.

William Waldegrave, then a middle-ranking Foreign Office minister, later remarked that the Thatcher government's attempts to derail German unification had been 'one of the sorriest episodes in British diplomatic history'. Christopher Mallaby, the British ambassador in Bonn, wrote streams of telegrams to London underscoring the unstoppable momentum towards unification, but Thatcher's foreign policy had detached itself from the government machine. She felt no need for advice; her instincts and prejudices had until now served her well. Her premiership entrenched the primacy of 10 Downing Street in setting foreign policy; global summits put her in close and regular contact with her peers abroad, whether at gatherings of European Community leaders or at the 'fireside chats' held by the Group of Seven leading nations. Thatcher had a deep suspicion that the FCO was often more concerned with the views of its allies abroad than the pursuit of the British national interest. Diplomacy by its nature usually involves some compromise, but Thatcher wanted to 'win'. On this occasion she paid a significant price. Her relationship with Helmut Kohl all but broke down.

German unification inevitably changed the power balance within the European Community. Thatcher refused to admit, however, that the post-war transformation of Germany – its embrace of democracy, an approach to defence verging on pacifism, a rules-based European and transatlantic alliance – marked a permanent shift. Where Thatcher saw a German Europe, others recognised the possibility of a European Germany. The immediate impact of her stubbornness was to leave her on the sidelines of American decision-making. George H. W. Bush and his secretary of state James Baker took on the role of statesmen in steering a path to German unification that was acceptable to both Gorbachev and most Western leaders. Washington's attention shifted from London to Bonn and then to Berlin. Thatcher saw the 'special relationship' as a way to co-opt American power, but at the end of the Cold War, she failed. The opening of the Iron

Curtain diminished Britain's importance in the eyes of American policymakers. Without the threat of communism, the role of faithful military ally lost some of its relevance. As the sole superpower, the United States would appreciate British support, but it would not need it. Thatcher's confidence about Britain's global reach had been seductive. The 1970s had broken the national spirit, and journalists who travelled the globe with the Lady during the 1980s could not recall a prime minister turning so many foreign heads – whether in Moscow's Red Square, while boarding a bullet train in Tokyo or when visiting Reagan in the White House. The magic, though, wore off. The collapse of communism was all she had ever wanted. When it happened, it was the end of her.

8

The Road to Bruges

Margaret Thatcher swept to power in May 1979 as a self-avowed
pro-European, at the head of an overwhelmingly pro-European
party and a nation that had lately voted by two-thirds to one-third
to remain in the European Community. History, language and
culture would ensure that Britain would never fall in love with the
continent, but the nation's pro-Europeans could be forgiven for
thinking the question had been settled. And yet. The seven years
since Edward Heath had signed the Treaty of Rome had been
largely lost – to the international economic turbulence caused by
OPEC's quadrupling of oil prices, to Harold Wilson's in-or-out
referendum in 1975 and to the economic and trade union troubles
that laid low his successor James Callaghan in 1979. Callaghan,
who had succeeded Wilson three years earlier, soon discovered
that the referendum had not bridged the divide within Labour.
The party's far left still regarded the European Community as a
capitalist conspiracy against the working classes and refused to
accept the result. Labour's foreign secretary David Owen produced a defensive post-referendum European strategy aimed
more at defusing internal party dissent than building alliances
with France and Germany. The passionately pro-European Roy
Jenkins was sent to Brussels to head the European Commission,
but he represented a lone voice among his colleagues in London.
The founding members had already come to suspect British
motives. When ministers backed further enlargement of the
Community to include Portugal, Spain and Greece, Paris and
Berlin suspected an attempt to dilute Franco–German ambitions

to deepen integration among the existing members. They feared 'wider' was being promoted as an alternative to 'deeper'.

Thatcher's Conservatives, installed with a secure majority in the House of Commons, were presented with an opportunity to make Britain's voice heard. Much later, she would suggest that her support for European engagement had been rooted primarily in economics – in the desire to be part of a burgeoning common market. This was a gloss on history that the record does not support. On the contrary, at the outset the Lady shared the hard-headed perspective that had prompted Harold Macmillan to lodge Britain's first application and Edward Heath to steer the nation into the club in 1973. Thatcher laid out the argument as clearly as any of her predecessors when, newly elected as Conservative leader, she campaigned for a 'Yes' vote in Wilson's referendum. 'The paramount case for being in', she told the House of Commons in April 1975, 'is the political case for peace and security.'[1] That security was a matter 'of working closely together on trade, work and other social matters which affect all our peoples. The more closely we work together in that way, the better our security will be from the viewpoint of the future of our children.' Europe would not be a substitute for the nation state, but 'it is only when we get and work together that we can achieve the larger objectives which we are seeking to achieve'.

Partnership in Europe, Thatcher continued, was vital to the preservation of Britain's place as a significant power on the world stage, because 'as a nation of fifty-five million, we would have some voice, but not enough'. Traditionally, Britain had been part of a larger grouping, but many of the Commonwealth nations had now set up their own trading preferences. 'It became vital that as those markets closed down, so we should be able to open up markets of equivalent or greater capacity elsewhere.' Lest anyone miss the point: 'The Community opens windows on the world for us which since the war have been closing. It is already strong and already a major influence in the world.'[2] Britain might now be a European rather than a world power, but by staying in the European Community it would retain a platform from which it could promote and defend its global interests. This was the case for engagement that had prompted Macmillan and Wilson to lodge the first applications to join. Membership was a multiplier of the nation's influence.

Four decades later, pro-Brexit Conservatives who styled themselves as heirs to Thatcher would seek to turn this argument on its head. Britain, they would say, could only recover a global role if it cut free from Europe and struck out on its own. Europe was redefined as a zero-sum game. The Lady herself would surely have scorned what Brexiters called 'Global Britain' as an empty proposition, but by the time of the 2016 referendum, English nationalism had brushed aside banal political truths.

The officials who greeted Thatcher in Downing Street would soon realise, however, that her attachment to the European Community was one of cold calculation rather than emotion. Heath had been prepared to imagine Britain's place in a federal Europe. His successor was an Atlanticist. Other leaders made an emotional connection to the European idea, but Thatcher, in the description of Charles Powell, 'thought the motivations of the Germans and the French were not ones we shared. That they had to, as neighbours, get together and hold hands . . . but we were a great partner with the United States.'[3] Europe mattered, but standing up to Soviet communism mattered most – and for that Britain needed a sure ally across the Atlantic. Whatever the Europeans did together, it must never be allowed to undermine NATO.

No one during that summer could anticipate the tempests that lay ahead. For Prime Minister Thatcher, Europe would become the place during the next decade where conflicting and contradictory impulses gathered and collided. The regular summits with other European leaders would show her both at her determined best and her belligerent worst. Europe would throw up the most curious, and ultimately lethal, paradox of her premiership. Here was a prime minister who would, through her enthusiasm for the single market, take Britain deeper into the process of European integration than her predecessors had ever imagined, and yet, even as she did so, she would also set a path for the nation's eventual departure.

Britain's natural place in the EEC might have been alongside France and Germany, setting, as one of three, the essential strategic direction of the Community. Its ties with Paris and Berlin would always struggle to match the intensity of the Franco–German partnership, yet both of those nations had good cause to forge a strong relationship with London. France and Britain had been friends and rivals since time immemorial and had for the last century been on the same side whenever it really mattered. France's view of the Community as an intergovernmental enterprise – a *Europe des patries* – rather than the supranational entity preferred by Germany, Belgium and the Netherlands, left it closer to London than to Bonn. If anything irked Thatcher, it was the adroitness with which French politicians managed to wrap up the single-minded pursuit of their own national interest in grandiloquent rhetoric about European construction. Germany's Atlanticism and its preference for liberal, open markets led it to regard Britain as a useful foil against France, and the feeling was mutual. France's decision in 1966 to leave NATO's military command structure had unsettled Bonn, testifying as it did to the abiding French suspicion of most things American. Greece,

Spain and Portugal would soon join the Community; the more members it had, the more ungainly the decision-making would become, unless a clear direction was set by the more powerful members. As a result, Heath and Callaghan had toyed with the idea of seeking an informal directorate.

Beyond Thatcher's personal coolness, two things conspired against the creation of such a troika. One lay in a genuine British grievance: the economic and industrial upheavals of the 1970s had left it as one of the poorer members of the Community in terms of income per capita, yet it was second only to Germany in terms of its financial contributions to the Brussels budget. The problem was a holdover from Britain's late entry to the European club. The design of the Common Market had belonged to France and Germany. The former insisted that an elaborate system of import tariffs and internal subsidies would serve the interests of French farmers, while the latter ensured that the emergent industrial powerhouses in Germany would have easy access to the markets of its neighbours. To make matters worse, once British entry began to seem inevitable, the French government had rushed to ensure that a new financial system for the Community was put in place before British accession.

The result was that Britain made a hefty financial contribution to the Community, while receiving relatively little back in the form of payments to its small agricultural sector. It had joined a club in which others had already set the rules to their own advantage. The problem had been recognised when Wilson sought to re-negotiate the terms of membership ahead of the 1975 referendum, but a deal struck to iron out the distortion had failed to make an impact. By 1979, transitional arrangements that had reduced the British contribution were coming to an end. It seemed obvious in London that a formula was needed that would cut the annual

238

contribution to Brussels and include a mechanism that would deal with the problem in the longer term. Unsurprisingly, other members were in no hurry to see their own payments rise – or subsidies to their farmers cut – for the benefit of Britain.

The second obstacle to closer engagement was one of political culture and temperament. In the House of Commons, politics is combat by another name. The Community's way of doing business is by consensus, even if it occasionally requires behind-the-scenes arm-twisting. The European Coal and Steel Community and the Common Market were products of a determination to put an end to war. The Brussels institutions – the Commission, the Council of Ministers and the Parliament – were structured to promote compromise. In Germany, this culture was wired into a post-war Federal Constitution designed to ensure the dispersal of power. Elsewhere, proportional voting systems encourage coalition-building within national assemblies. In Britain, the winner-takes-all electoral system promotes adversarial politics.

This clash of cultures was reinforced by the character of the new prime minister and the response of her European colleagues. Thatcher was a leader in search of enemies. She believed that decades of mushy compromise and a refusal to make hard choices lay at the heart of the nation's problems. Someone had to stand up for what was right, whatever the consequences. Cabinet ministers soon discovered that Thatcher would chair meetings by presenting her preferred conclusions and waiting for others to fall into line. It was soon apparent to fellow prime ministers and presidents that Thatcher's response to finding herself isolated was to relish the fight. British exceptionalism, after all, was at its best when standing alone. Could any other nation have turned a retreat so ignominious as that from Dunkirk into one of the great triumphs of history?

The opening shots in the battle over the budget were fired at a meeting of European Community leaders in Dublin in December 1979. Thatcher's first experience of EEC summitry had been six months earlier in Strasbourg. It had not endeared her to the occasions. The only woman among the nine leaders, she had been patronised by the French president Valéry Giscard d'Estaing. Diplomat David Hannay recalls Giscard's approach: 'It was "There, there, little girl. You don't really understand how this thing works."' Schmidt was also condescending, though 'not as bad as Giscard'.[4] The battle that began in Dublin continued through a procession of twice-yearly summits, until a settlement was finally reached in Fontainebleau in the summer of 1984. In its own terms, the deal was a fair one: a system of automatic rebates would return to Britain about two-thirds of its annual contribution, with the arrangements to remain in place until the next review of revenues and spending. The collateral damage along the way was considerable. The Foreign Office diplomat Stephen Wall would at one point describe the negotiation as 'the most long, drawn-out and bitter battle yet fought in the European Union'.[5] Britain was threatened with the abolition of the national veto that upheld the sanctity of vital national interests – the so-called 'Luxembourg compromise'. The other leaders also came close to bypassing British obstructionism by reaching an agreement outside of the Community's traditional framework. Thatcher never ceased demanding 'our money back'. A dangerous pattern was being set: however much she ranted and raged, Britain was not permitted to block the work of the Community. As Wall would observe: 'The negotiation split the EC as never before, soured Margaret Thatcher's relationship with her fellow heads of government, and led some of them to conclude that Britain was a "bad European".' Hannay is more forgiving: 'No British prime minister I worked for would have got as good a deal as she got.'[6]

Thatcher sometimes seemed to seek out enemies. The show-downs played well to her supporters in the media. Beating up the Germans and standing up to the French made for 'good copy', particularly for the newspapers controlled by Rupert Murdoch. The owner of the *Sun*, the *News of the World*, *The Times* and the *Sunday Times*, as well as Sky Television, Murdoch was a frequent visitor to Downing Street. So too was the equally anti-European Conrad Black, who in 1986 bought the Telegraph Media Group. The fights fitted Thatcher's self-image as a leader ready to take on all comers. In Brussels, her style jarred. The cost was a loss of confidence and trust. In 1982, *The Times*, which Murdoch had bought the previous year, was still taking a pro-European line. 'We are not bad Europeans,' it offered, 'unless we choose to present ourselves that way.'

Much of Thatcher's cabinet took the same view. As Chancellor of the Exchequer and then as foreign secretary, Geoffrey Howe pressed hard to blunt her belligerence. He was no starry-eyed European federalist, but he was attentive to the wider strategic importance of membership and understood that the purpose of the European enterprise was to create economic opportunities and improvements to security from which all would benefit. The best and brightest Foreign Office diplomats were kept busy defusing prime ministerial hand grenades, when they might have been building strategic alliances to advance British interests on her behalf. As the years passed, Thatcher found herself an increasingly lonely figure at EU summits. She was included in fewer and fewer of the informal bilateral get-togethers on the margins of the formal gatherings. The fault was not always on her side – the Council had more than its share of egos. But why, she seemed to say to herself, should she make the effort?

Giscard d'Estaing, France's president during the first two years of her premiership, was one of those French politicians for whom the phrase '*de haut en bas*' was invented. The writer Victor Hugo once remarked of Wellington's defeat of Napoleon at Waterloo that it represented 'the complete, absolute, dazzling, incontrovertible, definitive and supreme triumph of mediocrity over genius'. Giscard showed a similarly Olympian disdain for the nuts and bolts of politics. Aloof and self-aggrandising, he was a man for grand designs. The budget debate was one of those squabbles to be settled 'below stairs'. Thatcher reminded him, he was reported as saying, of his childhood nanny. Her relationship with François Mitterrand, Giscard's socialist successor, involved a hint of mutual fascination. The prime minister, Mitterrand once remarked, was a woman with 'the eyes of Caligula and the mouth of Marilyn Monroe'.[7] Thatcher later wrote that she thought him 'a self-conscious French intellectual, fascinated by foreign policy, bored by detail, possibly contemptuous of economics'.[8] She liked him, and she appreciated the early and unstinting support he offered following the Argentine invasion of the Falklands, which put to shame the hesitation of Ronald Reagan's Washington. There would never be a meeting of minds between the two leaders over Europe. For all France's determination to hold on to its national traditions, the Community was the place where it exercised European leadership and held Germany in check. In the minds of the French political elite, more Europe meant more France.

For a time, Thatcher established something of a rapport with West Germany's Helmut Schmidt, a social democrat, but one, to her mind, with sensible market-friendly and anti-communist instincts. She admired the resolve with which he backed the deployment in Europe of short- and medium-range Pershing and cruise nuclear missiles. However, Schmidt had no time for her complaints about the budget, and by Powell's account, he switched off. As for Mitterrand, 'He ostentatiously did other things, and used to spend his time at European Councils writing postcards to his grandchildren.'[9]

Schmidt's replacement in 1982 by the outwardly ungainly but politically much underrated Helmut Kohl produced at best a polite working relationship. On the face of it, that should have been otherwise. Kohl, like Thatcher, was a staunch Atlanticist. As much as Germany valued the European Community as the expression and guarantor of its break with the past, Kohl understood that the continent's security rested on America's presence as a bulwark against Soviet communism. Personal chemistry, or the absence of it, was a problem, according to Powell: 'He brought out in her all her fears about Germany. It was his manner, I think. It was the blustering, the being blustered by a German.'[10] Thatcher, Powell continues, would often regret behaving badly towards Kohl, but 'That's what it was. It really goes back to her source of fear, never properly articulated, that somehow Germany would rise again and behave as it had under Bismarck and the Kaiser and Hitler.'

The two drew different conclusions from their Atlanticism. For Thatcher, the imperative was that Europe avoided any action that might encourage the Americans to reduce their presence. Kohl, by contrast, saw no such contradiction: his vocation was to build what Thomas Mann had described as a 'European Germany' to put to rest fears of a 'German Europe'. He judged that the best way to persuade the United States to retain its commitment to the security of the continent was to demonstrate that Europe would play its part in the fight against communism.

Informal post-mortems following Thatcher's four-year budget fight heard some of the cleverest Whitehall officials conclude that it had been the only way to force Britain's partners – and France in particular – to budge. The sanctimonious refusal of other leaders to discuss net contributions to the Brussels budget was a convenient cloak over efforts to defend their own national interests. Britain's hefty payments to Brussels suited its partners, who saw their own contributions capped as a consequence. Against that, Thatcher's insistence that all she was demanding was the return of 'my money' underscored a fundamental difference in perspective. The argument for '*juste retour*' – the principle that nations should take out of the Community as much as they put in – offended the idea of solidarity and presented the Community budget as a zero-sum game.

As she battled for the British rebate, her fellow leaders were hatching plans for what the French often called 'the construction of Europe'. A decade earlier, the leaders of 'the Six' had signed up to a plan to turn the Community into the European Union. Among the ambitions was the creation of a single European currency. The project had been ratified three months before Britain formally joined, but Edward Heath had added Britain's name to the goal at the Paris summit in the autumn of 1972. As the idea resurfaced, along with the suggestion that Europe needed a clearer political identity, Thatcher bridled. What did these Europeans mean when they called for the creation of a 'political union'? And why did they want to create an economic and monetary union, when there were still lots of barriers to trade? Part of her scorned what she saw as empty rhetoric. Why couldn't they focus on pragmatic progress, such as creating a 'genuine common market' in goods and services, instead of insisting, as they did at the Stuttgart summit in June 1983, on issuing a new 'Solemn Declaration on European Union'. The clash between British pragmatism and continental vision had existed since the creation of the European Coal and Steel Community, but Thatcher's suspicions now met with a political dynamic in Paris, Rome and Bonn that was calling for another step change in the level of integration. To her mind, the goals ran far ahead of both her own concept of the Community and the readiness of the Tory party to pool national sovereignty. And the more combative she became in Brussels, the more the Eurosceptics in her party expected her to defend British sovereignty.

In the immediate aftermath of the budget deal struck in June 1984 in the grand surroundings of the Palace of Fontainebleau, it seemed that this tension between continental grand vision and British astigmatism could be managed. Britain wanted the completion of the single market, not least because its businesses had more to gain than most from the opening up of continental markets to service industries. Pressed by her ministers and mandarins to show a more constructive face at meetings of the European Council, Thatcher agreed that there had to be more to her European policy than saying 'No'. As she later recorded in her memoir, in the aftermath of the budget settlement she was prepared to couch her own ideas for Europe in language that sounded 'ostentatiously *communautaire*'. In a paper produced soon after the Fontainebleau summit titled 'Europe: The Future', the government called for a drive to create a genuine single market. This would include measures to harmonise industrial standards across the Community, remove non-tariff barriers to trade and promote the mutual recognition of professional qualifications in service industries. To disarm criticism that Britain saw Europe only through the lens of economics, Thatcher also set out plans for an expansion of European Political Cooperation to increase the Community's weight on the international stage. Expanded collaboration in matters of security would serve to strengthen the European pillar of the NATO alliance. Howe had set out a similar programme at the end of 1983, but with the budget dispute now over and Thatcher putting her name to the ideas, it looked for a moment as if Britain, albeit cautiously, was ready to contemplate 'more Europe'.

Hannay, who had been at the centre of the budget negotiations, was among those who believed that it had been essential to resolve the budget dispute: 'We could not have a satisfactory relationship until we had done something about the budget contribution.' The missed opportunity, he added, came after Fontainebleau. 'We never understood that the Franco–German relationship works because they did actually make concessions to each other. We never made any concessions. We just said, "You have to agree with us."'[11]

The convergence was around completion of the single market. Thatcher wanted a true free-trade area. Jacques Delors, the former French finance minister appointed to head the European Commission in January 1985, saw the single market as the platform for a broader push towards closer economic and political integration. Though Delors had not been Thatcher's first choice for the Commission presidency, she held him to be one of Europe's more 'sensible' socialists. Arthur Cockfield, a technocrat with considerable trade expertise serving as a cabinet minister in the House of Lords, was dispatched to Brussels to add British pragmatism to continental dreaming. Agreement on the single market would only temporarily obscure the fundamental difference of vision. Thatcher's future for Europe was essentially intergovernmental. Member states would work more closely together and dismantle impediments to cross-border trade and investment, without transferring much in the way of new authority to Brussels. Delors shared Monnet's vision of European institution-building and the pooling of national sovereignty. And along with the support of Mitterrand and Kohl, he could rely on the enthusiasm of the Italians.

Much later, when Conservative MPs put themselves at the head of the campaign to wrench Britain out of the European Union, they would direct much of their ire towards the mountains of new rules and regulations that underpinned the single market. The Commission and Council had deployed the single-market framework, they would say, in a power grab against governments. Delors had used majority voting in the Council of Ministers to extend the writ of Brussels deep into national life. There were instances that could be cited in support of this proposition. The European institutions, like all bureaucracies, wanted to accumulate power. The Brexiters, however, failed to understand (or pretended not to) that liberalising European markets would have been impossible without significant harmonisation of standards and norms across national borders, and that majority voting in the Council was the only way to disarm national vetoes that would otherwise have distorted the single market to protect favourite industries. Here was a paradox that Eurosceptics could never admit: Thatcher needed Delors. Liberalisation was only possible with greatly increased European regulation.

Thatcher's attempts to contain changes within the existing treaty were overwhelmed by Delors's energy, the ambitions of Kohl and Mitterrand and the keenness of Italian governments for European integration in order to stabilise their domestic politics. In 1985, the Italian prime minister Bettino Craxi assembled a majority of the member states for an intergovernmental conference to set the next steps towards a more cohesive Europe. Thatcher was outvoted at a summit in Milan in June 1985 and outflanked at a second gathering in Luxembourg in December. The Single European Act, which she signed in February 1986, set the goal of establishing a comprehensive single market by December 1992. It also revived the ambition of economic and monetary union, set the framework for cooperation in foreign policy and embedded freedom of movement as one of the pillars of economic integration. Some of this was just rhetoric, but the new treaty signposted the future direction of the Community and gave a foretaste of disputes to come. Kohl told the Bundestag that the leaders had 'taken a decisive step' towards closer integration. Above all, the summit threw into sharp relief the gap between the grand ambitions of some nations and the pinched incrementalism of the British. Thatcher later said she had underestimated the momentum; Delors, she observed ruefully, had emerged as 'a major player in the game'.[12]

'It thus looks like our damage limitation exercise is heading for success,' noted John Kerr, as the latest draft of the prime minister's speech was circulated in the Foreign Office.[13] Kerr, one of the brightest stars in Whitehall, headed the European department. A mandarin's mandarin, he excelled at Whitehall politics. Much of his department's time was spent damping fires started in Downing Street. In this particular case, the aim was to take away the fire-lighters from Number 10 before the event. Thatcher was scheduled to deliver the speech at the College of Europe in Bruges on 20 September 1988. Three months earlier, Delors had been appointed to lead a committee of central bankers that would map the route to a single European currency. Thatcher planned to mark out the chasm between what she saw as her own common-sense, practical Europeanism and the daydreams of those who imagined that vaulting rhetoric and grand visions would eventually lead to a 'United States of Europe'.

The first draft, written by Charles Powell, had fired a broadside at the federalists, gratuitously adding that Britain had done a better job than the French or Spanish in managing its withdrawal from empire. Powell had joined Number 10 from the Foreign Office some five years earlier, but what had been intended as a secondment had become something closer to a vocation. Powell's loyalty was to the prime minister rather than to his erstwhile department. He admired her courage and convictions and had an uncanny ability to anticipate her preferences. As draft followed draft, the language was softened. As Kerr indicated, most of it, while true to Thatcher's unflinching objections to anything faintly federal, remained within the bounds of what her fellow leaders would expect. The flavour was Gaullist rather than anti-European:

> My first guiding principle is this: willing and active
> cooperation between independent sovereign states is the best
> way to build a successful European Community. To try to
> suppress nationhood and concentrate power at the centre of a
> European conglomerate would be highly damaging and would
> jeopardise the objectives we seek to achieve. Europe will be
> stronger precisely because it has France as France, Spain as
> Spain, Britain as Britain, each with its own customs, traditions
> and identity. It would be folly to try to fit them into some sort
> of identikit European personality.[14]

De Gaulle could scarcely have complained. Kerr, however, had relaxed too soon. A couple of extra sentences were added by Number 10. Bernard Ingham, the prime minister's press secretary, flagged them to the media. They amounted to a scorching blast at Delors's ambition to build what Thatcher feared would be a superstate. Two weeks earlier, he had enraged the prime minister by extolling the role of 'social Europe' in a speech delivered at the annual conference of the Trades Union Congress in Brighton. Now came her retort: 'We have not successfully rolled back the frontiers of the state in Britain only to see them reimposed at a European level, with a European superstate exercising a new dominance from Brussels.'

Later, the Bruges speech would be seen by many as marking the point when Thatcher turned her back on Europe. Her words were explicitly otherwise: 'Britain does not dream of some cosy, isolated existence on the fringes of the European Community. Our destiny is in Europe, as part of the Community.'[15] Thatcher had not decided to leave; rather, she had found a new enemy to be vanquished. What she might not have realised was that she had given a licence to the hardening Euroscepticism in her own party and also for the right-wing media to turn their criticism of the Community into a crusade. Thatcher had been Murdoch's ally in breaking the power of the British printing unions; now they could make common cause against the 'statism' of Europe. The headline that filled the front page of the *Sun* set the battle lines: 'Up Yours Delors'.[16] The problem, Kerr would later say, was how difficult it was to get Thatcher to settle when every possible concession had been won from her fellow leaders. 'All you men! You are so weak!' she had shouted at her officials during one summit.[17] The reproach was directed at allies such as the Netherlands' Ruud Lubbers, as well as her own advisers. This was the same Margaret Thatcher who now settled an Anglo–French argument that had rumbled along for over a century. She agreed with François Mitterrand that the two governments should build a physical link between their nations. Construction of the Channel Tunnel began in the same year as her speech in Bruges. Europe had become her new battleground.

'I won't have the Belgians decide the value of the pound!'[18] Margaret Thatcher's outburst startled the guests at a private reception at Westminster in 1989. Hosted by the political journalists at

Westminster known collectively as 'the Lobby', it was a convivial affair. The mood shifted when a journalist had the temerity to suggest to the prime minister that she might soon be obliged to concede to the demands of her chancellor Nigel Lawson and agree to fix the pound's exchange rate against those of other European countries in the European Monetary System's Exchange Rate Mechanism (ERM). The Lady was visibly agitated. Lawson was wrong, she exclaimed. The media should pay less attention to briefings from the Treasury. Didn't they know that governments could not 'buck' the foreign exchange markets by fixing a rate for the pound? Her reason for singling out the 'Belgians' as the villains at such moments was never quite clear. The message was unambiguous: 'You shouldn't pay attention to the Treasury' was a reminder that the constitutional order was that the prime minister held the title of First Lord of the Treasury. Thatcher was not going to be bounced into a decision by the chancellor, even one so powerful as Lawson. Britain would never be part of Delors's grand project to replace national currencies with a single one. Thatcher had spent the previous few years selling off much of the state. The 'pound sterling', as she would often call it, was a national birthright. Each and every one of her predecessors since 1945 had been obliged, only sometimes successfully, to confront pressure to devalue the pound. The need to prop up sterling had been a constant brake on the economy. Yet for Thatcher the currency remained the vital emblem of national sovereignty.

True, she had been spared the speculative attacks on sterling that had tormented her predecessors. By the time she reached Downing Street, the taps had been opened on North Sea oil production. Rising oil and gas revenues freed Britain from the balance of payments crises that had haunted other post-war governments. James Callaghan would soon be reflecting ruefully that the economic and financial tide began to turn as soon as he signed the IMF agreement in 1976. By the early 1980s, the flow of petrodollars from the North Sea had put an end to the current-account and public borrowing crises. To the extent that the Thatcher government had a problem, it was that during her early years the pound had risen too far and fast. The prime minister's market-friendly economic policies, a ferocious squeeze on public spending and borrowing and her battles against the trade unions saw the pound return to favour among international investors. By the mid-1980s, however, sterling was being caught up in the foreign exchange turmoil caused by wild swings in the value of the dollar. The Treasury's experiment of steering the economy through the use of targets for the money supply had ended in dismal failure. As the economy boomed – stoked by Lawson's tax cuts – the Treasury looked to a stable pound as an anchor for policy. Lawson encouraged Thatcher to back sterling's membership of the Exchange Rate Mechanism, which provided fixed but periodically adjustable exchange rates for European currencies. Callaghan's government had signed up to the goal of exchange rate stability when the system was established in 1978, but had declined to fix a rate for sterling. While in opposition, Thatcher had mocked Callaghan as overly timid. Once in government, however, she had put the issue to one side.

An early apostle of the crude monetarism that had guided economic policy during the early 1980s, Lawson had watched the relationship between control of the money supply and the suppression of inflation collapse. A sharp rise in the value of the pound had made exports uncompetitive, and Britain lost a large slice of its manufacturing industry to foreign rivals. By the second half of the decade, Lawson had another problem. Eager to display his credentials as a reforming chancellor, he had stoked a fiscal expansion alongside a deregulatory boom – a surge in consumer credit and spending that would soon turn to economic bust. His priority was to stabilise the economy. He decided that the last weapon in his armoury was to fix the pound's value against the Deutsche Mark. The ERM allowed for some flexibility: sterling could move up and down within agreed limits and, if economic circumstances changed, the government could seek the agreement of other members to alter the rates.

The imperative for Lawson was to restore the credibility of the government's anti-inflation policy by associating the pound's fortunes with the solidity of the Deutsche Mark. For Thatcher, this was a step too far. She saw the ERM as a move towards the single currency that Delors was seeking. In truth, Lawson's attempt to link the pound's value to that of the Deutsche Mark, the franc, the lira and other currencies had nothing to do with the single-currency project. He shared the prime minister's deep antagonism for the Delors blueprint, but badly needed a credible framework for his economic policy. And he did not intend to be thwarted by the prime minister.

The battle over sterling between Thatcher and Lawson was waged over two years, with the chancellor attempting to 'shadow' the Deutsche Mark even as his prime minister blocked any formal move to join the ERM. On the chancellor's instructions, the Bank of England was told to intervene whenever sterling threatened to move outside the notional ERM band the Treasury had set. Though Thatcher was never officially told of the policy, she could scarcely have been unaware of Lawson's defiance. All the while, Mitterrand and Kohl pressed ahead with their plan for a European currency. As they began to make a reality of the single market in goods and services, Britain's partners expressed a new confidence that a currency union would herald Europe's arrival as an economic superpower. Lawson was a politician accustomed to getting his own way. His clash with Thatcher was about ego as well as the ERM. He enlisted the support of Geoffrey Howe. The foreign secretary had his own fears that Thatcher's increasingly strident opposition to any proposal from Brussels was taking Britain out of the European mainstream. In the summer of 1989, ahead of a European summit in Madrid, the two ministers met the prime minister in Downing Street to present her with an extraordinary ultimatum: if she didn't soften her views on the ERM, they would quit. Thatcher was forced into a tactical retreat. Treachery, she would later call it.[19]

No other ministers had been more central to Thatcher's project than Howe and Lawson. As chancellor throughout her first term, Howe had launched the programme of economic liberalisation that was to become the trademark of Thatcherism. He had kept his nerve amid the political backlash to a tough anti-inflation squeeze that had seen unemployment rise to an unheard-of three million. Mild-mannered, thoughtful and instinctively loyal, as foreign secretary he had sought to temper the prime minister's more destructive instincts, particularly during her battles in Brussels, and to open her mind to a less confrontational approach to the Soviet Union. He had ratcheted up notable successes on both counts but had never positioned himself as a threat to her authority. As the years passed, he was to discover that the reward for careful, intelligent logic was a response from the prime minister that measured on a scale from scornful to hectoring. The dressing-downs, absorbed without visible fuss by Howe, were not confined to their private meetings. Ministers and Whitehall officials alike would express themselves deeply embarrassed by the prime minister's habit of humiliating him in front of cabinet colleagues. 'She's a bully, plain and simple,' one of her senior officials remarked at the time.[20] Thatcher would later say that Howe had been too timid. Worse, he had been taken prisoner by the Foreign Office, a department to her mind more eager to please overseas governments than its own.

Yet she also feared that he was plotting against her. The passage of time and her churlish treatment of colleagues left her increasingly alone in Downing Street. And with isolation came paranoia. Howe, she thought, might topple her. Lawson provided intellectual heft and political gusto for the policies of privatisation and deregulation that signalled the decisive break with what was known as the 'Butskellite' post-war consensus. As self-confident as any in the cabinet, he showed none of Howe's diffidence. 'Nigel was well aware of his own virtues,' Thatcher would write in her memoir.[21] She had little to complain about: by selling off old state-owned utilities and liberalising the financial markets, Lawson gave form to her promise of a 'people's capitalism'.

Howe grew tired of picking up the crockery smashed during Thatcher's fights with Europe. Victory in the 1987 general election had cemented Thatcher's view that she was at once indispensable and invincible. Her autocratic style had seen the angry resignation of the defence secretary Michael Heseltine in 1986. Heseltine, one of the 'big beasts' of the cabinet and an obvious candidate for the future leadership, was passionate about British engagement in Europe. His presence on the backbenches at a time when the prime minister's disdain for Brussels was rising prefaced the emerging European divide within the Tory party. She felt less and less need for the advice of her ministers. Douglas Hurd, successively home and foreign secretary, would put it politely: 'Her very success was spoiling her judgement. She was less inclined to listen to anything but applause. In her the brake which in all of us imposes a pause between what we think and what we say was wearing dangerously thin.'[22]

In turn, the cabinet was increasingly reluctant to risk Thatcher's wrath by challenging her judgement. Downing Street began to resemble a regal court, an impression amplified by Thatcher's constant use of the royal 'we'. Some of those in her immediate circle – Charles Powell, her press secretary Bernard Ingham and one or two political aides – from time to time dared to offer contrary advice. Few others took the risk. During 1988, the government legislated to replace local authority property taxes – 'the rates' – with a new flat-rate community charge. Lawson spoke out against the change, telling her it was political 'madness'. Most of his colleagues saw the political danger of replacing a tax that was linked to the value of a property with a flat charge that would be paid at the same rate by dukes and dustmen alike, but they chose to save their courage for fights about their own departmental plans. When the poll tax was introduced, the people took to the streets, rioting in London and refusing to pay elsewhere. These angry protests would play a significant part in Thatcher's fall. She was not listening, insisting instead that there was 'work to be done' and that she planned to go 'on and on'.

Soon after the Madrid ultimatum, she took her revenge by moving Howe from the Foreign Office. Handed the role of leader of the House of Commons and the honorific of deputy prime minister, he was sidelined. To neutralise Lawson, she recalled to 10 Downing Street her former economic adviser Sir Alan Walters. He in turn made it plain that the government was not going to be seduced by the ERM. By the autumn of 1989, Lawson had resigned in protest at Walters's meddling. Political reputations are fragile things. Two years earlier, Lawson had been hailed as the guiding intellectual force in the government.

Thatcher's economic revolution was picking up imitators across the world, but it was going wrong at home. As growth stuttered to a halt and inflation soared, Lawson's legacy recalled a pattern familiar from the post-war decades: boom followed by inflationary bust. For her part, Thatcher was at once politically weakened and unwilling to temper her own instincts. The collision with her fellow European leaders, she would say later, was between two competing visions: her own of an open Europe of free enterprise, and the other of federalism, *dirigisme* and bureaucracy. It was also personal. John Kerr: 'Actually, the thing that really mattered was that she and Kohl did not hit it off. She didn't like him, and he didn't like her.'[23] In the autumn of 1990, her frustrations boiled over. Reporting to the House of Commons on the conclusions of a summit in Rome, she offered a parody of Delors's ambitions for a European superstate. And her answer to the Commission president? 'No, no, no!' she told MPs.[24] In Geoffrey Howe, something snapped.

Many years earlier, the Labour cabinet minister Denis Healey had compared Howe's parliamentary performances to being 'savaged by a dead sheep', yet Howe's short resignation speech in November 1990 was among the most devastating to be delivered in the House of Commons. 'The prime minister's perceived attitude towards Europe is running increasingly serious risks for the future of our nation,' he began. 'It risks minimising our influence and maximising our chances of being once again shut out.' Then followed a wounding description of how she treated her own ministers: 'It is rather like sending your opening batsmen to the crease, only for them to find, the moment the first balls are being bowled, that their bats have been broken before the game by the team captain.'[25] In a few words, Howe crystallised the anger and discontent that was running from the Tory backbenches to the cabinet.

Thatcher's isolation within her own government was matched by a popular backlash beyond Westminster against the poll tax and a darkening economic outlook. The Tory party is nothing if not ruthless. Three election victories counted for less than the prospect that she would lead the party to defeat in a fourth. Heseltine challenged her for the Tory leadership, and Thatcher failed by a small margin to win a decisive victory from Conservative MPs in the first ballot. Summoned one by one, a majority in the cabinet told her she would lose in the next round. After more than eleven years in Downing Street, she accepted her premiership was over. John Major and Douglas Hurd joined the contest, the former denying Heseltine the prize. On the day of her resignation, Thatcher reported to the Commons on her attendance at the Conference on Security and Cooperation in Europe, the gathering of international leaders that marked formally the passing of the Cold War. The Iron Lady could at least claim the end of Soviet communism. Her bravura performance that day – 'I'm enjoying this,' she exclaimed at one point – saw ministers staring at their feet as they sat crammed side by side on the front bench of the Commons. 'What Have They Done?' asked the headline in the *Daily Express*.

The answer would unfold over decades. The guiding emotions of Tory Euroscepticism still betrayed feelings at once of superiority and insecurity. The first was rooted in the exceptionalism of Britain's 'island story'. It could make its own way in the world without falling in with its neighbours. The second was fearful: Brussels was a dastardly plot calculated to subvert its freedoms and stifle its ambitions, but Britain could not afford to be left behind. From her starting point as a confident supporter of engagement in Europe, Thatcher had come to cleave to both of these emotions. With her resignation, the first fatal shots had been fired in the Tory civil war that more than a quarter of a century later would see Britain wrench itself out of Europe. Thatcherism and Euroscepticism merged. Her supporters would never forgive her defenestration.

9

The Bastards

The British journalists kicking their heels in the Dutch town of Maastricht during the early hours of a cold December morning in 1991 expected bad news. The summit talks among European leaders had run deep into the night. They were there to settle the terms of a new 'Treaty on European Union', and the expectation was that John Major would be either isolated or steamrollered into submission by his European partners. Instead, when a bleary-eyed Downing Street official finally appeared at the press centre, he was triumphant. It was 'game, set and match' for the prime minister. The treaty, at its heart a grand political bargain between France and Germany at the end of the Cold War, set out the path to a single European currency and a significant extension of the Community's remit into political and security affairs. Major himself hailed the accord as a great British success. 'We have surrendered nothing and we have lost nothing,' the prime minister said of the treaty. After months of tension, the talks had ended with handshakes rather than recriminations.

It was a victory of sorts. Maastricht, though, would also prove an inflection point in Britain's engagement with its own continent, the moment when the Conservative Party became consumed by 'Europe'. The treaty settled at Maastricht put in place the three-stage process that would lead by the end of the decade to the replacement of the Deutsche Mark, the French franc, the Italian lira and other European currencies with the euro. It created two new pillars of cooperation between European governments: in foreign policy and security, and in judicial and home affairs. It also established a remit for Brussels in the setting of social and labour standards across the Community – 'social Europe', Britain's fellow members called this. To signpost the widening of its responsibilities beyond economics, the European Economic Community was formally renamed the European Union. The agreement also codified the concept of European citizenship, distinct from the national identities bestowed by individual member states. None of the above were projects that could claim the enthusiastic support of Major's Conservative government. On the contrary, Britain was opposed to the single currency and the extension of social standards, and at best lukewarm about a bigger European role in foreign, defence and judicial affairs. The victory Major was claiming was essentially a negative one – about what Britain had avoided rather than what Europe had achieved.

In the exuberant view of his official, the prime minister had squared the circle. The triumph, as Downing Street saw it, was one of British exceptionalism. The rest of the Community was determined to take a new leap towards integration. The single currency was France's price for its consent to German unification, broader political cooperation Germany's price for agreeing that the Deutsche Mark could be subsumed into the euro. Britain had secured sufficient opt-outs and institutional protections to give it the best of both worlds. It could stand aside without sacrificing its place, and voice, in the councils of Brussels. For Major, the critical provisions exempted Britain from an obligation to join the euro – it could make up its mind when the proposed single currency was within plain sight – and left it permanently outside the remit of the Social Chapter. Maastricht formalised the new European strategy, allowing Britain to stand aside from projects viewed as inimical to national sovereignty, while ensuring it maintained its influence. Kim Darroch, a Foreign Office diplomat, recalls a sense that the government had found a new framework for the relationship. 'It felt that we were building a kind of model to British exceptionalism in the new European landscape. That we were able to have it both ways.'[1]

The strategy was driven by Tory party politics. Margaret Thatcher's implacable hostility to the single currency had been an important catalyst in her downfall. Her Eurosceptic supporters on the Tory backbenches, however, had since regrouped under her standard. Anticipating the party's future troubles, Maastricht had been preceded by a difficult negotiation between the prime minister and the Eurosceptics in his own party – some of them, such as the employment secretary Michael Howard, in the cabinet – about just how much he could agree to. The Maastricht balancing act, Major judged, would disarm the critics.

Thatcher, consumed with resentment about her defenestration and upset by Major's more positive tone towards Europe, had not made life easy for her successor. Just three months into his premiership, in March 1991, he was seeking the sympathy of US president George H. W. Bush. The two were meeting in Bermuda, and Bush was keen to be briefed on the progress of the negotiations that would lead to Maastricht. It was a mess, Major confided. Thatcher, he told Bush, objected to his closeness to the Germans. Monetary union was a big problem. The French wanted to tie Germany into Europe, and Kohl wanted to show that Germany was a good European. Major thought he could not win. At Maastricht, it seemed he had pulled it off.

Major's experience of foreign policy was slight. He had spent only three months as foreign secretary in 1989, before Thatcher moved him to the Treasury. Events allowed him precious little time to learn on the job when he replaced her in November 1990.

Within two months, he was taking the nation to war. A British military force of some 45,000 had been assembled in Saudi Arabia to support the American-led coalition preparing to expel Saddam Hussein's Iraqi army from Kuwait. Saddam seized control of the small Gulf state in August 1990, and had since defied calls from the United Nations Security Council to withdraw. Thatcher was prominent among those prodding Bush to lead the international effort to remove him by force. 'This is no time to go wobbly, George,' she famously told the president in a telephone call at the end of August, amid suspicions in Downing Street that senior members of his administration, including secretary of state James Baker, were overly hesitant about the use of force.

The debates between the White House and Downing Street continued into early November, when Baker travelled to London. The president, Baker told the prime minister, was determined to secure another United Nations resolution to provide unambiguous authority for military action. In his report of the encounter for Bush, Baker said that Thatcher remained 'very sceptical'. She warned that setting a deadline for Saddam would increase the risk of a chemical weapons attack on allied forces and that a new UN resolution would invite amendments that 'would restrict operational freedom'. A dozen years later, these roles would be reversed. It was Tony Blair who pressed George W. Bush to seek explicit United Nations approval before the second Gulf War. The failure to secure it fuelled debate about the legality of the war. In 1990, the elder Bush, defying Thatcher's impatience, secured precisely such a second resolution, bestowing on the conflict a legitimacy that was sorely absent in 2003.

The relationship between Major and Bush was the comfortable one of two politicians who shared a careful, deliberative approach to decision-making. The military success of the first Gulf War was preceded by an intense diplomatic effort by Washington to build the widest possible international coalition against Saddam. By the time the war began in January 1991, more than thirty-five nations backed the coalition. Beyond Saudi Arabia, those contributing troops included nations as diverse as France, Syria, Pakistan, Egypt, Australia and Canada. Critically, the military operation was halted once the Iraqi troops had been expelled from Kuwait. The elder Bush decided to resist the temptation to force regime change. The chaos across the region in the wake of the toppling of Saddam by George W. Bush in 2003 testified to his father's wisdom. For his part, the immediate aftermath of the 1991 war also saw Major score a significant diplomatic success. Defeated by the coalition, Saddam turned on Iraq's minority Kurdish communities. Indiscriminate attacks on the Kurds were soon leading television news bulletins across the world. In April, the prime minister presented to a European Community summit in Luxembourg a plan, to be enforced by Western air power, to create 'safe havens' for the Kurds within Iraq. After securing the backing of other European governments, he took the idea to Washington. Britain's view of itself as a bridge between Europe and the US typically saw it acting as a spokesperson for Washington in Brussels. Stephen Wall, the Foreign Office official serving as Major's private secretary, noted subsequently that the Kurdish initiative 'was one of very few occasions on which a British prime minister has acted as a bridge *from* Europe *to* the United States'.[2]

Most of the time, however, the traffic on the transatlantic bridge continued in the other direction. When Major met with Bush at Camp David in December 1990, the new prime minister was at pains to assure the president that Britain was opposing proposals tabled by France and Germany to transfer to the European

Community more responsibility for coordinating defence policy – a development that the Americans feared would undercut
NATO. Major said he had tabled counter-proposals to limit closer
European coordination to the Western Economic Union (WEU)
– an organisation that deferred to NATO. 'I don't favour the EC
having a defence role,' the White House note of the meeting
recalls Major saying. 'There may be neutrals in it [the European
Community], like Austria, that make it inappropriate . . . We do
not share the grand ambitions of some for an EC defence role.'
Three months later, when the two leaders celebrated victory in
the Gulf War at their meeting in Bermuda, Major shared his concerns that Britain might be unable to blunt the Franco–German
initiative, telling Bush that the defence proposals had a head of
steam, with Kohl seemingly supportive. The big problem was
France. Mitterrand was determined to press ahead, and Kohl was
no match for the French president.

Thatcher played the martyr for the swelling ranks of Tory
MPs who cheered her Boudicca-like defiance of the foreigners
on the other side of the Channel. Rupert Murdoch was, if anything, even more hostile to all things European. Conrad Black,
the Canadian-born owner of the Telegraph Media Group as
well as the weekly *Spectator*, encouraged Thatcher in her charge
of treachery against the ministers and MPs who had removed
her. So the victory of the pro-Europeans who had led the calls
for her departure was short-lived. Thatcher's nemesis Michael
Heseltine was as committed as any to be found in the Tory party
to Britain's place at the top table of European decision-making.
A richly successful self-made businessman, his resignation during
the Westland affair in 1986 had been a proxy for the European
struggle. He had wanted orders for military helicopters to be
placed with a European consortium, as the best way to protect

Britain's high-technology defence capabilities against absorption by American defence giants. Thatcher had wanted the order to go to the Americans. The argument marked out the ground on which she would eventually fall.

Heseltine saw Europe, as Thatcher once had, as a partner in rebuilding Britain's economic strength. Thatcher considered herself the agent of national rejuvenation. European 'corporatism' was an enemy of her let-the-market-rip approach to Britain's established industries. Thatcher was never a conservative in the small 'c' meaning of the word – a politician attentive to tradition and long-established institutions, civic engagement and little platoons. Her impulses – whether to smash the trade unions, privatise great swathes of the state, deregulate the City of London or champion the individual over notions of society – were those of a politician seeking enemies. As time passed, Europe became enemy number one. A new generation of recruits attracted by Thatcherism nudged Tory MPs in the same direction. As traditionalist 'Shire' Tories retired, their seats were more often than not taken by MPs marching under Thatcher's ideological standard.

The Lady had misread her successor. Major, cabinet colleagues would remark ruefully, had 'risen without trace', carefully avoiding at every step ideological labels that might make him enemies. 'He's whatever you want him to be,'[3] the campaign manager for another of the contenders to replace Thatcher remarked when the contest was under way. There was nothing soft about Major. In his insider's account of the European battles of successive British governments, the former diplomat Stephen Wall refers to him disposing of his enemies with a 'stiletto'.[4] For all that he was skilled at exuding reasonableness and common sense, Major had known hard times. The son of a music-hall performer who had grown up in Brixton in south London, he had no patience with fellow ministers who dismissed society's less fortunate as authors of their own troubles. 'He doesn't know what it is like to run out of money on a Thursday,' Major remarked acidly of Nigel Lawson.[5]

His views about Europe were essentially pragmatic. He was no Euro-dreamer, but nor was he the Eurosceptic Thatcher had imagined when she anointed him her chosen successor. His choice of Heseltine as his de facto (and later formal) deputy, the reappointment of the pro-European Douglas Hurd as foreign secretary and the choice of Chris Patten, a leading one-nation Tory, as Conservative Party chairman signalled that at the very least he wanted to repair the bridges with European partners blown up by Thatcher.

The goal, Major said in a speech in April 1991, was to put Britain 'at the heart of Europe'. Relations with Germany's Helmut Kohl were quite easily repaired. Major had none of the visceral fear of German power that kept his predecessor awake. As for the broader relationship with Europe, Major's view was grounded in realism. As he put it to the House of Commons in a debate rehearsing the negotiations at Maastricht: 'There are, in truth, only three ways of dealing with the Community: we can leave it, and no doubt we would survive, but we would be diminished in influence and prosperity; we can stay in it grudgingly, in which case others will lead it; or we can play a leading role in it, and that is the right policy.'[6] While Thatcher opposed the creation of a single currency on ideological grounds, Major's view, according to Wall, was grounded in realpolitik: 'Major saw that in some form the Euro was inevitable, and he was not going to fight an unwinnable battle to prevent Britain's partners from going ahead if they were so determined.'[7]

The change of tone did not dissolve suspicions in Bonn or Paris. It did persuade Kohl and Mitterrand to accept compromises that accommodated Major's political difficulties. Major, with his eyes on wayward Tory MPs, secured agreement that cooperation in foreign policy and defence should take place within a new 'intergovernmental' pillar of the Community, separate from the supra-national institutions in Brussels. National governments would retain a veto over decision-making. The same arrangement was agreed for the increased coordination of national policies directed against cross-border crime and terrorism. The explicit exemption of Britain from the Social Chapter further rewarded the change of rhetoric and the warmer tone. In succeeding years, fears harboured during the 1990s that the Community's push into foreign and defence policy undermined the transatlantic alliance were proved groundless. The WEU was quietly dissolved and the 'pillared' structure of Maastricht was dropped in subsequent treaties. Tony Blair would succeed in persuading the United States that a more coherent European approach to defence could strengthen rather than weaken NATO. Yet Major's success at Maastricht concealed an abiding tension. Britain could scarcely claim to be 'leading' Europe into the post-Cold War world when it was opting out of its most ambitious project. More immediately, Major soon enough discovered that negotiating Maastricht was much easier than navigating its passage through the House of Commons.

Four months after Maastricht, Major's general election victory defied the opinion polls that predicted that after thirteen years of Conservative rule, the voters were set on change. The nation had still to shake off the hangover from Nigel Lawson's economic boom, and the Labour leader Neil Kinnock had by most assessments done enough to restore the party to electability after its lurch to the left during the early 1980s. Beyond taking a more centrist economic stance, Kinnock had abandoned the policy of unilateral nuclear disarmament and reshaped Labour as a pro-European party. The social programme pursued by European Commission president Jacques Delors, the cause of the ire in Thatcher's Bruges speech, had rehabilitated Europe in the eyes of many on the left. Once seen as a capitalist club, Delors had rebranded it as a guardian of social standards. The voters, however, still harboured doubts about Labour's economic policies, and at the election they judged that the change from Thatcher to Major had been sufficient.

Major's victory was bittersweet. Thatcher won the 1987 election with a majority of 102; Major secured a margin of only twenty-one. That meant the government could be held hostage by a small number of its own MPs. Elevated to the House of Lords, Baroness Thatcher was ever more hostile to most things European. With a fair wind, Major might just have sustained the delicate balancing act he had pulled off at Maastricht. Events conspired against him. In June 1992, Denmark voted against ratification of the treaty in the referendum mandated by its constitution. This put the future of the treaty in doubt, as it could come into force only after each of the twelve governments had ratified it. The Eurosceptics demanded that in the wake of the Danish 'No', Britain should also decline to ratify. Then, just three months later, Major's government was hit by a financial hurricane.

The markets christened 16 September 1992 'Black Wednesday'. It was the day on which Major in effect lost the general election that he would fight nearly five years later, in 1997. The wall of international speculation against the pound broke the Bank of England, put $1 billion into the hands of currency speculator George Soros and, within a few hours, stripped Major's government of its credibility as a competent guardian of the economy. Sterling's devaluation and Britain's forced departure from the European Monetary

System's Exchange Rate Mechanism would prove a turning point in the Tory civil war over Europe. Major's defeat at the hands of the currency markets saw Tory antipathy towards the European Union solidify into the beginnings of the uprising that led to Brexit. With the Tory rebels mobilising against Maastricht, the government's failed attempt to keep the value of sterling tethered to the Deutsche Mark marked out the road for Tony Blair's victory five years later. Beyond that, there was a straight line to the referendum conceded by David Cameron on Britain's place in the EU. The reward was reaped in 2016 by Boris Johnson, Michael Gove and their band of Brexiters.

Thatcher had agreed to British membership of the ERM during the autumn of 1990, just weeks before her ejection from office. Weakened by the loss of Lawson, the unpopularity of the poll tax and darkening economic clouds, she had conceded to the advice of her then chancellor Major that the Treasury had run out of other options in its efforts to stabilise the economy after Lawson's inflationary bust. The economy was heading into recession and inflation was still close to 10 per cent. The crude monetarism embraced by the Treasury during the early 1980s had been thrown onto the intellectual scrap heap. The economy needed a reliable anchor against inflationary storms if the government was to restore its credibility. Fixing the pound's value against the Deutsche Mark, the argument ran, would rebuild the confidence of financial markets. The pound would fluctuate within fixed margins either side of a fixed rate of DM2.95. The initial impact of membership was encouraging. Inflation began to decelerate and interest rates were cut. And then things went wrong. The strains imposed by unification upturned Germany's policy priorities. The independent Bundesbank was focused on containing the inflationary pressures thrown up by the Federal Republic's absorption of the former East Germany. In Britain, recession and rising unemployment replaced inflation as the main challenges. So while the right policy prescription for Germany was relatively high interest rates, the rational approach in Britain pointed to cuts in borrowing costs. By the summer of 1992, this tension was playing out as pressure for a devaluation of sterling within the ERM.

Major had moved temporarily to Whitehall's Admiralty House during refurbishment of 10 Downing Street. Security in the prime minister's official residence was being upgraded after an IRA attack on the building had seen a heavy mortar explode in the garden, only yards from the Cabinet Office. The temporary accommodation, however, lacked the communications equipment – press agency news screens and markets data, secure telephone lines and the rest – normally available to the prime minister. The absence of timely information gave an almost comic quality to the crisis when ministers were summoned to respond to the storm that broke over sterling on 16 September. Kenneth Clarke, the home secretary, would later recount that, kicking their heels in the dark while Treasury and Bank of England officials rushed to and from Admiralty House, one small group of waiting ministers had sent out for a small transistor radio to keep track of the drama unfolding in the currency markets. Eddie George, the deputy governor of the Bank of England, arrived from Threadneedle Street clutching a small handset that displayed minute-by-minute exchange rate movements. Norman Lamont, the chancellor, darted back and forth from the Treasury.

Twice Lamont announced emergency increases in interest rates in an attempt to stem the flight from the currency. Nothing happened. In truth, the battle had been lost long before Major had summoned his cabinet colleagues to Admiralty House. They were there, Clarke would later say, simply to put their 'hands in the blood' – to share responsibility for the biggest economic defeat for the government since Callaghan's humiliation at the hands of the International Monetary Fund.[8] By early afternoon, when all were agreed that the game was lost and sterling could no longer be tied to the Deutsche Mark, the Bank of England had run out of money. It had been propping up the pound for months via secret arrangements with other central banks, notably the Bundesbank. In the first two weeks of September alone, the Bank had spent some $30 billion from its gold and foreign currency reserves in the attempt to hold the line. When the sums were finally done, they showed that for the first time since the war, the Bank's reserves showed a net deficit – to the tune of $14 billion. Buying back dollars and gold with a devalued pound cost taxpayers, at the Treasury's conservative estimate, some £3 billion. Senior Whitehall officials put the true cost at £5 billion. Politics counted for more than the numbers. The price of the 1976 IMF crisis had been Labour's defeat in the 1979 general election. The result of Black Wednesday was the shredding of the Major government's reputation for economic competence, the arming of his party's Eurosceptics and, in due course, an electoral defeat in 1997 to match that of Labour's Callaghan in 1979.

As had happened with Attlee in 1949 and Wilson in 1967, pride came before the fall. Linking the currency to the Deutsche Mark in 1990 had looked like sensible economics, but given the subsequent divergence of the two economies, it should have been obvious by 1992 that the chosen rate of 2.95 Marks was unsustainable. Britain needed lower interest rates to pull the economy from recession, while Germany was forcing rates up to pay for reunification. The answer should have been orderly realignment, with sterling fixed at a lower rate. Major's mistake was to mark out devaluation as defeat. The more aggressively the markets tested the government's commitment to defending the existing parity, the more immoveable he became. Days before Black Wednesday, speaking to Scottish members of the Confederation of British Industry, the prime minister bet the bank, and his reputation, on holding the line. 'All my adult life', he told the industrialists,

> I have seen British governments driven off their virtuous
> pursuit of low inflation by market problems or political
> pressures. I was under no illusions when I took sterling
> into the Exchange Rate Mechanism. I said at the time that
> membership was not the soft option. The soft option, the
> devaluer's option, the inflationary option, in my judgement
> that would be a betrayal of our future at this moment, and I
> tell you categorically that is not the government's policy.[9]

He mocked Wilson's devaluation in 1967, before recalling the words of the great economist John Maynard Keynes: 'There is no subtler, surer means of overturning the existing basis of society than to debauch the currency.' 'Debauch the currency': these were words to haunt him.

Black Wednesday was a foreign policy failure as much as an economic one, as clear an indication as could be imagined of a profound failure in Whitehall – mostly on the part of the Treasury – to engage properly with European partners. The pound was not the only currency under pressure. The French franc was in trouble, and the Italian lira had succumbed to devaluation. A broader adjustment followed sterling's departure. What this should have said to British ministers and officials was that the months and weeks leading up to Black Wednesday were a time to coordinate policy with fellow members of the ERM and, at the very least, to work closely with the German government and the Bundesbank. Instead the government stood aloof. The chancellor Norman

Lamont had never been an enthusiast for the ERM. Nor had he made an effort to build relationships in Europe, and as the crisis unfolded he did nothing to win friends and allies. On the contrary, to the extent that he engaged with his counterparts, he sought to browbeat Germany – and in particular the president of the independent Bundesbank Helmut Schlesinger – into cutting German interest rates, in the hope that this would reduce pressure on the pound. The exercise was entirely counter-productive. The Bundesbank did not take instructions from German politicians, let alone from a foreign government. Senior Treasury and Bank of England officials were equally reluctant to engage with their continental counterparts. The idea of building strong personal ties with the Europeans defied the Treasury's we-know-best instincts. It saw itself as a cut above mere continentals. The markets' final onslaught against the pound on Black Wednesday was triggered by some disobliging remarks about the solidity of the pound's value made by Schlesinger in the course of a newspaper interview. It was never entirely clear whether he was surprised by the market onslaught that followed.

Tory Eurosceptics were soon hailing the pound's devaluation as a moment of liberation rather than humiliation – proof, they said, of the dangers of attempting to fix exchange rates. The economic upturn that followed the pound's fall was held up as a signal that Britain should step back from its entanglements with the European Union and avoid any participation in the single currency. In truth, Black Wednesday marked another chapter in the sorry history of sterling's post-war slide. Successive devaluations did nothing to improve the competitiveness of the economy. Germany's superior economic performance was built on a strong currency. When the new Federal Republic was established, one pound sterling bought about twelve of the new Deutsche Marks;

by 2018, a pound was worth about two. None of this troubled those who were hostile to European engagement. Sterling was held to be a badge of nation. Black Wednesday had shown how dangerous it would be to join the proposed single currency. 'Save the pound' became the Eurosceptics' rallying cry.

The 'bastards', John Major called them. It was July 1993, and in his long battle to secure ratification of the Maastricht treaty, the prime minister had just survived a vote of confidence in the House of Commons. Major gave an interview in Downing Street to ITN's political editor Michael Brunson. The television lights had been switched off, but the tape was still running when the anger and frustration boiled over in an off-the-record, post-interview conversation with Brunson. The 'bastards' were the cabinet ministers who colluded with the rebel Tory MPs who had fought to derail ratification of the treaty. He did not name them, but political journalists were in no doubt as to their identity. Major had fumed against Michael Howard, Peter Lilley and Michael Portillo in private conversations with journalists at Westminster.[10] The exchange with Brunson, recorded by technicians at the BBC waiting to film another interview, revealed the poison that infected the upper reaches of his government. Asked by Brunson why he did not sack disloyal ministers, Major responded that he was hamstrung by his small majority in the House of Commons: 'We don't want another three more of the bastards out there. What's Lyndon Johnson's maxim?' The American president had decided against dismissing his FBI chief J. Edgar Hoover on the grounds that 'it's probably better to have him inside the tent pissing out than outside pissing in'. Major was in no doubt about Thatcher's role in stirring the rebellion. The 'bastards' were harking back to a golden age that had never existed.

The confidence vote was the last in a series of parliamentary battles that had begun more than a year earlier, in May 1992, when twenty-two Conservative MPs rebelled against the Maastricht Bill. The passage of the legislation had been suspended after the 'No' vote in the Danish referendum but was revived after that country reversed its decision in a second referendum. The Labour opposition, now led by John Smith, was in favour of the substance of the treaty, but the various opt-outs negotiated by Major provided political cover to take an opportunistic view of the votes in parliament. If the choice was between upholding its European credentials and bringing down the government by derailing Maastricht, Smith would choose the latter course. Repeated attempts to ambush the government as the legislation progressed through the House of Commons saw open collusion between the opposition and the growing number of Conservative rebels – encouraged all the while by Thatcher and, only slightly more discreetly, by the 'bastards' in Major's cabinet. Thirty Tory MPs joined the revolt at some stage in the passage of the legislation, while another ten abstained. The government's majority held only with the support of opposition MPs who were prepared to break with their own party leaders. In July 1993, the rebels inflicted a defeat on the government. Major rescued the legislation only by presenting it again in the form of a vote of confidence which, had he lost, would have left the Tory rebels responsible for forcing a general election the party was certain to lose. The government's opinion poll ratings, badly damaged by Black Wednesday, had slumped still further, and by-election defeats had already chipped away at its thin majority.

Surviving a scare that saw it backed only by the narrowest of margins in a referendum in France, Maastricht set in motion the creation of Europe's single currency, with Britain duly exercising its opt-out. Major had prevailed, but he had little to celebrate in his parliamentary victory. The battles over Maastricht had hardened anti-European opinion within the Tory party. Thatcher now presided over the sceptics as founder and patron of the 'Bruges Group', so named to recall her 1988 speech. For many of her supporters, fealty to the fallen leader and hostility to Europe were now fused in a mission to win control of the party. Norman Lamont, sacked as chancellor, derided Major as 'in office but not in power'.[11] Michael Portillo, the most ambitious of the 'bastards', was shameless in his preparation for a leadership bid. The sceptics had become a party within a party, and some of them were more intent on pulling back from Europe than sustaining the Conservatives in office. Backbench MPs such as William Cash, Iain Duncan Smith and Bernard Jenkin found their way into the television studios as torch-bearers for a movement that before too long would replace hostility to a particular European treaty with the demand that Britain quit the Union altogether.

For optimists in the West, the end of the Cold War and the largely peaceful dissolution of the Soviet Union created an unprecedented opportunity. The defeat of communism had been a triumph not just for the market economies of the capitalist West but for liberal democracy. The American political scientist Francis Fukuyama captured the mood in a best-selling book. *The End of History* foresaw the inexorable march of Western values across the world. The United States would act as the benign hegemon, guaranteeing security in an international system governed by rules. The European Community, or so many of its politicians thought, would serve as a 'normative' power, exporting its model of post-nationalist democracy and cross-border collaboration first to the new democracies in eastern and central Europe emerging from the former Soviet empire and later to its Middle Eastern and African neighbours. Painted with the broadest of brushes, this brave new world left behind both the nineteenth-century balance-of-power model of international relations that had ended in two world wars and the bipolar Cold War confrontation between two competing economic and political systems.

The optimism was not without cause. The demise of the Soviet Union had broken the Cold War deadlock in the United Nations Security Council, where resolutions tabled by the three permanent Western members – the United States, Britain and France – were no longer routinely vetoed by Moscow. China, following the path mapped by Deng Xiaoping, was beginning to integrate itself into the international economy. And the former communist states were lining up to be members of the European Union. George H. W. Bush's coalition-building and deference to the United Nations in the build-up to the first Gulf War gave further cause for hope. The demise of the Soviet Union left the United States as the sole superpower – the '*hyperpuissance*', in the description of the French foreign minister Hubert Védrine – but the hope was that it would use its power to underwrite the multilateral system.

As it turned out, what Bush declared to be a new international order was fracturing even as Fukuyama's book climbed the bestseller lists. The secession of Slovenia and Croatia from Yugoslavia during 1991 heralded a number of brutal Balkan wars marked by nationalism, ethnic cleansing and murderous attacks on civilian populations. The Serbian regime of Slobodan Milošević stood at the heart of much of the killing, most particularly in its brutal effort to block independence for Muslim Bosnia-Herzegovina. But this was a conflict without innocents, with atrocities inflicted on all sides and, by the end, one costing more than 130,000 lives. The United States and Europe offered a series of diplomatic initiatives and peace plans but intervened decisively only after outrageous acts of ethnic cleansing – including the massacre in 1995 of more than 8,000 Bosniaks by Bosnian Serbs in Srebrenica – sufficiently outraged Western public opinion.

Britain contributed peacekeeping troops to the United Nations' half-hearted attempts to separate the combatants and negotiate a political settlement. The RAF participated in sporadic NATO bombing strikes against Serbian forces threatening the UN force. Two former foreign secretaries, Peter Carrington and David Owen, were appointed successively to the role of United Nations mediator. But British policy leaned throughout towards caution. Douglas Hurd, the foreign secretary, was consistently reluctant to seriously confront Milošević's attempts to carve out a greater Serbia from the ruins of the former federation, taking territory from Croatia and Bosnia and absorbing Kosovo. In spite of the flagrant violation of international law, charges of genocide and the chilling echoes of the past evoked by the wholesale murder of communities on grounds of ethnicity, the British government judged the Balkans as being of limited strategic interest. At times, and in the familiar template of their relationship as friends and rivals, there was a measure of diplomatic and military cooperation with France, the other principal contributor to the peacekeeping force. But the government's focus was on avoiding action that might put the British peacekeepers at risk or drag Britain deeper into a multi-sided civil war.

British caution did nothing to warm the Major government's distinctly cool relationship with Bill Clinton, the new occupant of the White House. Major had hoped that Bush would secure a second term, and his support for the Republicans had not been lost on Clinton. Soon after defeating Bush in the 1992 election, Clinton had got wind that the Republican campaign had secured the help of Conservative Central Office in digging for information about his time as a Rhodes Scholar in Oxford some twenty years previously. While the Conservative Party looked for evidence that Clinton might have been involved in anti-Vietnam demonstrations, the Home Office was reported to have checked to see if the president had applied for UK citizenship in an effort to escape the Vietnam War draft. Major, who had been unaware of the cooperation, wrote to offer Clinton a personal apology.[12] In February 1993, a month after the presidential inauguration, he was duly rewarded with an invitation to the White House. The meeting was cordial, but the Clinton team made no secret of the fact that America looked to Germany and, to an extent, France as the key players in post-Cold War Europe.

Tensions in the relationship increased as Major, in tandem with the Irish prime minister Albert Reynolds, sought to start peace talks in Northern Ireland by drawing the republican side into a cease-fire. At the end of 1993, under pressure from the Irish-American lobby in Congress, Clinton lifted a long-standing bar on Gerry Adams, the leader of Sinn Fein, visiting the United States. The president's decision to grant Adams a visa overruled the advice of his State Department and the American ambassador in London, Raymond Seitz, and flew in the face of the US's policy towards organisations responsible for acts of terrorism.[13] It was seen in Downing Street as political game-playing at the moment when the government was seeking to maximise pressure on Sinn Fein to put aside its arms. The fury bubbled over in a note written by Roderic Lyne, Major's foreign policy adviser, to Anthony Lake, Clinton's national security adviser. Adams, Lyne said, was a leading figure in a movement that had 'murdered not only thousands of its own countrymen, but also one member of our royal family, one cabinet minister's wife, two close advisers to Margaret Thatcher and members of parliament, two British ambassadors – and small children in our shopping centres'.[14] Clinton claimed that by granting Adams a visa he had pushed him towards an IRA ceasefire. The following year, he became the first American president to visit Northern Ireland, and he later took a prominent role in Tony Blair's peace effort in the province. In the eyes of the Major government, however, his motives owed more to domestic politics than a genuine commitment to the Anglo–Irish peace process.

The Balkans were the source of a still deeper transatlantic breach. Kim Darroch, then an official in the British team dealing with the conflict, describes the episode as a 'massive European failure'. Darroch, who went on to become the chairman of the National Security Council and ambassador in Washington, says there was blame on all sides: 'We and the French put forces in, but with terms of engagement and a mandate that was such that they eventually became human shields for the Serbs as they conducted ethnic cleansing through Bosnia.'[15] The Americans were 'enraged'. Clinton declined to commit any American ground forces but wanted instead to lift, in the case of Bosnia, the United Nations arms embargo imposed at the beginning of the conflict and step up air strikes to halt Serbian advances. Major opposed a policy that Hurd suggested would simply create a 'level killing field'. Darroch continues: 'We had some of the most difficult encounters with the Americans I think we've had. They were accusing us basically of providing political cover for ethnic cleansing. We were saying: "Easy for you to say that from 33,000 feet. Why don't you put some people on the ground?"' The veteran American diplomat Richard Holbrooke, called in by Clinton to launch a new diplomatic initiative, sought to rebuild relations. But it took the Srebrenica massacre in the summer of 1995 to bring about the heavy NATO air attacks that forced Milošević to the negotiating table. Under Holbrooke's direction, the Dayton Accords in

November 1995 brought the fighting to an end. Repairs to the transatlantic bridge would have to wait until Tony Blair's election victory in 1997.

Major's relations with Europe were not much easier. The price of his success at Maastricht and a dwindling majority in the House of Commons was effective imprisonment by his own party. Beyond the hardcore sceptics who wanted to roll back the process of integration, a growing number of Conservative MPs had concluded that they would reject anything else that smacked of a transfer of national competencies to Brussels. The steady stream of backbench MPs who paid homage to Thatcher at her Belgravia apartment were encouraged to harass the government at every European turn. Major found himself on the margins in the councils of the Union. The replacement of the socialist Mitterrand by the centre-right president Jacques Chirac brought some warming of relations with Paris, but, as after Suez, Britain and France were heading in different directions. In Germany, Kohl's initial hope for Major's premiership turned to disappointment.

In mid-1995, the prime minister made a dash for freedom. He sought to shore up his premiership by resigning as Conservative Party leader and inviting opponents to challenge him. The Eurosceptic John Redwood picked up the gauntlet. Major won the ballot with the support of two-thirds of the parliamentary party, but that was not enough to restore his authority. Now defence secretary Michael Portillo planned to enter the fray but hesitated at the last moment. His ambitions, though, were undimmed and undisguised. He joined those waiting for Major's defeat in the election due by 1997. Before that, estrangement in Europe turned first to farce and then to humiliation. In 1996, an outbreak in British cattle of the lethal BSE, or mad cow disease, saw governments across the world impose a ban on imports of

British beef and beef products. The European Union did likewise. The Tory Eurosceptics, cheered on by Rupert Murdoch's and Conrad Black's newspapers, took the ban as a declaration of war. No such charge was laid against the United States, which had also barred imports of British beef. Major was panicked into a policy of non-cooperation in Brussels, instructing ministers and officials to block new initiatives and regulations until the ban was lifted. The absurdity of the strategy was evident almost as soon as it was announced. Before long the British ambassador in Brussels found himself vetoing measures that the government itself had initiated and steered through the EU's institutions. The policy was dropped behind the fig leaf of a European promise that all restrictions were strictly 'science-based'. Britain's standing in the EU had never fallen so low. Its partners were planning for the future. The imminent entry into the Union of Finland, Sweden and Austria required new treaty changes. Beyond that, governments were drawing a route map for the eventual admission of former communist states, including Poland, Hungary and the Czech Republic – a policy that both Thatcher and Major had championed.

For Britain's partners, enlargement meant new treaty provisions – and an opportunity to revise and strengthen the decisions made at Maastricht. Major had no room for manoeuvre. Stephen Wall was the senior British representative on the committee set up to negotiate the changes. Each week he would receive instructions from London as to the position he should take. The Foreign Office could have saved itself a lot of trouble, he later noted, by sending a one-line message: 'Just say "No".'[16] There was never anything on the agenda for which the government thought it could secure a majority of its own MPs.

For their part, the Eurosceptics were looking beyond the widely expected defeat at the hands of Tony Blair's Labour Party. Major was harried at every turn in Westminster and given not an inch of room to negotiate in Brussels. His anger and frustration poured out in private conversations with journalists about the treachery of cabinet colleagues. 'Bastards' now seemed a rather mild expression of his fury. The history and traditions of the Conservative Party had long seen power prized over ideology. Now a sizeable faction were prepared to hand over power to Tony Blair rather than compromise their loathing of the EU.

10

Back to the Desert

Tony Blair had been out of office for nearly a decade when the panel chaired by Sir John Chilcot delivered the official verdict on the war that wrote his political obituary. The conclusions of the Iraq Inquiry, published in the summer of 2016, were no less devastating for the interval. Blair had been Labour's most successful leader, winning three consecutive general elections. During a decade in office, he had remade the rules of centre-left politics, taking his party into political territory long owned by the Conservatives. Like Margaret Thatcher, he was among that select group of leaders who, rather than bending to the prevailing political winds, decide to change the weather. No matter. Tony Blair was also the prime minister who took the nation to war in Iraq.

In 2.6 million words filling twelve volumes, Chilcot and his colleagues laid bare every detail of the political bravado, systematic intelligence and diplomatic failures and military misjudgements that in 2003 saw Britain join the United States in the ruinous adventure to topple Saddam Hussein's regime.[1] The culprits? A powerful prime minister swayed by self-righteousness and driven by the conviction that Britain must stay close to Washington; a Secret Intelligence Service under a leadership that was too eager to please its political masters and stay close to the 'cousins' at CIA headquarters in Langley, Virginia; a flawed legal process; and a government unable and unwilling to plan for the consequences of removing Saddam. Never before had the nation's political and foreign policy establishments been subject to such forensic scrutiny. Iraq, the panel concluded, had been a war of choice. Saddam had posed no direct threat to the nation's security. The war was the product of messianic leadership, Chilcot argued, coupled to a 'sofa' style of decision-making in Downing Street that allowed the prime minister to bypass the traditional constraints of cabinet government. And once Saddam had been defeated, the occupation of Iraq had been bungled at almost every turn.

Chilcot, a former top civil servant, eschewed hyperbole and name-calling. Those – many of them in his own party – who charged that Tony 'Bliar' had wilfully tricked the nation into an illegal invasion were disappointed. Yet the absence of malice served to amplify the severity of the panel's judgements. No, Saddam's supposed weapons of mass destruction (WMD) were not an invention of the prime minister and his Downing Street clique. But neither, as Chilcot would say, had Blair been entirely 'straight' with the nation about the potential threat. He had been too eager to fall in with the plans of President George W. Bush; too ready to exaggerate the evidence he was receiving from the intelligence agencies; too sure of his own capacity to secure the explicit consent of the United Nations for the invasion; and too careless of post-war planning. The government's legal opinions at best had been massaged. Blair, in a favourite phrase, had decided that war was 'the right thing to do'. The prime minister's sin, and it was a grave one, was one of certitude – the abundant overconfidence and immoveable self-righteousness that substituted personal conviction for the due care a leader owes to the nation before sending its young men and women to war.

Blair has never recanted his view that the world is a better place without Saddam. But, just as Eden's premiership was defined by the calamity of the Suez expedition, so Blair's place in history would be framed by this war in the desert. The prime minister could have waited, Chilcot concluded, until the UN weapons inspectors had been able to conclude their search for WMD. Had he done so, the report might have added, the fracturing of the West could have been avoided. In 1956, Eisenhower's administration had warned Eden not to go to war without the support of the United Nations. The British prime minister had ignored him, and had then been caught in a storm of international opprobrium. In 2003, the tables were turned: it was Blair urging Bush to secure a resolution at the UN Security Council. Bush, like Eden had been in 1956, was impatient. Blair found himself co-conspirator in America's disastrous desert war.

Saddam Hussein had been a small blip on the radar screen when Blair took office in May 1997. The prime minister was an innocent abroad. Untutored in foreign policy and diplomacy, he carried instead a set of instincts. Coming from a new generation of leaders born after the end of the Second World War, Blair was unencumbered by the baggage of his predecessors. Empire was another country; Blair had been only six years old when Harold Macmillan gave his 'Wind of Change' speech announcing the dissolution of what remained. By temperament and political calculation he cast himself as a leader for the future. 'New Labour, New Britain', the 1997 general election slogan ran. There was no room for pipe-and-slippers nostalgia.

To the extent to which he had said anything about the world during his spell as leader of the opposition – his campaign for Number 10 had been rooted overwhelmingly in domestic politics – it was entirely conventional. 'Boilerplate stuff,' one high-ranking diplomat would say.[2] The two main partnerships for Britain were the European Union and the transatlantic relationship, he said in a speech in 1995. 'We need to use them to maximise our influence so that we can promote and protect our interests around the world, because we cannot do so alone. But to be effective we have to participate fully in each partnership.'³ The Foreign Office nodded in approval. This had been the received wisdom of the nation's diplomats ever since Macmillan had lodged Britain's first application for membership of the Common Market. For Macmillan, combining a close defence and security relationship with the United States with political and economic engagement in Europe had been the product of exhaustive calculation; for Blair, it was plain common sense. What the new prime minister added to the traditional formulation was ambition. Foreign affairs appealed to his ego. As Macmillan had observed, 'At home, you always have to be a politician; when you are abroad, you almost feel yourself a statesman.'

Within weeks of the election, Blair was heading to Hong Kong for the celebration of its handover to China. For the previous five years the governor, Chris Patten, had battled Beijing in a bid to entrench democracy in the colony. Blair seemed puzzled by the insistence of President Jiang Zemin that the handover marked the end of 150 years of Chinese humiliation. One of the prime minister's aides later recalled that 'Blair didn't have a clue what Jiang was talking about, not a clue about Britain's role in China.'⁴ All that said, the scale of Blair's election victory gave him a standing among other European leaders that was disproportionate to his youth and inexperience. In 1997, Helmut Kohl was approaching the end of his time in office. The centre-right French president Jacques Chirac found himself sharing power with a socialist prime minister, Lionel Jospin, after the left won control of the National Assembly. Blair and Britain were the zeitgeist. 'Cool Britannia', declared a *Time* magazine story, much to the prime minister's pleasure. Major's constant apology to other European leaders was that he could not carry his own party in the House of Commons; by contrast, Blair's control was near absolute. Like most of his predecessors, he would in time complain about the drudgery of interminable late-night summits in Brussels with his fellow European leaders, but the thespian in him relished the limelight. He invested in building personal relationships, blind to whether his counterparts hailed from the right or left. Spain's José María Aznar, Portugal's António Guterres and Sweden's Göran Persson were among the targets of his charm offensive. To the dismay of cabinet colleagues, he was among the first to congratulate Italy's populist media magnate Silvio Berlusconi on an election victory.

Britain was too small a stage for his talents. And summitry, he would tell visitors to Downing Street, offered a rare freedom. At home, policy choices had to be negotiated – his tense relationship with the chancellor Gordon Brown always came to mind – and, even then, decisions faced the harsh scrutiny of Whitehall's mandarins. Sitting with fellow European leaders in Brussels or in some far-flung retreat with his counterparts in the Group of Eight, he was unencumbered. Blair was also blessed by circumstance. The last years of John Major's premiership had been a miserable time for those who worried about Britain's prestige. Major's attempts to hold together a Tory party that was increasingly riven by division over Europe had seen the government driven to the margins of influence. His relationship with Clinton had been at best strained. Blair had only to smile to win applause.

If Blair was sure of anything, it was that he would not sit on the sidelines. He had been an eager cheerleader for Clinton's brand of centrist politics. The Democrats had won in 1992 and 1996 by staking out the political centre ground, and Labour's election campaign, with its promise to combine a rigorous economic programme with progressive social policies, borrowed heavily from the 'New Democrat' approach. Winning was what mattered. No previous Labour leader had secured two full parliamentary terms, but Blair intended to overturn that dismal record. When a reporter asked Clinton whether he had any advice for the new prime minister, Blair interjected: 'Well, he did one thing very right, which was to win again, and I hope I repeat that.'[5]

But how to win? Clinton was the most gifted politician of his generation, a man of mesmerising charm and an intuitive communicator. Whoever he was talking to – voter, journalist, foreign diplomat – they had no need to be told they commanded his complete attention. When, after a couple of minutes, he moved on, they knew it was only because of the responsibilities of his office. Clinton matched personal warmth with a sharp intellect and an insatiable appetite for knowledge. He devoured works of history, political science and philosophy. Blair, after a time, was almost as quick and as clever. And he knew better than most how to tell visitors to Downing Street what they wanted to hear. But he never matched Clinton's intellectual grasp.

To the extent that Labour's election victory saw a shift in the framework of foreign policy, the impulse at the beginning came from Robin Cook, the foreign secretary. Cook was no Blairite. Hailing from the 'soft left' of the party, he had never been in the vanguard of New Labour modernisers. Fiercely intelligent but an instinctive loner, he was viewed with suspicion by those close to the prime minister. The Foreign Office mandarins were irritated by his impatience with the formalities of office – someone else could meet the new ambassador from Lower Volta. Cook, though, signalled a shift in direction, setting out within weeks of the 1997 election a series of internationalist principles to recalibrate the compass for foreign policy. His addition of an 'ethical' dimension to the Foreign Office worldview attracted scorn from self-styled 'realists' among the foreign policy establishment. Governments cannot choose the states with which they are obliged to do business. And economics often collides with values in the shaping of diplomacy. A thriving business in selling weapons to some of the world's less pleasant regimes and close relationships with wealthy autocrats inevitably threw up the charge of hypocrisy. But Cook's fundamental view that Britain should be a force for good in the world fitted with Blair's expansive instincts. The Iraq War would see an abrupt parting of the ways. But both men believed that Britain had an important role in projecting values in the conduct of foreign policy.

Blair's starting point was that Britain should be a serious player in the geopolitical game. Early on, the ambition could seem gauche. Charles Powell had served as Margaret Thatcher's chief foreign policy adviser, over time becoming the most important figure in her inner circle. As chief of staff, his younger brother Jonathan Powell would play a similar role for Blair. He recounts a stumbling start. Soon after the election they jetted off to Denver, Colorado, for Blair's first meeting of the Group of Eight leaders, this one hosted by his pal Clinton. Powell and the press secretary Alastair Campbell were among the official party. Blair had signalled that he wanted Britain to make its mark at such gatherings. 'We were sitting on the grass in the sun and Tony suddenly said to me and Alastair, apropos of nothing, "Britain should be bigger." We both collapsed in laughter,' Powell recalls. At that point, 'He knew nothing about foreign policy. He wasn't interested in foreign policy – it wasn't his thing. Like all prime ministers, he learned on the job.'[6] Blair also understood the tie with domestic politics. Voters like their leaders to be respected abroad. Nigel Sheinwald was Britain's ambassador to the European Union before becoming Blair's foreign policy adviser and recalls that Blair 'was genuinely culturally comfortable in Europe . . . he could get as bored as anyone with European Council meetings but threw himself into it and saw the domestic advantage of looking like part of the leadership'.[7]

Before long, 'getting bigger' had been replaced by a subtler analysis. Britain should not seek to reclaim the great-power status of the 1950s, but it could be a nation whose voice was heard with respect in the world's capitals. Blair was still only forty-three when he entered Downing Street and arrived in office unburdened by the victory of 1945, which gave him an advantage over his predecessors. He was sometimes tripped up by his slight grasp of history, but ignorance could also be an advantage in escaping nostalgia. The nation's new role, he said, was to be at the 'crux' of international alliances. It could be at once America's close ally and Europe's leading player. 'We have got over our imperial past – and the withdrawal symptoms,' he told an audience at the Guildhall in November 1999. 'We have a new role – not to look back and try to recreate ourselves as the pre-eminent superpower of 1900, nor to pretend to be the Greeks to the Americans' Romans.'[8] Instead Britain should 'use the strengths of our history to build our future not as a superpower but as a pivotal power, as a power that is at the crux of the alliances and international politics which shape the world and its future.' To secure that role, Blair said, 'we have to reject creeping isolationism and an outdated view that a nation is only "independent" if it stands aloof'. Here was a formula to banish the demons of Suez.

Leaders measure each other not just by the traditional metrics of national power but by their political standing at home. The crushing nature of his election victory gave Blair ample advantage. President Chirac was hobbled by 'cohabitation' with the socialist prime minister Lionel Jospin. Helmut Kohl had been a giant of European politics, steering Germany to reunification, but his authority was fading, and in 1998 he would be replaced by the Social Democrat Gerhard Schröder. Clinton's presidency was drawing towards its close, mired in the scandal over his relationship with Monica Lewinsky. This made Blair 'the future'. His majority of 179 in the House of Commons – larger even than that enjoyed by Margaret Thatcher at the peak of her power – all but assured that he would be around for some time. That in turn meant time to shape his worldview.

Those who worked with Blair said he had not thought deeply about Europe before taking office. Like most of his generation, he took Britain's place in the European Union as a given. He had grown up in a borderless continent, spending part of his gap year working in a bar in Paris and acquiring a passable grasp of the language. For Blair, the ideological battles over sovereignty that had made the Tories unelectable were something of a mystery. In his mind, sovereignty was not an abstract notion, but the capacity to act. What mattered, as with membership of any club, was that Britain was among those writing the rules. 'Europe is not something that happened to us in 1973,' he had said while in opposition. 'We are Europeans. We are made up of wave after wave of settlers who came to these islands from Europe: Celts, Romans, Anglo-Saxons, Vikings and Normans.'[9] There was no romanticism in any of this. Blair did not dream of a 'United States of Europe'. The argument, as he would say in a speech in Warsaw in the autumn of 2000, was about collective power. Having a leading role in Europe was 'an indispensable part of influence, strength and power in the world', and Blair was interested in power. As Jonathan Powell puts it: 'Tony was determined to try to be a leader in Europe. Our aim was to be one of the big three from the very beginning – to insert ourselves into the Franco–German relationship.'[10] He had some success for a time, but more so with Schröder than Chirac, who, in Powell's description, 'didn't want the Brits interfering with the Franco–German relationship'.

The story that Blair told at the beginning of his premiership was persuasive. Britain had drifted to the margins of influence. Before being brought down by an excessive, and obsessive, opposition to European integration, Margaret Thatcher had danced on the global stage. Burning resentment at her defenestration and the ferocious opposition of Tory Eurosceptics had left John Major a prisoner of his party's divisions over Europe. By building bridges across the Channel, while refurbishing the relationship with Washington, Blair would restore Britain's influence. Europe was ready to listen. Blair was feted at his first formal summit of European leaders in June 1997 in Amsterdam. Britain's partners had grown used to it saying 'No' – Thatcher because she thought they were dangerous federalists, Major because he could not escape the shadow of the so-called 'bastards'. Now they looked across the table at a prime minister ready to say 'Yes'. Blair did not disappoint them. He dropped objections to a new Union treaty that had been raised by Major. And, with a nod to the trade union supporters of his own party, he signalled that Britain would now abandon the opt-out from the social provisions of Maastricht. Four years later, the Treaty of Amsterdam was followed by the Treaty of Nice. Britain, like other governments, had its demands and red lines, but it was no longer set on derailing the project. Europe, as one senior diplomat who had fought in the trenches for Thatcher and Major put it, was 'no longer the enemy'.[11]

The paradox was that even as the Conservatives complained that Britain was being bullied by Brussels, the nature of the Union was shifting in Britain's direction. The single market had capped the *dirigiste* instincts of the French, while an alliance between Germany,

Britain and the Nordic states had nudged it in the direction of a more open trade policy. The diplomat and intelligence chief John Sawers says that the essential political dynamics had changed from the time when Europe was essentially a Franco–German enterprise. The European Union had become a 'three-legged stool . . . On issues to do with defence and diplomacy, London–Paris was the key axis in terms of intervention and willingness to engage. In terms of future European integration and the whole European project, Paris and Berlin were the crucial drivers. On competition and open markets, London worked with Berlin.'[12] Britain and Germany also acted together in support of Atlanticism.

Early on, Blair signalled his intention to strengthen the bilateral relationship with France. The logic of close collaboration between the two nations was irresistible. Former imperial powers, they had both been stranded among the second rung of nations by the power shifts wrought by the Second World War. Both looked to interests beyond Europe. Peter Westmacott served as Britain's ambassador in Paris: 'There you had it. Same size, same history, dealing with a post-empire world, hanging on for grim death, both with decent armed forces and permanent seats on the Security Council, but both looking backwards with nostalgia and forwards with uncertainty. Very similar: rivals for 1,000 years.'[13] The mutual suspicions, though, often trumped the shared interests. Westmacott recalls a Parisian dinner during his ambassadorship that gathered together a dozen or so of the best and brightest of the French elite. Without warning, his host, a senior civil servant turned industry leader, halted the conversation: 'Now tell me, Mr Ambassador, why is it that the English hate us so much?'

The newly elected Blair wanted to challenge such assumptions. The Paris government had long pressed for a European Union defence capability, to operate alongside, but independently of, NATO. The United States was deeply suspicious, as had been the Thatcher and Major governments. France had broken with NATO during the 1960s, raising American suspicions about any European initiatives. Britain's view had reflected these concerns that separate European defence capabilities would undermine NATO. Efforts to make a reality of the Union's grandly named Common Foreign and Security Policy had come to nought. In 1998, Blair broke the deadlock by dropping previous objections to any new organisation. Travelling to St Malo in France for a bilateral summit with President Chirac, he lifted the UK's previous opposition to a proposal to create a 60,000-strong European Rapid Reaction Force. Cautioned by his officials about the likely reaction in Washington, the prime minister's response was: 'I'll sort out Clinton.'[14] Blair wanted Chirac to understand that there was substance to the government's policy shift, so for once he put Europe ahead of the United States. The protests from the White House and the Pentagon duly arrived in Downing Street soon afterwards, but they were not enough to disturb his close relationship with Clinton.

By 1999, he was being rewarded with the Charlemagne Prize for promoting European unity. Blair was following in the footsteps of Winston Churchill, Edward Heath and Roy Jenkins, and was suitably upbeat in his acceptance speech: 'I have a bold aim . . . that over the next few years, Britain resolves once and for all to end its ambivalence towards Europe. I want to end the uncertainty, the lack of confidence, the Europhobia.'[15] The second most important person in the government took a more sober view. Where Blair saw opportunity abroad, Gordon Brown, the chancellor, saw risks to his own project to redraw the parameters of Britain's economy and society. The prime minister enjoyed the international limelight; Brown's ambitions centred on marrying economic success to a fairer distribution of wealth and opportunity. The two men had won the election as partners, but for most of Blair's decade in office, prime minister and chancellor would be rivals at best. Brown was convinced that the leadership was rightfully his. Blair had 'stolen' it after the unexpected death of John Smith in 1994. Brown's version of a subsequent pact between the two men was that governing would be a joint project, and Blair would stand down from the premiership after a single parliamentary term. Blair had a different recollection of events. For much of the first term there was a rough-and-ready division of labour: Blair played on the international stage, while Brown burrowed away at domestic policy. On the single currency, though, they collided.

The European Union had three big projects during the closing decades of the twentieth century. On two of these – the creation during the 1980s of a single European market in goods and services, and the decision during the 1990s to extend the offer of membership to the new democracies of central Europe – Britain had been in the vanguard. Though she would later say she had been tricked, Thatcher championed the single market. Major and, subsequently, Blair were firm advocates of enlargement of the Union to bring in former communist states such as Poland, the Czech Republic and Slovakia, Hungary and the Baltic states.

It was the third project – the replacement of national currencies by the euro – that divided both the political parties and the nation. Thatcher's implacable opposition to the creation of a single currency had played a big part in her downfall. Major had papered over the cracks by negotiating an opt-out for Britain. It was left to the new Labour government to decide whether to exercise the option. Blair's view was shaped by the politics: if Britain was to be a leading player in Europe, as he intended, it must join. Brown's objections were born of economics and his desire to thwart the prime minister's grand projects. In the chancellor's view, Blair's premiership was a dress rehearsal for his own.

Facing the implacable opposition of Brown and looking over his shoulder at the Eurosceptic press, Blair deferred a decision about the euro during his first term, missing the single currency's launch date in 2000. His keenly prized second election victory in 2001 gave him the opportunity to swap sterling for a currency soon to be circulating in a dozen European countries. Brown said no. The history of past attempts to fix sterling's exchange rate was not a happy one, and Brown did not intend to have his own putative premiership held hostage to an irrevocable decision to join the euro. Blair blinked, knowing that by breaking with Brown he would also be inviting the wrath of the right-leaning press. The outcome was a messy compromise. Britain would indeed join when the economic conditions were right. But the judgement would be made on the basis of 'five economic tests' devised by the chancellor and his economic adviser, Ed Balls. The latter was a long-standing opponent of the single currency. The Treasury's intention was that the tests would never be passed.

Blair had won the 1997 general election on a promise that his party had left behind the shibboleths of old-fashioned state social-ism. Standing on the steps of Downing Street, he had recalled that he had campaigned as 'New Labour'. Now he would gov-ern as 'New Labour'. The same promise had been made to the Conservative-backing newspaper proprietors he had courted from the first day of his leadership – none more so than the anti-European Australian-born American Rupert Murdoch. Blair won the endorsements of Murdoch's newspapers. In return, Murdoch secured an open invitation to Downing Street. Blair feared his

influence and his wrath. For all the political capital he accumulated in his successive election victories, he was always loath to
confront Murdoch's myriad prejudices.

Roy Jenkins, one of the principal architects of Labour's con-
version to Europeanism thirty years earlier and a leader of the
party split in 1981 that saw the creation of the breakaway Social
Democratic Party, became an informal adviser to Blair. He soon
grew disillusioned with his reluctance to take political risks.
Perhaps, Jenkins and other critics would remark, it was no accident
that he reserved his most pro-European statements for speeches
delivered abroad – at Aachen, Ghent and Warsaw. Murdoch was
soon a frequent visitor to Number 10, and journalists invited to
regular off-the-record chats with Blair began to notice how he
tailored his remarks to their prejudices. Columnists from the
Financial Times were assured that he was determined to join the
euro. Those from the *Sun* were told he had no plans to give up
the pound.[16]

Blair saw no reason why Europe should get in the way of a close,
strong relationship with Washington. He never questioned the
conventional wisdom that sticking with the Americans gained
Britain leverage elsewhere in the world. Americans were like us;
we might disagree from time to time, but on basic values and
interests, the two nations were aligned. Getting on with the US
president was part of the prime minister's job description. John
Scarlett, chairman of the Joint Intelligence Committee during
Blair's premiership, says he saw the relationship as an instrument
of British influence: 'Tony Blair's approach was that if the United
States is on your side, you can do anything.'[17]

It helped, of course, that Bill Clinton was in the White House.
Blair first travelled to Washington in January 1993, the month of

Clinton's inauguration. Too junior at that point to make it to the Oval Office, he had soaked up the campaigning lessons offered by Clinton's team. He saw the political centrism – 'triangulation', the campaign strategists called it – that had propelled the Arkansas politician to the White House as a model for his own reshaping of New Labour. He had to wait another two years, and his own elevation to the party leadership in place of John Smith, to get an audience with Clinton. The two met at the American ambassador's residence in London's Regent's Park during a presidential visit to Britain. In the words of one of his officials, Blair was instantly 'star-struck'.[18]

Three more years, and in February 1998 he was back in Washington as prime minister. This time Clinton put on a show. The nineteen-gun salute at the White House was followed by a state dinner as glittering in its guest list as to recall the heady days of Kennedy's Camelot. Stevie Wonder jostled for space with Harrison Ford, Barbra Streisand with Steven Spielberg. Blair repaid the favour. With his host mired in a brewing scandal about his relationship with the White House intern Monica Lewinsky, Blair could not escape a question about it at the two leaders' closing press conference. He might have claimed immunity – something along the lines of not commenting on America's domestic politics. Instead: 'I've worked with President Clinton for some nine months as British prime minister. I have found him throughout someone I could trust, someone I could rely upon, someone I am proud to call not just a colleague but a friend.'[19] Clinton was in his debt. The two men got on. They were from a new generation of political leaders. Both saw in their experience an opportunity to reshape the politics of the centre-left after long periods during which conservatives had dominated politics. Before too long, president and prime minister were appearing at political roadshows designed to showcase their 'Third Way' progressive politics. Clinton was the master, Blair the apprentice. The pitch was to Middle America and Middle Britain, but soon enough they were joined by Germany's Schröder, Brazilian president Fernando Henrique Cardoso and Italy's Romano Prodi in preaching the gospel of their new social democracy.

Blair's familiarity with the military was slight. At school in Scotland he had been obliged for a period to enrol in the military cadet force. As soon as the opportunity arose, he had discarded the military fatigues for a place on the school's community service programme.[20] Now, as prime minister, he relished the chance to surprise people. Untutored he might be, but he was also determined to shed Labour's reputation as a party that was instinctively soft on defence. New Labour was a party of patriotism. And that meant strong defence. One of his first decisions, pressed on him by General Charles Guthrie, the Chief of the Defence Staff, was to announce a strategic review of defence policy. The end of the Cold War and a parallel crisis in the public finances saw Major's government cut deep into the defence budget. None of the services were spared, and the government scrapped all the tactical nuclear weapons that would have been used against Soviet forces in a war in Europe.

Blair's colleagues assumed that there were more cuts to come. This misread the prime minister and underestimated Guthrie. The general, a former special forces commander, had courted the Labour leader before the general election. The two men had breakfasted at Claridge's. If Britain was to have clout, Guthrie said, it needed armed forces that could fight. The Tory defence cuts had gone too far. Blair liked soldiers. They were 'doers', he once said. The review guaranteed the defence budget for the following years.

Blair would come to see the military as an ally. Guthrie fitted precisely the Hollywood image of the upper-class English officer whose cut-glass accent defied a storied military record. He had served in some of the bloodiest campaigns fought by the Special Air Service, the elite force that would be sent into the toughest battles. Most importantly, he understood politics and established an easy relationship with the prime minister. Blair chose as defence secretary George Robertson, a strong Atlanticist whose robust views on defence and security traced those of Ernest Bevin. Robertson would later become secretary general of NATO. Labour's first defence review gave a clue about Blair's intent: Britain's strategic ambition was 'to be a force for good in the world'.

Blair did not hesitate when he was asked by Clinton to send Britain's air force into battle alongside the Americans in the Middle East. The target was Saddam Hussein's Iraq. Since the end of the first Gulf War, Saddam had been playing cat and mouse with the United Nations inspectors charged with dismantling his programmes to build weapons of mass destruction. By 1997, responsibility for upholding the UN resolutions that had followed Operation Desert Storm had fallen largely on the American and British forces in the region. Much of the rest of the international community had become indifferent. Blair was alerted to Saddam's potential threat early in his premiership, sharing his concerns with Paddy Ashdown, the leader of the Liberal Democrats and a frequent visitor to Number 10. In November 1997, Ashdown noted them in his personal diary. 'I have now seen some of the stuff on this,' Blair had told him. 'It really is pretty scary. He [Saddam] is very close to some appalling weapons of mass destruction.'[21] During the same month, Blair used a foreign policy speech at the City of London's Mansion House to issue a direct threat to Saddam. The West wanted a diplomatic solution, but 'Saddam should not take this as a sign of weakness . . . He has made this fatal miscalculation before.'

In February 1998, Clinton and Blair discussed the possibility of bombing Iraqi military sites to enforce the UN resolutions. Later in the year, the UN's chief weapons inspector reported that the decommissioning process had reached an impasse. Blair sent British warplanes to join a series of US-led strikes against Iraqi military installations. Guthrie, who was with Blair in his Downing Street study when he authorised the action, would recall that the prime minister had been remarkably calm.[22] Downing Street officials later acknowledged that there had been a certain 'queasiness' about signing up with Clinton because of widespread speculation in Washington that the president wanted to divert attention from his political difficulties over the Lewinsky scandal. Blair seemed unperturbed. This was an important psychological moment for the prime minister. It also offered a premonition of the fights among Europeans about the 2003 invasion of Iraq. The air strikes lacked specific UN approval. The assumption was that Russia, France or both would have blocked a new resolution in the Security Council. Washington and London argued that Saddam's defiance of an earlier UN resolution provided sufficient grounds. The bombing brought sharp condemnation from France as a breach of the spirit of the St Malo declaration, signed just weeks earlier. The action seemed to confirm to the French that Britain would continue to put the United States before Europe. Blair was unapologetic. Prefacing the arguments that would see him join George W. Bush's Iraq War in 2003, Blair said that if Saddam defied the UN with impunity, it would put in question the entire multilateral security order.

The event that did most to form Blair's worldview was Slobodan Milošević's brutal campaign to drive ethnic Albanians from

Kosovo. The world had stood on the sidelines when the former Yugoslavia fell into civil war after the break-up during the early 1990s of Marshal Tito's federation. Britain's Conservative government had been particularly reluctant to intervene in the bloody conflict between Milošević's Serbia and Bosnia's Muslims. Milošević was eventually brought to heel by the Americans in the wake of the slaughter in July 1995 of more than 8,000 Bosnian Muslims – mostly young men and boys – by Bosnian Serb forces at Srebrenica. The US-sponsored Dayton Accords brought an uneasy peace to the region. By 1998, however, the Serbian leader had stepped up his repression of the majority Muslim population of Kosovo, shrugging off threats of renewed Western intervention as he sought to crush Kosovan independence fighters. Blair spoke out against this new round of ethnic cleansing. Clinton's secretary of state Madeleine Albright and Blair's foreign secretary Robin Cook were charged with leading a new round of diplomacy to stop the fighting. Milošević defied them.

NATO had 500 planes at its disposal when it began the bombing campaign calculated to bring Serbia to heel. The assumption in London, as much as in Washington and elsewhere in Europe, was that Milošević would not long withstand the onslaught. There was no appetite among the Western powers to send in troops. Clinton, facing heavy opposition in Congress to American involvement in a war of limited direct impact on its national interest, was clear from the outset: 'I do not intend to put our troops in Kosovo to fight a war.' Blair wanted the options left open. Both underestimated the Serbian leader's resilience and his determination to create facts on the ground. If he could drive out the ethnic Muslim population, Kosovo would become irreversibly part of Serbia. By early summer, NATO planes were running out of targets in Serbia and more than 400,000 Kosovan Albanians had been forced from their homes in what was fast becoming a humanitarian catastrophe. The conduct of the campaign, coordinated by NATO, was often chaotic, as the allies argued about appropriate targets. The Americans began to choose their own targets without reference to the British or anyone else. When the strikes were extended to Belgrade, the Chinese embassy in the Serbian capital was hit by a misdirected American missile. Meanwhile, in Guthrie's description, the bombs were 'turning big craters into bigger craters and rubble into smaller pieces of rubble'.[23]

Blair's response showed the certitude that would become a hallmark of later foreign policy decisions. More than once he drew comparisons between Milošević's ethnic cleansing and the Holocaust. 'It is time for my generation to reflect on the fight of our parents' generation against Hitler's evil regime,' he wrote in a newspaper article.[24] He rejected any idea of ceding ground to the Serbian regime: 'No compromise. No fudge. No half-baked deals.' Convinced of the righteousness of the cause, the prime minister enjoyed the international limelight. Flying to the Balkans with his wife Cherie Booth, he basked in the applause of those in the refugee camps. Visiting the Bulgarian capital Sofia, he invited comparisons between his own stand and William Gladstone's famous Midlothian campaign during the nineteenth century: 'Today we face the same questions that confronted Gladstone more than 120 years ago. Does one nation or people have the right to impose its will on another? Is there ever a justification for a policy based on the supremacy of one ethnic group?'[25]

There was a Manichaean quality about these statements that made realists in the Foreign Office blanch. Not because they disagreed with the sentiment, but because they also knew how often such grand statements of principle could collide with narrower interpretations of the national interest. Nor, in this instance, did

Blair's pulpit diplomacy endear him to his friend Clinton. The president had committed against ground troops. The logic of Blair's rhetoric was that the West should do whatever was necessary to stop Milošević. Clinton thought the prime minister was grandstanding. White House officials accused their Downing Street counterparts of promoting Blair's standing at the expense of Clinton's. Blair's aides spoke of a sourness in their exchanges. The view from the White House was rather different. On one level, this was simply about the amount of time the two leaders devoted to the crisis. For Clinton, it was one item on a long list. By the account of Sawers: 'From March through to July 1999, he [Blair] spent over half his time on managing the Kosovo war. Blair showed that fantastic combination of political energy and mastery of relationships and drive and communications skills and risk-taking.'[26] Yet the United States was the nation providing the serious firepower against Milošević. In any ground war it would bear the brunt of the casualties – and the generals in the Pentagon warned that a war with battle-hardened Serbian forces in the rough terrain of Kosovo might mean plenty of them. Ultimately, it was the president's, albeit belated, agreement with Blair to make a public statement hinting he was ready to consider sending ground troops to the region that persuaded the Serbian leader to throw in his cards after seventy-eight days of bombing. Afterwards, Clinton harboured something of a grudge. His respect for Blair did not extend to a readiness to see himself upstaged, even by so close an ally.

Once committed, Blair was relentless in pressing the case for the West to act. He was keen to frame the conflict in Kosovo as a test case for the post-Cold War international order. President George H. W. Bush had declared a new global order, in which great powers would cooperate in a rules-based international system. The

British prime minister now took it upon himself to set out some of those rules. Harold Macmillan had offered Kennedy his 'Grand Design'; now Blair offered the world a new doctrine.

The 'Doctrine of the International Community'[27] (he was never one to undersell his ideas) was unveiled while the Kosovo conflict was still raging. Delivered as a speech to the Economic Club of Chicago in April 1999, it marked a turning point in Blair's premiership. Early drafts of the speech were written by Lawrence Freedman, a leading British historian and expert in war studies, though Blair claimed personal authorship of the final version. Ironically, Freedman would later serve on the panel chaired by Sir John Chilcot that excoriated the prime minister's march to war in Iraq in 2003. At its heart, the doctrine called for a shift in the balance of international affairs in order to limit the capacity of individual states to challenge global rules and norms. Traditional notions of national sovereignty should henceforth be measured against a broader set of standards. Reclaiming the notion of inter-dependence – once Macmillan's favourite catchphrase – Blair's argument was that tyrannical rulers must take responsibility for the spillover effects of domestic repression. Borders had become more porous, and disorder in one nation had an impact elsewhere. When tyranny in one country 'produces massive flows of refu-gees which unsettle neighbouring countries, then they can prop-erly be described as threats to international peace and security'. From this flowed a responsibility on other states to intervene. The world had stood idly by during the ethnic slaughter in the African state of Rwanda and had been slow to act in Bosnia. Now the great powers should acknowledge an obligation to prevent such massacres. Kosovo shaped Blair's belief that Britain had a role in shaping a new settlement. This was rooted in the 'end of history' theory. The world was marching towards universal acceptance of liberal democracy and open economic systems. The role of the Western powers was to keep it on course. Liberal international-ism, as it came to be known, would redeem the unfulfilled promise made by Bush. That, anyway, was the theory.

Another war, this time in the West African state of Sierra Leone, hardened Blair's belief into an unshakeable conviction. The former British colony had been ravaged by civil war, and an attempt by Britain to support the government of the president Ahmad Kabbah had failed to stabilise the country. By the sum-mer of 2000, a United Nations peacekeeping operation was under threat, as the warlord leader of neighbouring Liberia, Charles Taylor, backed a rebel advance on Freetown, Sierra Leone's cap-ital. Taylor, who would later be found guilty of war crimes by the International Court of Justice, was ruling by terror after emerg-ing as the victor of a five-year civil war. Blair authorised the dis-patch of British troops to oversee the evacuation of British and other foreign nationals. This might have been no more than the story of another coup in another former British colony, but the Foreign Office feared it could have wider consequences. The fall of Freetown would represent the collapse of the latest in a series of UN peacekeeping operations and would have a ripple effect across West Africa. Wasn't this the sort of moment Blair had referred to when he talked about the responsibility of the international com-munity to restore stability in broken and failing states? Against this, there was little enthusiasm in London for an operation that would risk British lives. When patrolling British soldiers were captured by rebel forces, the Conservatives called for withdrawal. Blair consulted Guthrie, who offered a plan to free the hostages and stabilise the Kabbah government. It came with the risk of sig-nificant casualties, but Blair decided to take the gamble. Guthrie remembers that Blair 'didn't blink',[28] and the successful operation by special forces and paratroopers cost the life of just one British soldier. The rebels were forced to retreat and the UN mission was soon restored. Here was Blair's Chicago doctrine in action – or so it seemed – and the success of the mission marked another step on the road that would take him to Basra. 'On Sierra Leone,' he later recounted, 'there were those who said: "What's it got to do with us?" But I am sure that Britain's and Europe's long-term interests in Africa are best served if we intervene . . . to do what we can to save African nations from barbarism and dictatorship.'[29]

Tony Blair was in his hotel suite in Brighton, putting the final touches to a speech. It was September 2001, and the prime minister had travelled from London to the annual conference of the Trades Union Congress. He did not make a habit of mixing publicly with Labour's 'brothers' in the trade union movement, but fresh from that summer's general election victory he had decided to set out his stall for the second term. The speech was never given. The television flickering in the background showed a passenger jet crashing into the World Trade Center's North Tower. And then a second hit the South Tower. Within minutes the prime ministerial entourage was heading back to London.

The succession in Washington from Bill Clinton to George W. Bush unnerved Blair. Many in the senior ranks of the Labour Party were deeply hostile towards a new president who had reached the White House on an avowed platform of American unilateralism. After so easy and close a relationship with Clinton, how would he get on with the Republican former governor of Texas? The Third Way project had been calculated to lock conservatives out of power across the world. New Labour had put its money on Al Gore, Clinton's vice president. Bush in this respect was a measure of failure. There were other obvious divides. During his three years in Downing Street, Blair had styled himself as the international spokesman for Western intervention in trouble spots around the world. Bush had fought his campaign promising to disentangle America from its overseas commitments and was scornful of the multilateralism that was at the core of Blair's view of managed interdependence. In December 2000, during Clinton's farewell visit to Europe, Blair met the outgoing president at Chequers. 'Be his friend,' Clinton replied, when asked how Blair should handle his successor. There would be no hard feelings in the Clinton household. And that, in Blair's mind, was his job. Whatever the personal and political differences, it was the alliance that mattered.[30]

The traditional scramble to ensure that Britain's prime minister was the first European leader to meet the new president did not impress everyone in Downing Street. Cherie Booth spoke for the dissidents when she chided her husband for rehearsing every detail of the planned pilgrimage. When Blair's entourage argued about the present he would give Bush – a bust of Churchill was the eventual choice – Booth suggested a Downing Street ballpoint pen. A human rights lawyer, she was unimpressed by Bush's record as governor of Texas, when he consistently refused to commute the sentences of those on the state's death row. She made plain her strong objections to state killing when the two leaders met for a second time during 2001, this time at Chequers.[31] Others saw in the president's unapologetic unilateralism a worrying turn towards selfish, arrogant nationalism. This was not a leader likely to be impressed by Blair's Chicago speech. Blair was single-minded.

When the two leaders first met at Camp David in February 2001, their body language was not that of long-lost friends, but the prime minister opened the talks with an unexpected offer to the president. Most European governments – including Britain

– had opposed the new president's campaign pledge of a national missile defence system, a project reminiscent of Ronald Reagan's Star Wars. There were real fears that it would goad Moscow into a nuclear arms race. The foreign secretary Robin Cook raised objections with the prime minister, but Blair wanted to send a signal at this first meeting that their different political backgrounds would not get in the way of a strong relationship. The British government would give its approval for the required upgrade of US radar systems sited in the UK. What he asked in return was that the president sought to avoid an immediate breach with Moscow by including Vladimir Putin in consultations. Blair had taken the European side at St Malo but was not prepared to jeopardise Britain's close relationship with Washington by falling out with the new president. In return, he secured tacit US acquiescence for the Anglo–French plan for a European military force.

By the summer, the prime minister was hosting the president at Chequers and drawing public compliments from Bush: 'The thing I appreciate about the prime minister is that he is willing to think anew as we head into the future.' But the limits of Britain's influence were also obvious. Bush was unmoved by Blair's suggestion that he might think again about his campaign pledges to withdraw the US from the Kyoto Protocol on climate change and from the Anti-Ballistic Missile Treaty, a cornerstone of Cold War nuclear restraint. Officials accompanying Blair saw nothing in Bush of the commitment to a stable international order that had animated his father following the fall of the Berlin Wall. George H. W. Bush had gathered around him high-ranking officials such as James Baker and Brent Scowcroft, who were wedded to alliances as well as American leadership. George W. Bush's lieutenants carried no such commitments. America was setting off on its own. For all his charm, Blair was about to discover that he was powerless.

In the immediate aftermath of the collapse of the Twin Towers and the destruction of much of the Pentagon, Bush had been bundled onto Air Force One for his own safety. He was still in the sky when Blair spoke to the world from Downing Street. Britain, he announced, would stand 'shoulder to shoulder' with Washington in defeating those responsible: 'This is not a battle between the United States and terrorism, but between the free and democratic world and terrorism. We, therefore, here in Britain, stand shoulder to shoulder with our American friends in this hour of tragedy and we, like them, will not rest until this evil is driven from the world.' His aides would later say that 9/11 had been a potent demonstration of what Blair had said in his Chicago speech. The safe haven offered to Al Qaeda by Afghanistan's Taliban had spilled over into the biggest attack on American soil since the sacking of Washington by the British in 1814.

By offering unequivocal support at the outset, Blair calculated that he would maximise his influence in Washington. He had no qualms about joining an American-led effort to destroy the threat of Islamic terrorism. He was concerned that once the dust had settled, Bush would face immense pressure to act unilaterally without waiting for international endorsement. If Washington 'stepped out of the system', as the prime minister put it, the world would no longer be anchored by a system of rules.[32] On 20 September, Blair was in Washington as an honoured guest for Bush's first address to Congress after 9/11. Britain's military forces, he promised, would join the Americans in the coming war in Afghanistan against the Taliban and Al Qaeda. For his part, the president would be wise not to rush into reprisals – this was a moment to gather the widest possible coalition against the terrorists. Aware that the neoconservatives around the president were already calling for the response to reach beyond Afghanistan and to a confrontation with Saddam Hussein's Iraq, Blair sought to convince Bush that the focus should be on Al Qaeda and the Taliban. He returned to Downing Street persuaded – wrongly, as it would turn out – that the argument had been won.

At this point, Blair was at the height of his international authority. As Jonathan Powell says, 'We were busy being Greeks to Romans, trying to build an alliance and acting, as we thought, as the link to Europe.'[33] The first signs were indeed encouraging. As America spearheaded the fall of the Taliban in Afghanistan, Britain's prime minister became the most articulate spokesperson for an international effort to snuff out the threat from violent Islamists. His speech to the Labour Party conference in October, a few weeks after the Al Qaeda attack, prompted the Conservative-leaning *Daily Telegraph* to gush that this was Blair's 'finest hour'. Feted in Washington, he criss-crossed the globe, giving the same sermon in every city as he sought to broaden the coalition. Here was an opportunity to build a new settlement to confront the threat. The kaleidoscope had been shaken, he had told the Labour conference: 'The pieces are in flux. Soon they will settle again. Before they do, let us reorder the world around us.'

'Britain has lost an empire,' *The Economist* declared in January 2002, 'but has at last found Tony Blair.' The mischief that recalled Dean Acheson's admonition did not undermine the magazine's admiration for the prime minister. Amid criticism that his globe-trotting had led Blair to neglect domestic politics, *The Economist* said he could 'take pride' in the international role he had played since 9/11. Britain had joined America in the opening strikes against the Taliban and was leading the preparations for an international security force in Kabul. By winning the confidence of Bush, the magazine continued, Blair 'may even, for a moment, have realised the long-standing British dream of becoming the indispensable bridge between America and Europe'.[34] Blair had 'star quality' at a moment when other European leaders – Jacques Chirac, Gerhard Schröder – were preoccupied with domestic politics. The editorial did add a small note of caution: Blair's characterisation of Britain as a 'pivotal power' risked overstating British influence.

The prime minister's moral certitude also unsettled some of the old foreign policy hands in Whitehall. David Manning, his foreign policy adviser in Downing Street, was among those urging him to be cautious in his commitments to the US president. As much as Bush was personally appreciative, his close advisers – the vice president Dick Cheney, defence secretary Donald Rumsfeld and the neoconservative deputy defence secretary Paul Wolfowitz – were less impressed. Blair talked about internationalism and moral imperatives. He wanted to connect retaliation against the Islamist extremists with a new American-led effort to rekindle the peace process between Israel and the Palestinians. Bush's men had other priorities. What the world required, they thought, was an unambiguous display of American military might. Even before Al Qaeda had been driven from its camps in Afghanistan, they were planning to wage war on Iraq. Blair would soon be reminded of the ground rules of the cherished 'special relationship': Britain could expect a hearing for its assessment, but in matters of the American national interest, the decisions would always be taken in Washington.

By 2003, Britain had lost control. 'In most of the government, except perhaps in Blair's mind,' the senior diplomat Nigel Sheinwald recalls, 'there was a very high level of doubt about the Iraq operation. We were constantly believing we could somehow manage it. Manage the United Nations process. Trying to make it politically acceptable here, politically acceptable internationally, to get the international community together.' The problem, though, was in Washington. 'It never worked. It was always sticking plasters and inadequate remedies. Ultimately they really didn't need us. It was very clear at that critical moment. We were caught in a junior partner role with a huge amount of responsibility, which we never shook off.'[35]

The exchanges between Downing Street and the White House that would see British tanks and troops rolling into Iraq by the spring of 2003 were set out in detail by the Chilcot Inquiry. The picture that emerges from the minutes of the meetings between prime minister and president, the notes they exchanged and the transcripts of their telephone calls, is of a prime minister convinced that Britain should stick with its closest ally and a president who appreciated the support but was not to be budged from the path to war with Saddam Hussein. Blair's objective through this period reflected his fear after 9/11 that the United States would forsake leadership of a rules-based international system for a unilateral show of American power. The aim of British policy was to apply restraint in Washington: if Saddam was to be removed by force, it should be with the support of the United Nations. Blair wrote to Bush a month after the attacks: 'I have no doubt we need to deal with Saddam. But if we hit Iraq now, we would lose the Arab world, Russia, probably half the EU and my fear is the impact of all that on Pakistan. However, I am sure we can devise a strategy for Saddam deliverable at a later date.'[36]

The pull of the 'special relationship' sat alongside an unerring self-confidence. Blair had saved Kosovo and rescued Sierra Leone from chaos. In off-the-record conversations with journalists, he would say that holding Saddam to account for his defiance of the United Nations was 'the right thing to do', but also that it needed to be done in 'the right way'. Yet those closest to Bush had no interest.

NATO had responded to the 11 September attacks by invoking, for the first time in its history, Article 5, its mutual defence guarantee. 'We are all with you,' this declared to the Americans. Paul Wolfowitz travelled to NATO headquarters in Brussels, where he offered thanks but not reassurance. In the words of one senior diplomat, his message was that Washington was laying its own plans: 'Don't call us, and we probably won't call you.'[37]

'I will be with you, whatever,' Blair assured Bush in a note in 2002, as the drums of war grew louder.[38] Powell and Manning both advised the prime minister against making such a sweeping and apparently unconditional commitment. And rightly so. This was the promise that was later interpreted by many as proof that Blair would go to war, whatever the legal or diplomatic circumstances. In any event, it signalled that he had been swept up in his own role. He had been assembler-in-chief of the international coalition that had backed the toppling of the Taliban in Afghanistan. He had been instrumental in persuading Libyan leader Muammar Gaddafi to scrap his nuclear programme. Thus far Europe had stayed more or less united in its support for the Bush administration. Germany's Gerhard Schröder had signalled a major break with his country's post-war tradition by agreeing to contribute German forces to the coalition in Afghanistan. But even as Blair pledged his support to the US, the stresses were beginning to show in Europe. Stabilising Afghanistan was one thing; starting another war was a step too far for many of Britain's EU partners.

Blair would be roundly rebuked by the Iraq Inquiry for overplaying Saddam's alleged stocks of WMD. One of the Chilcot report's key findings was that there was no imminent threat when American and British forces launched the war in March 2003. More time could have been given to the UN weapons inspectors who were searching for the stockpile. But that there was such a

stockpile, no one in Downing Street doubted. The intelligence
services were convinced. None, according to senior Downing
Street officials, was more certain than Richard Dearlove, the
head of the Secret Intelligence Service – one of the officials crit-
icised in the Chilcot report. If Blair ever wavered in his belief
that Saddam held WMD programmes from before the first Gulf
War, Dearlove reassured him that the intelligence was incontrovertible.[39] But then Blair could not afford to waver. WMD was
the *casus belli*, the defiance of solemn United Nations resolutions
that gave the international community – and the British government – the right to intervene militarily. All the incentives were
thus to amplify and exaggerate the threat from such weapons.
And where does exaggeration cross the line into lying? Bush and
those around him were untroubled by such niceties. Saddam was
a threat and, after 9/11, the world's sole superpower was unwilling to brook such defiance.

Blair allowed no personal doubt that Saddam should be dealt
with, though part of him hoped that international pressure would
be enough. His main concern was to steer his ally in Washington
along a path that would keep the United States within the bounds
of the international community. The prime minister scored an initial success when, against the advice of Dick Cheney, Bush agreed
to go to the United Nations. In September 2002, the UN Security
Council passed a resolution calling on Saddam to comply with
its previous demands to give up his weapons of mass destruction
and sending in its own weapons inspectors again. The problem
would be that the resolution was ambiguous in its meaning as to
what might follow if the Iraqi leader defied the new inspection
mission led by Dr Hans Blix. The United States assumed it provided authorisation for war; Russia and France, among others,
took the view that another resolution would be required. Russian

president Vladimir Putin, seeking to rebuild his country's influence after its chaotic decline during the 1990s, was determined that Washington was not given a blank cheque. Even as he urged restraint in Washington, Blair felt that he had to make the case for war at home. By September 2002, he was telling the Trades Union Congress that the international effort to disarm Saddam through diplomacy and arms inspections could not be an excuse for permanent inaction. 'The challenge to all in the UN is this: the UN must be the way to resolve the threat from Saddam, not avoid it.'

Public opinion was at best lukewarm about the prospect of intervention, in spite of Downing Street's efforts to highlight the risks from Saddam's weapons stockpile by publishing hitherto secret intelligence information. These 'dodgy dossiers', as they would later be known, attracted sharp criticism from Chilcot's report, not because the information was false or invented but because they stretched to the very limits what little insight the spooks had into what was going on in Iraq. The information presented to the prime minister by Dearlove as rock solid was in fact distinctly flaky; the 'star' agent in Iraq was subsequently exposed as a fraud. The Joint Intelligence Committee failed to properly test conclusions drawn from small scraps of information. Robin Cook, moved from the Foreign Office to leadership of the House of Commons after the 2001 election, had stood full square behind the earlier interventions in Kosovo and Sierra Leone. But the march to war in Iraq he saw as a blatant abuse of US power. He questioned the legality as well as the ethics. When it came to the vote in parliament, he quit his cabinet post and delivered an eloquent denunciation in the House of Commons of Blair's course. Clare Short, the international development secretary, was another cabinet critic, though she voted in favour of the war, before quitting a few months later when Iraq fell into chaos.

Blair's defence was that every promise he made to Bush was conditional. Britain would stand alongside its ally to the extent to which Washington was willing to seek international legitimacy at the United Nations for the use of military force. By January 2003, however, he was desperately scrabbling for support for a second Security Council resolution to give authorisation for military action. He did not have the votes, and in any case he faced the threat of Russian and French vetoes. If he wanted to stick with Bush, legal grounds would have to be found for Britain to act on the basis of the first resolution. The only *casus belli* he could ever admit was the removal of Saddam's WMD. Those who spoke to him in the weeks before the war were left in little doubt about his wider strategic calculations. One way or another, the United States should be seen to be acting at the head of a coalition and, as a close ally, Britain had to play a part.[40]

Then there was the doctrine he had set out in Chicago. If Bush had not been making the case to confront Saddam, Blair would say with unflinching bravado, then he would have taken up the cause regardless. Sure of his own motives, the prime minister missed the rising opposition to the war of other European leaders. Some, especially among the new democracies that had emerged from the former Soviet Empire, were ready to back Washington almost without question. But France was far from alone, and essentially right, in seeing Bush's plan as a unilateralist assertion of American primacy rather than an effort to prop up the authority of the United Nations. Chirac grew frustrated at Blair's apparent refusal to consider the consequences for the Middle East of a war against Iraq. Kim Darroch, the Foreign Office diplomat who would later act as national security adviser and ambassador to the United States, was working in Downing Street at the time. Chirac, he says, was 'intellectually offended' about what he saw as the crass thinking behind Washington's approach. Britain, with France one of the former colonial powers, surely understood this. Chirac was right in his predictions of the consequences: 'What he was essentially trying to say to Tony Blair was "Look, the Americans just don't understand Iraq. If they think that going in and taking out Saddam Hussein is going to suddenly produce a Western government there, they are out of their minds."'[41] Darroch recalled that Chirac offered an accurate description of what would follow an American attack: 'What will happen is the country will divide up. The Shiites will form their own militias. The Sunni leaders will not accept any kind of Shiite, or even coalition, leadership in Baghdad and the whole thing will fall apart and any Westerners there will become natural targets.'

Much later, after the publication of the Chilcot report, Jonathan Powell reflected on the run-up to war. The notion of inevitability – that the course was fixed during Blair's meetings with Bush in 2002 – was the product of hindsight, he said.[42] Only weeks before the war, Blair's chief of staff was still uncertain as to whether British troops would join the Americans in the invasion. The decision had been taken only after the breakdown of talks at the United Nations Security Council about a second resolution. 'We were going to get them [the Americans] into an international coalition, and that would slow them down and make them do it in a sensible way,' Powell says of Number 10's strategy. The aim was to prevent them from 'lashing out' at Iraq. What happened? The plan went wrong. 'We got the first United Nations resolution and then we got stuck trying to get the second resolution.' The mistake, he continues, was political. 'Once we had gone down this path of trying to convince the Americans to look to the international community and not do it unilaterally, it was very hard to then just jump ship when things went wrong for us in the United

Nations.'[43] Sir Nigel Sheinwald was by then Britain's permanent representative in Brussels. 'We were caught in a junior partner role,' he says, 'with a huge amount of political responsibility, which we never shook off.'[44]

The impact of the Iraq War reached far beyond the stain it left on Tony Blair's reputation. Iraq's collapse into violent chaos, the sectarian conflict between Shia and Sunni Muslims and the rise of the self-styled Islamic State could all be traced back to the decision to destroy the Baathist regime of Saddam without a plan for what would replace it. Subsequent civil wars in Syria, Libya and Yemen attested to the extent to which the Iraq conflict had helped unglue the post-imperial settlement overseen by Britain and France after the First World War. There was nothing good to be said for the regimes of Saddam or Libya's Muammar Gaddafi, but nothing better for the power vacuum left behind by their removal. Just as the defeat in the desert fifty years earlier at Suez exploded Britain's post-imperial delusions, so the retreat from Basra in March 2009 shattered the notion that Britain remained a power capable of sustaining large-scale expeditionary forces in distant lands.

The courage of the troops deployed to Iraq, and later to Helmand province in Afghanistan, was not in dispute. There were never quite enough of them and they were never properly resourced. Through successive rounds of cuts in defence spending in the aftermath of the Cold War, military commanders and politicians sought to sustain the impression that Britain maintained 'full-spectrum' military forces, from its Trident nuclear deterrent, a powerful surface fleet, state-of-the-art fighter planes and bombers and sophisticated electronic intelligence, surveillance and target acquisition systems to readily deployable tank brigades. In truth, the effort to pose as a pocket superpower in the face of repeated budget cuts meant that many of these capabilities had been hollowed out. Iraq and Afghanistan pushed British forces beyond the limit. Shaming as it was, the deal eventually struck with Iraqi militia in southern Iraq to allow a peaceful withdrawal of British troops was an accurate measure of the diminution of Britain's military might.

The all-too-frequent arrival at RAF Brize Norton in Oxfordshire of the coffins of young British soldiers had a profound impact on the national psyche. The losses in Iraq were soon followed by mounting casualties from the war in Afghanistan, which had been supposed to be the 'good' war. The toppling of Saddam Hussein was a dangerous exercise in American unilateralism, but the forces that arrived in Afghanistan after the US drove out the Taliban carried a mandate from the United Nations. Some eighteen nations contributed to NATO's International Security Assistance Force (ISAF), with Britain initially contributing some 1,500 troops. The Taliban returned from their safe havens in Pakistan. ISAF's assumed role had been to provide basic security for the restoration of an Afghan government, but it now became the instrument of an experiment in armed nation-building. No one was more eager to take a bigger role than Britain's generals. They judged that a new mission to pacify the southern Afghan province of Helmand would exorcise the memory of the defeat in southern Iraq. In the phrase of the military commanders worried about cuts in army numbers, the choice was between 'using them or losing them'. The deployment was doomed. Imprisoned in isolated fortresses scattered across Helmand, the troops faced a deadly war of attrition. More than 450 had lost their lives before the mission was abandoned in 2014.

Iraq was a war of choice, undertaken in the absence of an immediate or direct threat to national security. Blair intended it to serve as a demonstration of how to make the world safe for Western liberal democracy. A million people joined an anti-war march in London, and he struggled to win the backing of parliament, relying on the votes of Conservative MPs to face down a rebellion in his own party. As Iraq descended into violent chaos after the toppling of Saddam's regime, opponents of the war were joined by many who had originally supported Blair's decision. Chilcot documented in damning detail the failure of the United States to plan for the aftermath of the war – and of Blair's government to press its ally to produce such a strategy. The can-do confidence that flowed from the defeat of the Soviet Union had hardened into hubris. The United States was the world's sole superpower. Europe, launching its own currency, seemed ever more self-confident. The United Nations had codified Western liberal values with the passage of 'Responsibility to Protect', a warning to autocrats and tyrants that the international community would not stand by in the face of oppression. But the United States and Britain had surrendered the moral high ground. Iraq's bloody civil war put paid to the notion that the West could export democracy on the tip of a cruise missile. So much for the Chicago doctrine.

The Iraq War challenged a basic assumption of the twin-pillared foreign policy Britain had forged in response to Suez. The premise was that Britain could leverage its influence in Europe in order to co-opt American policy in favour of British interests, and deploy its influence in Washington to assert leadership in Europe. Instead the fabled transatlantic bridge collapsed under the strain. By resolutely backing Bush, Blair lost his most important friends in Europe. The European Union was divided by the war, with Washington also winning the backing of many of the new members from eastern and central Europe, but France's Chirac and Germany's Schröder implacable in their opposition. France's threat to join Putin's Russia in using its veto at the UN scuppered

Blair's efforts to secure a resolution that would have given the war legitimacy. Chilcot's report offered no explicit judgement on the legality of the war in the absence of such a second resolution. It did challenge the way that the legal advice produced by the attorney general – initially ruling against the war – was conveniently changed to reflect political circumstances.

Britain's relationships with Berlin and Paris were badly damaged. His adviser David Manning says of Blair: 'I think to the very, very end he wanted to find a way of doing it [disarming Saddam], but with the international community behind it. The idea of doing it as a divided Western community was very unappealing to him, not least because it jeopardised everything he had achieved in Europe.'[45] In the weeks after Saddam's fall, Blair spoke angrily about the French veto. He told visitors to Downing Street that Chirac had tried to use Iraq to bring down his premiership.[46] It was a matter of jealousy. In truth, there had been substance to the French objections that he was unprepared to admit. Manning says the weapons inspectors should have been given more time – at least until the autumn of 2003 – but the problem was the Americans. 'We should have waited, I think. There was no way Bush was going to wait.'[47] The White House backed Blair's quest for a second United Nations resolution, but had never thought it an essential condition for war.

Whether, absent the Iraq conflict, Blair would have returned to the idea of joining the euro is moot. What was evident was that the war drained his political authority. He had carried the vote for war in the House of Commons only with the help of the Conservative opposition. Some eighty-four Labour MPs had voted against it and sixty-nine had abstained. This was no longer a prime minister who could risk a collision about the future of sterling with

Gordon Brown and a right-wing press in Britain that had become hostile to all things European. Blair's victory in the 2005 election testified to his residual authority, his undoubted political talents and the hopelessness of a Tory party now led by Michael Howard – its third leader since John Major's defeat – rather than to any great enthusiasm for the prime minister. Labour's majority in the House of Commons, which had been 167 in 2001, slumped to 66, and the party's share of the vote, at 35.2 per cent, was the lowest ever for a majority government.

Two years later, facing rising hostility among Labour MPs, Blair finally succumbed to Gordon Brown's impatience and stood down. There was precious little left of his European ambitions. Like Thatcher in her first months in office in 1979, Blair in 1997 had been offered an opportunity to establish Britain, along with France and Germany, as one of the continent's organising powers. Unlike Thatcher, he had initially sought to grasp it. He understood better perhaps than any post-war prime minister how engagement with the United States and with the continent of Europe should not be a choice. Yet as Roger Liddle, an adviser on Europe during Blair's first years in Downing Street, observed, when Blair came to write his memoir, Europe merited only twelve of 700 pages – proof, Liddle remarked caustically, that 'he does not think much of his European legacy'.[48]

Blair's enthusiasm for the euro was lost to his long-running power struggle with Gordon Brown. During the first term, this represented a failure of nerve, but by the second, Europe was being eclipsed by Blair's enthusiasm for the war in Iraq. Jack Straw, Robin Cook's replacement as foreign secretary, was never an enthusiast for Europe, pressurising the prime minister to promise a referendum if the Union pressed ahead with a new constitutional treaty. Blair was spared by opposition to the treaty in France and the Netherlands, but in any case his European policy was increasingly in thrall to the hostility to Brussels of the newspapers owned by Rupert Murdoch and Conrad Black. Without direction from Downing Street, ministers reverted to treating Europe as a zero-sum game. Curiously, Blair's personal relations with Chirac improved. Both left office in the summer of 2007, and Darroch remembers a valedictory meeting at the Elysée Palace. 'Chirac was in a very warm, let-bygones-be-bygones mood. He escorted Blair in the autumn sunshine across the gravel court in front of the Elysée and it was all very friendly and sepia-tinged.'[49]

The Iraq War also carried a lesson for France. Blair had been tripped up by opposition to the war in Paris and Berlin, but France likewise had failed to assemble a unified European front against Washington. Governments from Warsaw to Madrid had backed Bush. The conceit of the French after Suez had been that they could build a united counterweight to the United States in Europe. This was a moment when just such a common front was needed. For France, the American march to war in Iraq seemed not so much an effort to neutralise a real threat but more an assertion of US hegemony – a declaration that the '*hyperpuissance*', as Hubert Védrine had called it, could do as it pleased, regardless of international rules. The French had a point. The arrogance of American power was there for all to see in George W. Bush's National Security Strategy of 2002, which claimed a pre-emptive right to use force against potential enemies. It was underscored in his State of the Union address of January 2002. What became known as the 'axis of evil' speech singled out Iran and North Korea, as well as Iraq, as nations that would face the wrath of Washington. As it turned out, the toppling of Saddam Hussein would within a decade be followed by retreat.

But Europe was also a big loser. Blair had found it impossible to sustain a balance between Britain's loyalties to the United States and Europe, while France had discovered that it could not hold the continent together as an independent centre of power. The Anglo–French relationship, soaked in centuries of rivalry, had turned full circle since the Suez debacle. Rivals had become friends, then rivals again.

The world had changed. Britain remained one of its leading democracies in the Group of Eight and had a seat at the table of the larger G20. Permanent membership of the United Nations Security Council gave it a place at the heart of international diplomacy, and the Commonwealth lent it a voice in the developing world. At Brown's instigation, Britain was setting an example for the world's advanced democracies by committing to meet the UN's development spending target of 0.7 per cent of gross national income. And yet Blair had taken his eyes off the wider world as the rules of the geopolitical game changed. 'Gradually, then suddenly,' a character in Ernest Hemingway's *The Sun Also Rises* responds when asked how he had gone bankrupt. Twenty years after the fall of the Berlin Wall, those Western leaders who had thought that the defeat of Soviet communism had marked the permanent triumph of liberal market democracies might have said something similar. What Blair had not noticed was that the world had fundamentally changed since 1997. Liberal interventionism had imagined the inevitable advance of economic globalisation and of the democratic values of the West – the end of history. The Iraq War had struck a first blow against that presumption, but it was one of many. The global financial crash shattered the illusions about the permanence of liberal capitalism and the global prestige of the West. Russia emerged as a revanchist power under the rule of Vladimir Putin, and a fast-rising China rejected the invitation to become a stakeholder in a Western-designed international system. The world was witnessing the return of history.

There is a codicil to Tony Blair's premiership which, had Osama bin Laden not succeeded in destroying New York's World Trade Center, might have become the main narrative. He could have been remembered not as a prime minister too careless in going to war but as a peacemaker who brought to a close an ugly and seemingly intractable conflict that was much closer to home. His first trip as prime minister took him not to Washington, Berlin or Paris, but to Belfast and Northern Ireland's forgotten war. The province had lived with the violence for nearly three decades, after civil rights protests by the minority Catholic community during the 1960s had escalated into a war waged on the British state by the Irish Republican Army. The violence of the republicans was met by the equally brutal tactics of Protestant paramilitaries. In 1984, the IRA bombing of Brighton's Grand Hotel during the Conservative Party conference had come close to killing Margaret Thatcher. Five conference attendees, including an MP, had died in the assassination attempt. A few years earlier, the IRA had killed another MP, Airey Neave, a close adviser to Thatcher, as he left the House of Commons. In February 1991, mortar shells had landed just behind the prime minister's office in Downing Street. Only a year before Blair's victory in 1997, the IRA bombed the financial centre at London's Canary Wharf. Maintaining security required the deployment of 30,000 troops in Northern Ireland – this in a province with a population of only 1.6 million people.

Attempts to broker a political settlement between the majority Protestant unionist population and the Catholic nationalist community had come to nothing. In 1973, Edward Heath's government had tried to halt the violence with a power-sharing

327

agreement, only to see the accord brought down by militant unionists determined to keep the stranglehold on power they had been granted after the partition of Ireland in 1921. Against her pro-unionist instincts, in 1985 Thatcher had signed the Anglo–Irish Agreement with the government of the Republic of Ireland, in another attempt to give nationalists a significant voice in the affairs of the province. The war – waged by the IRA against the British state and by violent Protestant paramilitaries against the Catholic community – went on.

Another Labour prime minister, Harold Wilson, responded to the intransigence of unionists by asking officials to consider how to move Northern Ireland out of the United Kingdom. The idea fell by the wayside when the officials told Wilson that British withdrawal would start a civil war that would engulf the Republic as well as Northern Ireland.

Britain was alone among the world's leading democracies in facing an armed insurrection on such a scale. Though successive prime ministers insisted that the conflict was a purely domestic issue, they were acutely aware that it stained the United Kingdom's reputation abroad. David Manning, who was Tony Blair's foreign policy adviser before serving as ambassador in Washington, recalls that for many of Britain's allies, the army presence on the streets had the feel of a military occupation: 'I felt all the way through that Ireland was an open wound. It didn't really matter terribly whether you believed this was all very unfair. That wasn't the point. It was the perception.'[50]

The reputational damage was strengthened by the widespread view, especially in the United States, that the conflict reflected the British government's indifference to the fate of the Catholic community. On the East Coast of the United States, with its large Irish diaspora, Northern Ireland was widely regarded as a hangover from the days of colonialist oppression. The Irish communities in New York and Boston provided a steady stream of funding for Sinn Fein, the political wing of the IRA. Images of republicans being interned without trial and of IRA prisoners dying on hunger strike in Northern Ireland's vast prisons brought showers of criticism over British rule in the province. A significant slice of the East Coast political establishment claimed Irish antecedents. Britain saw Americans lending moral support to a terrorist movement. But in the US there was a suspicion of official collusion with Protestant paramilitary groups. Many in New York, Boston and Washington challenged the continuation of British rule over Northern Ireland. Ronald Reagan fell out with Margaret Thatcher over the issue, and Bill Clinton with John Major. The republican leaders – Gerry Adams and Martin McGuinness most prominently – were well known, but in the UK broadcasters were barred from transmitting interviews with them. Nigel Sheinwald saw the reputational impact first-hand while serving in the US capital: 'If you were representing Britain anywhere in the world, as I was in Washington in the 1980s, Northern Ireland was the millstone round your neck in reputational terms.'[51] Blair arrived in Downing Street imagining Britain as a beacon for progress and democracy. Northern Ireland told an altogether different story.

The groundwork for peace talks had been laid by John Major. Blair's predecessor had opened up channels of communication to Sinn Fein and the IRA and began negotiations with the Irish governments of Albert Reynolds and Bertie Ahern about the possible shape of power-sharing between unionist and nationalist parties. Major had taken considerable political risks to secure an IRA ceasefire. Two things were obvious to the members of the intelligence services who followed events in the province. The first was that the IRA would not succeed in driving the British out of Northern Ireland through violence, and its commanders had begun to understand this. The second was that the state could not defeat an insurgency that a sizeable portion of the population saw as a response to injustice. With the help of the US senator George Mitchell, Major set the parameters for future political talks. After a dispute over the granting of American visas to senior republicans, Bill Clinton joined Major's peace effort. The process broke down over the decommissioning of IRA weapons. The decision facing Blair following his election victory was how much political capital and personal energy to devote to reviving the effort.

The essential elements of a political settlement were never a mystery: power-sharing between unionists and nationalists in a devolved government in Belfast, the putting aside of the Republic's constitutional claim to the territory of Northern Ireland in exchange for a role in the affairs of the province, and embedded in this political framework, the principle of consent – agreement on all sides that the future constitutional status of the province would rest in the hands of the people. They could decide to remain within the United Kingdom or to join with the Republic in a united Ireland. If the outlines were evident, so too were the boulders strewn along the road after so many decades of violence. How to sequence negotiations and the decommissioning of weapons, how to deal with prisoners, how to treat historic crimes, and how, above all, to dispel sufficiently the mistrust and hatred between divided communities so that they could work together in government? Belfast was a city described by the high walls and barbed wire separating unionist and nationalist communities. Protestants and Catholics attended different schools. Nationalists were all but excluded from swathes of the public sector, including the police service. How could unionists be persuaded that the Union was safe, and nationalists be assured that the Westminster government accepted the legitimacy of their case for a united Ireland?

Blair brought to the negotiations self-belief, patience, political courage and an absolute determination to secure a settlement. He arrived in Belfast on the first of what would be many prime ministerial visits with the clarity of a politician addressing the conflict without prejudice. Labour's position had traditionally favoured the nationalist claim to a united Ireland, but Blair reassured unionists that the province would remain part of the UK for as long as a majority so wished. If republicans renounced terrorism, they would be included in the political process. In the summer of 1997, Blair was not sure whether he would succeed: 'If you ask me if the republicans have definitively decided to give up violence for good, the answer is probably no,' he said. That could change if they were drawn into talks. Either way, Blair was determined to show the US and the rest of the international community that Britain had given the republicans a chance; if they rejected it, they could no longer blame the 'British oppressor'. The gamble paid off. By the autumn of 1997, the IRA had declared another ceasefire and had joined talks chaired by Mitchell. When Blair sat down with Adams and McGuinness, he became the first British prime minister since partition in 1921 to meet the leaders of republicanism.

The Good Friday, or Belfast, Agreement, reached on 10 April 1998, saw Northern Ireland step out of the dark shadows of history. Blair was owed much of the credit, but so too were an array of other figures from across the sectarian divide. In the preceding months, Bertie Ahern, the Irish prime minister, and David Trimble, the leader of moderate unionism, shared the stage with the IRA leaders ready to exchange bullets for ballot boxes. George Mitchell played a pivotal mediating role. Bill Clinton, from the distance of Washington, made critical telephone calls to both sides during the final hours of negotiations. Behind the scenes, Jonathan Powell, Blair's chief of staff, kept the lights on as the essential go-between in discussions with republicans, moderate nationalists led by John Hume and Trimble's unionists. A former diplomat and one of the most trusted members of the team Blair had brought into Downing Street, Powell provided the conduit that linked Blair's political energy and insights to the complex machinery of political compromise.

Within weeks, the agreement won the overwhelming support of voters on both sides of the Irish border. Historic though it was, the accord was as much a beginning as a conclusion. Rejected by the more hard-line unionists of Ian Paisley's Democratic Unionist Party and challenged by dissident republicans, the text was shot through with constructive ambiguities. The history and enmities in Northern Ireland were not about to dissolve over one Easter weekend. For the next few years, Powell would never be far away from Belfast. The imperative, he later recounted, was to 'keep everyone in the room'. The eventual success of a peacemaking process that in 2007 saw the firebrand Paisley, for decades the standard-bearer of Protestant rule, share power with the former IRA commander McGuinness flowed from what Powell called a strategy of 'never letting the talking stop'.

11

Fog in the Channel

Britain's new prime minister, his officials would quickly learn, had come to view life as a procession of effortless triumphs. Born into a wealthy family in the 'stockbroker belt' of the English Home Counties, David Cameron had trodden a privileged upper-middle-class path from an exclusive preparatory school to Eton and Oxford. Spells at Conservative Central Office's research department and as a bag carrier and aide to Tory ministers were followed by a period in the private sector as a PR executive – positions shared out among young men and women of a certain social class rather than posts advertised in the situations vacant pages. Likewise, when the affluent and safe Conservative seat of Witney in Oxfordshire became vacant, Cameron seemed an obvious choice. Four years later, after his party's third consecutive general election defeat, he made an audacious bid for the Conservative leadership. Aged thirty-nine, he presented himself as a 'moderniser' who would drag the party into the twenty-first century and reset its relationship with an electorate that had been seduced by Blair's New Labour. There was nothing in his demeanour in May 2010 that said the premiership was anything other than pre-ordained. Of the world beyond Westminster, and Britain's place in it, Cameron knew little.

The Number 10 officials who gathered to greet Cameron on his first day as prime minister were struck by his casual entitlement. He was handed the secret codes needed to authorise the firing of Britain's Trident missiles in the event of nuclear war. 'There was no sense of awe,' one official remarked of Cameron's introduction to his new responsibilities.[1] Yet this was not a politician arriving in office with a grand plan to steer the nation in a new direction. Why did he want to be prime minister? Cameron had been asked by a television interviewer before the election that had seen him defeat Labour's Gordon Brown. Another Conservative leader would have responded with a declaration of intent to transform the nation's fortunes, but Cameron was insouciant. 'Because I think I'd be good at it,' he replied. Good at it. So, in one dimension, he was to prove. Cameron showed himself to be entirely comfortable in the role. Power, one official remarked, fitted him 'like an expensive suit'.[2] He was ready to take risks. The general election had left him short of a majority in the House of Commons. Brown sought initially to assemble a coalition with smaller opposition parties that would keep him in office, but Cameron's 'big, bold offer' to Nick Clegg's Liberal Democrats of a five-year partnership secured the prize for the Conservatives. Yet it was soon clear enough that while Cameron would be good at *being* prime minister, he would never quite grasp that this was not at all the same as being a *good* prime minister. Into that gap would fall the fateful decision to gamble the nation's future on a referendum that would in the end leave Britain rudderless and diminished.

To the extent that Cameron took office with a set of foreign policy instincts, they pulled him in the direction of retrenchment. After the wars in Iraq and Afghanistan that had marked out Tony Blair's premiership and the global financial crash that had emptied the Treasury's coffers, this was unsurprising. Grand hopes of nation-building had been lost to the desert dust of Basra and Helmand. For some time, Cameron had privately expressed doubts about the war in Afghanistan, a conflict in which British soldiers were dying for little apparent purpose. Blair's liberal interventionism was a doctrine that spoke more easily to the idealism of the centre-left than to the pragmatism of a British Tory. Then, of course, there was George Osborne. A long-standing friend and ally, Osborne's role was to provide Cameron with a governing strategy. It started with the harsh fiscal austerity the new chancellor deemed essential to bring down the budget deficit. The gap had reached more than 10 per cent of national income – three or four times what the Treasury would consider 'safe'. Osborne was clear the armed forces could not escape the axe. There would be moments during the following years when Cameron would break his own rules – notably when he was drawn to support military intervention to remove Muammar Gaddafi's regime in Libya and, in an effort foiled by parliament, to join the United States in an attack on Bashar al-Assad's Syrian regime. But, as with his policy towards Europe, Cameron set out with other ambitions.

Gordon Brown's three-year premiership had turned out to be an awkward interlude. The former chancellor had waited a decade for the keys to Number 10. The premiership, he believed, had been promised to him by Blair as long ago as 1994, when the death of John Smith had seen the two competing for the succession. Brown had stepped back, on the promise, he would later say, that Blair would make way for him after a first term. Blair had a rather different memory, but by 2007, ten years into his premiership, the consequences of the Iraq War weighed too heavily. Elected as a leader to unite the country, now he divided it. In 2007, he gave in to the pressure from his party to step down.

The big surprise was that Brown arrived in office without a clear agenda. Surely, during all those long nights plotting to seize the crown, he had also mapped out a strategy for his premiership? Ten years at the Treasury had provided a matchless grasp of the domestic policy challenges. Yet, within months of his arrival in

Downing Street, it was obvious that there was no grand plan. And abroad, he was left to pick up the pieces of his predecessor's wars. An ignominious withdrawal from Iraq – the last British troops left their base in the city of Basra in September 2007, under the cover of a secret agreement with local Shia militia – had been accompanied by an ill-judged military build-up in Afghanistan. Britain had agreed to take a lead role in the NATO force that was charged with defeating the Taliban and building a rudimentary democracy. History – the 1842 retreat from Kabul during the First Anglo–Afghan War – might have cautioned against the enterprise. But the chaos into which Iraq had fallen had not yet destroyed the optimism of the generals who claimed that with enough military force and sufficient financial aid, Afghanistan could be moulded into something resembling a Western-style democracy. British commanders had cheerfully lobbied for their troops to take up the role of subduing the Taliban in Helmand province. Soon enough they found themselves pinned down, often in remote outposts, by an enemy revitalised by the cause of expelling foreign forces. Brown and his advisers knew the war could not be won – at least not with the resources the NATO coalition was ready to invest. But it was too soon to admit defeat. The generals blamed their own tactical misjudgements on inadequate forces and equipment. Brown took most of the brickbats.

Towards Europe, Brown showed a grudging engagement. He understood the logic of Britain's membership of the European Union but would never be comfortable with the consensual politics that were at the heart of EU decision-making. By temperament, he understood politics as a battle between competing values and ideologies. His political style was well suited to the House of Commons. The consensualism that was designed into the semi-circular layouts of most European parliaments – and indeed the new assembly in Scotland – was a foreign country. During Blair's premiership, Brown framed his regular trips to Brussels for meetings of finance ministers as win-or-lose, claiming supposed victories for British policy and belittling the initiatives of European colleagues. He was proud to have thwarted Blair's attempts to take Britain into the single currency – all the more so as the future of the euro came into question during the economic hurricane that followed the global financial crash.

David Miliband, Brown's foreign secretary, took a broader view. A committed multilateralist, he saw Britain's role as a convener of like-minded democracies. He was anxious to repair the damage to its European relationships inflicted by the Iraq War. His predecessor Jack Straw had started in that direction, working closely with his German and French counterparts to bring Iran into international negotiations over its nuclear programme. Straw, though, was never an enthusiast for Europe, while Miliband leaned instinctively towards the continent. He dispensed with Blair's characterisation of Britain as a bridge between Europe and the United States. Bridges, as the German chancellor Gerhard Schröder had once told Blair, invite people to walk over them. Miliband considered that the closer engagement he sought in Europe would of itself raise Britain's influence across the world.

Gordon Brown's legacy would be salvaged at least in part by the bankers who brought down the world's financial system. When the collapse of the American investment bank Lehman Brothers triggered the global crash in the autumn of 2008, the British prime minister was the only Western leader who was schooled in the intricacies of international financial markets. A decade of attending meetings at the International Monetary Fund, strong contacts in the American economic establishment and a desperate need to find a purpose for his premiership conspired to give him a leading role in the international effort to stabilise the world economy. The real and present danger was that draining confidence in the financial markets would see the world slide into a deep depression, as it had done during the 1930s. Action by individual governments – even those as powerful as the United States' – would be insufficient to restore confidence. China had to be part of the story; so too other emerging economies, such as India, Brazil and South Africa. What was needed was a coordinated effort to allow fiscal policies to take some of the strain, in addition to the world's central banks injecting sufficient money into global markets to prevent a spiral into deflation. Brown had a mission for his premiership.

The London summit of the G20 leaders in April 2009 would prompt claims from Brown's friends that he had effectively saved the global financial system. The diplomacy that preceded this gathering of the leaders of the most important industrialised and rising nations was intense. And the summit itself could not paper over transatlantic differences regarding the extent to which governments should borrow more to stimulate the world economy. For all that, it was a classic exercise in multilateralism – recognition that the open international financial system could be stabilised only if governments of all stripes acted in concert. The alternative was a return to the beggar-thy-neighbour protectionism that had driven the world into deep recession during the 1930s.

The symbolism counted. The promise that governments would inject more than a trillion dollars into the global economy included a repackaging of previous commitments. The simple fact of the meeting and the diplomacy that preceded it produced a level of agreement that did much to rebuild confidence. It was enough, one senior diplomat remarked, 'that all these people agreed to sit down together in one place'. Brown had intended to focus on domestic policy as prime minister. If his premiership left a mark on history, it was in the realm of international affairs. A year later, defeated in the general election, Brown might have been compensated. Influential figures on the international monetary scene promoted him as a candidate to take over the prestigious role of managing director of the International Monetary Fund. A small-minded Cameron refused the government's backing. The job went to France's Christine Lagarde.

Cameron held up Harold Macmillan as a role model. In opposition, he had a painting of his fellow Old Etonian above the desk in his House of Commons office. The comparison cast the new prime minister as a patrician one-nation Tory with a social conscience. In truth, the similarities were slight. Macmillan's social liberalism was rooted in personal sight of the impact of the Great Depression on the poor during the 1920s. By the time he reached the highest office, he had spent decades being schooled in domestic and overseas affairs. A veteran of the First World War, he had been a prominent adviser during the Second World War, working closely with Eisenhower and de Gaulle. He had served in several offices of state, including as chancellor. The experience had left him acutely aware of Britain's slipping place in the world and, after Suez, of the pressing need to build overseas alliances. For Cameron, foreign policy was a foreign country.

Several months after the election, a senior Number 10 adviser offered some telling insights. Cameron, this official said, worked hard enough and was comfortable taking decisions. He accepted advice from Osborne and had built a good working relationship with his coalition partner Clegg. He was a 'quick read', finding it easy to follow the arguments in official briefings and to take decisions. Missing, the official continued, was a prospectus or much sense of intellectual inquiry. He was, well, 'shallow'.[3] And what did he think about the world? In the prime minister's mind, the adviser offered, 'the world is somewhere where you take your holidays'. It was a crushing observation, reminiscent of a scene from the television satire *Yes Minister*. At the time it seemed unfair. Time would show it to have been depressingly prescient.

Cameron devolved the framing of domestic policy to George Osborne. The chancellor was the 'ideas man', the chief executive to Cameron's non-executive chairman. He was also the political strategist, a close student of the way that Blair had transformed the fortunes of the Labour Party. In forging a five-year coalition with Clegg to secure a stable House of Commons majority, Cameron had shown his willingness to take political risks. Osborne, however, set the policy terms of the agreement with the Liberal Democrats. The legacy of the crash was a rising mountain of debt, with annual public borrowing rising above 10 per cent of national income. 'We're all in this together,' the chancellor would say of the austerity programme he had designed to pull Britain out of the economic abyss. The goal was to cast the coalition as an essentially moderate enterprise; public spending cuts and tax increases were measures taken in sorrow, not anger. Cameron had taken on board Brown's ambitious overseas aid target as an emblem of his commitment to soften his party's reputation for being uncaring. For the rest, though, he accepted Osborne's judgement that the nation's overseas commitments could not escape the axe. The armed forces had been placed front and centre during Blair's term, a vital instrument of his doctrine of liberal interventionism. Now, battered and exhausted by two wars, they had to fight for their budgets.

Arriving without a settled worldview, the new prime minister brought with him one institutional innovation. Blair's so-called 'sofa government' had prompted severe criticism from various inquiries into the Iraq War. Informal decision-making militated against careful decision-making, the argument ran. Cameron's answer was to pull together the Whitehall machinery handling foreign policy, defence, intelligence and domestic security under one roof. Chaired by the prime minister, the new National Security Council followed the model of the United States, bringing together senior ministers and relevant officials and spooks from across government. Set up by Sir Peter Ricketts, the former head of the Foreign Office and one of Whitehall's shrewdest diplomats, it was a sensible reform, not least because it united the various strands of government dealing with domestic Islamist terrorism with those directing Britain's contribution to the fight against Al Qaeda and other jihadi groups in the Middle East. A committee, though, would never be a substitute for a policy. And Cameron showed little interest in digging deep. Another official recalls an early meeting of the NSC being devoted to the relationship with China. Several papers had been prepared as to how the government might handle a rising power that was at once commercially important and a serious strategic threat. The prime minister showed little interest, with the exception of the discussion as to whether he should risk the wrath of Beijing by meeting the Dalai Lama. Cameron thought yes, and the meeting was duly arranged. Beijing responded with an eighteen-month freeze on high-level contacts. China policy was henceforth delegated to Osborne. The chancellor decided to downgrade the strategic risks in pursuit of business opportunities. Within a couple of years, Cameron was doffing his cap to Beijing, as Osborne declared that Britain would be China's 'best friend' in the West.

Cameron's first big foreign policy speech was defensive. Policymakers at home and overseas had begun to talk of a drift towards 'strategic shrinkage', as the government focused on cutting the deficit and the prime minister put himself at the head of a campaign to 'sell' British business overseas by leading large overseas trade delegations. In the first of his annual addresses at the City's Mansion House, he insisted that restoring the nation's economic health by cutting the deficit was as much about increasing Britain's heft in world affairs as about rebuilding at home: 'What I have seen in my first six months as prime minister is a Britain at the centre of all the big discussions. Producing the ideas, consulted for our experience and respected for the skills we bring and our capacity to find solutions. So I reject the thesis of decline.' Britain was not 'shuffling apologetically off the world stage'. His references to the twin relationships with the United States and Europe were entirely conventional: he would nurture the 'deep and close relationship' with America and 'strong and active' membership of the European Union. His aim was to project a policy of hard-headed internationalism, eschewing military adventurism. A policy 'more commercial in enabling Britain to earn its way in the world once again, more strategic in its focus on meeting the new and emerging threats to our national security'.[4] The practice, Cameron discovered, was not so easy. Among early initiatives was an attempt to 'reset' relations with Russia's Vladimir Putin, which had been badly damaged by the Russian regime's murder in London of the exiled Alexander Litvinenko. The former intelligence officer had been killed in 2006, poisoned with the radioactive substance polonium-210. Cameron engineered a temporary thaw, but Putin's invasion of Ukraine in 2014 put an end to the effort.

On withdrawal from Afghanistan, Cameron was in tune with both the public mood and the economic circumstances. Getting out had broad, though not universal, support across Whitehall's foreign policy and defence establishments. The nation had tired of war. The tactics deployed by the Taliban – lethal improvised explosive devices that could destroy all but the most heavily armoured vehicles – saw a steady stream of dead and wounded soldiers arriving back in Britain. The war's strategic goal, if there ever was one, had dissolved into expediency. As in Iraq, Britain found itself as a junior partner in a conflict in which it could not take any of the big decisions. They all belonged to Washington. Barack Obama had fought the 2008 US presidential election on a pledge to bring American troops home. Once in office, he had been persuaded by his generals to agree to a temporary surge in the number of US forces in order to allow them to redraw the battlefield with the Taliban. But he had taken a lot of convincing, and the surge had been accompanied by a deadline for withdrawal. The numbers would be cut again once the immediate objectives had been achieved. The president had heard the Taliban's boast that if the Americans had the military advantage, the Afghans had the time. Soon enough, the Taliban judged, US public opinion would turn against the war. They were right. By 2014, America and its allies had settled on a strategy. They would declare victory and head for the exits, leaving the Afghan government to fight for its own future, with the help of a small number of Western advisers and training staff.

As sensitive as Cameron was to the charge that Britain had stepped back from the world, the message from the government's spending review was unequivocal. Fiscal austerity would take precedence over self-confident globalism. Deep cuts in the Foreign Office's budget heralded a smaller diplomatic footprint. As the foreign secretary William Hague opened new 'micro-embassies' in small and emerging economies such as Paraguay, the FCO's big diplomatic posts in Europe were being hollowed out, with ambassadors across the world told that their first priority was to provide an on-the-spot sales force for British business. Diplomats who were accustomed to assuming a wider role in shaping the contours of international relations were handed annual targets to improve Britain's trade balance.

A promised strategic defence review pointed in the same direction. Ministers on the National Security Council reported that the government was conducting two parallel conversations with itself. The first focused on the array of new threats facing the country, from the spread across the Middle East and much of Africa of jihadi groups affiliated to Al Qaeda and other violent groups to the alarming level of cyber-attacks on the British government and sensitive industries from countries such as Russia, China, Iran and North Korea. The second demanded that the Foreign Office and the Ministry of Defence contribute to swingeing cuts. Hague was anxious not to signal a retreat from the world, but the circle could not be squared. National security adviser Peter Ricketts recalls that the government had been 'Disguising decline . . . Right up until 2010, when William Hague came in and said, "We are not going to have any nonsense about strategic shrinkage." The 2010 review was supposed to show that there was no strategic shrinkage going on, but by then that was getting quite hard to sustain.'[5]

In the event, the defence budget was reduced by about 15 per cent over the lifetime of the parliament. In deference to appearances, Cameron insisted on holding on to the most prized emblems of international status: a planned £30 billion modernisation of the Trident nuclear missile system and the construction of new aircraft carriers, both projects that had been set in motion by Gordon Brown's government. As much as the decisions were intended as a statement of Britain's commitment to global security, closer examination told a different story. Trident's modernisation would be paid for by shrinking the navy's surface fleet, and the aircraft carriers by reducing the number of American F-35 warplanes that would fly from them. Likewise, increased funding for anti-terrorism efforts, cyber-capabilities and the intelligence agencies were paid for by cuts elsewhere. The RAF lost fighter planes, the navy lost ships and the army lost soldiers. As a maritime nation, Britain prized its command of the seas, but the scrapping of the Nimrod programme left it without any aircraft for vital maritime surveillance. The Harrier jump jet force was retired. The navy lost its existing carrier, HMS *Ark Royal*, and the fleet was reduced to nineteen surface ships, the smallest since the Napoleonic Wars. The slimmed-down military would be able to deploy a maximum of 30,000 personnel in any overseas operation, compared to the 45,000 that had been available for the Iraq War in 2003. The complaints of the military chiefs were echoed by semi-public expressions of disquiet in Washington. The 'pocket superpower' pretence was threadbare.

Politicians are rarely accused of consistency. So it was with Cameron after the start of what was briefly thought to be an 'Arab Spring' for democracy. In January 2011, angry protests against an unpopular regime in Tunisia lit a match for uprisings across the Arab world. Vast demonstrations in Cairo's Tahrir Square saw Egypt's authoritarian ruler Hosni Mubarak suffer the same fate as Zine El Abidine Ben Ali had in Tunisia's Jasmine Revolution. The Libyan dictator Muammar Gaddafi also found his absolute authority challenged by a popular uprising in the east of the country. Western governments – briefly and over-optimistically – saw the possibility of the democratic transformation of a region that had stubbornly refused to throw off the habit of authoritarianism. Cameron's initial reaction was cautious. In February, he travelled to the Gulf, at the head of a delegation of defence industry leaders selling arms to the local autocrats. The optics, as diplomats call them, were scarcely good as people took to the streets in Tunisia, Egypt and Libya, demonstrating against autocratic rule. As Gaddafi's military advanced on the eastern city of Benghazi, intent on crushing the Libyan rebellion, a prime minister who had scorned liberal interventionism reversed himself. What prompted the turnabout was never truly clear. Cameron had obviously been stung by the juxtaposition of television images of his meetings with Arab autocrats with those of crowds marching for freedom and human dignity. Some in Downing Street thought his decision had been coloured by the wars in the former Yugoslavia during the 1990s. Gaddafi's brutal repression stirred uncomfortable memories of the murderous behaviour of Serbian leader Slobodan Milošević. Cameron had been an adviser in the Conservative government that had opposed tougher international intervention to prevent the slaughter and ethnic cleansing of Bosnian Muslims.

Cameron was not alone. A few months earlier, he and the French president Nicolas Sarkozy had signed a bilateral treaty updating the defence cooperation between the two nations that had begun with the St Malo declaration in 1998. France, like Britain, was struggling to sustain the reach of its military, and it made sense to share the burden. Picking up negotiations started by Gordon Brown, Cameron signed off on arrangements that would see the two nations coordinate the deployment of carrier-led naval task forces. Joint training exercises would allow them to deploy a Franco–British expeditionary force. Most sensitively, the treaty established a project for nuclear warhead testing – the first time that Paris and London had shown a willingness to share nuclear secrets since their parting of the ways over Britain's Polaris decision in the early 1960s.

Cameron's and Sarkozy's enthusiasm was not shared by Barack Obama. The US administration saw only a limited national interest in what happened in Libya. A president who had promised to bring home troops from the Middle East, Obama was not inclined to send more. There was also irritation in the White House at the sequencing: Cameron had just announced deep cuts in Britain's military capabilities, and now wanted to pull the US into a new conflict. 'If you Europeans want to rattle sabres in Libya, you will have to pay for your own blades,' one of Obama's officials remarked, in response to the calls for military intervention.[6] Closer to home, many of the prime minister's advisers harboured their own doubts. The first aim of the proposed intervention was to prevent the slaughter of the people of Benghazi, but what then? General David Richards, the chief of the general staff, and John Sawers, the head of the Secret Intelligence Service, both had direct experience in the region. Both were sceptical about an open-ended intervention. Was the aim to tilt the balance in the civil war towards the rebels, to force regime change or simply to safeguard Benghazi? A UN Security Council resolution suggested the latter – Russia would go no further before wielding its veto – but once French and British warplanes began bombing Gaddafi's forces, mission creep became inevitable. Cameron wanted regime change but had no plan for what would come next.

For Sarkozy, Obama's stance was a spur to action, a chance to break the yoke of dependency on the US. Europe would show it could act alone. Here was the dream of every French leader since Suez. However, the reality was not quite so simple. Neither France nor Britain was prepared to put troops on the ground, and an air campaign would require help from the US for surveillance, targeting and intelligence. A compromise was negotiated with the White House: the US would give active support for the first week of bombing, before command and control of the operation passed to NATO. Washington would, in Obama's description, 'lead from behind'. This was a phrase the president would come to regret. It was meant to signal that America would not always be the first to put its military in harm's way, that sometimes it would operate in a support role for allies. Instead the words were taken as a signal of retreat and a sign of weakness.

Wars that start well often end badly. So it had been with Iraq. Within a week of the first airstrikes in Libya, Gaddafi's advance eastwards had been halted and much of his military destroyed. But the rebels were not strong enough to follow through with a decisive blow against the regime. France and Britain were drawn in to supply arms, intelligence and training for the rebels. It took another six months for the anti-Gaddafi forces to seize Tripoli. Captured, Gaddafi was summarily killed. Sarkozy and Cameron travelled to Benghazi to enjoy the adulation of the anti-regime crowds. 'What next?' someone asked. No answer. Cameron had acted without thinking ahead. Neither France nor Britain was ready to take responsibility for the peace. Libya was a state stitched together after empire. Gaddafi had ruled as an absolute dictator. The country lacked the institutions and structures of a modern state. Before long, it had fallen into what became an essentially tribal civil war. By then, Cameron and Sarkozy had found other priorities.

Syria told another dismal story. In August 2013, its leader Bashar al-Assad was alleged to have used chemical weapons against rebel forces seeking to overturn his regime. If proven, this crossed a 'red line' that had been set down by Barack Obama. The US president had been reluctant to intervene directly against Assad's brutal suppression of the uprising in Syria. Too many regional actors – Iran, Iraq, Turkey and Saudi Arabia among them – had interests in the conflict. The American focus was on the jihadis of the self-styled Islamic State, but Assad's flouting of international law by using long-banned weapons was a step too far. As the United Nations sought to check the veracity of the reports, Obama prepared for strikes against Syrian military installations. Sarkozy was eager to join the operation, and French warplanes were put on alert. Cameron also wanted to participate, but Whitehall's mandarins were cautious, not least because Washington was sending mixed messages as to the scale and timing of its planned reprisals. The public mood had turned against military intervention, even in response to such horrific crimes. Cameron realised that he needed the consent of MPs, and the House of Commons was recalled from its summer recess.

The rejection by the House of Commons of any military action marked the end of Cameron's flirtation with foreign policy activism. Beyond the political humiliation of such a defeat on a major issue of foreign policy, the 285–272 vote put a question mark over Britain's willingness to take a lead on the international stage. The wars in Afghanistan and Iraq had taken their toll on national self-confidence, weakening public support for armed intervention in the other nations' conflicts. Ed Miliband, who had replaced Gordon Brown after Labour's 2010 election defeat, refused the backing of his party in what some saw as an act of public penance – an attempt to dissociate himself from 'Blair's wars'. Dozens of Conservative MPs defied the whip and voted with the opposition. It was clear, Cameron told MPs after the vote, 'that the British parliament, reflecting the views of the British people, does not want to see British military action. I get that and the government will act accordingly.'[7] William Hague took the defeat badly: according to one senior diplomat, 'it knocked the stuffing' out of the foreign secretary. Two years later, he resigned from the job and announced his intention to stand down as an MP at the next election.

In March 2014, nine months later, Russian tanks crossed the Ukrainian border to secure Moscow's annexation of Crimea. Russian special forces and irregular troops moved into eastern Ukraine. The Russian aggression overturned the foundation of the post-war European order: the assumption that the continent's borders could never again be changed by force of arms. The invasion was also a flagrant violation of the 1994 Budapest Memorandum – an agreement that guaranteed the territorial integrity and security of the newly independent Ukraine in return for its willingness to scrap its nuclear weapons. Russia was among the three guarantors, along with the United States and Britain. The United States and the European Union responded to the aggression with sanctions.

As in Libya, Barack Obama made it clear that while the United States would be supportive, the Europeans were expected to take the lead in seeking a resolution. British diplomats initially played a lead role in framing the European sanctions package, but Cameron then retreated to the shadows, leaving the diplomacy to Germany's Angela Merkel and French president François Hollande. Foreign Office officials could not recall so important an event when Britain had effectively absented itself from the diplomacy that followed. The prime minister, it seemed, had lost his enthusiasm for the international stage. For a while during 2014 and 2015, he would look further afield, when he flirted with the idea that Britain could position itself as best friend in the West to Xi Jinping's China. But this was dangerous play-acting rather than serious foreign policy.

*

Cameron's relationship with Obama was cordial but cool. In 2009, Gordon Brown had won the unseemly race between European leaders to be the first to secure an Oval Office audience with the new president. The two men had worked closely together in response to the global financial crash. Brown's chairmanship of a summit of the G20 group of rich and emerging powers in London had been widely applauded. But Whitehall worried that there was something cold about Obama. America's first black president did not share the instinctive Atlanticism of most of the Wasps (White Anglo-Saxon Protestants) who had dominated the Washington foreign policy establishment. What the president wanted to know, his advisers said, was what was Europe contributing to global security? A state visit to Britain saw him establish an unusual rapport with the Queen, but generally speaking Obama was unsentimental about the ties between the US and UK. The bust of Winston Churchill that had sat in the Oval Office during George W. Bush's presidency was quietly moved. The most pressing demands on American foreign policy now came from wars in the Middle East and from the impact on Asia of China's rise. A personal friendship with the Queen did not prevent a strikingly hard-headed assessment of America's national interest.

For his part, Cameron accepted the assumption of the British defence and foreign policy establishments that the relationship with Washington was essential to the nation's security. This establishment view of the 'special relationship' was set out in a confidential paper that circulated in Whitehall during the months before Cameron's election victory. It was one of 'life's harsh truths', the author began, in the weary tone of a senior mandarin bothered too often by politicians, that the government had to measure the weather over the Atlantic from time to time. There would be no harm in repeating the exercise during the strategic defence review that would follow the election. No harm, that is, as long as the terms were clear from the outset. 'This should be the traditional policy review,' it emphasised, 'identifying alternatives, but in the final analysis sticking to the status quo. And our soul-searching should be done very much in private.'[8] The note might have been taken from the script of an episode of *Yes Minister*. Policy reviews are fine, as long as they do not change things.

Fifty years after Macmillan had repaired the relationship, the essential tenets had not changed. Britain, these held, was the net beneficiary. For the US president, the alliance was important but ultimately optional. There was much more at stake for the occupant of Downing Street. Even after the fall of the Berlin Wall, Europe still sheltered under the US security umbrella. The United States' presence in Europe – embedded in NATO – was essential reassurance against an assertive Russia. It served as guarantor of European cohesion. Washington provided critical intelligence about terrorism and filled yawning technological gaps in Europe's defences. In Britain's case, it also supplied a strategic nuclear deterrent. Churchill once remarked that 'No lover ever studied the whims of his mistress as I did those of President Roosevelt.' Sixty or seventy years later, much the same might have been said of the attention paid to Washington by the foreign policy establishment in London. Proximity was power. The connections supplied British diplomats and generals with a standing they would otherwise have lacked. The Foreign Office, the Ministry of Defence, the intelligence services – all drew prestige from the dense web of bureaucratic connections and personal relationships. Surely, the beneficiaries argued, this favoured position was well worth the occasional political embarrassment when a prime minister was lampooned in the press for seeming too slavish in his or her devotion to the Americans. What such judgements did not measure was the extent to which British policy might be bent towards the priorities of the Americans even when Britain's strategic interests pointed firmly in another direction.

Europe would be Cameron's undoing. He had decided at the start of his leadership that his party's post-Thatcherite obsession with Brussels stood in the way of his determination to wrench the Conservatives back to the political centre ground. Voters were worried about the health service, education, living standards and jobs. While Tory MPs were talking about Europe, the electorate drew the conclusion that they were more interested in talking to themselves. Cameron had watched as endless arguments about Europe had driven the party to the political margins. His two predecessors, William Hague and Michael Howard, had put Europe at the centre of their general election campaigns. And lost. Soon after becoming leader, he described supporters of the anti-European United Kingdom Independence Party led by Nigel Farage as 'fruitcakes, loonies and closet racists, mostly'.[9] The Tories, Cameron said, should stop 'banging on about Europe'.

Much earlier, Cameron had been at the Treasury, working as an adviser to the chancellor Norman Lamont when sterling crashed out of the European Exchange Rate Mechanism. When Lamont announced on 16 September 1992 that the billions of dollars thrown at the foreign exchange markets by the Bank of England had been wasted, Cameron was pictured standing behind him. In the years that followed, he had watched the bitter parliamentary battles over the ratification of the Maastricht Treaty and seen John Major tortured by the hard-line Eurosceptics. Tony Blair's crushing electoral victory in 1997 had seen the Conservatives swing to the right. William Hague set it as his personal mission to 'save the pound' from Blair's enthusiasm for the euro. The Tory defeat of 1997 was followed by an equally devastating collapse in 2001.

If Cameron understood that the Conservatives had to speak to voters about the real preoccupations of their daily lives, from the beginning of his premiership he sometimes seemed to be in the thrall of the Eurosceptics. Kim Darroch recalls Cameron's first European summit in 2010. The proceedings were uneventful, but the prime minister had earned some kudos among his new colleagues by helping to untangle some drafting disputes about the final communiqué. He was visibly pleased with himself, counting the summit a success – until one member of the British media asked whether his obvious enjoyment had tempered his sceptical views of the Union. 'There was a pause and then [Cameron] said "Well", and started listing all the things he didn't like about Europe.'[10]

Hague had softened the edges of the strident Euroscepticism that had seen him lead the party to defeat in 2001. Emotionally, he was with the nostalgists who thought Britain should look beyond its own continent to rebuild and revitalise relationships on the global stage. Much of his time at the Foreign Office was spent nurturing bilateral ties with far-flung nations. Embassies were opened in capitals from which British diplomacy had long since retreated. Relationships with the Arab states of the Gulf were revived. Officials were put to work examining if the Commonwealth could be resuscitated as an instrument of British reach and prestige. The Liberal Democrat Lord William Wallace served as a Foreign Office minister in Cameron's coalition. He was struck by how many Conservatives still signed up to 'the myth of Commonwealth'. The idea that 'India is going to give us a special deal because they are grateful for what we have done for them demonstrates the degree of delusion'.[11] Hague's worldview, his officials would say, had a distinctly Elizabethan tilt: untied from Europe, it imagined, Britain could flourish again as a buccaneering maritime nation, capable of making an impact in every corner of the globe. Unconstrained, Britain could show the world what it was made of. The foreign secretary allowed pragmatism to percolate the romanticism. Over time, he began to understand how the support of other European states acted as a multiplier of British power, providing leverage in the promotion of its projects and interests. But he was never entirely comfortable among his European peers, and the aloofness was noticed. More than a century earlier, Lord Palmerston had dismissed the worth of established, permanent alliances. Hague, one of his European counterparts would remark, had been born a century too late.

In 2010, Britain was viewed in Brussels as a semi-detached partner. It stood outside the eurozone and the Schengen system of open borders, and had opted in to only some of the provisions in the Maastricht Treaty that deepened the integration of security, law and justice. Hague challenged the conventional wisdom in the Foreign Office that Britain should keep a seat at every European table. For its part, the Tory party had a new generation of Eurosceptics at Westminster. They had grown up with Thatcherism and had little sense of the role played by European integration in securing the peace in Europe in the struggle with Soviet communism. When they reread Thatcher's Bruges speech, they alighted on her defence of Britain's right to make its own political choices but ignored the passages that argued with equal vigour that she would not retreat to the sidelines – that Europe belonged to Britain as much as to the continent. William Wallace caught a glimpse of the neuralgia. As Whitehall prepared for the centenary commemoration of the First World War, a memorandum circulated to ministers emphasised that the events should not

give 'credence to the myth that European integration is the outcome of the two world wars'.

Cameron's Bloomberg speech in January 2013 came in two parts.[12]
Nick Clegg, his coalition partner, refused to allow the promise of
a referendum to be presented as government policy. Cameron was
obliged to separate his critical but generally positive reflections
on the EU from the pledge that, should the Conservatives win an
overall majority at the next election, the voters would be able to
make up their minds in a referendum. At its core, the prime minister promised a new settlement between the United Kingdom and
the European Union, with a referendum to ratify or reject that
agreement by the end of 2017. Many of his demands on Brussels
might have been plucked from the wish lists of prime ministers
past. The government wanted to see a completion of the single
market, powers flowing to national capitals rather than in the
other direction, more democratic accountability for European
institutions and less intrusion into national life. More specifically, Britain wanted a set of guarantees that the integration of
the eurozone would not be at the expense of the rights and interests of those nations outside the single currency. The government,
Cameron said, wanted reform that would be good for Europe as
well as for Britain. The prime minister's European peers were not
taken in. Britain, they could see, wanted to go further along the
road of opt-outs and exemptions. Later, after the Leave side had
won the 2016 referendum, Cameron would say that in offering a
plebiscite he was responding to rising – all-but-irresistible – public pressure. The opinion polls at the time told a different story.
According to Ipsos MORI, the proportion of voters citing Europe
as 'one of the most important' issues rarely rose above 10 per cent
between 2010 and 2015 – scarcely irresistible.

The speech had been drafted and redrafted in Downing Street over weeks and months. Cameron had first raised the prospect of offering the pledge during the previous summer. William Hague was an enthusiast. George Osborne saw the dangers; the government, the chancellor argued, could weather the Eurosceptic storms without taking such a huge risk. Kenneth Clarke, the champion for a lost generation of Tory pro-Europeans, was appalled. Beyond an intense dislike of referendums – the 'device of demagogues and dictators', Margaret Thatcher had called them, invoking Clement Attlee's description on the eve of the 1975 vote called by Harold Wilson – Clarke, like Osborne, saw a danger that the vote could well be determined by the public mood rather than a considered argument about the pros and cons of EU membership. He considered resigning from the cabinet, but in the event decided to stay. Others expressed weary resignation.

Cameron's assertion that he was responding to a palpable and legitimate demand in the country for an opportunity to decide whether to remain part of an EU that had changed beyond all recognition since 1975 threw a veil over what was an attempt to make the government's life easier among its own supporters. Clarke recalled that Cameron told him that the offer of a referendum was the only way to pacify the Conservative Party in the run-up to the 2015 general election. European leaders were shocked at the prime minister's readiness to gamble Britain's place in Europe on the vicissitudes of public opinion. Aides to Angela Merkel said that she thought Cameron 'more than foolish'. Donald Tusk, then Poland's prime minister and subsequently president of the European Council of Ministers, voiced his concerns directly to the prime minister. Cameron, Tusk later disclosed, had assured him that all would be well: the Conservatives would not secure a majority in the 2015 election, so would have to go into coalition again with the Liberal Democrats. The smaller party would block a referendum.

Soon after becoming prime minister, Cameron was asked to name his favourite children's book. 'When I was younger', he replied, 'I particularly enjoyed *Our Island Story* by Henrietta Elizabeth Marshall . . . It is written in a way that really captured my imagination and which nurtured my interest in the history of our great nation.'[13] Published at the turn of the twentieth century, Marshall's heroic history, oblivious to the darker moments in the nation's past, charts England's unique role through the centuries as the champion of freedom and liberty and architect of democratic institutions. Cameron's Bloomberg speech picked up on the exceptionalist flavour. 'It's true that our geography has shaped our psychology,' the prime minister said. 'We have the character of an island nation – independent, forthright, passionate in defence of our sovereignty. We can no more change this British sensibility than we can drain the English Channel.'[14]

Yet Cameron, in his way, was proposing to do just that. Number 10 officials urged that the threshold for a decision to leave should be significantly higher than 50 per cent because of the profound constitutional consequences. Such ideas were brushed aside. Cameron's vanity told him he would win. The *Financial Times* reported a conversation during 2014 with Herman Van Rompuy, the former Belgian prime minister and president of the European Council. By then the prime minister had also agreed to the demand of the Scottish National Party for a plebiscite on Scottish independence. 'I will win this [the Scottish vote] easily and it will put to bed the Scottish referendum question for twenty years. The same goes for Europe,' Cameron told him.[15]

The prime minister had learned nothing from experience. Each concession to the Eurosceptics on his own backbenches brought forth another demand. In 2005, in his campaign to win the party leadership, he had promised to break the link in the European Parliament with other mainstream centre-right parties, such as Germany's Christian Democrats. In 2009, Conservative MEPs duly withdrew from the European People's Party (EPP) and set up a new group of centre-right parties, the European Conservatives and Reformists. The new arrangements put the Tories in dubious company with right-wing populist parties, but the consequences reached well beyond the seating plan for the Brussels parliament. The EPP was the forum for frequent informal gatherings of the leaders of the main centre-right parties in Europe – gatherings at which they could kick off their shoes, open another bottle of good wine and strike informal deals. Merkel was assiduous in her attendance; so too were other figures such as Nicolas Sarkozy. Cameron, without much thought, had cut himself off from influence.

The Eurosceptics cheered and then demanded more. Cameron had once promised a referendum on the Lisbon Treaty – a pledge that was pre-empted when Gordon Brown's government ratified it before the 2010 election. The sceptics demanded a legal provision that any further European treaty that transferred sovereignty from Westminster would be subject to a referendum. The Sovereign Grant Act became law in 2011 and served to embolden rather than placate Cameron's critics. By now it was clear that a substantial minority of Conservative MPs – estimates varied from forty to eighty – would be satisfied by nothing less than withdrawal from the European Union. Another sizeable group, alarmed at the rise in support for UKIP in the opinion polls, demanded a guarantee against British participation in any new European projects. Clarke reminded Cameron that appeasement would only lead to further concessions. He did not listen.

Cameron had intended the Bloomberg speech to put the Europe debate to rest until after the 2015 election; instead, it gave encouragement to his opponents by signposting a route that could lead to Britain's departure from the Union. Within months, ninety-five backbench Conservative MPs had signed a letter demanding a new law that would reassert the sovereignty of British over European law – legislation that would have made a mockery of Britain's signature of the Treaty of Rome by challenging the primacy of European law in areas where sovereignty had been pooled, such as trade. The leading Eurosceptic MP John Baron indicated that the letter was a signal that the rebels had the prime minister on the run, telling the *Financial Times*: 'You'll remember that the word referendum wouldn't even pass David Cameron's lips and then a letter was signed by 100 MPs and we got him to agree to a referendum.'

Cameron had, in effect, surrendered policy to the strange concoction of exceptionalism and insecurity that drove the sceptics' hostility to the Union. Britain's influence over the direction of the EU during the preceding decades had been immense, yet Cameron adopted the defensive crouch of a leader always on the losing side, unwilling even to hint that Europe had been working in Britain's national interest. Frustrated officials in 10 Downing Street privately complained that every decision was now held hostage to the prime minister's fears of a backbench rebellion. Any initiative that might require legislation – even if it was self-evidently in the national interest – had to be weighed against Cameron's ebbing authority. Foreign Office diplomats talked of paralysis. In the days after the Bloomberg speech, one of the prime minister's most senior Downing Street advisers was asked about its significance, and shook his head in dismay.[16] It would have been much worse, a colleague remarked, if the government had not depended on the votes of Nick Clegg's Liberal Democrats. The fact of the coalition precluded more concessions.

The promise of a referendum was ineffective in staunching rising voter support for UKIP in the run-up to the 2014 elections for the European Parliament. On the contrary, it conferred a legitimacy on both Nigel Farage's party and the rebels on Cameron's own side. Tory MPs who had once called for a halt to the transfer of powers to Brussels now felt emboldened to demand their repatriation or to join Farage in arguing it would be best to quit altogether. From the ageing membership of their constituency associations, Conservative MPs heard the arguments that had echoed through the decades: Britain was an island nation that looked to the world, not to Europe. The Commonwealth – and the Anglosphere – was Britain's natural home. And yes, Britain had won the war.

Nigel Farage peered through the same rose-tinted spectacles at an imagined past, but he added anger to the mix. If the halcyon days of the 1950s had been lost, someone had to be to blame. By 2014, Farage had broadened the assault. The product of an expensive public-school education who had had a career in the City of London before taking up the Eurosceptic cause during the 1990s, the UKIP leader was an unlikely 'man of the people'. Farage, however, coupled a natural facility to connect with voters with a shrewd grasp of political strategy. As the country paid the price of the financial crash, UKIP presented itself as a populist insurgency against the elites and the economic establishment, standing against Osborne's fiscal austerity, big business and immigration, as well as the Eurocrats of Brussels. The repeated attacks on immigration often teetered towards racism, but the party insisted all the while that it stood on the right side of patriotism. Farage also saw the potential of tapping into working-class discontent in the

Labour strongholds of the Midlands and the north of England. Labour's leader Ed Miliband had taken the Labour Party to the left. His appeal was to socialist-minded voters in the middle-aged metropolitan classes, rather than to workers in the towns that had been left behind by globalisation. UKIP, in Farage's description, had become 'the fox in the Westminster henhouse', taking support from Conservative supporters in the Home Counties and making inroads among disgruntled voters in hard-pressed working-class communities. Euroscepticism merged with English nationalism and, at the extreme, dog-whistle racism.

Immigration was the key that opened the door to UKIP's electoral success, turning the argument over Europe into a bitter conflict about culture and identity. When the first group of formerly communist states from eastern and central Europe joined the European Union in 2004, Tony Blair's government was one of only three – alongside Sweden and Ireland – to waive the right to apply temporary restrictions on immigration from the new member states. The economy was booming, and the Treasury saw the arrival of workers from the likes of Poland, the Czech Republic, Hungary and the Baltic states as an important addition to the British labour market. Mervyn King, the governor of the Bank of England and subsequently a cheerleader for those calling for Britain's departure from the Union, was at the forefront of those arguing that Britain should throw its doors open to Polish plumbers in order to hold down wage increases and thus curb inflation. The exodus from the former communist states, however, exceeded all expectations. The tens of thousands of new arrivals expected each year were subsequently counted in the hundreds of thousands. Large numbers headed for London, but many others settled in small towns in England, taking low-paid jobs that went unfilled by the indigenous population. In 2007, they were joined by new arrivals from Romania and Bulgaria. Despite pressure on schools, hospitals and other local services, the initial response was relatively muted. The economy was growing, incomes were rising and Gordon Brown implemented new funding arrangements for local services to take the pressure off small communities.

What changed everything was the financial crash and the squeeze on public spending introduced by Cameron's government. Brown's immigration funding scheme was among the first to be scrapped. Suddenly, communities faced wage freezes, falling living standards, cuts in public spending and less job security. The Polish plumber, the Romanian fruit-picker and the Lithuanian warehouse worker were easy targets for Farage's populism. UKIP became the party of English as much as British nationalism. Immigrants were portrayed as stealing jobs from local populations, driving down wages for the low-paid, claiming welfare benefits and jumping the queue for scarce social housing. The culprit, according to UKIP, was the European Union's insistence on the free movement of workers. The political elites and big business were part of the conspiracy. The flaws in this argument were manifest. The evidence showed that immigrants from Europe were overwhelmingly net contributors to the economy, paying more in taxes than they received in public services, with few relying on welfare. About half of the annual net increase in immigration was attributable to migrants from non-EU countries, notably Pakistan, India, Nigeria and Bangladesh; in crude economic terms, these were the communities that were most likely to be a temporary burden on the state. Such facts were lost to the increasingly strident claims that England's identity was at stake and that communities were being overwhelmed by the immigrants from Europe.

Cameron had given UKIP a target to aim at. Net immigration, including workers from Europe and arrivals from the rest of the world, was running at above 200,000 a year. He promised a severe squeeze. The numbers, he promised, would be reduced to 'the tens of thousands' in net terms. Arriving in Downing Street, he was told by officials that the goal was unattainable, not simply because he had no control over the numbers coming from the European Union but also because the government was power-less to influence the decisions of those leaving Britain. The new prime minister was left with a pledge that would be broken during every year of his premiership. In the narrative that was shaped by Farage, English workers were paying the price for the cheap labour demanded by big business and for the nannies and house-keepers employed by the London rich. Nothing could be done as long as Britain remained in the EU. The 2014 elections for the European Parliament saw UKIP emerge as the largest party, with the Conservatives driven into third place. The ratchet of Euroscepticism had turned up another notch.

This was the first of several prime ministerial miscalculations. Securing the reforms he had promised in the Bloomberg speech, still vague as they were, would require the support of Britain's partners. Cameron did nothing to win himself allies. The financial crash was followed by a crisis in the eurozone that threatened the very existence of the euro, as weaker economies such as Spain, Portugal, Italy and Greece struggled to escape the burden of ris-ing public debt and large current account deficits. The demands for help from these so-called 'Club Med' governments collided with an insistence of Germany and other northern European states that they would not bail out weaker partners. Berlin pre-scribed austerity for all, before German taxpayers put any of their funds at risk. Over weeks and months of crisis – economic col-lapse in Greece threatened its very democracy – compromises were made, but harsh rhetoric and hard terms saw relationships stretched to breaking point. The fear in 2013 was of yet another external shock. And Cameron, in promising a referendum, had taken the pin from a hand grenade. Many other governments faced populist insurgencies. What if Britain voted to leave? Might it prove contagious? In seeking to solve his own political problem, Cameron had brushed aside without a thought the risks for Britain's partners.

Germany's Angela Merkel would be the pivotal figure in any renegotiation of Britain's terms. The British assumed, rightly, that Berlin would do its best to keep the UK in the European club. For all their differences about the direction and pace of European integration, the two nations shared the same liberal-minded Atlanticist outlook, and Britain was a useful foil for Berlin's much closer but rarely smooth relationship with Paris. Merkel, though, was dismayed by Cameron's decision. During a visit to Britain two months before the Bloomberg announcement, the prime minister told her that the demand for a referendum had become politically irresistible. She was unpersuaded. What disturbed her – and the same sentiments were heard in many European capitals – was that even as it proposed to gamble on a plebiscite, Cameron's government forever refused to make the case for the Union. Merkel was not naive – when European leaders turned up in Brussels for their regular summits, each and every one had their national interest front of mind. What was missing in the British approach was any recognition of a broader, long-term interest in the success of the Union. France and Germany had created the Common Market as a vehicle for reconciliation. Nations such as Portugal and Spain saw it as the guarantor of democracy. For the Baltic states, it underwrote independence from the Soviet Union.

For Cameron, the bargain was entirely transactional, win or lose. Merkel had seen the same short-termism in his decision to leave the

EPP. A leader who was keen to be a serious player in Europe would not have given up the influence afforded by membership of this club of European centre-right parties. Cameron had cut himself off from the informal deal-making that routinely preceded the regular Brussels summit. He paid a heavy price for this in December 2011, at a Brussels summit called to put in place new fiscal rules to restore market confidence in the future of the eurozone.

To a greater or lesser degree, other European leaders recognised a commonality of interest that reached beyond the outcome of this or that negotiation about trade policy, budget contributions or farm subsidies. 'Solidarity', this was called, though the word was often deployed by governments in pursuit of narrower interests. 'The construction of Europe', as the French called it, had its own intrinsic worth. Cameron never admitted such a sentiment. Nor, to be fair, had his predecessors in Downing Street. When, in 2011, eurozone leaders offered to include other EU governments in their discussions on the future development of the currency area, Sweden, Poland and the rest took the opportunity. Sourly, Cameron told his fellow leaders that he had no wish to be at the table when they were discussing the single currency. Beyond occasional shouting from the sidelines, he showed no appetite for helping to stabilise the euro, even though he acknowledged that Britain too would suffer if the enterprise failed. 'The eurozone is at a crossroads,' he remarked in 2012. 'It either has to make up or it is looking at a potential break-up. Either Europe has a committed, stable, successful eurozone with an effective firewall, well-capitalised and regulated banks, a system of fiscal burden sharing and supportive monetary policy across the eurozone, or we are in uncharted territory which carries huge risks for everyone.'[17] Yet no one, he might have added, should expect an outstretched hand from the British side of the

Channel. The Treasury was ready to extend some financial help to the Republic of Ireland, one of those worst hit by the crisis. But the rest of the eurozone should solve its own problems. Britain would look after itself.

Merkel could see that Cameron was undermining his own position in a future referendum campaign. The right-wing press in Britain was filled with invective and invention about the EU. The *Sun*, the *Daily Mail* and the *Daily Telegraph* filled their pages with alleged plots to subvert British freedoms. If the German Wehrmacht was not marching along Whitehall, well-heeled Eurocrats were issuing regulations that would ban British pork pies and steal the catch of the Cornish fishing fleet. Ministers rarely pushed back, preferring instead to promise that they were going into battle against the Eurocrats. How could a government that had routinely presented the Union as a nuisance, if not a direct threat to British nationhood, Merkel once asked Cameron, reinvent itself as a champion of European integration during a six-week referendum campaign?[18] Cameron, driven by political opportunism, had not thought through the contradiction. Similar doubts about the referendum were heard in Paris and Brussels.

Cameron's lecturing tone towards his fellow European leaders was scarcely well received. The British government seemed to be congratulating itself for staying out of the euro even as its economy struggled with a slump in output and a ballooning budget deficit. This was the frame of mind that led the prime minister into isolation at the summit in Brussels in December 2011. The nations in the eurozone wanted the EU to underpin new rules for budgetary discipline within the monetary union – a so-called 'fiscal compact'. For this they required the consent of governments outside the single currency, including Britain's. Cameron, fearful of giving his approval to anything in Brussels that might attract the wrath of his backbench MPs, decided to try to strike a bargain: Britain would lend its support to the changes in return for some protection for financial institutions in the City of London. The proposal was a profound misjudgement. To some in Berlin it smacked of blackmail. French president Nicolas Sarkozy was outraged. The prime minister had badly misread the politics. When he presented his ultimatum to the summit in the early hours of the morning, he was told brusquely that Merkel and Sarkozy had already found a way around a British veto. They would draft a new agreement that would sit alongside the existing treaties.

Wrapped up in Cameron's grandstanding was a genuine policy point. As the crisis drove the eurozone nations closer together, there was a risk that their decisions would disadvantage Britain. But Cameron had not listened carefully enough to Merkel. She was prepared to be helpful where she could be, but she would not be bullied by the British. Cameron duly wielded his veto, and the rest of the Union ignored him. In the description of one of the diplomats, the prime minister had delivered 'a masterclass in how to lose a negotiation'.[19] Back in London, the script was rewritten by Downing Street to cast futile isolation as a great victory. Britain had stood firm and said 'No!' The Tory Eurosceptics cheered the prime minister to the rafters in the Commons. A Number 10 aide laconically recalled a famous headline from *The Times*: 'Fog in the Channel – continent isolated'.[20] There was something almost pathetic about the occasion.

Cameron's failure to understand the limits of Merkel's support would be a recurring theme. 'He just cannot understand', a Foreign Office diplomat observed, 'that charm does not cut it. They [other European leaders] have domestic politics too.' A glimpse of the frustration with Cameron's style came to light a few years later, in a leaked recording of comments made by Radosław

Sikorski, the Polish foreign minister. In an expletive-laden assessment, he derided British 'posturing' in Brussels and Cameron's policy of appeasing the Tory Eurosceptics: 'His whole strategy of feeding [his critics] scraps in order to satisfy them is, just as I predicted, turning against him. He should have said "Fuck off", tried to convince people and isolate [the sceptics]. But he ceded the field to those that are now embarrassing him.'[21] The Polish foreign minister was a long-standing Anglophile and, like Cameron, an alumnus of Oxford University's raucous Bullingdon Club. He spoke, however, to a perception of the British that was becoming fixed in the minds of politicians and policymakers on the other side of the Channel.

The 2015 general election, as a senior Downing Street official would later remark, was a contest Cameron was unlucky enough to win. The prime minister had expected to return to Downing Street at the head of another coalition with Nick Clegg's Liberal Democrats; instead a collapse in support for Clegg's party and a poor campaign by the Labour leader Ed Miliband gave Cameron a small majority of twelve seats in the House of Commons. Now he would have to redeem the pledge he had assured other European leaders he would avoid.

Well before Cameron formally tabled his demands for the reform of the Union in order to make it more attractive to British voters, it was evident in other European capitals that the changes would not rewrite the essential rules of the relationship. Angela Merkel's red line – the preservation of the framework of existing European rules – was almost universally endorsed by her partners. When Edward Heath had taken Britain into the club in 1973, he had been obliged to accept the rules. Cameron would not be allowed to rewrite them and, as the Tory Eurosceptics demanded, remove the primacy of the European Court of Justice in matters of EU law. The so-called four freedoms – the free flow across borders of goods, services, capital and people – underpinning the single market were indivisible. Britain might be offered, for example, emergency arrangements to deal with disruptive surges in migration, or language that would disassociate it from the grand ambitions for European unity of its partners, but it would not be allowed to fundamentally reset the Union's rules. Cameron himself had constrained what other governments could offer by ruling out treaty changes as too time-consuming. In the description of the soon-to-be-president of the European Council Donald Tusk, 'What he was asking for was impossible to achieve within the Union's treaties.'

The renegotiation that followed in the winter of 2015 culminated in thirty hours of hard negotiation at a leaders' summit in Brussels in February 2016. The eventual bargain reflected the Treasury-driven effort to secure guarantees that Britain would not be disadvantaged by increasing integration within the eurozone. Cameron was given assurances that members of the single currency would not be allowed to ignore the views of non-members when setting rules for the entire Union. The twenty-seven also agreed to an 'emergency brake' that would allow the British government to impose temporary restrictions on the access to welfare benefits of workers from other member states. In a nod to British exceptionalism, the agreement permitted the UK to disavow the long-term goal of ever-closer union of the peoples of Europe.

The safeguards for the City of London were on their own terms significant. The benefit changes and the opt-out from an ever-closer union represented a genuflection to the concerns of Conservative backbench MPs, but this was scarcely the 'new settlement' that Cameron had promised. Nor would any of it mean much to British voters who would soon be asked whether they wanted to remain in the European Union. In the event, the deal hardly registered beyond Westminster. Cameron freed his cabinet from collective responsibility for the duration of the referendum campaign, as Harold Wilson had done in 1975. His close friend Michael Gove and five others took him at his word and set up the official 'Vote Leave' campaign. They were joined by Boris Johnson, the outgoing mayor of London, who had returned to parliament in 2015 in pursuit of the prize for which he had entered politics – Cameron's job in Downing Street.

The opinion polls at the beginning of 2016 showed a small majority for remaining in the Union. But the margin – with a little more than 40 per cent for Remain and 37 or 38 per cent for Leave, with the rest undecided – was too slight to be comfortable. Cameron was betting that when it came to polling day, voters would opt for safety. The Treasury, the Bank of England and almost every international economics organisation were predicting a costly economic shock if the nation voted to leave. Osborne's Treasury painted a lurid picture of lower growth, rising unemployment and tax increases.

Cameron was also betting on himself. Two years earlier, he had agreed to the demand of the SNP for a referendum on independence. There had been some scares during the campaign, but ultimately the Scots had taken the 'safe' course and backed staying in the Union by 55 to 45 per cent. What such comparisons ignored, however, was that the pro-independence side had started with support of only a little above 30 per cent. A large number of Scots had not been swayed by the threat of severe economic dislocation if they voted for independence.

The Leave campaign stirred nostalgia with neuralgia – a longing for an imagined past mixed with a fear of the future. Its promise to 'Take Back Control' harked back to Churchill and the 'Big Three', when a Britain detached from Europe thought that it could hold its own at the top table of world affairs. Much of the language in the campaign – about restoring sovereignty, reclaiming Britain's global reach and defending democracy – echoed the debates of the 1950s, when Britain stood aloof from the creation of the Common Market. The Treaty of Rome, in the mindset of English nationalists, mocked the freedoms of Shakespeare's 'precious stone set in a silver sea'. The real force of the Brexit campaign, however, lay in its unashamedly populist claim to speak for 'the people' in their struggle with the elites – not just the Eurocrats in Brussels but the British political establishment and the business leaders who had conspired to 'shackle' Britain to the European Union. Michael Gove encapsulated this pre-enlightenment mindset when he declared during the campaign that Britain had had enough of the 'experts' who predicted dire economic consequences if Britain voted to leave. The Brexiters, as they styled themselves, spoke for 'the people' – those who wanted to leave the European Union.

This assertion of British exceptionalism seeped into an ugly English nationalism that was redolent of the xenophobia championed by Enoch Powell in the 1960s and 1970s. In the United States, the Republican presidential candidate Donald Trump demanded that all Muslims be treated as suspect. The Brexiters cast Turkey as the threat: Johnson and Gove made the entirely false claim that it would soon join the European Union. The claim that Britain would be overrun by millions of Turkish migrants became a pillar of their campaign. A second pillar – that the £350 million sent to Brussels each week could be diverted to the National Health Service – was equally mendacious. The net contribution was far below that. Johnson had never been a politician troubled by truth. The two deceits were merged into the populist trope that the nation was menaced by 'outsiders'.

The Leave campaign co-opted a handful of prominent Labour figures to the cause, with the MP Gisela Stuart appointed chair. Highlighting the supposed threat from the future entry of Turkey and the Balkan states, Stuart crystallised the xenophobic message: 'Instead of giving an extra 88 million people – more than our entire population – access to the NHS,' she declared, 'I believe it would be safer to take back control. We should give our struggling NHS the £350 million we send to the EU every week.'[22] The foreigners, in other words, were taking money that could otherwise be channelled to hard-pressed hospitals. The Remain side sought to generate fear – sometimes overblown – about the economic costs of breaking with Europe, but the Leavers mobilised more powerful emotions about culture and identity. The great surge in refugees fleeing the civil war in Syria during 2015 – Germany had felt obliged to allow about a million refugees to cross its border over the year – gave a rough credence to the scare stories about Turkey.

These were not arguments rooted in facts or reason. Gove made anti-intellectualism his trademark. The myriad independent institutions and experts predicting that departure from Europe would do severe damage at once to the economy and national prestige were, quite simply, wrong. Why? Because they were part of the conspiracy of the elites – mainstream politicians, big business, establishment intellectuals – against the people. For its part, Nigel Farage's UKIP led an even more anti-migrant campaign. Here, five months before the presidential election put Donald Trump into the White House, Brexiters were road-testing the proud mendacity of his campaign strategy.

It was a campaign that matched the national temper. The costs and consequences of the global financial crash and the government-imposed austerity that followed had fallen largely on the less advantaged. Labour leader Jeremy Corbyn, a maverick rebel from the far left of the party who had been chosen by party activists to replace Ed Miliband after Labour's defeat in the 2015 general election, refused to allow his party to mount a vigorous pro-European campaign in disadvantaged, largely Labour-voting areas, thereby adding credibility to the Leave side's crusade against elites. Nostalgia played to the affluent elderly of the English Home Counties – voters with memories of a more glorious past who had never properly come to terms with membership of the Union. Anti-immigrant nationalism chimed with the resentment of working-class voters in the small cities and towns of the Midlands and the north that would swing decisively towards Brexit. On the eve of the poll, an editorial in the *Financial Times* captured the deep frustrations of the Remain side: 'This is no time to revert to Little England. We are Great Britain. We have a contribution to make to a more prosperous, safer world. The vote must be Remain.'

At this point, the mood in 10 Downing Street was nervous but still positive. Cameron thought he would scrape through. The messages arriving from other parts of the country – the Midlands and the north-east, as well as swathes of southern England – were a lot less optimistic. Johnson and Gove's campaign had cut through with the simple demand to take back control. 'The question of Britain's role in the European Community hangs like an axe over the head of the Conservative Party,' the political commentator Joe Rogaly had written in the *Financial Times* a quarter of a century earlier, when Margaret Thatcher battled her senior ministers about the relationship with Brussels. As Cameron appeared outside Downing Street to announce his resignation on the morning after the referendum, he could reflect that the civil war in the Conservative Party that Rogaly had predicted had claimed its third prime minister in succession. Thatcher's 'No, no, no!' to

Jacques Delors's plans for more European integration had played a large part in her downfall. During the years that followed, John Major's government had been harried to defeat by the rising swell of Euroscepticism that followed the Lady's departure. Cameron, who had promised to banish the party's obsession with the EU, was the author of his own destruction. The enormous cost of his careless referendum pledge would be borne by the country. Britain had decided to cut itself loose from its most important economic partner and surrender any role in shaping the political future of its own continent.

The vote was not just about Europe or the EU. The skill of the Leave side lay in the way it gathered the myriad grievances of a disgruntled nation into a single vote. Many Leave supporters were making a broader protest about the indifference towards their lives of the political elites. Others were rebelling against the globalisation and technological innovation that had swept away traditional jobs and replaced them with the insecurity of the 'gig economy'. That said, the Leave campaign, rooted in nostalgia for what the Brexiters now called 'Global Britain', saturated at times with references to Britain's victory in 1945 and gripped by a need to reassert parliamentary sovereignty, produced uncanny echoes of the 1950s. Europe was fine for the French and the Germans, but Britain's sights were on the world. In the Britain of 2016, many, particularly those living in smaller towns and cities, had grown fearful of the future. 'Take Back Control' had unlocked the power of the past.

Four days after the referendum, Cameron travelled to Brussels for his last summit of the Union's leaders. The mood was downbeat but even-tempered. Jean-Claude Juncker, the president of the European Commission, echoed a point that had often been made by Merkel: 'My impression is that if you, over years, if not decades, tell citizens that something is wrong with the EU, that the EU is too technocratic, too bureaucratic, you cannot be taken by surprise if voters believe you.'[23] There were also polite warnings that Britain should not expect the remaining EU states to be generous in negotiating a new settlement. Enda Kenny, the Irish prime minister, foreshadowed what would become a crucial difficulty when he said that any deal must respect the open border between Northern Ireland and the Republic agreed in the Good Friday or Belfast Agreement. Donald Tusk fired a warning shot about Britain's future access to the single market, telling journalists that 'There will be no single market à la carte.'

Long-standing European officials reflected on the painful irony of the referendum result. None had been more enthusiastic about the creation of the single market than Britain's Conservatives, they recalled, nor about the rapid enlargement of the Union to include the former communist states of eastern and central Europe. Yet it was from these policies – the increased regulation to level the playing field in the single market and the influx of workers from the new member states – that Cameron claimed his difficulties had flowed. There had never been much in the way of consistency about Britain's troubled relationship with the rest of its own continent.

12

Alone

Everything changed on 23 June 2016. No one, before the vote, had grasped the seismic scale of the decision to quit the European Union. This was a step that, beyond cutting ties with Brussels, imperilled the very future of the UK union. A defeated David Cameron appeared in Downing Street to announce his departure from the scene. His resignation was probably inevitable, given that he had seen the referendum as an exercise in party management. But it was also evident that he wanted to escape the mess as quickly as possible. 'I do not think it would be right for me to try to be the captain who steers our country to its next destination,' he said. 'It's called jumping ship,' a cabinet colleague on the pro-European side remarked.[1] When Boris Johnson and Michael Gove, the leaders of the Leave campaign, appeared before the cameras on the morning of 24 June, they looked shell-shocked rather than triumphant. Johnson sought to sound reassuring about a vote that would wrench the nation from the club it had joined forty-three years earlier: 'We cannot turn our backs on Europe,' he offered. 'We are part of Europe. Our children and grandchildren will continue to have a wonderful future as Europeans, travelling to the continent, understanding the languages and cultures that make up our common European civilisation.' For Johnson, backing Brexit had been about personal ambition: establishing his claim to the leadership. 'We [the Leavers] will be crushed,' he had told the prime minister at the start of the campaign.[2] Winning was not part of the plan.

Westminster and Whitehall were in shock; Remainers and Leavers alike were unprepared. The assumption on both sides had been that although the outcome would be close, head would prevail over heart, economic calculation over the palpable anger of much of the electorate. The vote tore down one of the twin pillars of Britain's foreign policy. It overturned an economic model that had seen the country become a platform for global companies operating across the twenty-eight-nation European Union. Britain in effect was denying the identity it had embraced in the decades after Suez: that of a leading European power with worldwide interests. In practical terms, quitting the Union would invalidate thousands of regulatory agreements and norms that had been shared with Britain's European partners.

Psychologically, it would upend decades-old assumptions. Brexit put a question mark over the future of the United Kingdom itself. The Brexiters had mobilised a majority of the English, but Scotland voted by a wide margin to remain. The future of Northern Ireland was put in doubt. Like Scotland, it had voted Remain. Suddenly, a Britain that had entered the twenty-first century as the flag-bearer for globalisation was turning in on itself. Brexit Britain was fractured and divided. The great cities in England, led by London, had mostly backed Remain, while smaller cities and provincial towns had leaned towards Leave. The nation had divided between the elderly voters looking to reclaim the past and the pro-Europeanism of the overwhelming majority of young voters. The affluent and well-educated were Remainers, the left-behinds Leavers. These splits would dominate politics for the foreseeable future. They would leave Britain a nation marooned.

The timing of this great leap into the unknown was still more confounding. Had Britain decided to strike out on its own fifteen or twenty years earlier, it would have done so at a time of international stability. Globalisation was opening up new markets across the world, democracy was on the march into hitherto authoritarian states, and the United States, as the sole superpower, underwrote international security in the manner of a benign hegemon. By 2016, all these assumptions had been shattered. Britain voted to cut itself loose from its own continent at a moment that was more uncertain than any since 1945. The shifts in global power now saw China challenge Western hegemony, Russia seek to destabilise Europe and autocrats rise to power in states such as Turkey, Brazil, the Philippines and India. Islamist terrorism was a shared threat. The credibility of the West and faith in liberal, open international markets had been shredded by the 2008 financial crash. Globalisation was in retreat. How, European leaders such as Angela Merkel asked, could a nation such as Britain think it would fare better alone?

Every foreign policy document produced in Downing Street for the previous fifty years had said that Britain's interest lay in upholding and promoting the rules-based international order. Now it was forsaking multilateralism for bilateralism, demolishing the European pillar of its foreign policy at just the moment when the second, Atlantic pillar faced its own serious challenges. Donald Trump's 'Make America Great Again' unilateralism was in many respects energised by the same grievances – stagnant incomes, rising employment insecurity, fears of immigration, growing inequality – as the Brexit campaign. Trump, elected to the presidency in November 2016, would pronounce himself an ally of the Brexiters. The irony that escaped Johnson and his supporters, however, was that Trump's determination to focus on America's narrow national interests would disarm Britain. The nation's security had been embedded in the North Atlantic Treaty Organisation since 1949. Now the United States had a president who asked: 'What's the point of NATO?'

*

'Brexit means Brexit.' So Theresa May declared during her campaign to succeed David Cameron as Tory party leader and prime minister in July 2016. This short phrase would later serve as an epitaph for an ill-starred premiership. By the time she was forced to quit Downing Street three years later, she had been unable to untangle its meaning. The country had voted by the narrow margin of 52 to 48 per cent to quit the European Union, but the binary choice presented on the ballot paper paid no heed to the complexity of leaving. Nor did it answer the obvious question as to what sort of departure it would involve. The Tory-led Leave side had made ambiguity an article of faith during the campaign. The less that was said about the end point of Brexit, the fewer the opportunities for pro-Europeans to expose the risks and contradictions. Did the country want an arrangement such as that enjoyed by Norway or Switzerland, which preserved many of the economic ties to the other twenty-seven – the old 'common market' – while breaking with the political goals of the Union? Ardent Brexiters such as Daniel Hannan, a Member of the European Parliament, backed such a compromise. Others imagined a more decisive rupture that would see Britain retreat to the far-flung margins of its own continent – a relationship with Brussels comparable to that enjoyed by, say, distant Canada.

There had been clues during the referendum campaign but no real answers. For his part, David Cameron had not wanted to admit the possibility of defeat. No one on the Remain or the Leave side had produced a serious assessment of what it would take to disentangle Britain from more than forty years of integration with Europe. Large swathes of policy – agriculture, the environment, employment rights, financial services regulation, competition, aviation and data protection among them – had effectively been transferred to joint decision-making in Brussels.

Was it all to be unravelled? The Leavers had acted during the campaign as if Britain could simply walk away. Nothing was further from the truth. 'It's a bloody mess,' one senior official in the prime minister's office observed on the morning after the vote. 'This will take a decade to sort out.'

And what of the other union? At the heart of the Good Friday Agreement that ended the thirty-year-long war in the province was an irrevocable commitment to an open border between Northern Ireland and the Republic. Pulling down the watchtowers and dismantling border posts had been an essential element in damping down the clashes between unionists and nationalists. Cross-border trade and investment provided the underpinnings of prosperity in both north and south. More important than the economics was the political symbolism: an open border presented the citizens of the island of Ireland with a choice of identity. Shutting down that option would invite the return of the politics of grievance and, quite possibly, violence. Yet Brexit would indeed create a 'hard border' between the Republic, which was remaining in the EU, and the north. Unless special arrangements were made for Northern Ireland or the government opted to remain in the single market and the customs union, trade across the frontier would have to be policed.

In Scotland, the Remain vote was more than 60 per cent. Confronted with the prospect of being torn out of the EU without a say, the ruling SNP argued with some force that the people of Scotland deserved another independence referendum. Such was the price of hubris. Cameron had led Britain out of Europe and stirred the demands of Scottish nationalists for a second referendum.

To add another layer of complexity, two distinct currents of opinion on the Leave side had merged into one during the campaign.

The first, a servant to nostalgia, saw Brexit as the platform for a wider global role for Britain, a nation now free of the regulatory and other encumbrances of EU membership. A larger version, some said, of Singapore; or a return to the swashbuckling adventurism of the first Elizabethan age. The second impulse pulled in the opposite direction. Brexit was an opportunity to throw up the barricades against the world beyond, imposing strict limits on immigration and shielding British industry from the harsher winds of globalisation. If the first of these attracted more affluent Tory Brexiters in the south of England, the second appealed to the UKIP-supporting voters in some of the nation's most depressed towns and cities, who saw Brexit as an act of revenge against the ruling elites. As for the House of Commons, two-thirds of MPs across all parties had been on the Remain side of the campaign. Now these MPs were expected to put into law a policy they thought damaging to British security and prosperity. 'How can I vote to damage my country?' asked one pro-European minister.[3]

Whitehall had not prepared for Brexit. Cameron had been unwilling to admit the possibility he might lose. Contingency plans might leak. So while Jeremy Heywood, the cabinet secretary, and other senior officials across the big departments of state had considered the consequences – and understood the scale of the task ahead in the event of a Leave vote – Cameron had barred detailed planning. It was easier, one of the mandarins would later confide, to share Cameron's hubris than to imagine the enormity of the challenge. True, the Treasury had produced assessments of the likely damage to the economy, business and living standards of a pro-Brexit vote. The economics establishment – the Bank of England, the International Monetary Fund, the Organisation for Economic Cooperation and Development, as well as the Treasury – agreed that giving up privileged access to its principal market would cost Britain dearly in terms of investment, trade, competitiveness and economic growth. The impact need not be immediate, not least because the Bank of England moved swiftly to reassure the financial markets that it would forestall a deflationary spiral with looser monetary policy. Instead the losses would be cumulative over several years: lower growth, a fall in the value of the pound, a standstill in investment, weakening living standards and a sharp drop in business confidence.

Theresa May's political ambitions had never been a secret. She had harboured hopes for the premiership since her days of student politics at Oxford. A cautious, careful politician, she had stood outside the 'chumocracy' of young men at the heart of Cameron's Downing Street. She had campaigned on the Remain side of the referendum debate, though colleagues complained that she had kept a deliberately low profile – an insurance policy, everyone assumed, in case of victory for the Leavers. She had never shown much interest in, or enthusiasm for, foreign policy or matters European. Her six years at the Home Office at once took her close to the record for longevity in the post and confirmed a lack of interest in global affairs. If anything had defined her time in Cameron's government, it had been her fierce advocacy of tougher controls on immigration and a studied preference for more security at home rather than military adventurism abroad. Previous prime ministers had taken the fight against terrorism to Iraq and Syria. She saw the bigger risk from British-born, self-radicalised jihadis responsible for most of the terrorist attacks in the UK. Officials reported that at meetings of the National Security Council she would roll her eyes when the younger men – Cameron, Osborne and Clegg – talked excitedly about bombing missions in Libya, Iraq or Syria.

At the moment of Cameron's departure, May's chances of taking the crown were uncertain. Once the shock of the Brexit vote cleared, Johnson was up and running as the favourite for the succession, with Gove leading his campaign. The path to Number 10 was cleared for May, however, by a very public falling-out between the two most prominent Leavers. May presented herself as a 'safe pair of hands' to steer the government through what would undoubtedly be rough waters. This put a 'Remainer' at the head of the party. Some of the miscalculations that followed, which ultimately doomed May's premiership, were rooted in this tension.

The officials who greeted May in 10 Downing Street took away two early impressions. The first was that the new prime minister preferred to operate within a tight circle of advisers, discouraging wider debate and keeping her own thoughts closely guarded until decisions had to be taken. The second was that she was anxious to demonstrate to the Tory party that she could be entrusted with the task of taking Britain out of the European Union. 'She's secretive and indecisive,' one senior official judged of her first few days as prime minister.[4] She was also untrusting of the civil service. Her two closest advisers, Nick Timothy and Fiona Hill, acted as gatekeepers. Johnson was given the job of foreign secretary and another Brexiter, David Davis, was chosen to head the Department for Exiting the European Union, a new unit set up to take charge of negotiations with Brussels. The mandarins at the FCO, May's advisers thought, were too 'pro-European' to be entrusted with the task, while the prime minister was keen to limit Johnson's influence. The big decisions, she decreed, would be taken within Number 10.

This mix of secrecy and anxiety would lead the prime minister into a series of strategic blunders that ensured Britain's departure from Europe would be anything but smooth. The first of these saw the prime minister set out hard 'red lines' that would limit her room for manoeuvre in negotiations with the other twenty-seven EU states. The second was an assumption that a settlement could be agreed with Brussels and then steered through parliament without the support of opposition MPs – that Brexit would be the sole property of the Conservatives, in spite of the party's wafer-thin majority in the House of Commons. The third was a rush to trigger formal, time-limited negotiations with the twenty-seven before the government had reached its own settled position on the nature of Brexit.

By the time May spoke to the Tory party conference in Birmingham at the beginning of October, she was offering a Brexit calculated to win the plaudits of the Eurosceptic party faithful, but one that inevitably would seriously disrupt the economic relationship between Britain and the EU. Her crowd-pleasing 'red lines' decreed that Britain would no longer accept the Union's freedom of movement rules or allow British law to be decided by the European Court of Justice. May played to the gallery: 'We are not leaving the European Union only to give up control of immigration all over again. And we are not leaving only to return to the jurisdiction of the European Court of Justice. That's not going to happen. We are leaving to become, once more, a fully sovereign and independent country – and the deal is going to have to work for Britain.'[5]

None of this had been discussed in advance with the cabinet nor with Philip Hammond, whose role as chancellor would be to minimise the economic cost of Brexit. Hammond was horrified when, sitting in the conference hall, he heard May promise what was in effect a 'hard' Brexit that would sever industry's complex supply chains across Europe. And few noticed the central contradiction at the heart of her position that would later derail her government. May had, in effect, promised that Britain would leave the Union's single market and the customs union. But she was also pledging to retain the open border between north and south that was central to the peace agreement in Northern Ireland. The two promises were incompatible.

Britain had not surrendered its independence to the European Union. If proof of that were needed, it was supplied, ironically, by the decision to leave the EU. Reclaiming the sovereignty that had by choice been pooled with other EU members, however, would come at the price of giving up real power and influence. Taking back control of 'our laws, our borders and our money' effectively ruled out favourable access to the single market and membership of the EU's customs union. It would also close down British participation in the data-sharing and border-alert schemes that had become an integral part of security operations against international terrorism and crime syndicates, a prospect that alarmed the nation's security chiefs. The elaborate networks of supply chains that defined Britain's economic relationship with its European partners would be broken. Foreign investors in Britain would no longer be able to depend on frictionless access for their goods and services to the rest of the continent. Trade with the EU27 would require Britain to reach agreement on an entirely new set of arrangements. May, unimpressed by the advice of her officials that she should proceed cautiously, also announced that the formal process of withdrawal, as set out under Article 50 of the Union's treaty, would begin in March 2017. The two-year time limit on those negotiations meant in turn that the nation would leave at the latest by the spring of 2019.

The strategic error here was to surrender negotiating leverage to the EU27. The officials advised that Mrs May should defer invoking Article 50 until she had had preliminary talks with other

European leaders – above all with Angela Merkel – on how the negotiations should be structured. Once the clock started ticking, they warned, the pressure to compromise would fall disproportionately on Britain. The cost of falling out of the EU without a deal at the end of the two years would be much higher for Britain than for its partners. The prime minister overruled them, defying the experience of officials who had spent their careers learning the ways of Brussels.

The exasperation across Whitehall was palpable. Neither of her two closest aides, Nick Timothy and Fiona Hill, had experience of the European Union. When decisions were taken, they were driven by narrow political calculation. It was soon obvious that, given the division among Conservatives over what shape Brexit should take, May had made a mistake by freezing out opposition parties. By the end of the year, Sir Ivan Rogers, who served as Britain's permanent representative to the European Union, had resigned in frustration at the prime minister's refusal to accept the obvious. With only three months left before her self-imposed timetable to begin formal negotiations with Brussels, he revealed in his resignation letter that May had not yet decided on her core negotiating objectives. Diplomats who remained in Whitehall privately voiced agreement with Rogers. The EU27, they said, were preparing a trap that would give Brussels complete control over the progress of talks. May was walking into it. In the years that followed, Sir Ivan would produce a series of coruscating commentaries on the prime minister's failure to grasp the basic rules about negotiating with the EU. He was struck, he said later, by the ignorance of his political masters. Many senior ministers thought a trade deal with the EU27 'had to be negotiated, agreed and ratified before we left and in operation the day after legal exit, and that we had to have a plethora of new trade deals with other global players in force as well. Plenty of such lofty promises were made in the referendum campaign. They were, and have been proven, total fantasy.'[6] The result of such 'extraordinary' and 'culpable naivety' had been that the terms of the negotiation were dictated by Brussels. Much of what Sir Ivan said publicly continued to be conveyed sotto voce to May by still-serving officials in Downing Street. She did not listen.

The reaction to the referendum vote among Britain's friends and allies was one of disbelief, dismay and, in many cases, anger. Mark Rutte, the Dutch prime minister, was scathing. England, he said, 'has collapsed politically, monetarily, constitutionally and economically'. Cameron sought to blame Britain's partners for the vote, charging that they had not made sufficient concessions on the rules that governed the free movement of people. Others described the referendum outcome as an act of national self-harm. Germany's Angela Merkel voiced sadness at the decision, but her officials insisted that she had told Cameron from the outset that the rules could not be rewritten to suit one member state. It was evident that, wherever the relationship eventually settled, Britain would be diminished. If it had a constant reputation abroad, it was one for careful pragmatism calculated to preserve its prestige and influence. Britain spoke for political stability. Until the Brexit vote. From Washington to Tokyo and Berlin to Madrid, the view among policymakers was that leaving the Union would reduce Britain's influence in the world. It would cut economic connections with its biggest trading partners and from the political councils that so often shaped its interests. Barack Obama, White House aides said, saw the vote as a terrible mistake. Many of the Brexiters promoted a stronger relationship with Washington as an alternative to entanglement with Europe. The view of the White House was that Britain had made itself a less useful partner. The

Obama administration began to make Berlin its first calling point in Europe.

Britain had learned after 1945 the importance of international rules for a nation with global interests and a declining capacity to defend them. It had been instrumental in the creation of the big multilateral organisations – the United Nations, the Bretton Woods institutions and NATO – that provided it with leverage in the pursuit of its foreign policy objectives. By submitting to rules, Britain was enhancing its capacity to safeguard its interests. After missing the bus at Messina, successive governments had also come to understand how the European Union provided additional weight in Britain's dealings with others, a forum through which it could leverage national influence. Allies understood this. On a visit to London during the referendum campaign, Obama had spoken directly to the British electorate: if Britain wanted to hold on to a privileged position in Washington, it should keep its capacity to shape decision-making on its own continent. Instead emotion overturned self-interest. The rise of China and the revanchism of Vladimir Putin's Russia in central and eastern Europe heralded a return to a great-power competition in which even the strongest European nations would struggle to act alone. Deep cross-border collaboration within the framework of the EU was vital in the fight against terrorism.

Germany, France, Italy and other European governments had their own selfish concerns. They feared being caught up in the forces unleashed by Britain's referendum. Europe was still recovering from the crisis that had shaken the euro to its foundations in 2011 and 2012, and from the political turmoil over migration after a large influx in 2015 of refugees from war-torn Syria. Germany alone had seen the arrival of about a million, most from Syria but many also from Afghanistan and Iran.

Reduced to chaos by civil war, Libya had become a jumping-off point for migrants from sub-Saharan Africa seeking to cross the Mediterranean to Italy and Spain. Merkel's decision in August 2015 to open Germany's borders to the migrants had proved hugely controversial both at home and among its neighbours. The appeal of parties such as UKIP was not unique to Britain. Anti-migrant populist groups, such as the National Front in France and Alternative for Germany, were challenging establishment politicians across the continent, many of them carrying much the same message as the Brexiters.

The immediate fear was that Britain's decision could prove contagious, turning it into the first of many breakaway states. Marine Le Pen's National Front in France and the League, Italy's far-right nationalist party, had also made Brussels a target. Now they might flirt with withdrawal. The twenty-seven governments agreed at the outset that whatever offer was made to Britain must demonstrate the high cost of leaving the club. The Union needed a 'demonstration effect' to discourage further departures. Merkel was among many leaders who genuinely regretted the British vote and, initially, hoped it might yet be reversed. But the German chancellor was insistent that to the extent that Britain withdrew itself from the rules of the club, it must also lose the benefits. She told visitors in no uncertain terms that the *acquis*, the framework of European laws and regulations that bound the governments of the Union in common purpose, could not be bent or broken.

Anticipating that Britain would attempt a strategy of divide and rule, the twenty-seven also established a rigid framework for the negotiations. Leaders would not bargain independently with May. Instead the European side would be led by Michel Barnier, formerly a senior French commissioner, on the basis of guidelines agreed in advance by all governments. Critically, the talks would be broken into two parts. Discussions about the future trading arrangements between the two sides would not start until the practical terms of the divorce had been settled. This would include a financial settlement to cover Britain's outstanding obligations to the Union and a guarantee that the Irish border would be kept open. Barnier did not waver. The concessions that had been promised by the Brexiters proved illusory.

For her part, May was inattentive to the politics in other European capitals. Lacking interest in, or experience of, the political dynamics of Europe, she decided that the focus of her efforts around Brexit would revolve around the unity of her party. For a time, the internal troubles of the opposition seemed to offer reassurance. The Labour leader Jeremy Corbyn privately counted himself as a Eurosceptic, even though a substantial majority of Labour MPs stood firmly on the Remain side. He had campaigned only half-heartedly for the party's official pro-European position. But as negotiations with Brussels approached deadlock, Labour MPs began to bypass Corbyn and press for a soft version of Brexit that would maintain close economic ties. May, in turn, had no clear strategy. 'Theresa Maybe', *The Economist* dubbed her in early 2017.[7] And she closed her eyes to the risk that withdrawal from Europe would threaten the United Kingdom, refusing to give the Scottish parliament and the Wales and Northern Ireland assemblies a role in the Brexit negotiations.

By the time formal negotiations opened in the spring of 2017, three things were obvious: the government had not agreed a position that bridged the prime minister's stated determination to remove Britain from European law while maintaining privileged access to its markets; cabinet ministers were deluded as to what

Britain could achieve in the talks; and both the cabinet and the Tory party at Westminster were divided as to how far the government should lean towards a 'clean break' with Brussels – the 'hard' Brexit sought by a growing number of Brexiters – or towards a maintenance of frictionless trade and investment flows – the 'soft' Brexit favoured by pro-European ministers such as the chancellor Philip Hammond. Boris Johnson at the Foreign Office spoke for the delusions. The government's approach to negotiations was a have-our-cake-and-eat-it strategy, he announced. This drew an appropriately caustic response from other European capitals. Xavier Bettel, the prime minister of tiny Luxembourg, caught the mood with the observation that as a full member of the European Union, Britain had always been asking for special 'opt-outs . . . Now they are out, and want a load of opt-ins.'[8] Johnson was often as insistent privately as publicly that Britain could leave the Union and retain all its advantages. Diplomats at the Foreign Office reported that his response to advice that said otherwise was to 'cover his ears with his hands and hum the national anthem'.[9]

Those who had led the charge for Brexit were united in their scant knowledge of the way Europe worked. Dominic Raab, who would at various times be Brexit secretary and then foreign secretary, confessed that he had not realised how much of Britain's trade with the continent passed through Calais – a potential bottleneck in the event of tariffs or trade restrictions. Johnson had been Brussels correspondent for the *Daily Telegraph* during the 1990s. His self-chosen role had been to expose the European Commission's 'conspiracies' to undermine British sovereignty – supposed regulations demanding 'straight' bananas and the like. The facts were never allowed to get in the way of a 'good story'.

Michael Gove had declared during the referendum campaign that if the country backed Leave, the British government would 'hold all the cards' in subsequent trade negotiations. It was soon obvious that precisely the opposite was true. Gove brushed it all off. The Brexiters, a Downing Street insider offered, took a faith-based, pre-Enlightenment stance. Foreign Office diplomats and ambassadors overseas complained that Johnson's reluctance to properly read official briefings for meetings was matched by his refusal to accept policy analysis that collided with his inexplicable confidence that Europe would bend to Britain's will. His counter-parts were baffled and increasingly irritated by the presumptuous-ness. The Italian foreign minister Paolo Gentiloni was lectured by Johnson on the quantities of Prosecco imported by Britain. He expected in return to win Italy's support in any negotiations about the City of London's access to European financial markets. Gentiloni was appalled.[10] The EU was about trade, the Brexiters told themselves. When push came to shove, the German govern-ment would have to listen to its car manufacturers, the French and Italians to their wine growers, and so on. The analysis entirely missed the political commitment in Berlin, Paris and elsewhere to protect the cohesion of the Union.

Invited in 2017 to speak at the Munich Security Conference, Johnson exposed the embarrassing gulf between the two sides. He took to the stage to announce how much Britain was looking forward to 'liberation' after forty years under the yoke of the EU. In the audience were senior politicians from eastern and central European nations that had suffered decades of repression under Soviet communism and had joined the European Union as a way to entrench their freedom. Many were angered by Johnson's ana-logy. 'Disgraceful' was the description of one envoy from central Europe. German ministers were deeply offended by the foreign secretary's habit of drawing parallels between Berlin's influ-ence within the EU and Adolf Hitler's ambitions for European domination. Jean-Marc Ayrault, France's foreign minister, noted that Johnson had 'told a lot of lies'[11] during the referendum campaign, while his German counterpart, Frank-Walter Steinmeier, described Johnson's behaviour as 'outrageous'.[12]

All the while, Britain's capacity to shape international debates and decisions drained away. In November 2017, Sir Simon Fraser, a former head of the Foreign Office, set out the concerns that were echoing through Whitehall. 'It is hard to call to mind a major foreign policy matter on which we have had decisive influence since the referendum,' he told an audience at Chatham House. 'Our political establishment commands little respect abroad, and the negative economic consequences of Brexit are beginning to show.' As for Johnson's stewardship of the Foreign Office, 'Successful foreign policy calls for careful analysis and sustained effort, not soundbites and wishful thinking.'[13]

The Brexiters' naive belief that bilateral deals with both the EU and the world's most dynamic economies could be struck within a year or so were rooted in the past. Their worldview was one in which tariffs were the principal impediment to trade, but the reality was that free trading arrangements relied to a much greater degree on regulatory alignment and shared standards and norms. And anyway, Britain drew most of its overseas income from financial and professional services that were never subject to tariffs. This territory was much harder to navigate. If proof of this were needed, it was that Canada and the EU had taken seven years to come to such an agreement. Nor would the Brexiters accept the basic truth that the relationship between Britain and the EU was asymmetric; about 45 per cent of Britain's trade was with the EU27, but for its partners the comparable figure was less than 10 per cent. Britain would be the big loser if the process broke down, the more so because another sizeable chunk of its trade depended on deals negotiated by Brussels with countries such as Brazil, South Korea and Canada. But the Brexiters would not be shaken from their complacency. The initial response of the financial markets to the referendum vote had been damaging but not calamitous. The economic losses would soon emerge, accruing during the next three years as business investment stalled and consumer confidence dipped. The absence of the immediate shock predicted by the Remain side, however, helped to perpetuate the illusion that Britain could weather the storm.

The pattern was set: overconfidence, a failure to grasp the scale of the task and an assumption that Britain would have a relatively easy ride in negotiations. It seemed not to occur to ministers that Article 50, the section of the Union's Lisbon Treaty setting out the terms under which a member would depart, had been written in such a way as to ensure that the country leaving would be disadvantaged. The evidence suggested that they had not taken the trouble to read it. Wolfgang Schäuble, Germany's veteran finance minister, mocked Johnson's shallow grasp of the way the Union worked and offered to send him a copy of the Lisbon Treaty. Ironically, Article 50 had been drafted by one of Britain's smartest diplomats. Sir John Kerr – later Lord Kerr – had had a career spanning the top diplomatic posts, serving as ambassador in Brussels and Washington, before becoming the permanent under-secretary of the Foreign Office. Later, he was co-opted as one of the authors of the Lisbon Treaty, signed in 2009. Kerr, a strong pro-European, could scarcely have imagined that a few years later Britain would invoke Article 50 – and that he would lead a powerful group in the House of Lords in vigorous opposition to the government's mishandling of the subsequent negotiations.

Missing amid the cacophony was any sense that the government had an organising vision for Britain's relationship with the world after Brexit. For all the occasional stresses and strains, the balancing act between the United States and Europe served as the reference point for Britain's relationships with nations across the globe. But no longer. Leaving the EU would downgrade ties with Europe. Did this mean that Britain would fall helplessly into the arms of the Americans? Or would there be an entirely new foreign policy architecture? Neither May nor Johnson offered an answer. Instead they talked of Brexit foreshadowing a transformation into 'Global Britain'. More pertinently, just as the government set about casting off from Europe, a new US president had begun to undermine the relationship with Washington.

It was left to the Queen to convey these concerns when she spoke at a dinner in the gilded splendour of the ballroom at Buckingham Palace. Few of her 170 guests on that evening in June 2019 could have guessed the monarch's diplomatic mission. The guest of honour at the state dinner – an event at the very pinnacle of the pomp and pageantry bestowed by Britain on foreign leaders – was Donald Trump, the forty-fifth American president. After more than two years in office, Trump had established himself as the most controversial president in modern American history. Beyond the royal palace, demonstrators were planning what they promised would be the largest-ever protest against a visiting leader. Jeremy Corbyn and the Liberal Democrat leader Vince Cable had pointedly refused to dine with Mr Trump. So too had John Bercow, the speaker of the House of Commons.

Senior Whitehall officials whispered that Theresa May had been too eager in issuing the invitation for a state visit when she had travelled to the White House following Trump's inauguration in January 2017. The relationship since then had been far from smooth. The president, at once capricious and wholly at odds with the essential liberalism of British and European democracy, had caused nothing but trouble for May. A shorter trip in 2018 had seen large crowds gather in central London to demonstrate against his presence. Now, as the prime minister contemplated what were to be the last weeks of her premiership, she gritted her teeth as Trump was feted by the great and the good of the British establishment as if he was a cherished friend and ally. The Queen, who had spent a lifetime meeting and greeting world leaders, many of them ruthless dictators and autocrats, was unfazed. Trump's visit coincided with a series of events to mark the seventy-fifth anniversary of the D-Day landings in Normandy. The Queen focused her remarks on how the Second World War had strengthened the unique bonds between the two countries and on the vision Franklin Roosevelt and Winston Churchill had shown in setting a new path for international relations. The great statesmanship of these leaders, she told the assembled dignitaries, had been shown in their creation of an international framework to guarantee peace and freedom: 'After the shared sacrifices of the Second World War, Britain and the United States worked with other allies to build an assembly of international institutions, to ensure that the horrors of conflict would never be repeated.' Next came a polite but precise message for Trump: 'While the world has changed, we are forever mindful of the original purpose of these structures: nations working together to safeguard a hard-won peace.'[14] Britain, she might have added, remained committed to the multilateral rules and institutions that Trump had thus far scorned.

Trump had won his election only a matter of months after the Brexit referendum. The maverick New York property developer, once a registered Democrat, had seized the Republican Party nomination. Then he had beaten Hillary Clinton in the race for the White House. In its way, the election was America's Brexit – a rejection of the existing political elites by a large slice of the electorate. Trump's hijacking of the Republican Party invited parallels with the Eurosceptic coup in the Conservative Party. His victory at the polls drew on the same strains of working-class anger and nationalist nostalgia as the Brexit vote. The British Leavers promised to 'Take Back Control'. Trump promised to 'Make America Great Again'. Both were looking back to the 1950s: the president to an era when, outside the Soviet bloc, America's writ went unchallenged around the world; the Brexiters to a time when Britain thought it could count itself above its European neighbours. The pitch in each case was to disgruntled voters who had seen their economic security upturned by globalisation and their cultural identities destabilised by immigration.

The two campaigns also appealed to crude nativism. Trump's target was illegal immigration from Central and Latin America. The Brexiters directed their fire at migrants from eastern and central Europe, and at a wholly imaginary threat that Europe would soon be overrun by tens of millions of Turkish migrants. Neither campaign paid homage to the facts, and both succeeded in raising the fears of voters. Nigel Farage, the UKIP leader, was feted by the president-elect at Trump Tower in New York. Trump's belligerent unilateralism saw him repudiate the multilateral institutions created by the US after the Second World War. Brexit, in his mind, was a similar reassertion of national sovereignty.

Trump's periodic interventions in the British debate on the side of the Brexiters were a nuisance for the government and embarrassing for the prime minister, but much more dangerous for Britain was his palpable disdain for the post-war international order. Trump declared such 'globalism' as a threat to the US national interest. He had pulled the US out of the Paris climate change agreement and repudiated Barack Obama's support for the nuclear deal between Iran and the world's leading powers.

More, he was questioning the value of Washington's long-standing alliances. The irony here was that while Trump had been a cheerleader for Brexit, the fact of Britain's departure from the EU weakened its voice in Washington. The frustration showed in the doomed effort to save the Iran nuclear deal. In May 2018, Boris Johnson, the foreign secretary, was dispatched to Washington to make a last-ditch appeal to the White House. Trump declined to make time for him. Johnson's efforts to persuade Mike Pompeo, the secretary of state, Mike Pence, the vice president, and Ivanka Trump, the president's daughter-cum-adviser, were in vain. Kim Darroch, the UK's ambassador to Washington, cabled back to London that 'We did everything we could across government to save the deal . . . There has been no stone unturned in our attempt to persuade and shape the administration's view.' A year later, this cable was among a batch of communications from the Washington embassy leaked to the press. The notes, in the manner of private dispatches from overseas ambassadors, were candid in their description of the capricious and inept nature of the Trump regime. The president, furious, all but forced Darroch's resignation from his post by way of a series of angry tweets. Johnson, by now in a race for the succession to Theresa May in 10 Downing Street, declined to back the ambassador. Trump's treatment of a close ally was unprecedented. Such was the new balance of power between London and Washington. Darroch resigned from his post.

The threat to Britain from the new 'America First' policy was hard to understate. 'Existential', in the description of a senior Foreign Office diplomat. If the US cut itself loose from its international moorings, its close ally would be left marooned. Successive British governments prided themselves on being Washington's most reliable ally within NATO. The president now questioned why the US should continue to defend Europe, when most of

NATO's European members failed to meet their commitments to spend at least 2 per cent of their national incomes on defence. Other presidents, of course, had complained that the US was bearing too much of the burden of European defence. None had suggested that the alliance itself was in question. What could that mean for Britain's nuclear deterrent, which, under the agreement reached by Kennedy and Macmillan at Nassau in December 1962, was still formally attached to the alliance?

The day after the Buckingham Palace state banquet, May welcomed Trump in Downing Street. She presented him with a framed typescript draft of the Atlantic Charter signed by Winston Churchill and Franklin D. Roosevelt in 1941. The Second World War, the charter declared, was being fought in the name of freedom and democracy. Its eight principles, including disavowing expansionism, protecting borders, underwriting self-determination and ushering in greater international cooperation, would be the foundation for post-war peace. These were lofty ideals unfamiliar to Trump. The gentle pestering continued when the president joined a dozen other leaders for a D-Day commemoration service in Plymouth. Each signed a proclamation pledging to continue to cooperate in upholding the values and freedoms for which so many young soldiers had died in 1944.

The Brexiters struggled to add substance to the much-trumpeted promise that a 'Global Britain' would soon be striking new alliances and deals across every continent. Canada, Australia and several other nations indicated that they would be ready to negotiate agreements, but only after Britain had settled its post-Brexit relationship with the EU. In any event, Britain had scarcely been cut off from trading with the rest of the world during the decades of its EU membership. Germany's place in the Union had not prevented it from becoming the world's biggest exporter to a fast-rising China. The Brexiters suggested that Britain had somehow been held back by Europe, but bilateral deals with, say, Japan or South Korea would simply replicate arrangements already in place via the EU. A trade deal with the United States – promised by Trump – would be lopsided. As much the larger of the two economies, the US would hold the stronger negotiating cards. The same lopsided balance of power also defined the relationship with Xi Jinping's increasingly assertive regime in Beijing. David Cameron and his chancellor George Osborne had sought to forge a much warmer relationship with China. But it was evident that Beijing, like Washington, was in no mood to be indulgent. Tensions over Xi's efforts to dilute democratic protections in Hong Kong saw stern warnings from Beijing that Britain risked being cast into the wilderness. Such are the realities of geopolitics. Britain had been weakened by Brexit.

The contradictions in May's negotiating position and the hollowness of 'Global Britain' would have been even more apparent had May faced a credible opposition. Instead Labour was effectively disarmed by the leadership of Jeremy Corbyn. He had always sat outside mainstream Westminster politics. His worldview – fiercely anti-American and deeply suspicious of Europe – had not changed since the 1970s. Determined to block the rupture with Brussels sought by hard-line Brexiters, pro-European Labour MPs found it impossible to craft a coherent position for their party. Most found it impossible to imagine circumstances in which the country would choose Corbyn as its prime minister.

May was an instinctively cautious politician. In the spring of 2017, she decided to gamble. What she needed, her advisers told her, was a Commons majority sufficient to face down the Brexiter rebels on the Conservative backbenches who were already threatening to derail her negotiations with Brussels. By April 2017, the opinion polls showed the government to be far ahead of the opposition. The prime minister had inherited an effective majority of seventeen; if she could double or triple that, she would have the political authority she needed. She called an election for June 2017. Instead of the increased majority she had expected, her wooden performances, a badly organised Tory campaign and a protest vote for Corbyn saw May lose her majority. 'Theresa May's Failed Gamble', declared *The Economist*, above a photograph of an ashen-faced prime minister.[15] Her political authority shredded, she was sustained in power by a pact with Northern Ireland's Democratic Unionist Party, its ten MPs among the most Eurosceptic at Westminster. Now, more than ever, May would need the support of opposition MPs to push through parliament an agreement that maintained a close economic relationship with Europe. Yet Brexit became even more a negotiation among the Tories, a struggle between hard-line Brexiters uninterested in the economic consequences of crashing out of the EU without a deal with Brussels and cabinet moderates, led by Hammond. May was in office, but not in power.

For month after month, the government was pulled in different directions, while Barnier and his negotiating team in Brussels looked on in strained incomprehension. The frustration on the European side was eloquently expressed by Donald Tusk, the president of the European Council. A self-declared Anglophile, Tusk was among those in Brussels who refused to give up hope that Britain might revise its decision to leave the Union. Watching the infighting among Conservatives, he told the Brussels media that he hoped God had reserved 'a special place in hell' for those in Britain 'who promoted Brexit without even a sketch of a plan of how to carry it out safely'. The message from Barnier was consistently polite but firm: unless Britain gave up its red lines on the single market and customs union, it would leave the European Union with the promise of an economic partnership scarcely more privileged than Canada's.

Hammond's Treasury reported on the heavy economic cost of surrendering ready access to Britain's biggest market. Manufacturing supply chains would be wrecked and the country's service industries effectively shut out of the EU27. The City of London was already seeing a steady flight of international bankers to Dublin, Paris, Luxembourg and Frankfurt, and Whitehall began to understand the vast complexity of disentangling itself from regulations and norms established over four decades. Business regulation, much of competition policy and environmental standards had been contracted out to Brussels. Without an accord of sorts to manage Britain's departure, planes would not fly, mobile phones would not work across borders and imports and exports of vital medicines would come to a halt. All the while, hard-line Brexiters in May's cabinet and on the Tory backbenches at Westminster clung on to the idea that Britain could sail out of the EU without hitting so much as a squall. Formally at least, the prime minister stuck by the statement of the government's position delivered at Lancaster House in January 2017, in which she had insisted that Britain could break from Brussels while continuing to enjoy unique trade benefits. For its part, Barnier's team was calm, clear-headed and unbending.

With the Article 50 clock running down, the prime minister began to realign her demands with the limits set by Brussels. The softening of her supposed 'red lines', however, in turn invited collision with the fundamentalists in her party. Talks with the EU were put on hold for months at a time, while Downing Street sought to persuade and cajole the Tory rebels. For a moment, in the summer of 2018, it looked like she had rallied the cabinet behind a shaky compromise. The Chequers agreement, negotiated at a day-long cabinet meeting held at the prime minister's country house, sought to blend continued access to the single market in traded goods with the freedom for Britain to strike its own trade deals with third countries such as the US. Within days, however, the concessions cost her the departure of two cabinet ministers: David Davis, the minister in charge of Brexit, and Johnson at the Foreign Office. Both alleged that the prime minister's stance would 'trap' Britain inside the EU's customs union indefinitely. Deploying the increasingly unruly rhetoric that he had made a trademark in describing the relationship with Brussels, Johnson charged the proposals would leave Britain as a 'vassal state' of the EU.

Those concerned with the nation's security and its capacity to defend its interests and citizens abroad had other concerns. NATO represented the first line of Britain's defence, but diplomats, intelligence agencies and defence chiefs were acutely conscious of the value of European cooperation, especially in countering terrorism and international criminal networks. Officials said that Alex Younger, the head of the Secret Intelligence Service, was particularly outspoken in his demands to the prime minister that a deal with the EU27 should safeguard British access to the vast trove of data collected by the Schengen nations – information vital to the fight against Islamist and other terrorist groups. Challenges from a more assertive China and an increasingly revanchist Russia, the multiplicity of cyber-attacks on British business and government departments, and threats from the expanding international network of Islamist jihadis spoke to an increasingly disordered world. This was not the moment for Britain to break off cooperation with fellow European governments. In a speech in 2018, John Sawers, a former head of the Secret Intelligence Service, said publicly what many serving officials were saying privately:

> The emerging world order that we have to reckon with is one where power sweeps aside rules. Interests overwhelm values. And Britain is leaving the European Union. Just at a time when America is stepping back from its enlightened leadership in the world, at a time when great power politics is resuming its dominance at the cost of the rules-based international order, as Europe faces its biggest political challenges for seventy years, Britain is marching boldly out of our big protective regional grouping to face the cold winds of the modern world on our own. I find it hard to believe that this is in our long-term interests.[16]

The 599-page withdrawal agreement – the terms of the divorce – that May finally agreed with Barnier's team in November 2018 was at once prosaic, vital and explosive. Vital because the page upon page of legalese about Britain's remaining financial obligations to the Union (a £39 billion exit bill), the future rights of EU citizens in Britain and British citizens in the EU27, and special arrangements to ensure that a subsequent settlement of the trading and political relationship would maintain an open border between Northern Ireland and the Republic of Ireland were integral to any divorce settlement. Prosaic because an attached 'political statement' setting out the parameters for the eventual economic and political relationship was at best broad-brush in its aspirations, leaving many of the most difficult problems to future talks. In the meantime, things would carry on as they were, under a transition period lasting until the end of 2020. Explosive because the proposed deal exposed brutally the contradictions that had from the beginning been inherent in the Conservatives' approach.

The swelling ranks of Tory MPs who had grown weary of the talks and called increasingly for a 'clean break' with Brussels also judged that the proposed arrangements for the Irish border represented another Brussels 'conspiracy' to keep Britain within the EU's customs union and subject to European regulation indefinitely. On the other side of the line, pro-European Scottish Nationalist, Liberal Democrat, Labour and a handful of Conservative MPs judged that the proposed accord would leave Britain too far beyond the single market, the recipient of some 45 per cent of the nation's exports.

The collisions between Tory diehards and supporters of a compromise deal with Brussels turned to open civil war within the Conservative Party, and there were rising calls from opposition MPs for any settlement with Brussels to be submitted to a second referendum. None of the various factions, however, could muster a parliamentary majority. Senior civil servants talked of paralysis across Whitehall and a complete breakdown of collective cabinet responsibility. The prime minister, hoping in vain for the support of Northern Ireland's Democratic Unionists, tried three times to get the agreement through the House of Commons, only to be defeated on each occasion by large majorities comprising opposition MPs on one side and Tory rebels and Democratic Unionists on the other – the former seeking a 'softer' and the latter a 'hard' Brexit. Facing open challenges to her leadership, in spite of winning a vote of confidence among Conservative MPs, and paralysis in the House of Commons, May was forced to ask other European governments for successive extensions of the Article 50 negotiating process beyond the original deadline of 29 March 2019. The Conservatives had split twice before over matters of trade and protection: during the battle over the Corn Laws during the 1840s and over imperial trade preferences during the opening years of the twentieth century. The party seemed to have forgotten its history.

The first rule of politics is to learn to count. May had signed up to a deal for which there was no majority in the House of Commons, and all the while the parameters of the debate were shifting. She offered to resign in an attempt to corral her own MPs into backing her deal, but it made no difference. After the third rejection, she bowed to the political realities and resigned in June 2019. Britain's frustrated European partners, keen to avoid a chaotic 'crash-out' Brexit, agreed to set a new deadline of 31 October 2019.

This was the moment Boris Johnson had been waiting for. In his final pursuit of the crown, he took up the cudgels of English nationalism. Brexit became a crusade against the efforts of the European elites, with their co-conspirators in London trying to imprison Britain permanently in the Union. His campaign added rancour to xenophobia: the pro-Europeans were trying to subvert 'the will of the people' and were guilty of acts of treachery. He based his leadership bid on a promise he could never keep: that come what may, with or without an agreement with the twenty-seven, Britain would leave the Union by the latest deadline of 31 October. The pledge was impossible to redeem. Withdrawal required legislation and thus the approval of MPs. Johnson, like May, would not have a majority, least of all for the 'no-deal' Brexit he now suggested was a real possibility.

Johnson was brazen in his duplicity. His career was studded with instances where he had been caught speaking less than the truth. Some years earlier, the Conservative leader Michael Howard had sacked him from the shadow cabinet for lying. Yet somehow he had bounced back. The overwhelming choice of the party faithful, he was installed in Downing Street in late July. As prime minister he abandoned all pretence that Britain would seek a close economic partnership with the Union after Brexit – and found himself caught in the parliamentary impasse that had paralysed his predecessor.

The extraordinary events that followed took Britain to the edge of political and constitutional breakdown. In an effort to thwart an attempt by MPs to seek any further extension of the Brexit deadline, Johnson announced an extended prorogation of parliament – a move denounced by, among others, the former Conservative prime ministers John Major and David Cameron as an attempt to squash legitimate democratic debate. Defeated in the House of Commons, the prime minister removed the whip from twenty-one centrist Conservatives, only to face the indignity of the resignation from ministerial office of his talented brother, Jo Johnson. Opposition MPs took their case to the courts. Judgements handed down successively by the Scottish High Court and the UK's Supreme Court found that the prime minister's prorogation had been unlawful. The courts ruled that he had, at very best, misled the Queen in seeking royal assent for the prorogation. Parliament returned, with the speaker of the House of Commons John Bercow determined to give opposition MPs their voice by upending the rules that had hitherto debarred them from tabling legislation.

Johnson found the way to a no-deal Brexit blocked by law. He fared only slightly better in his attempts to reopen the package negotiated by his predecessor. Barnier signalled a willingness to adjust the EU's stance on the Irish border, but Johnson was obliged in return to accept provisions, rejected by May, that would impose a new virtual 'border' in the Irish Sea between Northern Ireland and the rest of the UK. The Democratic Unionists, fearful that the province was being put on the road to eventual Irish reunification, said no. Deadlock now led inexorably to a general election. 'No ifs or buts,' Johnson had promised on the steps of Downing Street – Britain would leave the Union on 31 October. It was another broken promise.

When the nation voted for a new parliament in December 2019, the opinion polls showed it was still evenly divided about Britain's place in Europe. If anything, there was a slight tilt in favour of Remain, but Johnson went into the election with several advantages. The division between Corbyn and his party about whether Labour, if elected, would call another referendum on Brexit left the opposition without a clear policy. Corbyn was deeply unpopular, especially in the Labour heartlands of the Midlands and the north – places where the left-behinds had voted in some numbers for Brexit and where Johnson now focused his campaign. And to the extent that there was a Remain vote, it was shared between Labour, the Liberal Democrats, the Scottish Nationalists and the Green Party. Johnson's 'Get Brexit Done' proved a powerful campaign slogan, just as 'Take Back Control' had during the 2016 referendum campaign. Never mind that getting Brexit done in any real sense would require negotiations stretching over many years to come. Returned to office with a large majority of eighty, the prime minister duly signed and dispatched the withdrawal agreement that saw Britain's membership of the EU officially end on 31 January 2020.

There was no coincidence in his choice of venue to set out his worldview following Britain's departure. On 3 February 2020, the prime minister took to the podium in the baroque splendour of the Painted Hall at the Old Royal Naval College in London's Greenwich. Above him, Sir James Thornhill's ornate painted ceiling recalled the nation's great maritime victories and the moment in 1689 when the ascent to the throne of William and Mary cemented England's victory over Catholic Europe. The Glorious Revolution, he said, marked 'the settlement of a long and divisive political question about who gets to sit on the throne of England'. Brexit was a similar moment. After all the arguments of the recent past, Britain was about to cut loose again. 'This is the newly forged United Kingdom on the slipway.'[17] The grandiloquent rhetoric of this call to arms said nothing of the destination. Where were the Spanish galleons to be plundered by England's valiant buccaneers? The prime minister was untroubled by such omissions, living in a world freighted not so much with history as post-imperial illusions.

Afterword

The Search Resumes

Two months after the retreat from Suez, Anthony Eden jotted down some private reflections on the debacle. The significance of the misadventure, he concluded, was not so much that it had changed the course of the future, but that it had revealed the harsh realities of the present. Britain could not continue in this manner. The task of navigating this unwelcome truth would be left to Eden's successors, starting with the reassessment made by Harold Macmillan. Ultimately, their conclusions led to Britain joining the European Economic Community.

Brexit, like Suez, was an attempt to chart the future by reaching back to the halcyon days of history. Just as Eden had hoped that post-imperial Britain would cling on to its great-power status, the central claim of the Brexiters was that the nation could recover the freedom of action they imagined it had enjoyed before it signed up to Europe. Not for them Macmillan's notion of interdependence or the benefits of collective action. The process of adjusting to reality may take longer this second time around: Suez was a single shattering event, while the impact of Brexit will be felt over many years. The delusion that Britain can do as it pleases, however, is destined to be shattered again. The country's place in the world will always be shaped by its history, but it cannot, as the Brexiters would have it, remain frozen in history.

The Britain of 2020 could still claim many innate strengths and membership of some exclusive international clubs. But, as after Suez, it was lost. In ending more than four decades of close engagement with its European neighbours, it had reopened Dean

Acheson's question about its place in the world – a question most thought had been settled by Edward Heath's signature on the Treaty of Rome. Joining the European Community – a decision taken hard on the heels of the withdrawal of British forces from East of Suez – defined Britain as a European power, albeit, like France, one with a global outlook and interests. By pulling up the European anchor, Britain left itself without a role.

The international weather was less hospitable than that faced by Macmillan after Eden's departure from Downing Street. Most obviously, as a consequence of the redistribution of power in the world, the intervening decades had seen a further erosion of Britain's relative economic and military position. The landscape post-Suez was described by the Cold War confrontation between the United States and the Soviet Union, and by the recovery from the war of Britain's European neighbours in the EEC. The fear of Macmillan and his successors was that Britain would find itself locked out of these power blocs. Sixty years later, the world was a markedly more unstable place. The Pax Americana – the post-war guarantor of the West's, and Britain's, security – was fracturing. The emerging era – some called it the 'new international disorder' – looked set to be shaped by great-power antagonism between the United States and China and by the military adventurism of Vladimir Putin's Russia. Much of the Middle East was in flames, with Syria and Libya torn apart by civil war, Lebanon on the brink and Iran in permanent confrontation with the US. Rising nationalism was challenging the liberal internationalism that had seemed to be the legacy of the West's victory in the Cold War. Before the Brexit referendum, David Cameron's government had imagined that Britain could be China's 'best friend' in the West. By 2020, Beijing's expansionist foreign policy and disregard for international rules presented a broad challenge to Western democracies.

For its part, America had turned inwards to embrace Donald Trump's belligerent isolationism. In short, the stable, rules-based international system of the second half of the twentieth century, which had assured a long era of relative peace, was giving way to one of great-power competition that more closely resembled the balance-of-power system of the nineteenth century. Britain would have to find its new place during times that were more dangerous than any seen since 1945.

Beyond trumpeting the return of sovereignty, the champions of Brexit never settled on the nation's new role. Some imagined that, freed from European regulation, Britain could reinvent itself as a swashbuckling economic entrepôt sitting at the edge of the continent – a bigger, European version, they said, of Singapore. These free-traders, however, stood alongside English nationalists whose ambition was to slam the door on migrants and throw up barriers to protect domestic industries. Others conjured up the restoration of the so-called 'Anglosphere' to which Margaret Thatcher had been so attached – the 'special relationship' with the United States extended to Australia, New Zealand and Canada. Others still looked to the Commonwealth as a surrogate for empire, while searching out the economic opportunities presented by China and other rising states. A competing group comprised those who had backed Brexit on the assumption that all the economic connections with the EU could be preserved, even as Britain repatriated sovereignty. In summoning up something called 'Global Britain', Boris Johnson was merely throwing a rhetorical cloak over a cacophony of often contradictory ideas.

Johnson was a prime minister without a compass. In the words of an official who worked with him daily in government, he was unconcerned with charting a steady course. He showed ebullient disregard for inconvenient truths and strategic choices. The

political gods did not look kindly on such braggadocio. The outbreak of coronavirus – the Sars-like infection that had started three
months earlier thousands of miles away in China's Wuhan province – had by the end of February 2020 swept across Europe and
landed in Britain. Europe began to lock down. Johnson's instant
response was true to character. Dismissing the fuss, he assured the
nation that Britain's 'world-beating' epidemiologists and pharma-
ceutical companies would soon dispatch the virus. The assumption seemed to be that Brexit had inoculated the nation against
misfortune. As he spoke, COVID-19 took hold across the UK,
laying low the prime minister himself as the government put the
economy into an unprecedented lockdown. Johnson recovered,
but the cost of his overconfidence was measured in thousands
of lost lives. Brexit had been about recovering national borders.
Pathogens have no respect for such niceties.

Johnson had marked May 2020 in his diary as an occasion for
a joyous celebration of British exceptionalism, marking the defeat
seventy-five years earlier of Nazi Germany and the leadership of
his hero Winston Churchill in standing alone against the fascist
menace. Instead, the nation was hidden away at home in fear of
falling victim to COVID-19. The government's response to the
danger was hesitant and shambolic. The death toll in Britain was
higher than that faced by its European neighbours. British exceptionalism now marked out national failure rather than the innate
superiority assumed by the prime minister.

Brexit did nothing to change the facts of global power. Whatever
else, Britain would have to remain anchored in the West. The
nation still depended for its territorial security on the US-led alliance represented by NATO. Outside Europe, it would have to
show a special fealty to Washington. Yet, with nearly half of its
trade conducted with the 27 members of the EU, the nation's vital

economic interests could not be detached, post-Brexit, from those of its continental neighbours. Whatever the final arrangements for the economic and political relationship between Britain and the EU27, and however many trade deals London signed with third countries, engagement with Europe would remain a *sine qua non* of national prosperity. The tragedy of Brexit was that by throwing up fresh barriers to these exchanges, it promised to weaken Britain's relative economic performance. The country would also pay a political cost. The EU had acted as a multiplier of British influence, with Brussels providing a platform from which Britain could pursue its national interests in its dealings with the US, China and India alike. Absent from the councils of Berlin, Brussels and Paris, the nation lost political and economic leverage in negotiating with the rest of the world.

That was not to gainsay Britain's strengths, whether they be its deep democratic traditions at home or its long experience and connections across the world. The country would keep its seat on the Security Council for as long as others disagreed as to who was next in line. Britain's prominent role in NATO sat alongside membership of the Group of Seven democracies and leadership of the Commonwealth. Its position of sixth or seventh in the league table of world economies paid for armed forces with an expeditionary reach matched in Europe only by France, while its language, culture and history were a sustained source of soft power. So too was the largest budget for development aid among comparably rich states. Britain's intelligence services and diplomats, in the phrase coined by Douglas Hurd, have long punched well above their weight.

These were formidable assets. The vital missing ingredients were a framework – a grand strategy, as foreign policy practitioners would call it – in which to deploy them and a realistic appraisal of the reach of a middle-ranking power. How, in future, to gather allies if and when Vladimir Putin's regime murdered Russian émigrés living in the UK? How to win the backing of the international community in the stand-off with China about the preservation of democracy in Hong Kong? How to forestall an assumption in Washington that, outside the EU, Britain was a 'soft touch', too weak on its own to defy the wishes of the United States?

The unavoidable dependence on the US for security and on European economic ties for prosperity shaped the deliberations of the senior Whitehall officials put to work in the summer of 2020 to come up with a new foreign and defence strategy. Their brief, one mandarin remarked wearily, was to give some sort of meaning to the prime minister's rhetorical flights of fancy.[1] The striking characteristic of the review was the paucity of choices. Certainly, these officials concluded, there was room to strengthen and extend Britain's network of bilateral relationships around the world. There might also be opportunities to act as a convener of new groupings of like-minded nations – to set up a new club of liberal democracies perhaps. But the US and Europe loomed large in every choice. In the case of Washington, the priority was to remain a demonstrably useful ally, notably by maintaining the defence budget. In the case of Europe, the need was, well, to build a new relationship that would serve, if not as a surrogate for EU membership, as at least an effective substitute. The focus, in the first instance, would have to be on rebuilding bridges to Paris and Berlin, but Britain would also need some form of arrangement that would allow it to work with the EU's institutions. The nation's most pressing security concerns – whether international terrorism, cyber-attacks by hostile states or attempts by Russia and China to destabilise the West's democracies – were also Europe's. If Britain was to be effective in the fight against, say, jihadi terrorism, it would need continued access to the intelligence resources of the European Union.

Missing was a willingness on the part of Johnson's government to think afresh – to imagine a world in which Britain's contribution to the international order abandoned the old obsession with keeping up appearances and pretending that Britain could continue to play the part of a pocket superpower. Such thinking would have started by questioning why national prestige demanded that tens of billions of pounds should continue to be spent merely to hold on to the illusion of an independent nuclear deterrent. Might some of the cost be better spent on bolstering Britain's contribution to international security by reversing the long decline in the navy's surface fleet, by providing sufficient operational aircraft for the RAF and ensuring that a smaller army would have a technological edge over potential adversaries? Shouldn't Britain focus more on sustaining the skills of its intelligence and diplomatic communities, and less on 'prestige' projects such as aircraft carriers? Those looking for a single word to define the weaknesses of British foreign and defence policy after 1945 could not improve on 'overreach' – the consistent refusal of governments to align their perception of Britain's standing in the world with the diminished resources it could gather at home. Such realism, however, sat uncomfortably with the sepia-tinged imaginations of the architects of Britain's withdrawal from the European Union, in which Britannia would always be a 'world-beater'. Johnson would leave it to future leaders to take on the familiar task of closing the gap between grand international ambitions and constrained domestic capacity. This prime minister could never draw the distinction, made seventy years earlier by Sir Henry Tizard, between pretending to be a great power and acting as a great nation.

Brexit carried a more particular, existential danger: that leaving the EU could be the catalyst for the eventual break-up of another union. History might eventually record that the referendum of 2016 was a vote not just about Britain's relationship with its European neighbours, but about the future of Britain, and the United Kingdom. Most obviously, the withdrawal agreement with Brussels unpicked the economic relationship between Northern Ireland and the rest of the UK. Goods and people would continue to cross the border between Northern Ireland and the Irish Republic without checks or hindrance. Trade between the province and the rest of the UK, however, would be subject to new controls. With a border now drawn in the Irish Sea, a united Ireland did not seem quite so distant a prospect. The sharper rupture, though, was between London and Edinburgh. In 2014, the people of Scotland had rejected independence in a referendum. Two years later, however, they voted by a bigger margin to remain in the European Union, only to find their decision overridden by the pro-Leave vote in England. The terms of the UK Union had been rewritten, in effect, by English Conservatives. Scotland, came the message from London, would have to do as it was told. Support for Scotland's nationalists surged. Would it be Britain alone or England alone?

Select Bibliography

Libraries of books have been written about the actors and events in this book. Listed below are some of those I have found most useful, alongside the web addresses of the official archives from which I have most frequently drawn. The list is far from comprehensive.

Worthy of special mention are Peter Hennessy's superb histories of the early post-war decades; the late Hugo Young's brilliant account of Britain's tortuous relationship with Europe; Keith Kyle's magisterial *Suez*; the collection of essays, edited by Roger Louis, on the not-quite-so-special Atlantic relationship, brought together by the Ditchley Foundation; and Michael Charlton's wonderful interviews with the architects of Britain's ultimately ill-fated attempt to reconcile itself with its own continent.

Richard Neustadt's two short books provide an illuminating and, for a Brit, brutal description of the hard-headed nature of the United States' view of the fabled 'special relationship'. Stephen Wall's insider accounts of Britain's troubled ties with Europe are essential reading for anyone wanting to map the route to Brexit. Half a dozen archives with excellent digital collections offer a window onto history as it happened.

Acheson, Dean, *Present at the Creation*, W. W. Norton and
    Company, New York, first published 1969, reprinted 1987
Ashdown, Paddy, *The Ashdown Diaries, Volume Two 1997–1999*,
    Allen Lane, London, 2001

Bales, Tim, *The Conservative Party from Thatcher to Cameron*,
  Polity, London, 2010

Beckett, Andy, *When the Lights Went Out: Britain in the Seventies*,
  Faber & Faber, London, 2009

Benn, Tony, *Out of the Wilderness, Diaries 1963–67*, Arrow,
  London, 1989

Bennett, Gill, *Six Moments of Crisis: Inside British Foreign Policy*,
  Oxford University Press, Oxford, 2013

Blair, Tony, *A Journey*, Hutchinson, London, 2010

Brinkley, Douglas, *Dean Acheson: The Cold War Years 1953–71*,
  Yale University Press, New Haven and London, 1990

Brinkley, Douglas, 'Dean Acheson and the Special Relationship',
  The Historical Journal, 33, 3 (1990)

Brown, Gordon, *My Life, Our Times*, The Bodley Head, London,
  2017

Burk, Kathleen and Cairncross, Alec, *Goodbye Great Britain:
  The 1976 IMF Crisis*, Yale University Press, New Haven and
  London, 2002

Butler, David and Kitzinger, Uwe, *The 1975 Referendum*,
  Palgrave Macmillan, London, 1976

Callaghan, James, *Time and Chance*, Collins, London, 1987

Campbell, John, *Edward Heath: A Biography*, Pimlico/Random
  House, London, 1994

Catterall, Peter (Ed.), *The Macmillan Diaries: The Cabinet Years,
  1950–1957*, Macmillan, London, 2003

Catterall, Peter (Ed), *The Macmillan Diaries, Vol. II: Prime
  Minister and After, 1957–1966*, Macmillan, London, 2011

Charlton, Michael, *The Price of Victory*, BBC, London, 1983

Chilcot, John (Chair), *The Iraq Inquiry: Report of a Committee of
  Privy Councillors*, HC264/265, HMSO, London, 2016

Clarke, Peter, *The Last Thousand Days of the British Empire:*

Churchill, Roosevelt, and the Birth of the Pax Americana,
Bloomsbury, London, 2009

Clinton, Bill, *My Life*, Hutchinson, Random House, London, 2004

Colman, Jonathan, *A 'Special Relationship'? Harold Wilson,
Lyndon B. Johnson and Anglo–American Relations*, Manchester
University Press, Manchester, 2004

Colville, John, *The Fringes of Power, Downing Street Diaries, Vol. II*,
Hodder and Stoughton, London, 1985.

Cradock, Percy, *Know Your Enemy: How the Joint Intelligence
Committee Saw the World*, John Murray, London, 2002

Daddow, Oliver J. (Ed.), *Harold Wilson and European Integration*,
Frank Cass Publishers, London, 2003

Dalton, Hugh, *High Tide and After: Memoirs 1945–1960*,
Frederick Muller, London, 1962

Denman, Roy, *Missed Chances: Britain and Europe in the Twentieth
Century*, Cassell, London, 1996

Donoughue, Bernard, *Downing Street Diary: With Harold Wilson
in No. 10*, Jonathan Cape, London, 2005

Dumbrell, John, 'The Johnson Administration and the British
Labour Government: Vietnam, the Pound and East of
Suez', *Journal of American Studies*, vol. 30, no. 2, Cambridge
University Press, 1996

Eden, Anthony, *Full Circle: The Memoirs of Anthony Eden*,
Houghton Mifflin, London, 1960

Elliot, Francis and Hanning, James, *Cameron: The Rise of the New
Conservative*, Fourth Estate, London, 2007

Freedman, Lawrence, *The Official History of the Falklands
Campaign. Volume 1: The Origins of the Falklands War*,
Routledge, Abingdon, 2005

Freedman, Lawrence, *The Official History of the Falklands Campaign.
Volume II: War and Diplomacy*, Routledge, Abingdon, 2007

Garnett, Mark, Mabon, Simon and Smith, Robert, *British Foreign Policy Since 1945*, Routledge, Abingdon, 2018

Garton Ash, Timothy, *In Europe's Name: Germany and the Divided Continent*, Random House, New York, 1993

Greenstock, Jeremy, *Iraq: The Cost of War*, Heinemann, London, 2016

Hannay, David, *Britain's Quest for a Role: A Diplomatic Memoir from Europe to the UN*, IB Tauris, London, 2012

Healey, Denis, *The Time of My Life*, Michael Joseph, London, 1989

Heath, Edward, *The Course of My Life*, Hodder and Stoughton, London, 1988

Henderson, Nicholas, *Mandarin: The Diaries of Nicholas Henderson*, Weidenfeld and Nicolson, London, 1994

Hennessy, Peter, *Having It So Good: Britain in the 1950s*, Allen Lane/Penguin, London, 2006

Hennessy, Peter, *Never Again: Britain 1945–51*, Vintage, London, 1993

Hennessy, Peter, *The Prime Minister: The Office and Its Holders Since 1945*, Allen Lane/Penguin, 2000

Hennessy, Peter, *The Secret State: Whitehall and the Cold War*, Allen Lane/Penguin, London, 2003

Hennessy, Peter, *Winds of Change: Britain in the Early Sixties*, Allen Lane, London, 2019

Horne, Alistair, *Macmillan: 1957–86*, Macmillan, London, 1996

Howe, Geoffrey, *Conflict of Loyalty*, Macmillan, London, 1994

Hurd, Douglas, *Memoirs*, Little, Brown, London, 2003

Jay, Douglas, *Sterling: A Plea for Moderation*, Sidgwick & Jackson, London, 1985

Jenkins, Roy, *A Life at the Centre*, Macmillan, London, 1991

Kavanagh, Dennis and Seldon, Anthony, *The Major Effect*, Macmillan, London, 1994

Kenny, Michael and Pearce, Nick, *Shadows of Empire: The Anglosphere in British Politics*, Polity, London, 2019

Kissinger, Henry, *The White House Years*, Little, Brown and Company, Boston, 1999

Kyle, Keith, *Suez: Britain's End of Empire in the Middle East*, Weidenfeld and Nicolson, London, 1991

Lamb, Richard, *The Macmillan Years, 1957–1963*, The Emerging Truth, John Murray, London, 1995

Liddle, Roger, *The Europe Dilemma: Britain and the Drama of European Integration*, IB Tauris, London, 2014

Louis, Wm Roger and Bull, Hedley (Eds), *The Special Relationship: Anglo–American Relations Since 1945*, Clarendon Press, Oxford, 1986

Major, John, *The Autobiography*, HarperCollins, London, 1999

Mayne, Richard, Johnson, Douglas and Tombs, Robert (Eds), *Cross Channel Currents: 100 Years of the Entente Cordiale*, Routledge, London, 2004

Monnet, Jean, *Memoirs*, William Collins and Sons, London, 1976

Moore, Charles, *Margaret Thatcher: Vol. I, Not for Turning*, Allen Lane, London, 2013

Moore, Charles, *Margaret Thatcher: Vol. II, Everything She Wants*, Allen Lane, London, 2015

Naughtie, James, *The Accidental American: Tony Blair and the Presidency*, Macmillan, London, 2004

Neustadt, Richard E., *Alliance Politics*, Columbia University Press, New York, 1970

Neustadt, Richard E., *Report to JFK: The Skybolt Crisis in Perspective*, Cornell University Press, New York, 1999

Newhouse, John, *Imperial America: The Bush Assault on the World Order*, Alfred A. Knopf, New York, 2003

Ogilvie-White, Tanya, *On Nuclear Deterrence: The Correspondence of Sir Michael Quinlan*, Routledge, London, 2011

Patten, Chris, *Not Quite the Diplomat: Home Truths About World Affairs*, Allen Lane, London, 2005

Pimlott, Ben, *Harold Wilson*, Harper Collins, London, 1993

Powell, Jonathan, *Great Hatred, Little Room: Making Peace in Northern Ireland*, Bodley Head, London, 2008

Riddell, Peter, *Hug Them Close: Blair, Clinton, Bush and the Special Relationship*, Politico, London, 2003

Roberts, Richard, *When Britain Went Bust: The 1976 IMF Crisis*, OMFIF Press, London, 2016

Roll, Eric, *Crowded Hours*, Faber & Faber, London, 1985

Salmon, Patrick (Ed.), *Documents on British Policy Overseas, Series III, Volume VII: German Unification 1989–1990*, Routledge, London, 2010

Seitz, Raymond, *Over Here*, Phoenix/Orion, London, 1998

Self, Robert, *British Foreign and Defence Policy Since 1945*, Palgrave Macmillan, London, 2010

Stephens, Philip, *Tony Blair*, Viking/Penguin, New York, 2004

Stephens, Philip, *Politics and the Pound: The Conservatives' Struggle with Sterling*, Macmillan, London, 1996

Straw, Jack, *Last Man Standing*, Macmillan, London, 2012

Thatcher, Margaret, *The Downing Street Years*, Harper Collins, London, 1993

Thatcher, Margaret, *The Path to Power*, Harper Collins, London, 1995

Wall, Stephen, *The Official History of Britain and the European Community, Vol II: From Rejection to Referendum, 1963–1975*, Routledge, London, 2012

Wall, Stephen, *The Official History of Britain and the European Community, Vol III: The Tiger Unleashed, 1975–1985*, Routledge, London, 2019

Wall, Stephen, *A Stranger in Europe: Britain and the EU, from Thatcher to Blair*, Oxford University Press, Oxford, 2008

Wallace, William, 'British Foreign Policy after the Cold War', *International Affairs*, vol. 68, no. 3, London, July 1992

Wright, Patrick, *Behind Diplomatic Lines: Relations with Ministers*, Biteback, London, 2018

Young, Hugo, *This Blessed Plot: Britain and Europe, from Churchill to Blair*, Macmillan, London, 1998

Ziegler, Philip, *Wilson: The Authorised Life*, Weidenfeld and Nicolson, London, 1993

WEBSITES

National Archives, Kew, London: nationalarchives.gov.uk

US National Archives: archives.gov

Hansard: parliament.uk

National Security Archive, George Washington University, Washington DC: nsarchive.gwu.edu

Office of the Historian, Department of State, Washington, DC: history.state.gov

The Margaret Thatcher Foundation: margaretthatcher.org

The John F. Kennedy Library and Archive: JFKlibrary.org

Notes

PROLOGUE

1 Cited in Young, Hugo, *This Blessed Plot: Britain and Europe from Churchill to Blair*, Macmillan, London, 1998, p. 24.
2 Speech at Columbia University, 11 January 1952.
3 'Britain, the Commonwealth and Europe', Conservative Central Office, October 1962.
4 Neustadt, Richard E., *Alliance Politics*, Columbia University Press, New York, 1970, pp. 111–12.
5 Hansard, 8 April 1975, c. 1027.
6 Speech at the Lord Mayor's Banquet, 22 November 1999.
7 Self, Robert, *British Foreign and Defence Policy Since 1945*, Palgrave Macmillan, London, 2010, p. 117.
8 Neustadt, *Alliance Politics*, p. 5.
9 Young, *This Blessed Plot*, p. 1.
10 Charlton, Michael, *The Price of Victory*, BBC, London, 1983, p. 307.

1. BROKEN DREAMS

1 Anthony Logan, *Financial Times*, 8 January 1986.
2 The protocol is published in Avi Shlaim, 'The Protocol of Sèvres, 1956: Anatomy of a War Plot', *International Affairs*, Vol. 73, No. 3 (1997).
3 Colville, John, *The Fringes of Power: Downing Street Diaries Vol. II*, Hodder and Stoughton, London, 1985, p. 364.
4 National Archives, CAB 128/30, CM 56, 54th Conclusions, 27 July 1956.
5 'CIA Confirms Role in 1953 Iran Coup', National Security Archive, Washington, Electronic Briefing Book No. 435, 19 August 2013.
6 Catterall, Peter (Ed.), *The Macmillan Diaries: The Cabinet Years, 1950–1957*, Macmillan, London, 2003, p. 587.
7 'Factors Affecting Egypt's Policy in the Middle East and North Africa', 20 April 1956, JIC (56), 20 Final.
8 National Archives, CAB 128/30, CM 56, 54th Conclusions, 27 July 1956.
9 Ibid.
10 Office of the Historian, 'Message from Prime Minister Eden to President Eisenhower, 27 July 1956', *Foreign Relations of the United States, Suez Crisis*, Vol. XVI.
11 Kyle, Keith, *Suez: Britain's End of Empire in the Middle East*, Weidenfeld and Nicolson, London, 1991, p. 148.

12 Ibid.

13 Office of the Historian, 'Letter from President Eisenhower to Prime Minister Eden, 31 July 1956', *Foreign Relations*.

14 Ibid.

15 Louis, Wm. Roger, and Bull, Hedley (Eds), *The Special Relationship: Anglo–American Relations Since 1945*, Clarendon Press, Oxford, 1986, p. 275.

16 Eden, Anthony, *The Reckoning: The Eden Memoirs*, Cassell, London, 1965, p. 513.

17 Hansard, HOC, Vol. 557, cc. 1602–18, 2 August 1956.

18 Hennessy, Peter, *The Prime Minister: The Office and Its Holders Since 1945*, Allen Lane/Penguin Press, London, p. 233.

19 Kyle, *Suez*, p. 320.

20 Ibid., p. 295.

21 Kyle, *Suez*, p. 290.

22 Logan, *Financial Times*, 8 January 1986.

23 Shlaim, 'The Protocol of Sèvres, 1956'.

24 Logan, *Financial Times*, 8 January 1986.

25 See Kyle, *Suez*, p. 388.

26 *Observer*, 4 November 1956.

27 Kyle, *Suez*, p. 256.

28 Office of the Historian, *Foreign Relations of the United States, Suez Crisis, Special Watch Report of the Intelligence Advisory Committee*, 28 October 1956, Vol. XVI.

29 'The American Presidency Project: Radio and Television Report to the American People on the Developments in Eastern Europe and the Middle East', national radio and television address, 31 October 1956, available at UC Santa Barbara.

30 Louis, *The Special Relationship*, p. 277. See also Office of the Historian, 'Memorandum of a Discussion at the 302nd Meeting of the National Security Council', 1 November 1956.

31 Hennessy, *The Prime Minister*, p. 243.

32 Neustadt, *Alliance Politics*, p. 26.

33 Hansard, HOC, Vol. 562, cc. 1456–63, 20 December 1956.

34 Office of the Historian, *Foreign Relations of the United States, Suez Crisis, Memorandum from the Secretary of State's Special Assistant for Intelligence*, 5 December 1956, Vol. XVI.

35 Kyle, *Suez*, p. 426

36 Ibid.

37 Ibid., p. 467.

2. GREEKS AND ROMANS

1 Colville, John, *The Fringes of Power*, p. 204.

2 Crossman, Richard, 'The Making of Macmillan', *Sunday Telegraph*, 9 February 1964.

3 Catterall, *The Macmillan Diaries*, p. 187.

4 Acheson, Dean, *Present at the Creation*, W. W. Norton and Company, New York, 1969, reprinted 1987, p. 387.

5 Watt, David, *The Inquiring Eye*, Penguin, London, 1988, p. 85.

6 Speech at Westminster College, Fulton, Missouri, 5 March 1946, winston-churchill.org.

7 See the National Archives, 'UKUSA Agreement', GCHQ files HW80/1-HW80-10.

8 Speech at University of Zurich, 21 September 1946, winstonchurchill.org.

9 Winston Churchill, 'Humble Address on the Death of President Roosevelt', House of Commons, 17 April 1945.

10 Louis, *The Special Relationship*, p. 52.

11 Hansard, HOC, Vol. 417, cc. 421–558, 12 December 1945.

12 Dalton, Hugh, *High Tide and After: Memoirs 1945–1960*, Frederick Muller, London 1962, pp. 74–5. See also Louis, *The Special Relationship*, pp. 51–2.

13 Hansard, HOC, Vol. 417, cc. 421–558, 641–739, 12/13 December 1945.

14 Ibid.

15 Lord George-Brown, *In My Way: The Political Memoirs of Lord George-Brown*, Gollancz, London, 1971, p. 243.

16 Louis, *The Special Relationship*, p. 45.

17 See Garnett, Mark, Mabon, Simon, and Smith, Robert, *British Foreign Policy Since 1945*, Routledge, Abingdon, 2018, p. 95.

18 Louis, *The Special Relationship*, p. 54.

19 Hewitt, Gavin, 'Strains on the Special Relationship', BBC News, 20 April 2016.

20 Cited in Ruane, Kevin, *Churchill and the Bomb in War and Cold War*, Bloomsbury, London, 2016, p. 57.

21 National Churchill Museum, 'The Bright Gleam of Victory', speech at Mansion House, 11 November 1942.

22 Michael Howard, 'The 1995 FCO Annual Lecture, 1945–1995: Fifty Years of European Peace', FCO Historians, October 1995.

23 National Archives, CAB 129/53, C(52) 202, 18 June 1952.

24 Office of the Historian, 'United States Objectives and Programs for National Security', National Security Paper NSC-68, 1950.

25 Louis, *The Special Relationship*, p. 261.

26 See the American Presidency Project, UC Santa Barbara, 'Declaration of Common Purpose by the President and the Prime Minister of the United Kingdom', 25 October 1957.

27 Office of the Historian, 'Memorandum of a Conference with the President, White House, Washington, October 22, 1957', *Foreign Relations of the United States, 1955–1957, Western Europe and Canada*, Vol XXVII, p. 311.

28 National Archives, C. (58) 77, 10 April 1958, 'Anglo–American Relations', note by the Secretary of State for Foreign Affairs.

29 Louis, *The Special Relationship*, p. 87.

30 Office of the Historian, 'Information Memorandum from the Assistant Secretary of State-Designate for European Affairs (Burt) to Secretary of State Haig, 21 May 1982', *Foreign Relations of the United States, 1981–1988*, Vol. XIII, 283.

31 Catterall, Peter, *The Macmillan Diaries Vol. II: Prime Minister and After*, Macmillan, London, 2009, p. 239.

3. A THOUSAND YEARS OF HISTORY

1 Denman, Roy, *Missed Chances: Britain and Europe in the Twentieth Century*, Cassell, London, 1996, p. 196.

2 Catterall, *The Macmillan Diaries Vol. II*, p. 313.

3 Kyle, *Suez*, p. 267.

4 Speech to the College of Europe, Bruges, 20 September 1988; margaret-thatcher.org.

5 Ibid.

6 National Archives, 'Future Policy Study, 1960–70', FP (60) 1, Cab 129/100, 24 February 1960.

7 Young, *This Blessed Plot*, p. 73.

8 Acheson, *Present at the Creation*, p. 385.

9 Charlton, *The Price of Victory*, p. 21.

10 Ibid., p. 81.

11 Ibid., p. 67.

12 Ibid., p. 70.

13 Ibid., p. 67.

14 *Documents of British Policy Overseas*, Foreign & Commonwealth Office, 2nd Series, Vol. I, 1986, pp. 6–7.

15 See Denman, *Missed Chances*, p. 188.

16 Charlton, *The Price of Victory*, p. 115.

17 Ibid., p. 117.

18 Young, *This Blessed Plot*, p. 83.

19 Denman, *Missed Chances*, p. 199.

20 Young, *This Blessed Plot*, p. 118.

21 Cited in Bogdanor, Vernon, 'From the European Coal and Steel Community to the Common Market', Gresham Lecture, 12 November 2013.

22 Hennessy, Peter, *Having It So Good: Britain in the 1950s*, Penguin/Allen Lane, London 2006, p. 594.

23 Hansard, HOC, 27 June 1950, Vol. 476, cc. 2104–59.

24 Statement by Edward Heath, Paris, 10 October 1961, available at CVCE, EU, University of Luxembourg.

25 Hennessy, *Having It So Good*, p. 615.

26 Bennett, Gill, *Six Moments of Crisis: Inside British Foreign Policy*, Oxford University Press, Oxford, 2013, p. 86.

27 Speech at Labour Party conference, 3 October 1962.

28 See Young, *This Blessed Plot*, p. 163.

29 Anthony Eden, speech at Columbia University, January 1952.

30 Conservative Central Office, 'Britain, the Commonwealth and Europe', October 1962.

31 Catterall, *The Macmillan Diaries Vol. II*, p. 431.

32 Available at University of Luxembourg, CVCE.eu.

33 Catterall, *The Macmillan Diaries Vol. II*, p. 535–9.

4. A VERY BRITISH BOMB

1 Catterall, *The Macmillan Diaries Vol. II*, p. 523.

2 Acheson, *Present at the Creation*, p. 385.

3 For a detailed account of the Westpoint speech, see Neustadt, Richard, 'Dean Acheson and the Special Relationship: The West Point Speech of December 1962', *Historical Journal*, Vol. 33, No. 3 (1990), pp. 599–608.

4 Ibid.

5 Catterall, *The Macmillan Diaries Vol. II*, p. 523.

6 Neustadt, *Alliance Politics*, p. 52–3.

7 Louis, *The Special Relationship*, p. 91.

8 Ibid., pp. 118/19.

9 Ibid., p. 120.

10 Hennessy, *Having It So Good*, p. 182.

11 Ibid., p. 329.

12 Ibid., p. 339.

13 See the National Security Archive, 'Consultation Is Presidential Business: Secret Understandings on the Use of Nuclear Weapons', NSA Electronic Briefing Book, No. 159.

14 Colville, *The Fringes of Power*, p. 345.

15 Garnett, *British Foreign Policy Since 1945*, p. 119.

16 Louis, *The Special Relationship*, p. 105.

17 Lamb, Richard, *The Macmillan Years, 1957–1963: The Emerging Truth*, John Murray, London, 1995, p. 298.

18 See Neustadt, *Alliance Politics*, p. 38.

19 Office of the Historian, Letter from Kennedy to Macmillan transmitted via outgoing telegram, Department of State, to US Ambassador, London, 8 May 1961.

20 Neustadt, Richard, E., *Report to JFK: The Skybolt Crisis in Perspective*, Cornell University Press, New York, 1999, p. 134.

21 Ibid., p. 77.

22 Office of the Historian, Department of State, 20778, Memorandum of Conversation, 19 December 1962.

23 John F. Kennedy Presidential Library, 'Kennedy–Macmillan Joint Statement, Nassau, 21 December 1962'.

24 National Archives, Cab. 128/36 (62), 76th Conclusions, 22 December 1961.

25 Charlton, *The Price of Victory*, p. 283.

26 Catterall, *The Macmillan Diaries Vol. II*, p. 527.

27 Ibid., p. 528.

28 Neustadt, *Alliance Politics*, p. 35.

29 Louis, *The Special Relationship*, p. 97.

30 Charlton, *The Price of Victory*, p. 294.

31 Neustadt, *Alliance Politics*, p. 111.

32 See Lamb, *The Macmillan Years, 1957–1963*, p. 319.

33 Margaret Thatcher Foundation, 'Letter to Reagan (Trident nuclear deterrent)', 11 March 1982.

34 Ibid.

35 Ronald Reagan Presidential Library and Museum, 'Letter to Prime Minister Margaret Thatcher of the United Kingdom Confirming the Sale of the Trident II Missile System to the [*sic*] Her Country', 11 March 1982.

36 Press conference at NATO summit in Warsaw, 9 July 2016.

37 Interview with author.

38 Garnett, *British Foreign Policy Since 1945*, p. 152.

5. POWER AND THE POUND

1 Office of the Historian, Telegram from the Embassy in the United Kingdom to the Department of State, 16 October 1964. *Foreign Relations of the United States, 1964–68*, Volume XII, Western Europe, 230.

2 Ibid.

3 Speech at the Guildhall, 16 November 1964.

4 Healey, Denis, *The Time of My Life*, Michael Joseph, London, 1989, p. 280.

5 Speech at Labour Party conference, Scarborough, 1 October 1963.

6 Speech at Birmingham Town Hall, 19 January 1964.

7 Hansard, HOC, Vol. 653, cc. 32–167, 5 February 1962.

8 *The New Britain*, Labour Party Manifesto 1964.

9 Dumbrell, John, 'The Johnson Administration and the British Labour Government', *Journal of American Studies*, Vol. 30, No. 2, Part 2, August 1996, p. 214.

10 Office of the Historian, 'Telegram from the Embassy in the United Kingdom to the Department of State', 16 October 1964.

11 Hansard, HOC, Vol. 704, cc. 629–705, 16 December 1964.

12 Benn, Tony, *Out of the Wilderness: Diaries 1963–67*, Arrow, London, 1989, p. 108.

13 'The Wind of Change', speech to the South African parliament, Cape Town, 3 February 1960.

14 Interview with author.

15 Self, *British Foreign and Defence Policy Since 1945*, p. 70.

16 Colman, Jonathan, *A 'Special Relationship'? Harold Wilson, Lyndon B. Johnson*

and Anglo–American Relations, Manchester University Press, Manchester, 2004, p. 31.

17 Ziegler, Philip, Gresham College Lecture, 21 February 2006; see also Ziegler, Philip, *Wilson: The Authorised Life*, Weidenfeld and Nicolson, London, 1993.

18 Office of the Historian, 'Memorandum of a Telephone Conversation between President Johnson and Prime Minister Wilson, 10 February 1965'. *Foreign Relations of the United States 1964–68*, Vol. II, Vietnam, January–June 1965.

19 Ibid.

20 Quoted by Davies, Peter, 'Sterling and Strings', *London Review of Books*, 20 November 2008.

21 Office of the Historian, *Foreign Relations of the United States, 1964–1968*, Vol. V, Vietnam, Circular 137167, 17 February 1967.

22 Dumbrell, 'The Johnson Administration and the British Labour Government', p. 231.

23 Healey, *The Time of My Life*, p. 334.

24 Davies, 'Sterling and Strings'.

25 Office of the Historian, 'Memorandum from the President's Special Adviser for National Security Affairs (Bundy) to President Johnson, 3 June 1965'. See also 'Memorandum from Francis M. Bator to the President's Special Assistant for NSC Affairs, 29 July 1965'.

26 National Archives, Cabinet Papers, CC (68), 7th Conclusions, 15 January 1968.

27 Hansard, HOC, Vol. 756, cc. 1787–911, 17 January 1968.

28 Bennett, *Six Moments of Crisis*, p. 101.

29 Hennessy, Peter, *Winds of Change: Britain in the Early Sixties*, Allen Lane, London, 2019, p. 31.

30 Young, *This Blessed Plot*, p. 190.

31 Ibid., p. 192.

6. MISSED CHANCES

1 Campbell, John, *Edward Heath: A Biography*, Pimlico/Random House, London, 1994, p. 335.

2 Young, *This Blessed Plot*, p. 220.

3 Michael Cockerell, 'Ted Heath and Me', *Guardian*, 19 July 2005.

4 Campbell, *Edward Heath*, p. 335.

5 Young, *This Blessed Plot*, p. 228.

6 Ibid., p. 226.

7 Hansard, HOC, Vol. 823, cc. 1732–2033, 2076–217, 27/28 October 1971.

8 Louis, *The Special Relationship*, p. 97.

9 Heath, Edward, *The Course of My Life*, Hodder and Stoughton, London, 1988, p. 493.

10 Office of the Historian, *Foreign Relations of the United States, 1969–1976*, Vol. E-15, Part 2, 'Message from British Prime Minister Heath to President Nixon, 25 July 1973'.

11 Office of the Historian, 'Message from British Prime Minister Heath to President Nixon, 4 September 1973'.

12 Kissinger, Henry, *The White House Years*, Little, Brown and Company, Boston, 1999, p. 961.

13 Interview with author.

14 Beckett, Andy, *When the Lights Went Out: Britain in the Seventies*, Faber & Faber, London, 2009, p. 147.

15 Butler, David, and Kitzinger, Uwe, *The 1975 Referendum*, Palgrave Macmillan, London, 1976, p. 12.

16 Young, *This Blessed Plot*, p. 280.

17 Ibid., p. 291.

18 *Sun*, 7 June 1975.

19 *The Times*, 7 June 1975.

20 Young, *This Blessed Plot*, p. 290.

21 Interview with author.

22 Speech at Labour Party conference, Blackpool; available at britishpolitical-speech.org.

23 Seitz, Raymond, *Over Here*, Phoenix/Orion, London, 1998, p. 213.

24 National Archives, 'Britain's Decline, Its Causes and Consequences', Diplomatic Report no. 129/79, FCO, HM Ambassador at Paris, 31 March 1979.

7. COLD WARRIOR

1 Interview with author.

2 Ibid.

3 Thatcher, Margaret, *The Path to Power*, HarperCollins, London, 1995, p. 57.

4 Margaret Thatcher Foundation, speech at Kensington Town Hall, 19 January 1976.

5 Margaret Thatcher Foundation, letter to President Carter, 2 October 1979.

6 Moore, Charles, *Margaret Thatcher, Vol. 1: Not for Turning*, Allen Lane, London, p. 442.

7 Thatcher, Margaret, *The Downing Street Years*, HarperCollins, London, 1993, p. 156.

8 Margaret Thatcher Foundation, speech accepting Donovan Award ('The Defence of Freedom'), 28 February 1981.

9 National Archives, cited in *The Times*, 1 May 2014.

10 Freedman, Lawrence, *Britain and the Falklands War*, Institute of Contemporary British History, Basil Blackwell, Oxford, p. 23.

11 Bennett, *Six Moments of Crisis*, p. 169.

12 Hansard, HOC, Vol. 21, cc. 633–68, 3 April 1982.

13 Ibid.

14 Ibid.

15 Margaret Thatcher Foundation, Falklands: Henderson Valedictory Despatch

('US Policy in the Falkands Crisis with Some Valedictory Comments on US/ UK Relations'), 27 July 1982.

16 Thatcher, *The Downing Street Years*, p 198.

17 Office of the Historian, 'Transcript of a Telephone Conversation between President Reagan and British Prime Minister Thatcher', *Foreign Relations of the United States, 1981–88*, Vol. XIII.

18 Hansard, HOC, Vol. 25, c. 738, 15 June 1982.

19 Thatcher, *The Downing Street Years*, p. 235.

20 Interview with author.

21 Hansard, HOC, Vol. 971, cc. 620–736, 25 July 1979.

22 Moore, Charles, *Not for Turning*, p. 452.

23 Private conversation.

24 Wright, Patrick, *Behind Diplomatic Lines: Relations with Ministers*, Biteback, London, 2018, p. 1.

25 Interview with author.

26 Moore, Charles, *Margaret Thatcher, Vol. II: Everything She Wants*, Allen Lane, London, 2015, p. 129.

27 Interview with author.

28 Thatcher, *The Downing Street Years*, p. 444.

29 Interview with author.

30 Ibid.

31 Margaret Thatcher Foundation, 'Press Conference after Andropov's Funeral', 14 February 1984.

32 Margaret Thatcher Foundation, 'Return to Moscow', Margaret Thatcher's memoir, 16 March 1985.

33 Margaret Thatcher Foundation, 'Record of a Meeting between the Prime Minister and President Reagan at Camp David, 22 December 1984'.

34 Ibid.

35 Moore, *Everything She Wants*, p. 252.

36 Interview with author.

37 US National Security Archive, 'Session of CC CPSU Politburo, Outcomes of Margaret Thatcher's Visit, 16 April 1987'.

38 Hurd, Douglas, *Memoirs*, Little, Brown, London, 2003, p. 381.

39 National Archives, Ref. PREM 19/3175. See also Salmon, Patrick (Ed.), *Documents on British Policy Overseas, Series III, Volume VII: German Unification 1989–1990*, Routledge, London, 2010, p. 79, text and footnote.

40 US National Security Archive, 'Record of Conversation between Mikhail Gorbachev and Margaret Thatcher, 23 September 1989', written by Anatoly Chernyaev. See also 'The Thatcher–Gorbachev Conversations', National Security Archive Electronic Briefing Book No. 422, posted 12 April 2013.

41 Speech to the College of Europe, Bruges.

42 Wright, *Behind Diplomatic Lines*, p. 188.

43 Salmon, *Documents on British Policy Overseas*, pp. 164–5.

44 Hurd, *Memoirs*, p. 382.

45 Timothy Garton Ash, 'Britain Fluffed the German Question', *Guardian*, 21 October 2009.

46 Interview with Nicholas Ridley, 'Saying the Unsayable About the Germans', *Spectator*, 14 July 1990. Available at the Margaret Thatcher Foundation.

8. THE ROAD TO BRUGES

1 Hansard, HOC, Vol. 889, cc. 1020–150, 8 April 1975.

2 Ibid.

3 Interview with author.

4 Ibid.

5 Wall, Stephen, *A Stranger in Europe: Britain and the EU from Thatcher to Blair*, Oxford University Press, Oxford, 2008, p. 5.

6 Interview with author.

7 *Observer*, 25 November 1990.

8 Thatcher, *The Downing Street Years*, p. 730.

9 Interview with author.

10 Ibid.

11 Ibid.

12 Thatcher, *The Downing Street Years*, p. 558.

13 Speech to the College of Europe, Bruges.

14 Ibid.

15 Ibid.

16 *Sun*, 1 November 1990.

17 Interview with author.

18 Stephens, Philip, *Politics and the Pound: The Conservatives' Struggle with Sterling*, Macmillan, London, 1996, p. 104.

19 Thatcher, *The Downing Street Years*, p. 840.

20 Private conversation.

21 Thatcher, *The Downing Street Years*, p. 309.

22 Hurd, *Memoirs*, p. 399.

23 Interview with author.

24 Hansard, HOC, Vol. 178, cc. 869–91, 30 October 1990.

25 Hansard, HOC, Vol. 180, cc. 461–66, 13 November 1990.

9. THE BASTARDS

1 Interview with author.

2 Wall, *A Stranger in Europe*, p. 111–12.

3 Private conversation with author.

4 Wall, *A Stranger in Europe*, p. 110.

5 Private conversation with author.

6 Hansard (HOC), Vol.199, cc. 269–320, 20 November 1991.

7 Wall, *A Stranger in Europe*, p. 114.

8 Stephens, *Politics and the Pound*, p. 147.

9 Speech to Scottish Confederation of British Industry, Glasgow, 10 September 1992.
10 Conversation with author.
11 Hansard, HOC, Vol. 226, cc. 281–85, 9 June 1993.
12 Major, John, *The Autobiography*, HarperCollins, London, p. 498.
13 Seitz, *Over Here*, pp. 279–81.
14 Released by National Archives, December 2018; see *Financial Times*, 28 December 2018.
15 Interview with author.
16 Wall, *A Stranger in Europe*, p. 157.

10. BACK TO THE DESERT
1 Chilcot, John (Chair), *The Report of the Iraq Inquiry: Report of a Committee of Privy Councillors*, HC264/265, HMSO, London, 2016.
2 Private conversation.
3 Speech to Friedrich-Ebert Foundation, Bonn, 30 May 1995.
4 Private conversation.
5 Press conference, Downing Street garden, 29 May 1997.
6 Interview with author.
7 Ibid.
8 Speech at the Lord Mayor's Banquet, 22 November 1999.
9 Stephens, Philip, *Tony Blair*, Viking/Penguin, New York, 2004, p. 210.
10 Interview with author.
11 Private conversation.
12 Interview with author.
13 Ibid.
14 Private conversation.
15 'The New Challenge for Europe', speech delivered at Aachen on receipt of the Charlemagne Prize, 13 May 1999.
16 Author's conversations with Tony Blair.
17 Interview with author.
18 Private conversation.
19 Remarks at White House, 6 February 1988.
20 Stephens, *Tony Blair*, p. 119.
21 Ashdown, Paddy, *The Ashdown Diaries: Volume Two, 1997–1999*, Allen Lane, London, 2001, p. 127.
22 Stephens, *Tony Blair*, p. 157.
23 Ibid.
24 'It Will Be Peace, On Our Terms', *The Times*, 7 May 1999.
25 Speech at University of Sofia, 17 May 1999.
26 Interview with author.
27 'Doctrine of the International Community', prime minister's speech in Chicago, 22 April 1999.

28 Stephens, *Tony Blair*, pp. 169–70.

29 Prime minister's speech at Lord Mayor's Banquet, 22 November 1999.

30 Stephens, *Tony Blair*, p. 187.

31 Ibid., p. 196.

32 Ibid., pp. 196–200.

33 Interview with author.

34 *The Economist*, 10 January 2002.

35 Interview with author.

36 Tony Blair, letter to George W. Bush, 11 October 2001, published in Chilcot, *The Iraq Inquiry*.

37 Stephens, *Tony Blair*, p. 205.

38 Tony Blair, letter to George W. Bush, 28 July 2008, published in Chilcot, *The Iraq Inquiry*.

39 For advice of intelligence chiefs, see Chilcot, *The Iraq Inquiry*.

40 See Stephens, *Tony Blair*, pp. 209–37.

41 Interview with author.

42 Ibid.

43 Ibid.

44 Ibid.

45 Ibid.

46 Stephens, *Tony Blair*, p. 235.

47 Interview with author.

48 Liddle, Roger, *The Europe Dilemma: Britain and the Drama of European Integration*, I. B. Tauris, London, 2014, p. 177.

49 Interview with author.

50 Ibid.

51 Ibid.

11. FOG IN THE CHANNEL

1 Interview with author.

2 Ibid.

3 Ibid.

4 Prime minister's speech at Mansion House, 15 November 2010.

5 Interview with author.

6 Private conversation.

7 Hansard, HOC, Vol. 566, cc. 1555–6, 29 August 2013.

8 Ministry of Defence paper made available to author.

9 LBC radio interview, 4 April 2006.

10 Interview with author.

11 Ibid.

12 Prime minister's EU speech at Bloomberg, 23 January 2013.

13 Prime minister's speech on Scottish independence, 7 February 2014.

14 Prime minister's speech at Bloomberg.

15 See *Financial Times* magazine, 22 January 2016.
16 Private conversation.
17 *Financial Times*, 17 May 2012.
18 Private conversation with German officials.
19 Private conversation.
20 Ibid.
21 *Financial Times*, 23 June 2014.
22 Statement issued by Vote Leave campaign, 27 April 2016.
23 *Financial Times*, 23 June 2014.

12. ALONE
 1 Private conversation.
 2 Interview with *The Times*, 13 September 2019.
 3 Private conversation.
 4 Ibid.
 5 Speech at Conservative Party conference, 5 October 2016.
 6 Speech at Trinity College, Cambridge, 10 October 2018.
 7 *The Economist*, 7 January 2017.
 8 See Stephens, Philip, 'Britain's Latest Brexit Strategy: Any Deal Will Do', *Financial Times*, 22 March 2018.
 9 Private conversation.
10 Ibid.
11 Reported by Reuters, 14 July 2016.
12 'Johnson Appointment Divides Opinion', *Financial Times*, 14 July 2016.
13 Speech at Chatham House, 7 November 2017.
14 The Queen's speech at US State Banquet, 3 June 2019; royal.uk.
15 *The Economist*, 10 June 2017.
16 2018 Sir Edward Heath Charitable Foundation Lecture, Salisbury, 19 October 2018.
17 Prime minister's speech, Greenwich, 3 February 2020.

AFTERWORD
 1 Conversation with author.

Index